Hegel

Hegel

An Intellectual Biography

Horst Althaus

Translated by Michael Tarsh

Polity Press

English translation © Polity Press 2000
First published in Germany as *Hegel und die heroischen Jahre der Philosophie*
© Carl Hanser Verlag 1992.

This translation published in 2000 by Polity Press
in association with Blackwell Publishers Ltd.

Editorial office:
Polity Press
65 Bridge Street
Cambridge CB2 1UR, UK

Marketing and production:
Blackwell Publishers Ltd
108 Cowley Road
Oxford OX4 1JF, UK

Published in the USA by
Blackwell Publishers Inc.
Commerce Place
350 Main Street
Malden, MA 02148, USA

ISBN 0-7456-1781-6

A catalogue record for this book is available from the British Library and
has been applied for from the Library of Congress.

Typeset in 10 on 12 pt Sabon
by Ace Filmsetting Ltd, Frome, Somerset
Printed in Great Britain by MPG Books, Bodmin, Cornwall

This book is printed on acid-free paper.

Contents

Contents

Translator's Note

The following text is an abridged version of the German original, particularly with regard to material likely to be of more direct interest to a German audience. The abridgements were made in agreement with the author and the German publisher. The bibliography has been developed and extended in relation to English-language translations and publications.

1

Origins

When Hegel was born in Stuttgart on 27 August 1770 the very landscape of the place seems already to have left a powerful mark upon the character that would subsequently emerge. Hegel was born a native of Württemberg, and always continued – even in later years as a salaried official of the Prussian state – to consider himself as a Württembergian.

According to family tradition the Hegels were descended from immigrants from the Steiermark or Kärnten region, persecuted Protestants who had sought protection in Württemberg in the middle of the sixteenth century. One of these immigrants was a Johann Hegel, potter by profession, who had settled in Grossbottwar in the Neckar region and eventually managed to become mayor of this little town. His numerous descendants in Württemberg included the Pastor Hegel who baptized Friedrich Schiller and the philosopher's father, Georg Ludwig Hegel, ducal secretary and later counsellor of state. The philosopher's grandfather had been chief intendant in Altensteig in the Black Forest, whilst his mother, Maria Magdalena, came from an old Stuttgart family of the seventeenth century which had spawned theologians, lawyers and officials, and which could be traced back on the maternal side to the Württemberg reformer Johannes Brenz.

For a young man with the family background that Hegel possessed and the interests that he would later develop, Württemberg in the latter half of the eighteenth century was an extremely auspicious place in which to be born. Alongside Saxony and the Saxon-Thuringian principalities, the state of Württemberg could boast the most developed educational system in the 'Holy Roman Empire of the German Nation'. Prussia at the time still lagged far behind in this respect, and the only teachers it could call upon in any abundance were retired soldiers and war-wounded veterans who were very poorly remunerated for their educational services.

The exemplary educational institutions were all to be found in Saxony and Württemberg. Saxony could draw on schools in Meissen, Grimma and Schulpforta to supply its future state officials and civil servants, and especially the clerics and high-school teachers whom the country constantly required, and the philologists who, having read their Homer and developed an elegant Latin style, would leave their institutes of learning feeling properly equipped for any post or task. There was a highly developed system of financial assistance available which was administered in accordance with two essential criteria for selection of candidates: the steadfast faith and appropriate behaviour of a good Lutheran Christian, and the grammatical mastery of the classical languages. If things were in good order here, then it was felt that everything else could be left to take care of itself.

In Hegel's time the Swabians of Württemberg represented the only Protestant German community south of the river Main which occupied a self-enclosed territory with jurisdiction of its own, and that since 1565, the year in which, after protracted sectarian conflicts, the State Assembly irrevocably declared the Lutheranism of the Augsburg Confession as the sole official religion of state. In this respect the Württemberg Swabians clearly distinguished themselves from the Swabians who still occupied ancient Habsburg territory under remarkable arrangements and structures of political rule which, dissociated from one another as they largely were, never succeeded in developing into any cultural or political unity. So-called 'Austrian Swabia', together with Vorarlberg and Breisgau, formed part of lower Austria and was governed until 1752 from Innsbruck, and subsequently from Freiburg. The region in question, with its various flatlands on the upper Danube as well as in the north, belonged amongst the outlying territories of the Habsburg crown, although it also boasted a number of 'Free Cities' and principalities. But under the rule of Karl Eugen the idea of 'Swabia' came increasingly to be identified with Württemberg because the dukedom, with its approximately 500,000 inhabitants, constituted a strong centralized state in marked contrast to the scattered Swabian settlements beyond its borders with their largely Catholic populations. On the one hand an absolutist regime of an eighteenth-century monarch with leanings towards the Enlightenment and a centralized, pragmatic and secularized system of public administration, and on the other an antiquated expression of Imperial rule with strong feudal remnants that tamely resisted the state and its all-powerful monarchy. What the categories of 'state', 'monarchy' and 'feudalism' effectively signified as political and historical factors at this time can be most fruitfully studied in relation to Swabia, where these forms all coexisted with one another, variously in cooperation or conflict as the case might be. In addition Württemberg was characterized by the presence of a state church which since the Reformation had continued to exercise its undiminished influence, through all other political changes, and which still closely controlled the lives of its subjects from the cradle to the grave.

Württemberg is a country rich in towns, but, with the exception of the princely residences of Stuttgart and Ludwigsburg, there is little real separation between 'town' and 'country' as such. The countryside effectively begins in the towns and penetrates deep within them, its plots and allotments already forming part of the latter, its rows of houses incorporating stables for cattle and store-rooms for agricultural equipment used out in the fields beyond the town. Even in 1849 Friedrich Theodor Vischer could describe Tübingen as a rather 'dirty and desolate little village' where cows were still being driven through the narrow streets. Stutttgart is not like Dresden any more than Lessing is like Schiller, and even less like Leipzig which already appeared to Goethe, even before Hegel was born, as a 'little Paris'. None the less, the princely residence of Stuttgart and its roughly twenty thousand inhabitants was a comfortable and attractive place, with its parks, gardens, promenades and businesses, with its stores and shops serving the demands of court, and formed a striking contrast with the surrounding countryside. The area around the New Palace, the English Garden which faces towards Cannstatt, the neatly regular streets in the suburbs and the Residential Palace in Ludwigsburg, all these are classical expressions of the eighteenth century.

It is difficult to free ourselves from the image of Franz Eugen's Württemberg as a kind of educational forcing house – not least because of Schiller's early experiences there which drove him to abandon the state and its residential capital. Nor were the characteristic features of political absolutism lacking here either: witness the exercise of arbitrary government, the examples of financial extravagance, an established culture of court 'mistresses' with Franziska von Hohenheim as the conspicuous centre of attention, and the fortress of Hohenasperg which essentially functioned as a political prison. The fate of the poet Schubart, whom the Duke had deviously tempted to set foot in Württemberg territory and then confined to prison there under the most wretched conditions for ten years, had shocked people throughout the German lands of the 'Empire', including Frederick the Great, who eventually succeeded in getting him released. But the political system was largely felt to be an artificial intrusion, and hardly exercised any deeper effects upon the predominantly agricultural life of the country. The memory of the precious 'System of Ancient Law' (*Das gute alte Recht*) had never completely disappeared. The latter very much represented the feudalism which Hegel would later bitterly reject, but it also stood for the other more attractive aspect of a system where the estates could still offer some resistance to the power of the absolute monarch.

But it was precisely this absolutist power which encouraged modernizing tendencies in the educational system in contrast to the ecclesiastical monopoly of influence that had formerly prevailed. What the Duke expected from the Karlsschule was less a supply of young blood for the pulpit or schoolroom, something which in Swabia had been abundantly available for centuries already, but rather, in addition to military officers, a reliable source of trained doctors and professional people for the technical and administrative elite of the country. And he would enlist such people wherever they could be found. As a pupil at the Karlsschule Schiller, for example, had studied medicine and natural sciences without even considering theology as an option.

None the less, the pragmatically oriented educational policy so in evidence here was much less characteristic of Württemberg generally. It would be a long time before it could even begin to compete with the theological traditions of Swabian education. The prospective theologian had to embark upon a path that led from minor seminaries to the University of Tübingen, and typically speaking from schools like those at Maulbronn or Babeuren to the Tübingen Stift. And, as in Saxony, there was also a highly developed system of financial support for the selected students. They would eventually arrive at an ecclesiastical institution without further pretensions, namely a seminary expressly designed to lead to the eventual ordination of an officially accredited preacher, the archetypal figure in whom the 'Swabian system' would find its ultimate fulfilment!

And this was also the path which Hegel's father, the secretary of the ducal finance office, imagined for his eldest son. Wilhelm entered the German School at the age of three, and the Latin School at the age of five, but the original plan to send him finally to one of the Württemberg seminaries which prepared students to enter the university was dropped. Instead he attended the Stuttgart *Gymnasium* from the age of seven – only the year before the family had moved from the less select Eberhardstrasse to new and prosperous quarters in the Röderschen Gasse.

This was both a backward and a forward step. It was a backward step in so far as it deviated from the standard Swabian pattern of optimal educational choice; but it was something of a forward step from the perspective of Stuttgart court society and its conventions, since the *Gymnasium* Illustre paid generous tribute to more elevated educational aims. According to his station, Hegel's father, if not exactly a man of the ducal court, was certainly a man of the ducal administration. But the *Gymnasium* was not the foremost school in Stuttgart. It was the Karlsschule that attracted the best teachers and the personal attentions of the Duke, and it was here that Hegel's brother Ludwig was sent. There was no question of sending Hegel there on account of the practical orientation of the teaching and Hegel's professed intention to become a minister. Unlike Schelling and Hölderlin and other young students from the smaller towns and regions of the area, Hegel did not find himself forced into entering one of the cloister schools in the country.

At the *Gymnasium* Hegel showed himself to be an exemplary student who responded to the authority of his teachers and specifically sought out further personal contact with them. This was particularly true for his class teacher Löffler, who had once presented the eight-year-old Hegel with the Eschenberg translation of Shakespeare's works, and whom Hegel liked to accompany on his walks.

Hegel showed himself meticulous in complying with his duties at school. Plato and his Socrates, together with Homer and Aristotle, were naturally the focus of daily attention on his part. Amongst the Greek tragic poets he was particularly inspired by Sophocles' *Antigone* as well as Euripides. He read the classical authors like Livy, Cicero and Longinus (whom he also translated) and Epictetus. His early experience in reading Greek came with the study of the New Testament. And since the young Württemberg schoolboy was already expected to become a cleric in due course, he had to study some Hebrew as well, a subject for which the curriculum allowed two hours' study a week, just the same as for Greek. As far as more recent German literature was concerned Hegel acquainted himself with Goethe's *Werther*, Lessing's *Nathan the Wise* and Schiller's play *Fiesco*. But the book which seemed to have particularly absorbed his attention at this time was *Sophie's Journey from Memel to Saxony* by Johann Timotheus Hermes, a vast novel in six volumes describing the adventures of a young woman during the Seven Years War and the Russian occupation of East Prussia. The author allows himself, very much in the manner of Fielding or Richardson, to discourse at length about the realities of everyday life, with vivid scenes set in taverns and domestic houses featuring cooks and stable boys, and post-horses in the country, etc. Hegel found it impossible, as he confesses in his diary, to tear himself away from the book, which was indeed one of the most popular literary works of the century. Schopenhauer later took the opportunity of pouring contempt on Hegel's judgement: 'My favourite book is Homer, Hegel's is *Sophie's Journey*.'

Hegel essentially used his personal diary from the very beginning to record rationalistic precepts and observations, and rather precocious ones at that for someone of his age. There is no evidence here of participation in youthful pranks or transgressions of any kind, and Hegel the schoolboy and student seems never to have been young at all. Early on he responds to the problems and difficulties which social life can bring with a rather disarming good-humouredness. Harmless camaraderie, games of chess and card-playing with very low stakes characterize his spare time and clearly give much enjoyment. He looks on pretty girls with pleasure, but only at a safe distance. Failing to go to church one Sunday was the extent of his boldness, and merits a corresponding entry in the diary. He was even prepared to visit a Catholic church and observe proceedings there in order to compare it all with his own Lutheran background. He praised the priest's sermon on that occasion, though not without recording his considerable antipathy to the ceremony of the Mass itself.

The burning question as to who would give the final school address at the end of the year – 'On the Corrupted State of the Arts and Sciences amongst the Turks' – was settled diplomatically by the authorities through entrusting the task to five pupils. As the top of his year Hegel was the last one to speak at the annual ceremony, something he did with all due solemnity, and much praise for his teachers of course. The address revealed all the characteristic stylistic features of a school speech. There is one point, however, which is rather more than a standard gesture of humility and seems to express a genuinely heartfelt Hegelian sentiment: 'We can already learn to see now, although it is too late for some, that such neglect [of study and learning] will procure the disadvantageous effects that our teachers have warned about.' In other words: what we ourselves neglect to do is lost for ever, and through our own deed.

That seems the appropriate tone for a self-searching Lutheran sinner with downcast eyes, one who none the less is sure of delivery from the errors and the confusions of youth and already desirous of attaining a maturity which will protect him from the errors he must remorsefully admit to now. A eulogy for a maturity which apparently cannot be acquired too early and for a rationality of outlook which should be seriously cultivated from the first. This confession, and the insights it harboured, represents more than a rhetorical topos and honestly reflects the attitudes of a precocious young man expressing his own experience on leaving school. He gladly recognizes that it is far better to live in Württemberg than in the Turkish Empire and is more than willing to offer heartfelt thanks to the Duke and his teachers for that.

2

The Tübingen Stift

Hegel entered the portals of the University of Tübingen in the autumn of 1788. His matriculation papers specify the exact date as 27 October and enter him in the Faculty of Theology. There had never been any real alternative as far as Hegel was concerned. This course had already been decided upon long before he graduated from the Stuttgart *Gymnasium* and it was in complete accordance with his father's wishes.

Hegel had already made a successful application for a specific grant to support his studies and this, together with specific permission from the Duke, allowed him to enrol at the University Stift or seminary without further ado. The Stift, originally founded by Duke Ulrich, was located in a former Augustinian monastery that had been dissolved in 1547 and was now used to train and educate prospective Lutheran pastors and high-school teachers who were native citizens of Württemberg.

The 'Ephor' or Director of the Stift was the same Jacob Friedrich Abel who had once been Schiller's teacher in Stuttgart. The actual day-to-day running of the institution was largely in the hands of the so-called 'Repetenten'. The characteristic discipline of a seminary was maintained throughout the essentially semi-monastic institution. The various punishments and rewards which the students had acquired were carefully added up three times a year to provide a powerful yardstick for assessing their overall performance. All transgressions were punished with specific disciplinary measures called 'Caritionen', which ranged from threats to withdraw the standard wine ration at meal times to actual periodic incarceration.

With its barely three hundred students the University of Tübingen at this time was a supremely undistinguished institution, essentially little more than a training ground for people who would eventually serve in the churches and schools of Württemberg, while students destined for professions in the law or medicine would attend the Karlsschule in Stuttgart instead. The Enlightenment culture of the time, to which even a place like Tübingen was not entirely immune, was still essentially Enlightenment in the tradition of Christian Wolff, and knowledge of Kant's *Critique of Pure Reason*, which had already appeared in 1781, was largely the secret prerogative of more forward and precocious minds. And Hegel himself was certainly not amongst these. But quite irrespective of Kant or Wolff, Rousseau or Herder, the university teachers like Storr and Schnurrer, Flatt and Rösler effectively exercised their own narrow authority in the lecture halls. They gave priority to Christian dogmatics over exegesis or ecclesiastical history, and emphasized simple biblical faith of an orthodox or pietistic kind. These exemplary teachers of traditional theology presented the young Hegel, who had already accepted the superiority of Greek culture as a student at the Stuttgart *Gymnasium*, with the theoretical and practical reality of 'Christianity', as a phenomenon of 'world history', as a new principle in relation to the classical world.

Hegel reacted to the academic teaching at Tübingen with his own enormous capacity for lethargy. This was lethargy as an escape mechanism, as a means of intellectual survival. The Hegel of these years in Tübingen revealed a certain idleness, a general tendency to allow things to go their own way. This is also true for the numerous occasions on which he transgressed the Seminary rules (as many as eighteen times in 1790): he was punished and reproached by the administration for failing to attend lectures, for neglecting the accepted dress code, for going on drinking expeditions at night and sleeping in till the following midday, and for absenting himself from prayers. A year later he was punished with solitary confinement for leaving the Stift without permission and returning late from vacation.

The official documents up till 1791 remark upon a certain deterioration in his conduct but continue to praise his intellectual abilities and industry. His frequent absence from lectures is also duly noted. It seemed rather characteristic of the Stift that, without being generally permissive, it none the less permitted a certain leeway for the students. One could not really describe the standard punishments as draconian in character, and the nocturnal studies which Hegel preferred were obviously accepted as some compensation for his various absences.

Hölderlin, exactly the same age as Hegel, had also entered the Stift the same year. Although he was also enrolled to study theology, his thoughts dwelt constantly upon the land of Greece and the ancient Greeks themselves, upon their gods, temples and works of art. In his own immaculate appearance he was said to resemble a youthful 'messenger of the gods' himself! For his part Hölderlin had pursued the preferred Swabian educational path, passing directly from the cloister school at Maulbronn to the university in Tübingen. He suggests that he was originally placed above Hegel in the so-called 'Location' (a ranking list in terms of academic performance) since we find him reluctantly admitting to his mother in 1790 that he has now fallen behind Hegel and Märklin in his studies. The relevant documents do not actually confirm this but they do show that Hegel himself was demoted and placed behind the same Märklin, a fellow student of his from Stuttgart. Leutwein, a year ahead of Hegel and a good friend of his at the time, ascribed this demotion to a certain spirit of independence on Hegel's part, which was certainly not encouraged at the Stift. Hegel had not exactly recommended himself to the authorities by what Leutwein calls his 'eccentric behaviour', something further underlined by his irregular attendance at lectures. Leutwein expressly reproaches Hegel with a general 'desultoriness of approach', with inconsistent industry, wide-ranging but disorganized reading, and a constant tendency to change the focus of his interests.

In Hegel's mind, however, the real reason for his demotion lay in the Stift's interested concern with Märklin's uncle, who later became director of the Denkendorf seminary. The demotion seems to have left Hegel with a 'permanent sense of hurt' which he none the less succeeded in concealing outwardly. Even in Berlin in later years Hegel would still ask after his friend Märklin's circumstances whenever he received visitors from Württemberg. The young man with whom Hegel had found himself in such intense competition at the Stift later became the Abbot of Heilbronn. As far as the philosopher's later life is concerned, Leutwein himself drew a positive conclusion from Hegel's supposed setback at the university: 'If he had remained third in his year, Berlin would certainly never have got to look on him and he would not have given the German fatherland so much to talk about.'

This demotion seems to have spurred Hegel on to overcome his former lethargy and idleness and he now showed a capacity for hard work unusual for him. Intellectual energies that no one had suspected in him were suddenly released almost at a stroke. There was no more time now for retiring to bed early and he began to spend weeks on end studying at night. The blow which had befallen him had become an inner incentive for change.

He may have been disadvantaged with respect to Märklin because of his own lack of familiarity with the latest intellectual currents and trends. And perhaps the decision to demote him was not particularly unfair anyway, since Hegel had preferred to spend his nights drinking and playing cards with boon companions rather than discussing the philosophy of Kant which Märklin himself was studying at the time. Hegel, who was quite familiar with near contemporary works like the vast picaresque novel *Sophie's Journey* or with Hippel's *Life Story*, had not yet attained such heights, and even if he had read the relevant texts he did not feel confident enough to express an opinion about them. His own preferred authors at this time were Plato and Aristotle, and certain pieces by Schiller, Spinoza, Jacobi, Herder and, above all, Rousseau. The French Revolution had already stormed the ramparts of the Ancien Régime in the name of Rousseau, and it was not long before news of these events began to penetrate the threshold of the Stift. The general call for 'freedom' soon found speedy and enthusiastic acceptance amongst the students there.

Everyone was talking of the new coming century as if it would prove the century of freedom itself. Hegel was looked upon as one of the most ardent advocates of the Revolution. The pages of his *Stammbuch* or personal album are filled with typical exclamations of the time which, though entered in another hand, obviously reflected Hegel's own sentiments: 'Vive la liberté', 'Vive Jean-Jacques', and Schiller's *In tyrannos* or 'Death to Tyrants' – the celebrated motto with which the poet had recently prefaced his play *The Robbers*. According to Johann Eduard Erdmann, Hegel must have been regarded at the time as a republican with Jacobin sympathies. These sympathies were further strengthened when Schelling entered the Stift in the autumn of 1790. By then Hegel had acquired the equivalent of a doctorate of philosophy.

Five years younger than Hegel or Hölderlin, Schelling was born in Leonberg, the son of a Lutheran pastor and a theologian by early training. He graduated from the cloister school in Bebenhausen. With Schelling the idea of the 'Golden Age of Swabia' actually became a legend. He was only fifteen years old when he entered the Stift, had already 'skipped' three school years, and now impressed everyone with his knowledge of languages and his unparalleled ability to synthesize ideas in bold and unpredictable ways. In short he was everything that Hegel was not. Schelling was the authentic 'genius' in the romantic *Sturm und Drang* sense of the word who effortlessly put Hegel and Hölderlin in the shade. In total contrast to either of them, Schelling was a precocious offspring of the Swabian clerical aristocracy.

But the image of the 'trinity of friends' is a deceptive one. It is an image that can only be artificially constructed in retrospect. Not one of the three, who actually chanced to share a room with one another shortly before Hegel's departure from Tübingen, had any inkling of the future in which they would come to be seen as bonded together for ever.

Schelling's entry to the Stift significantly strengthened the republican faction there. Clearly marked out as he was by his volatile temperament and the infective enthusiasm he could lend to any subject, Schelling was immediately suspected by the Duke of organizing student demonstrations at which the 'Marseillaise' had been sung by the participants. When the Duke visited the Stift personally to investigate the matter he presented Schelling, who had almost automatically assumed responsibility for everything, with the offending German translation of the song and said: 'There is a fine little song composed in France and often sung by Marseille bandits. Is the young man familiar with it?' Schelling gave the remarkably self-possessed reply: 'Majesty, all of us transgress in so many ways', and the Duke, who regarded himself as a good Christian, was quite lost to find an appropriate response.

Compared with the self-confidence of Schelling, Hegel had something of the fellow traveller about him, and appeared even rather awkward and recalcitrant in nature. One can only speculate about what finally encouraged him to start organizing his time more productively and gradually focusing his own wide-ranging reading and writing, something which had certainly already been noticed by the authorities at the Stift. He was clearly regarded there as something of an eclectic who possessed a great deal of knowledge in many areas but which he seemed quite unable to bring together. Eclecticism is understood in this context as a manifestation of uncontrolled and undisciplined reflection, in contrast to that practical knowledge and understanding of the ways of the world so highly prized in a princely residential town, an understanding that needs no scholarly learning and presupposes a certain loss of that rural innocence which we would assume the students from Maulbronn, Denkendorf and Bebenhausen initially brought with them to Tübingen

But is this opposition between reflection and naïve simplicity, supposedly mirroring the opposition of town and country, really valid? Could one plausibly describe a young man like Schelling as naïve? A character like his seems rather to reveal evidence of a certain over-cultivation than any of the characteristic features of the humble Swabian student from the Neckar valley. As far as Hegel's character was concerned the rather 'old-fashioned' impression which he made on his student contemporaries was not a matter of affectation. It was certainly the butt of affectionate humour, as we can see from Hegel's personal album in which his friend Fallot from Mömpelgard drew a little picture of a bald, bent and bearded Hegel on crutches, together with the words 'May God Preserve the Old Man'.

If a successful caricature is capable of revealing something of the inner and outer characteristics through exaggeration, then Fallot's casual sketch testifies to Hegel's apparent infirmity, his ungainliness, his total lack of elegance. With regard to Schelling the contrast could hardly be a more glaring one. Hegel's appearance of premature age was probably due more to his general awkwardness than to his precocious and comprehensive knowledge or the pedantic fashion in which he pursued his studies. In fact there were many others who effortlessly outshone him academically at the Tübingen Stift, as he was rather painfully aware. Hegel faltered along behind the others. The sermons which he, like all the theology students, had to preach were fairly disastrous. These were held, according to custom, during meal times amongst the students and formed part of the daily devotion at table along with readings and accompanying exegesis from Scripture. The chosen speaker received special board that day. The manner in which Hegel delivered his sermon was halting and difficult to follow. On his leaving certificate he would eventually read, in Latin, that 'he did not excel as a preacher'. If this prospective cleric had ever wished to rise to eminence within the hierarchical Württemberg ecclesiastical establishment, then the outlook was not promising.

In fact one of his principal interests at the time appears to have been one Auguste Hegelmeier, the daughter of a recently deceased professor of theology and a very attractive young woman who was well aware of the great impression she made upon the students. Hegel liked to join in with her other admirers who would gather of an evening in the tavern to spend an hour in her company. But things went no further than this. Hegel's sister relates that he never 'aroused any particular hopes for the future' amongst the opposite sex and she probably had good reason for thinking so. Hegel's prospects as far as a Church position was concerned were hardly secure, given his decided lack of talent in the pulpit and his consequent doubts about his suitability as a minister anyway.

According to a later report by his friend Leutwein, Hegel tended at the Stift to 'wander around in a cavalier fashion in the realm of knowledge', to occupy his time with subjects which were sometimes peripheral or unrelated to the official curriculum, sometimes far in advance of its requirements. He retained his fondness for making copious excerpts, just as he had in Stuttgart. He would take a single sheet of paper, inscribe a suitable title for his excerpt in the top margin, and insert the page in the appropriate file. We know from his later lectures on the history of philosophy that he occupied himself intensively with Aristotle at a very early period and was particularly irritated to have to work with an almost unreadable ancient edition (the Basle edition of 1531 or possibly 1550) without an accompanying Latin translation of the text. The dialectical Aristotle meant as much to Hegel at this time as the Gnostic systems did to Schelling, as Albert Schwegler reported in his reminiscences of Hegel published in 1839. Hölderlin chose the lines of Pylades in Goethe's *Iphigenie* when he came to inscribe Hegel's personal album: 'Enthusiasm and love are the pinions to mighty deeds!' Immediately below the quotation someone had also written Lessing's Spinozan motto in Greek: *hen kai pan*. 'The One and All' was a shared formula of Hegel and Hölderlin which Schelling too could enthusiastically endorse.

3

Between Monarchy and Republic

Naturally there were very considerable differences of political opinion between Hegel and his father in Stuttgart: the partisan of the new revolutionary convention in France and the civil servant in the Duke's employ could
hardly be expected to see eye to eye on things. And yet there do not seem to
have been any great profound tensions in the relations between father and
son. During the months before and immediately after his official examination Hegel's closest personal contact appears to have been with his friend
Stäudlin. The writer and lawyer Gottfried Friedrich Stäudlin was twelve years
older than Hegel, and had made something of a name for himself as editor of
the first Swabian *Musenalmanach* or literary and cultural journal. In his capacity as a reviewer for this journal Stäudlin had come into some conflict
with Schiller who edited a rival publication of his own called 'Anthology',
although Stäudlin subsequently managed to patch up the quarrel to some
extent. This was something that would soon prove to be of considerable
personal significance for Hölderlin since, through Hegel's mediation, the poet
himself had formed a very close friendship with Stäudlin. And it was through
him that Hölderlin first made the personal acquaintance of Schiller when he
came from Jena to visit Württemberg. As a result of this meeting Schiller
recommended Hölderlin to his older friend and patron Frau von Kalb as a
possible private tutor ('Hofmeister') for her son. Thus it was that Hölderlin
came to leave Tübingen for Jena, where he would eventually be followed
first by Schelling and later by Hegel. It was therefore Stäudlin who can be
credited in part with shaping the future relationship of the three friends from
Tübingen.

At this time Hegel was having to consider his own immediate future options. This he duly did, though without any signs of apparent urgency. He
had already made some tentative moves in this direction before the examination, making the relevant enquiries through various intermediaries. Thus a

certain Herr von Sinner, who, though not himself a personal acquaintance of Hegel, had learned about him through another graduate of the Stift called Hauff, had mentioned Hegel's name in response to the enquiries of the von Steiger family in Berne who were currently seeking an appropriate personal tutor. The family had initially considered another graduate of the Stift called Schwinzdraheim for the position, and Herr von Steiger desired more detailed information about the candidate. Sinner took the necessary steps but, on learning about the supposedly questionable 'conduite' of the candidate, he advised against employing him after all and suggested Hegel in his place. It appears that Sinner may have been trying to ingratiate himself with von Steiger by strongly advising against the one candidate in favour of the other and imagined that he could arrange everything himself without more ado. For the patrician von Steiger this was clearly not nearly enough, however, and he made further enquiries through another intermediary, a teacher from Berne called Rütte, who contacted Johannes Brodhag, the proprietor of The Golden Ox in Stuttgart, in the idea that he might have had direct personal experience with the suspect candidate. In the end Rütte received the same report of Schwinzdraheim's 'dubious reputation' along with a corresponding recommendation of Hegel. The Stuttgart proprietor went further and enquired at the Ducal Consistory whether Hegel would be permitted to leave Württemberg to take up such a post. In order to speed things along Brodhagen even went to see Hegel himself at home. At first Hegel hesitated because he considered the proposed salary of 15 louis d'or a year to be too low: he suggested instead 25 louis d'or 'along with some corresponding perks' and requested in any case a fortnight in which to consider the matter.

There were also other people who entertained some reservations about Hegel's tutoring prospects: Ephor Schnurrer for one. Even before Hegel had passed the examination in his presence Schnurrer had written to the former student Scholl in terms which reveal something of his estimate of Hegel's character: 'I really doubt whether he [Hegel] has learned properly how to make those kinds of sacrifices which are inevitably coupled, at least at the beginning, with the position of private tutor.'

Here we see a man who in his capacity as a university teacher clearly knew Hegel's personal character rather well, candidly expressing the difficulties attendant upon the career of private tutoring in general and particularly in relation to Hegel himself. Being a private tutor at this time meant serving as a very subordinate employee in educational matters, and being a useful and advantageous adjunct to some noble family. Such service could range from the most agreeable personal intimacy between teacher and student on the one hand to the lowly status of a lackey on the other. A personal tutor could be the educator of princes, or simply a travel companion for young gentlemen on tour, something which Lessing did not regard as beneath him and which Herder had considered a great privilege. Everything really depended upon chance and luck, as well as upon personal aptitude, tactfulness and a general capacity to fit in with other people. On the other hand the possible advantages of such employment could easily be outweighed by the particular difficulties it brought with it.

Hegel had good reason therefore to request a fortnight's reflection and to try and discover, so far as possible, something of the conditions and circumstances with which he would have to reckon. The time of his own original Jacobin enthusiasm was certainly behind him and republican Berne probably did not appear a particularly enticing prospect. But the prospect of assuming an official clerical post was equally unattractive to this newly qualified young theologian with a very poor reputation for delivering sermons (duly noted in his final university report). If Hegel needed time to reflect and consider other possible options, his hesitancy revealed the extremely ambiguous feelings he harboured about the offer of employment in Switzerland. However, on 11 September Hegel was able to write to Rütte in Berne that 'no further impediments now stand in the way of my accepting this position in the von Steiger household'.

On account of the impending examination he had to postpone his arrival in Berne until the first week of the following month. He asked von Steiger to request official permission from the relevant ecclesiastical authorities for him to leave Württemberg, confirmed an increase in his proposed salary of 5 louis d'or, and promised to contribute his utmost 'towards the education of the daughter of Herr Hauptmann'.

On 20 September, only ten days after Schnurrer's letter to Scholl, Stäudlin reported to Schiller: 'From his friend Magister Hegel he [Hölderlin] has learnt that you yourself are currently in a position to offer a similar tutoring position in the Jena area. Since Hegel has already accepted the engagement as house tutor in Berne and definitely abandoned any other intentions he may have had, H[ölderlin] has with the greatest urgency asked me whether you yourself might put in a good and influential word on his behalf with regard to the said position.'

The letter reveals the nature of the choice: K. F. von Steiger or Charlotte von Kalb, Berne or Jena – the town which represents the world of practical politics or the town which represents Schiller. Hegel had decided in favour of the Republic of Berne.

Hegel did not have to produce his own dissertation in Tübingen. He graduated after successfully defending a dissertation 'De Ecclesia Wirtembergicae Renascentis Calamitatibus' written by Le Bret, the Chancellor of the University. He had similarly matriculated as 'Magister' by defending the dissertation 'De limite officiorum' by Professor Böck rather than anything written by himself. In both cases, therefore, the task was to defend an existing position, which appears to possess authority by virtue of its established existence: simply an authority which justifies its existence in and of itself, and a justification which also and simultaneously supports the rationality of what exists with its authority! There is no sign of any opposition or resistance here on Hegel's part. Magister and Candidate Hegel kept conspicuously and scrupulously to the traditional rules. The idea of expressing and defending one's own theses in the circle of one's academic colleagues was something more characteristic of Schelling than of Hegel. So too Hegel's friend and rival Märklin had already distinguished himself by a knowledge of Kant's philosophy which Hegel would not acquire for a long time yet. Perhaps we should give credence therefore to the final university report which Hegel received on 20 September 1793. It states that while Hegel was 'not without competence in philology' ('non ignarus'), he certainly did not appear very promising in philosophy ('Philosophiae nullam operam impendit').

4

The Tutoring Years

Hegel's decision to leave for Berne and experience the life of a house tutor for himself was a crucial step for him. In the first place it marked the end of his years as a student, a time which he had passed in a rather distracted and unsettled way. Of course it also marked his departure from his homeland in the Dukedom of Württemberg and the beginning of a very different life in a republican Swiss city-state.

During the long reign of Karl Eugen the state of Württemberg had suffered a major decline. In the last twenty-three years the Duke had attempted to heal the wounds which he had himself inflicted on the country during the previous thirty-three through the financial extravagance of the Court, the oppressive burden of taxation, arbitrariness in government and acts of personal brutality. This was no easy prospect and indeed he never succeeded in accomplishing it. Even amongst the other German potentates and princes of the time, Karl Eugen enjoyed no enviable reputation. It says a good deal about his regime that the Emperor and the governments of Prussia, England and Denmark were all called upon at one time or another to act in defence of the Württembergian Constitution which the Duke had violated so ruthlessly. It was the Estates which had made this appeal as protectors of the 'Old System of Rights' against a government which for all its efforts had never quite been able utterly to destroy the idyll of Swabian freedom. In 1770, the year in which Hegel was born, the Duke was forced to accept the so-called 'Adjustment' and make numerous concessions to the older liberal demands of the Swabian tradition. In 1793, the year in which Hegel departed for Berne, the government of Karl Eugen finally met its end. The victorious progress of the revolution in France had also begun to make itself felt in Tübingen in the form of processions and demonstrations, in the defiant planting of 'freedom trees', in the founding of republican clubs: it was obvious that the time of the old order was over.

Whether any great hopes were to be entertained with regard to the Republic of Berne was another matter entirely. And it is difficult to know whether Hegel harboured any such hopes when he set out on his journey to Switzerland.

At that time Berne was certainly still the most powerful of the Swiss republics, a city state whose past, without its rulers remotely realizing the fact, was far more illustrious than its future would ever be. The Grand Council in Berne represented something like the sovereign power in an absolutist state; its members were elected, but only from out of the ranks of the ruling and similarly prospective families of the city. Every ten years, at Easter time, the vacant places had necessarily to be filled appropriately. Hegel was in a good position to observe and record the proceedings and the attendant circumstances at first hand.

Karl Friedrich von Steiger, in whose service Hegel was employed as personal tutor to his six-year-old son and eight-year-old daughter, belonged to one of the families of the ruling oligarchy of Berne. Hegel's employer and master of the household was a member of the Grand Council and a nephew of Christoph Steiger, whose tenure as Councillor marked the beginning of a protracted struggle against the political pretensions and abuses committed by the Berne oligarchy, and one in which the old system slowly but surely met its end.

The Berne residence of the von Steigers was Junkerngasse 51. The house had been sold that year to the von Steigers by the family Wattenwyl, and the family had therefore only recently moved in. The family property at Tschugg in the Vogtei Erlach region lay in the Jura mountains between the lakes Bielersee and Neuenburgersee. It was here that Hegel spent his first tutoring years during the summer and the winter months. The obvious familial pride displayed by the von Steigers, in a town well used to the manifestations of rank and privilege, was hardly calculated to encourage a smooth relationship between the parties, and there seems to have been little personal warmth or sympathy involved on either side. Hegel's official title as 'House Tutor', as expressed in the original written negotiations, was, despite the highly respectable residences of the von Steigers, somewhat exaggerated; and in his Berne passport Hegel was merely described as 'Gouverneur des enfants de notre cher et féleal citoyen Steiguer de Tschougg'. There is nothing whatever to suggest that the von Steigers regarded their tutor as any different from all the other similar graduates of educational institutions who were simply eager to secure their daily bread and find some advancement where they could. He must have appeared to them as another modest and straightforward young man, a Swabian with German with a knowledge of Greek and Latin (though this was certainly not required for the daughter), and with some history, geography, geometry, literature and the requisite Reform-Protestant instruction. And there is nothing whatever to suggest that the modest young tutor in their employ ever caused them to think otherwise of him. But there is plenty to suggest that the master of the house trusted his Swabian tutor with various other duties in addition.

The position certainly offered some corresponding advantages. It allowed Hegel plenty of time for private study and the residence at Tschugg put a large library at his disposal which he exploited to the full. It is impossible to discover whether Hegel ever frequented the imposing classical reading room of the Berne City Library, but it is difficult to imagine that he did not given that it was situated in the close vicinity of the von Steigers' Berne residence. One of Hegel's principal activities ever since his early school years in Stuttgart was his practice of making substantial excerpts and gathering all sorts of written material, perhaps with a view to some special and particular use in the future. The von Steigers spoke French amongst themselves and this undoubtedly encouraged him in his active knowledge of the language as well. Otherwise the dominant influence during these Berne years for Hegel proved to be the study of the Scottish political economists.

Hegel's acquaintance with English writings in the field of political economy would eventually be revealed in its own way at the beginning of 1799 with his close study of and commentary upon Sir James Steuart's *Investigation into the Principles of Political Economy* (a German translation of which had appeared with Cotta). Steuart was a political economist of moderate views who belonged to the last phase of the English mercantile system of economic thought. Steuart's two-volume work, originally published in London in 1767 under the title *An Essay on the Science of Economy for Free Nations*, discusses subjects like population, agriculture, industry, trade and commerce, gold, coinage, borrowing rates, travel and communications, the banking system, the monetary exchange system, public credit and the tax system – all of them themes which appear rather remote from the previous concerns of this Württembergian theologian and dutiful subject of the state. Not questions concerning the proper Pauline-Lutheran doctrine of 'Justification by Faith' or the coming of 'The Kingdom of God', but issues of land cultivation and agricultural production, of exports and imports, of tariffs and property rights, etc. Although Steuart himself was already operating with distinctions like the cost of production and the cost of selling, with the principles of supply and demand, this did not prevent his fame subsequently being eclipsed by Adam Smith's *Wealth of Nations* in 1776. Hegel's first acquaintance with the field of national and political economy reflected a stage of economic thought which had already been undermined and rendered obsolete by the new doctrine of free trade, although it was certainly one that recognized a secure and fundamental role for 'property' in the sphere of the state and civil society. We can clearly see here the original source of observations which will appear explicitly in Hegel's writings in Berne and Frankfurt, when he writes, for example, that:

> In the states of modern times the security of property is the hinge upon which the entire body of legislation turns, the point to which most of the citizen's

rights are related. In many a free republic of the ancient world [on the other hand] the constitution of the state itself exercised control over the right to private property, the very thing which is the central concern of all our authorities and constitutes the pride of our states . . .

This passage clearly reveals the double-edged character of Hegel's critical analysis. The actual day-to-day life of the von Steiger family also provides Hegel with a particularly vivid picture, quite apart from any theoretical reflections, of the social and political world of a great house at the centre of a once powerful republic already on the wane – a little version of the story described by Gibbon in his *Decline and Fall of the Roman Empire*, a copy of which Hegel had found in the Tschugg library. In Berne there was open access to witness the political deliberations and observe developments as they unfolded, something which he certainly took advantage of himself, and the kind of open political processions and celebrations that were also to be seen here were quite unknown in Württemberg.

During these otherwise rather tedious years in Berne Hegel seems to have spent his evenings socializing and probably even singing with friends around a regular table in the tavern: at least this is what is suggested from the correspondence which Hegel later carried on in Frankfurt with the painter and artisan Sonnenschein. Johann Valentin Sonnenschein, a native of Ludwigsburg, whose artistic creations include the Laurel Room of the Stuttgart palace known as 'Die Solitüde', had left the service of the Duke of Württemberg for reasons of health and moved with his wife and child to Switzerland, where he became a teacher at the School of Art in Berne. 'We often sing "The joys of radiance divine" [Schiller's famous lines later set by Beethoven] in your memory', as he wrote to Hegel on 13 November 1797 long after the latter had already left the city, in order to remind him of the evenings they had once spent together. However, the most interesting acquaintance which Hegel made in Berne was certainly that with Konrad Engelbert Oelsner. As a direct witness of the revolutionary events of 1792, and a man personally acquainted with men of all political persuasions, Oelsner, who was the ambassador of the City of Frankfurt in Paris, used his *Letters from Paris* to express his fears about the possible collapse of the new French republic. Hegel himself drew Schelling's attention to these letters, which had appeared in Archenholz's historical-political journal *Minerva* and indeed must be counted amongst the first eye witness reports of the French revolutionary scene to appear in German.

Otherwise Hegel was busy during this Berne period with fulfilling various other duties which his employer had entrusted to him. In Tschugg he had temporarily assumed the function of general supervisor for von Steiger's affairs with an obligation to keep his employer fully informed about all developments in his absence. Thus in the summer of 1795 Hegel reports that work on laying gravel down in the front yard cannot be completed yet because the workers are otherwise employed with the crops. He also informs von Steiger about the return of his wife from the spa, and expresses his general satisfaction with the progress of the children in his charge. Everything communicated in precise detail in the distanced and objective form appropriate to his position.

It is a striking fact that nowhere in the surviving letters from this period does Hegel explicitly refer either to the revolutionary events unfolding in France or to the effects of the same in Berne, even though the Revolution was taking an increasingly drastic turn at this time. On 16 October 1793 Marie Antoinette was sent to the guillotine, only to be followed by Robespierre on 28 June 1794. Apart from a single reference to the defeat of 'Robespierre's faction' in one of his letters to Schelling, Hegel says nothing about the developments. Hegel's remark, in the same letter of 24 December 1794, that 'you will certainly already be aware that Carrier has gone to the guillotine' seems to treat the fact as a natural result and inevitable consequence of events. One must of course remember that throughout this period in Berne Hegel found himself physically at the very centre of the counter-revolutionary movement in Switzerland, which through the coalition with Austria and Prussia was actively taking strong measures to hinder the influence of revolutionary-minded individuals and of revolutionary ideas in general. In addition Hegel was actually living under the roof of von Steiger, one of the most vigorous supporters of the conservative cause, in the very midst therefore of the anti-revolutionary party. The typical Prussian admiration for the Berne Republic, an attitude that had been expressly shared by Frederick the Great, was founded not least on the political manoeuvrings of the von Steigers who were long-standing confidants of the government in Berlin. But the reason for Hegel's reticence in this respect could also lie in his awareness of the powers of censorship at the time. He constantly had to reckon with the possibility that his correspondence would be intercepted and read by the authorities. We can probably surmise as much from his recommendation to Schelling in the postscript to his letter of 16 April 1795 where he says: 'Be so good as not to stamp your letters to me in future, for that way they will arrive more safely.'

While he was living in Switzerland Hegel made a couple of major excursions: one to Geneva in May 1795 and one to the Bernese Alps in July 1796. In his personal diary Hegel provided a quite detailed description of his tour of the Swiss mountains in the company of three other house tutors from Saxony, by the names of Thomas, Stolde and Hohenbaum. The travellers set off early on the 24 July at four o'clock in the morning and eventually arrived at Thün around ten o'clock. There they boarded a boat to Interlaken where they commenced their journey through the Bernese Alps on foot. Their route led them over Grindelwald and Scheidegg to Meringen, then further on through the Berne region as far as Andernmatt and thence over Flüelen to the lake of Vierwaldstättersee towards Lucerne.

Hegel's trek through the mountains was hardly comparable to Goethe's trip through the same region which proved to be such a moving experience of living nature for him. Hegel's descriptions of the journey nowhere reveal any sense of awe or astonishment in the face of the overpowering might of the mountains around him. Even the glacial formations of Grindelwald could hardly stir his interest in their geological constitution. And why not? 'The sight of them presents nothing of further interest to the view. One can only really describe it as another kind of snow which offers nothing of any further interest for the spirit.' Here we see Hegel the house tutor, who also happens to be a certified graduate of theology when required, testing out the physico-theological proof for the existence of God in the harsh presence of a nature devoid of vegetation and finding the demonstration wanting! As he contemplates the upper slopes of the region in all its barren bleakness the Enlightenment notion of a nature perfectly fitted to serve our human needs and purposes strikes him as an absurdity: 'I doubt whether the most devout of theologians would dare to ascribe the virtue of utility for man to nature herself in these mountain regions . . .' The sheer 'might and necessity of nature' cannot properly be understood or appreciated in Hegel's eyes, whereas at least the waterfalls at the Staubbach present us with 'an image of free and spontaneous play' and thereby introduce a lighter tone into the otherwise gloomy dereliction of this mountain world.

The path taken by our four mountain tourists followed a route which was particularly popular at the time. While it was not dangerous, it was certainly exerting and rather uninspiring. By the end of it all Hegel had procured for himself a pair of extremely sore and painful feet. The food along the way was not always particularly enticing either, and Hegel was hardly disposed to regard the grilled marmot he was offered in the local inns as a culinary delicacy. However, Hegel was pleased to record one thing at least, namely that he now understood the local language of these Alpine dwellers rather better than he did that of the Bernese townspeople. And after all, in order to know what such people think, one must possess some 'knowledge of the older form of the German language' which has survived in these regions better than it has in Germany itself.

5

Schelling's Apprentice

~~

It is impossible to learn very much about Hegel's relationship to Schelling in the period immediately after they left the Tübingen Stift since there is no surviving evidence of letters exchanged between them from this time. The situation with Hölderlin, who appears early on as Hegel's correspondent, however, is rather different. Hegel led an extremely secluded life as a house tutor in Berne and he took time to learn to get accustomed to his new situation and accept the rather limited and limiting conditions, at least from an external point of view, of his position.

Schelling, who had yet to sit his final examination at the Stift, had already composed a piece on the biblical story of creation, under Schnurrer's supervision, in 1798. In it he synthesized elements of Kantian rationalism with Herder's notion of original sin and the fall of man as a poetic expression of the origin of evil. Schelling once again pursued a similar approach to this question on a broader scale in his essay entitled 'On Myths, Historical Legends and Philosophemes of the Ancient World', which appeared in the fifth number of *Memorabilien*, a journal dedicated to philosophy and the history of religion. The journal was edited by Heinrich Eberhard Paulus, who was born in 1761 in the same Diocese of Leonberg as Schelling, and had now begun to play the role of advocate for Schelling's ideas, although in later years he would actually become one of the philosopher's most bitter opponents. On reading an advertisement for the essay Hegel decided to set pen to paper himself and express his own interest in the subject to Schelling.

The letter in question represents the first obvious renewal of the earlier connection between the two, which had been interrupted by Hegel's departure from Württemberg, and also betrays an extremely cautious perspective on the latter's part. Various shared attitudes of the earlier period are rehearsed. Nothing at all is to be expected from Tübingen, says Hegel, clearly assuming that Schelling will naturally agree with him on this. For Tübingen simply signified Storr, the culture of orthodox mediocrity, as well as Schnurrer and all the other teachers at the Stift: 'Unless and until someone like Rheinhold or Fichte is appointed to a position there, nothing significant will come of the place. There is nowhere I can think of where the old system of thought is so obstinately perpetuated as it is there . . .'

But we also learn a little more from this letter. There seems scant trace of his earlier sympathies for the first manifestations of the revolutionary cause; on the contrary, he now writes that 'the whole sorry tale of the Robespierre faction' can be seen for what it is. The fact that French newspapers are forbidden in Württemberg does not seem to disturb him in the least.

The letter also has a more personal side to it which does reveal something of Hegel's attitudes to the current state of affairs in Tübingen. He is particularly interested to learn about Renz, a name that also appears later in his correspondence with Schelling. Hegel thinks that something should be done to assist this former *Primus*, or top student, who was in Hegel's year at the Stift, and suggests he might be able to find him a position in Saxony. Hegel also mentions a certain Reinhard. Nine years older than Hegel, this Karl Friedrich Reinhard had also been a student of theology at the Stift where he had pursued Oriental Studies under Schnurrer. He had subsequently entered the service of the new French government and made numerous friends amongst the partisans of the Revolution, particularly amongst the Girondists. He had made the acquaintance of Sieyès by writing a specially commissioned piece on the Kantian philosophy for him. When Schelling told Hegel that Reinhard currently occupied 'a post of considerable importance in the Département des Affaires Étrangères' he could hardly have imagined that this was only the beginning of an impressive political career which would eventually lead to Reinhard's appointment as French foreign minister. It would be the former Tübingen student Reinhard, son of a minor prelate from Schorndorf, who would formally grant Napoleon the full control over the Directory.

Even if we did not possess Hegel's other theological writings from Berne, we could learn from another letter to Schelling, written only a few weeks later, that Hegel had begun studying Kant in earnest for himself at the beginning of 1795. Hegel complains of his current isolation from the literary and intellectual scene, and laments the connected fact that he does not really have the possibility of acquainting himself properly with the unfolding contemporary debates concerning the significance of Kantian philosophy. He wholeheartedly shares Schelling's conception of the current alternatives: 'Either Kant or Orthodoxy', but also adds a characteristic personal observation of his own: 'The power of orthodoxy cannot be broken as long as the profession associated with it is so intimately connected with worldly advantages and so closely tied in with the totality of the state.' The 'orthodoxy' in question is the dominant theological faction of the time, a 'system of mediocrity' supported and maintained by 'a gang of moaners and sycophants'. But Hegel even expresses a much more distant and reserved attitude to Fichte whom he accuses of making things easier for such people through the recent publication of his *Critique of All Revelation*: 'From the idea of God's holiness he constructs what he should and must do in virtue of his moral nature, and thereby has only reintroduced the old style of dogmatic demonstration.'

But Hegel's ideas are still in too great a state of flux here, and our knowledge of the details too insufficient, for us to be completely sure about Hegel's general position at this time. He is principally concerned at first with familiarizing himself with the intellectual scene and only gradually developing his own views. He clearly feels in need of Schelling's assistance and instruction and shows himself more than ready to subject himself to the latter's criticisms. At this time Hegel unreservedly recognized the superiority of his younger friend in the intellectual sphere and regarded him as a kind of teacher, indeed as something more than this, as his mentor in all the relevant and important areas of current philosophy. That is why he asks for Schelling's understanding for his own limitations and relatively sparse rate of production.

This was no artificial or stylized gesture of modesty on Hegel's part but was a natural expression of his own character and his external circumstances at the time. It also expressed his response to the brilliant confidence which was so characteristic of Schelling and so untypical of himself.

It is only from Hegel's letter that Schelling now gets to learn something about Hölderlin, the third member of this group of friends. Hegel tries to explain the reason why Schelling has not heard anything by letter from Hölderlin himself, who had departed for Jena in the meantime. He should not take it as coldness, Hegel assures him, and reports that there is no doubt about Hölderlin's 'growing interest in cosmopolitan political ideas' now that he is attending Fichte's lectures. Without expressly intending to do so, Hegel found himself something of an intermediary here, attempting to mediate between the extreme and alternative positions of his two friends. As such a mediator he can honestly proclaim the common ideal and aspiration they had shared at Tübingen: the realization of 'The Kingdom of God'. Naturally this was no longer to be understood in the usual sense intended by 'theologians of profession', and by the traditional Church of devout believers, but in terms of the very different programme proposed by Kant and Fichte: 'Reason and Freedom shall remain our rallying cry and the Invisible Church our unifying bond.'

In his provisional and still tentative way, Hegel succeeds here, without expressly trying to do so, in spontaneously articulating a major theme of his thought to come. For the average Lutheran Christian of the time it could not but appear as a stone of offence. The suspect conjunction of 'Freedom' with 'Reason' could hardly expect to meet with an enthusiastic reception on the part of the orthodox. But the real scandal lay in the idea of the 'Invisible Church', an expression which sounds like something from the mystical writings of Jakob Böhme. The 'Invisible Church' is a crucial concept, which releases its full measure of critical force against the existing regime of the 'Visible Church' and all the powerful material and sacramental means at its disposal.

Schelling's reply of 4 February 1795 proved to be an enormous encouragement for Hegel in his isolated position in Berne, and offered him an ample opportunity for engaging with the ideas expressed in it. Hegel goes so far as to say, in a letter of 16 April, that he already descries an entire 'system' of thought here, indeed more than this, 'a *completion of knowledge* which will procure for us the most fertile results'. There is a certain self-confidence on Hegel's part in evidence here as he shows himself more than ready to collaborate with Schelling in effecting a transformation of the currently prevailing atmosphere of thought, though he clearly accepts his friend's leading role in the project. Naturally we see Hegel here still in search of himself, but he is emphatic about one thing: 'I expect a revolution in Germany to ensue from the Kantian philosophy and its consummation.' He is grateful to Schelling for affording him insight into Fichte's new doctrine of knowledge and all the previously unparalleled consequences that will flow from it. The most important thing is that 'mankind is here represented in his own eyes as something worthy of respect'. The reason why this has taken so long to accomplish and the identification of those responsible is also clear. Religion has acted as an ally of despotism in preaching its 'contempt for the human race' and the task now is to disseminate ideas about how things should develop in future and thus to dispel the attitude of resigned indifference of men towards their own fate.

A sense of idealism and undisturbed optimism clearly animated both correspondents at this time. Hegel explicitly mentions the names of Kant, Fichte and Schiller as the authentic harbingers and messengers of the 'Invisible Church'. The correspondence also frequently casts Hölderlin in the natural role of future apostle in this prophetic vision. The content of their message consists essentially in trusting in the transformative power of ideas. Hegel is especially enthusiastic about the writings of Theodor Gottlieb von Hippel to whom he owes, so he tells Schelling, the general orientation of his thought: 'Strive towards the sun, my friends, that the salvation of the human race may all the sooner grow to fruition. What use the hindering leaves or the boughs of the tree? Strike through them and cleave to the sunlight!'

The original sympathy for the French revolutionaries which Hegel felt in his Tübingen days has receded considerably in Berne. But although Hegel's role as onlooker naturally deters him anyway from any kind of direct political engagement, his correspondence with Schelling still expresses great interest in Reinhard's career and considerable admiration for this former student of the Stift now risen to some eminence through the Revolution. Perhaps for a short period of time Reinhard came to represent Hegel's own hopes for the future.

The cooling of Hegel's initial revolutionary ardour represents a certain taking stock of events on his part, as well as the firm formation of specific views which will remain largely unchanged in the time to come. His personal experiences combine with the conclusions he has begun to draw from the fate of events in France. For the French situation casts its own light on the predicament of Württemberg under Karl Eugen and his immediate successor. For the 'orthodoxy' of the Württemberg church is also closely bound up with the political interests of the state, of despotism, and that means with the ideology of 'contempt for the human race'. This is the fundamental point of Hegel's agreement with Schelling who was equally repulsed by 'orthodoxy' and 'despotism' and sought a corresponding refuge in 'philosophy', pre-eminently that of Kant and Fichte. Hegel finally expressed the conclusions he had drawn from his experiences in Württemberg in his 'theological' and thoroughly unofficial papers under the title of his essay 'The Positivity of the Christian Religion'. 'Positivity' here characterises every concept and practice that has become fixed and ossified in the course of history as opposed to whatever its original intention and meaning might have been. Hegel thinks here of the Spaniards, advancing with the crucifix in their hands, exterminating entire generations of native Indians in the Americas in the name of Christianity, or of the supposed science of 'theology' which developed from the needs of the Church to become an effectively 'godless' discipline.

As his revolutionary hopes began to fade the Hegel of the essay on the 'Positivity of the Christian Religion' sees religion essentially reduced to an expression of 'orthodoxy', the state to an expression of despotism, and both of them directly connected with one another. While he was in Berne Hegel communicated few details about his general 'method' in the letters he wrote to Schelling. He was still testing his way in this respect and his relevant thoughts were tentative. 'My own labours', he wrote on 21 July 1795 to Schelling in Tübingen, 'are hardly worth talking about.' He was still expecting stimulus and intellectual encouragement from Schelling and did not feel bold enough to hazard any critical judgements of his own about his friend's work: 'You will not expect any observations about your latest piece. I am only the pupil here.'

And this was quite true: nothing had become firm in Hegel's mind as yet, and nothing could prematurely be exposed to public view. Hegel was not willing to communicate anything to Schelling that he was still unsure about or had insufficiently thought out – whereas Schelling, on the contrary, was pouring out his ideas like a boiling flood of lava and was even now in Tübingen actively preparing to take issue with Fichte himself. What strongly bound Hegel and Schelling together at this time was the shared belief in the advent of a new epoch which would emerge to do battle with the forces of 'orthodoxy' in the name of 'philosophy'. Hegel's own study of Kant's thought was principally directed towards his book on *Religion within the Bounds of Reason Alone* which he hoped to use as a basis for thinking through Kant's own concept of 'positive religion'. This book helped to reveal the prospect of just such a new epoch in the history of the world in Hegel's eyes, and one which neither he nor Schelling ever imagined would be born in Württemberg. Just as Märklin had proved to be far ahead of Hegel in studying Kant in Tübingen, even now Hegel's progress in this direction is painfully slow and deliberate. On account of his various duties in the von Steiger household Hegel's study of Kant's work and of Schelling's early writings was subject to constant interruption.

By the time Schelling's period of study in Tübingen came to an end, the tone and character of the correspondence between them had begun to change. Theoretical questions retreat somewhat behind discussions of Schelling's travel plans and all the relevant preparations for them, and soon detailed reports about his visits to Stuttgart, Leipzig and Jena, and a special trip back to Württemberg which he made from Thuringia. While Schelling was travelling around in the personal company of the Riedesel family, Hegel was living in a state of increasingly depressed isolation in the Jura. Schelling recognized these phases of depression on Hegel's part, which would also recur repeatedly in the future. He attempted to encourage his friend and urged him to move and quit his position as soon as possible. Hegel certainly needed just such an external appeal at this time, and it seems to have represented a further stimulus which strengthened his own intention of leaving the household of the von Steigers.

6

Jena contra Tübingen

At this time Kant, Reinhold and Fichte represented the eminent triple point of reference for both Schelling and Hegel in their struggle against the Tübingen faction of Schnurrer, Storr and Flatt. There was a moment when Hegel seems to have considered the possibility of offering his services for a position as *Repetent* back at the Stift, but the name of Renz, the Vicar of Maulbronn, was soon mentioned in the same connection and any chance Hegel may have had, despite his general feelings about Tübingen, were immediately dashed anyway. The subject is briefly mentioned in his correspondence with both Schelling and Hölderlin, but it seems fairly clear that the three of them had long since recognized that there was only one real alternative for them: it was Tübingen or Jena.

The important name most closely connected with Jena at the time was that of Karl Leonhard Reinhold, a native of Vienna who had progressed from would-be Jesuit seminarian to become a Protestant and a Kantian. He had actually introduced himself in Königsberg to the author of the *Critique of Pure Reason* who actively encouraged him to teach the principles of Kantian philosophy in Jena, an activity which contributed enormously to its dissemination. Members of the younger generation who had been influenced by Kant and Kantianism put great hopes in Reinhold. Students responded well to his teaching, and he began to make a considerable name for himself. His lectures must have been particularly stimulating and the man who gave them had, after all, earned the conspicuous favour of the father of critical philosophy himself. In 1794 Reinhold decided to accept a call to the University of Kiel, and Fichte took his place in Jena.

Fichte had obtained the chair of philosophy at the principal University of Saxon-Weimar not least through the decisive support of Goethe. Fichte's academic activities were initially extremely successful and before long the numbers of those attending his lectures had grown to around five hundred.

But his very success in the post almost automatically called forth a host of opponents on the university scene. At first only a few isolated voices were raised against his persisting influence, but the number of agitators ready to defame the man gradually increased and their attacks became more and more vocal. It cannot really be said that Fichte himself was entirely without responsibility in this, for he made things extremely easy for his opponents and gave them plenty of material to suggest that he was a dangerous character from the political point of view. It is not particularly difficult to see how Fichte's claim that 'the aim of all governments is to render government superfluous' could easily be interpreted as a call for anarchy or revolution. And once Fichte felt it necessary to launch an open attack on three specific student fraternities on account of 'the extremities of their crude behaviour and general lack of discipline', his happy period in Jena was definitely and abruptly at an end. As a result he had to suffer broken windows and see his wife verbally abused in the street. The Senate of the University remained largely unmoved and Fichte was only able to procure some peace for himself by taking official leave with the Duke's agreement in the summer of 1795.

During this entire period Fichte had entertained the thought of emigrating to France. He wanted the opportunity to continue work on the *Doctrine of Science* at leisure and for this he required time to himself free from all official duties. His opponents were not entirely wrong to see him as a sympathizer with the French Revolution. In the draft of a letter which Fichte wrote at this time we read:

> My system is the first system of freedom; and just as that nation [the French] have torn themselves free from the external chains which fetter mankind, my system of thought also tears man free from the thing in itself, from all external influence, and posits him according to first principles as an absolutely independent being ... I would more gladly bear the title of French citizen, if the nation in question saw fit to confer this upon me.

Hegel in Berne and Schelling in Tübingen had watched the growing influence of Fichte's doctrine and the spectacle of its sudden demise soon afterwards at the hands of its enemies. This constitutes one of the main subjects of Hegel's correspondence with Schelling. After receiving and immediately studying a copy of Fichte's *Foundation and Outline of the entire Doctrine of Science*, Schelling could write to Hegel about it at the beginning of January 1796 in the most extravagant and enthusiastic terms: 'How fortunate I feel if I may be one of the first to welcome this new hero, Fichte, in the land of truth! – Blessed be this great man! It is he who shall finally accomplish the work!'

This Fichte, friend of the French, champion of 'the rights of man' and secret partisan of the revolution, effectively 'exposed' as such in public by his enemies during the great 'atheism controversy', this Fichte has almost disappeared from the general consciousness on account of the ardent speeches he later directed against Napoleon in his famous *Discourses to the German Nation*. A new image simply came to displace the old. But both aspects properly belong to the same Fichte. The side of his earlier work which had influenced and impressed Schelling more than anything else was the crucial emphasis he laid on the doctrine of the 'ego'. The 'ego' is everything and outside the ego is simply the 'non-ego'. Even if there were no other certainty in experience, there would still remain the one *unique* and unassailable certainty that 'I = I'. according to Fichte the 'absolute ego' can never come into contradiction with itself. And if it ever seems to do so, this is a sure and certain sign that it has not yet properly been conceived in accordance with the form of the pure ego, i.e. in and through itself alone, and is falsely grasped instead, as if it were determined by external things. But this should not be the case, since man is his own end and must determine himself and never permit himself to be determined by anything alien or other than himself. Or as Fichte expressed it in his first lecture he delivered at Jena, *On the Vocation of the Scholar*: 'Man must always be at one with himself. He should never enter into contradiction with himself.' Fichte contemplates the entire range of experience in terms of three steps which he denominated thesis, antithesis and synthesis and dissolves it into so many 'acts of the ego': the positing of the ego and the positing of the non-ego are the central acts which constitute what Fichte calls transcendental philosophy, a philosophy in which the ego comes to experience the true nature of its own consciousness.

This system of thought exerted an enormous influence upon Hegel and Schelling at this time. And indeed it probably influenced Schelling even more than Hegel. Schelling is far in advance of Hegel when he expresses the results of his own Fichtean reflections in his letter to Hegel of 4 February 1795 in the following formula: 'God is nothing but the absolute ego.' Hegel on the other hand expressed a number of decisive reservations about Fichte and was certainly not prepared to share Schelling's then uncritical admiration for Fichte. We remember how Hegel had already complained in his letter to Schelling of the end of January 1795 that Fichte had 'reintroduced the old dogmatic style of demonstration'. This is all something that Hegel still has to consider and reflect upon in more detail.

And for Hegel that means: what is the point of combating the dogmatism of his Tübingen teachers if it is only going to re-emerge in a new form within philosophy itself? And it also means that, in this regard at least, Fichte has only fallen back to a pre-Kantian standpoint himself.

7

Between Berne and Frankfurt

The years which Hegel spent in the rather anonymous role of house tutor with the von Steigers actually proved to be quiet and uneventful ones. The post itself, it very soon became clear, fell somewhat below his expectations. His original hesitation before accepting the position appeared justified in hindsight. None the less, there is no doubt that Hegel regarded his choice as far preferable to entering the service of the Church. The full extent of his principal reasons are clearly revealed by his remarks on the political and the ecclesiastical regime in Württemberg as expressed in his correspondence with Schelling.

The hopes he had initially entertained with respect to the Berne position can partly be explained as a reaction to the domestic situation as he perceived it, and the idea of living for a while in a republic must have seemed attractive to Hegel. His time there gave him some opportunity to participate in social life and as a foreign visitor he was able at least to observe local political developments. Although he was fairly disillusioned by what he saw in this respect, he amply exploited his circumstances if only to expand his empirical knowledge of the country and its government. If in spite of his rather depressing situation Hegel made no real attempt to find escape with another position elsewhere, this suggests a certain lack of motivation on his part. However, once Hölderlin had contrived to find him an appropriate alternative, he lost no time in accepting another position as house tutor in Frankfurt am Main.

Hölderlin himself had not remained long in the house of Charlotte von Kalb. His unsettled state of mind did not encourage him to spend a long time in any one place, and he had now moved on to become house tutor with the Gontard family in Frankfurt. This decision would soon grant him the greatest experience of his personal life, just as it would later cast him into the utmost despair. Hölderlin wished to see Hegel established in a similar professional position in his immediate vicinity, and Hegel responded to his mediating efforts with alacrity and enthusiasm. Thus Hölderlin was entrusted by Hegel with making all the preliminary arrangements with the Gogel family in Hegel's interest as he saw fit. Hegel expected to be reimbursed for his travel expenses by money transfer or on his arrival in Frankfurt. Naturally he expressed his willingness to accommodate himself to Herr Gogel's wishes 'concerning the instruction and particular supervision of the children'. Hegel was pleased to find that the instruction 'for children of this age would consist in those areas of knowledge deemed requisite for any educated person'.

When he finally had the opportunity Hegel could hardly wait to leave Berne and bemoaned the fact that he would have to stay in the von Steiger household at least until the end of the year. As it turned out, he seems to have conspired to return to Stuttgart in the autumn to visit his father and the rest of the family.

When he arrived home on this occasion he was in a very depressed mood, and it was obvious that the years in Berne had left their mark on him. His sister noted at the time: 'he came back in a rather introverted state, and was at ease with himself only in his intimate circle'. In the circumstances his sister and some of her friends obviously did their best to raise his spirits. Nanette Endel, a young woman then learning the art of dress-making, referred to this period much later in a poem she wrote for Hegel's fifty-seventh birthday: 'Many fair hours we spent together then / And many a wreathe we wove'. She still remembered the roasted chestnuts which her 'friend' had offered her and how she thanked him by straightening his necktie for him every morning. The family would send him out to market to do the household shopping with a thaler clasped in his hand. The end of the year was celebrated by a solemn reading in the small circle of family and friends. All of them hung on Hegel's words as he read to them from the autobiographical novel *Agnes von Lilien* by Karoline von Wolzogen. Hegel, who certainly enchanted his listeners on this occasion, would seem, according to the reminiscences of Nanette Endel, to have been transported himself by reading the work. This novel by Schiller's sister-in-law appealed to him as strongly as Hermes's *Sophie's Journey* and Hippel's *Life Course* had done earlier.

The relationship between Hegel and Hölderlin, in spite of enormous differences of character between them, was more profound than that between Hegel and Schelling, even though Hegel closely shared the latter's intellectual and reflective tendencies. While he was in Berne Hegel had generally looked to Hölderlin for support in the first instance. And Hölderlin himself felt Hegel's character as 'a calm and reasonable man' to be a 'very wholesome' influence on him, as he wrote to his friend Neuffer on 16 February 1797, in the first few weeks after Hegel's arrival in Frankfurt. He found he could orient himself with respect to Hegel on those occasions when he felt he no longer understood either the world or himself. And Hegel seemed to be someone who was indeed capable of steadying Hölderlin's volatile personality.

The Gogel family with whom Hegel was employed lived in the Rossmarkt area of Frankfurt and Hölderlin himself lived nearby. It is clear that they saw one another on a daily basis. Hegel was soon introduced into Hölderlin's circle of friends, where he became personally acquainted with the poet's brother who was temporarily visiting the town, and where he first met Isaak von Sinclair, who had also studied in Tübingen and was now living with his mother in the small nearby town of Homburg. The subsequent story of Sinclair's life, which would be so closely entwined with that of Hölderlin and also culminated in a personal crisis, once again clearly reveals how ominously the suspicion of 'republicanism' continued to hang over so many of those who had once studied at the Stift. The charges that were later made against him, to the effect that he had been actively involved in a conspiracy against the life of the Duke of Württemberg, landed Sinclair in prison for five months after enduring a trial for 'high treason', although they were to prove groundless in the end. None the less, the case revealed the kind of reputation which Sinclair, the friend and confidant of Hölderlin, then enjoyed. Perhaps the classic case of the pure republican was Reinhard, but Hölderlin was touched by the same enthusiasm. The 'republican sympathies' Hegel had exhibited at Tübingen, in so far as we can talk of such a thing, had certainly suffered something of a blow during his stay in Berne. None the less, for Hegel this early republican period was not entirely lost for good – he would later incorporate the insights he originally gained from it, though without the accompanying illusions, into his developing conception of politics.

Hegel's new position in the Gogel household proved a genuine piece of good fortune for him and there was certainly no comparison with his former life in Berne. 'Here in Frankfurt I feel I am becoming more equal to the world', he now writes to his friend Nanette Endel in Stuttgart, and his friend the painter Sonnenschein can report to everyone back in Berne that Hegel is flourishing in Frankfurt. Hegel himself felt it was like returning home from exile. Frankfurt was a cosmopolitan place with a patrician oligarchy like Berne, but without the glorious past and pretensions of that city. It had become an increasingly important and strategically placed centre for trade. The city had left behind its past role as traditional host for imperial coronations, but the associated ceremonies and festivals as described by Goethe in his autobiography *Poetry and Truth* were still fresh in the public mind. It was here that Goethe had come of age as a writer, had composed his earliest poems and first discovered the material from the Faust legend.

Hegel's period in Frankfurt was disturbed by events in the Gontard household where Hölderlin had fallen in love with Susette Gontard and now found himself caught up in a hopeless situation. Hegel had been introduced to the Gontard family himself as a friend of the poet. He was not merely a detached observer of the unfolding story but was inevitably involved in it himself, even acting as a messenger between the two lovers in their predicament. At the beginning of 1799 Susette Gontard wrote to the poet, now banished by her husband from the household: 'Next month you will be able to try again, you can perhaps find out through H[egel] whether I shall be alone again.'

On 15 January 1799 Hegel received a letter from Stuttgart. His sister informed him of the death of his father. It was a full seven weeks later, on 9 March, that Hegel travelled back to Stuttgart to deal with his father's estate. Since the deceased had left no final testament, the inheritance was shared equally between the children. Hegel's third amounted to 3,154 gulden, 24 kreuzer and 4 pennies. He returned to Frankfurt on 28 March with this modest sum which would none the less help him to change his course in life. After almost six years as a tutor he could now consider giving up his current position, following Schelling's example and preparing himself for an academic career. It was typical of Hegel's tardiness that he waited for almost another two years before he actually left Frankfurt for good.

8

Theological Writings

The Hegel of the Berne years was not simply a theologian in a formal sense, for he genuinely felt himself to be a theologian (by vocation), although it is clear that he was only willing to spend a period as a domestic tutor in order, as he says himself, to avoid having to take up a clerical position. And thus it was that his studies in Berne, and immediately after his return from Switzerland, initially remained focused principally upon theological questions. Hegel's Berne manuscripts and his later Frankfurt ones can be regarded as a unity since it was only in Frankfurt that he properly carried out and completed the projects he had begun in Berne. All in all, these writings represent a series of theological-philosophical studies in which, while remaining within the existing academic conventions, the author decisively moves away from everything that his Tübingen teachers of theology had stood for. The themes of these writings – *Folk-Religion and Christianity, The Positivity of the Christian Religion, The Spirit of Christianity and its Fate,* together with the sketches for *The Spirit of Judaism* and a piece on *Religion and Love* – were still developed in the standard terms appropriate for a would-be clerical candidate. But from the theological and dogmatic point of view Hegel's questions and answers alike are decidedly marginal with respect to ecclesiastical orthodoxy. This is true from the perspective of Gottlieb Christian Storr, Hegel's instructor in dogmatics at the Stift, who defended an explicitly 'supranaturalist' position in accordance with conservative Lutheran orthodoxy and in direct opposition to all currents of the Enlightenment. It was equally true from the perspective of Storr's disciple Johann Friedrich Flatt, who was also quite happy to be described as a biblical-apologetic supernaturalist. In Tübingen Flatt had been the first person to give lectures on Kant's critical philosophy, if only because he saw in him a suitable opponent to be vanquished by means of special 'revelation'.

As far as the content of his studies is concerned, Hegel presents us here with little that is radically new. In his essay now known as *The Life of Jesus* Hegel is principally concerned with examining the question of the historical Jesus. He treats Jesus as a historical figure and attempts to read off from him the characteristic signs of the time in which he lived, as an itinerant teacher who frequented the Jewish religious sites and places of worship, a man who was initially supported by the mass of the people and then rejected by them, and who directly challenged the priestly class and gathered a company of convinced and dedicated followers about him. He appeared in their eyes as a victorious champion of virtue over vice, of love over hatred, of truth over falseness, of freedom over enslavement. Hegel is not in the slightest interested in Jesus as a supposed worker of miracles. Throughout his narrative Hegel clearly sides with the rationalists in this respect. A Jesus who really performed miracles could not possibly stand before the bar of rational criticism. And to inspire faith in himself Jesus had no need to work miracles anyway.

All of this represents the kind of theology which has already assimilated everything that Lessing and Reimarus had achieved before him in the relentless struggle against so-called 'orthodoxy'. Jesus is envisaged here in all his vigorous humanity and concrete reality, as one who contested and indeed finally overcame the destiny of the Jews. The words with which Jesus takes his leave of the disciples are simply virtuous exhortations derived from reason itself: 'You have now become men who are finally capable of trusting in yourselves without the need of alien leading-strings', says Jesus, transparently echoing Kant. And he adds the following: 'When I myself am no longer to be found amongst you, then from henceforth may your own developed sense of morality be your guide.' It is only natural, therefore, that Hegel's account ends simply with the death and burial of Jesus. This biographer cannot bring himself to follow his crucified subject along the path which leads from the grave to the resurrection, and thus our would-be Swabian cleric omits any description of the culminating miracle of the faith. And indeed for a Jesus whose teaching essentially reflects a moralizing interpretation of Kant's 'rational faith' and aims simply to establish a corresponding 'folk-religion' in accordance with it, there is no absolutely need for a resurrection in the first place.

As a kind of moral teacher, Jesus thereby comes to resemble merely a Socrates amongst the Jews. Both of them gathered followers about them, and both were condemned to death by the authorities. Neither actually succeeded in transforming their teachings into an effective public rather than merely private religion in their respective communities. Jesus failed as a teacher of a new morality, and Socrates made himself hated as a seducer of the people. It was precisely Hegel's interest in the historical Jesus that threatened to transform his own position into one directly opposed to the traditional dogmatic self-understanding of Christianity. Indeed in his essay on *The Positivity of the Christian Religion* Hegel seems clearly to have courted this danger. It was as if dangerous contraband were being smuggled over a heavily guarded border into enemy territory.

The question concerning the 'positivity' of religion always includes for Hegel the question concerning the concomitant decline of religion. What is the significance of the fact that the way in which a religion now appears can be so utterly remote from its original self-understanding? Hegel understands 'positive' religion here essentially in opposition to and in contrast with 'natural' religion. Hegel assumes that while there is only one true natural religion, there are many positive religions. In view of the many different forms in which positive religion can manifest itself, a purely universal concept of 'human nature' no longer appears adequate. Otherwise it would seem impossible to explain how a religion like Christianity has managed to adapt itself to so many various kinds of customs and culture, something for which it has been both condemned and praised alike: 'under the banner of the cross the Spaniards were able to murder entire generations of people in America, while the English have simply intoned their Christian hymns in honour of their God'. While the womb of the Church has given rise to 'the highest examples of art and the most impressive achievements of science', it has also led men 'to banish the beautiful products of art for the sake of the Church, and to condemn the human pursuit of scientific knowledge as a godless enterprise'.

Hegel silently proceeds here to bring together many different and quite varying phenomena under the rubric of the positivity of the Christian religion, all of them as examples of alienation from authentic reality. The fact that the Christian can now regard a 'slave' as his brother does not betoken any readiness to embrace Christian communism. And why not? Because the 'principles of a shared community of goods, if it were to be pursued with any rigour, would hardly encourage the spread of Christianity in the world'. The reality is quite different:

> In the Catholic Church the accumulated wealth of the monasteries, of the clerics, of the churches has continued to exist; little of it finds its way to the poor, and even when it does, it does so in a form which only sustains the penury in question, with the most unnatural consequence that the wandering thief who spends his nights on the street finds himself better off than a conscientious and industrious worker.

In view of such circumstances the state is absolutely required to supply the deficiencies of the Church. To allow the Church to assume control over the state as the political authority would be courting serious danger, even for the Church itself. All regulation of the citizen's life must be removed from the sphere of the ecclesiastical authorities. The idea of an 'Invisible Church' now emerges over against the Church as a specific institutional organization directly and closely associated with the rest of social life.

For all his excursions into such dangerous territory Hegel still clearly intended to present his approach as impeccably Christian in character, without at the same time having to suppress his own convictions. Hegel recognizes as a matter of method that intrinsically irreconcilable elements cannot be combined without producing the phenomenon of positivity. Hegel expresses himself audaciously enough in these writings but he avoids giving gratuitous offence. What he says here has been expressed before by others far more sharply and provocatively. His theological writings would not necessarily prevent him pursuing a professional clerical career if he had wished to. And what he says in his *Fragments on the Spirit of Judaism* would not be unacceptable to Lutheran orthodoxy: 'Mosaic religion [is] a religion born out of misery for a life of misery. [It is] unsuited to the happiness that expresses itself in joyful play.' Hegel can write:

> The fate of the Jewish people is the fate of Macbeth who stepped beyond the pale of nature itself and relied upon the help of alien beings, who, in their service, trampled down and murdered everything that was holy in human nature, was eventually abandoned by his gods (for they were gods and he was their slave) and found himself utterly destroyed in and through his own faith.

In this Hegel merely seems to be repeating, in a new variation, the old and unquestioned topos of Christian dogmatics, with all its later consequences, that the Jews themselves were responsible for the death of Jesus. Hegel continued to maintain this view of Judaism and the Jews and indeed extended it in certain ways, so that he was also able to appropriate the idea, standard enough in the Christian Church, of the Jews as the unconscious agents of future salvation. It thus became a case of 'both/and' in the dialectical sense. The idea of 'dichotomy' as a valid principle for comprehending nature and history was thereby methodically exploited to the full. 'Judaism' and 'Greece' therefore come to be regarded as two world-historical phenomena which are irreconcilable with one another. In the essay *The Spirit of Christianity and its Fate*, which Hegel began in Frankfurt and accurately expresses his views in this respect, he writes: 'The mighty tragedy of the Jewish people is no Greek tragedy, and it can arouse neither pity nor fear, for these feelings can only emerge from contemplating the fate of an inevitable transgression on the part of a beautiful nature; the former can only arouse a feeling of horror.'

It would probably not to be too difficult to discover similar thoughts in other theological authors expressed in a slightly different way. If Hegel is merely evincing acceptable opinions with an eye to a possible clerical position, then we cannot profitably ask after the originality or otherwise of his views in this respect. Hegel will not have to change a great deal in this written material in the future, although he will find it necessary to articulate his thoughts methodically. He already considers the movement of 'dichtomy' as a dialectical process which subjects everything to itself, where we cross from one moment of experience to its opposite in order to find ourselves in the other and thus return to ourselves. The theologian can write: 'In love what has been separated still exists, but no longer as separated.' The experience of 'love' here signifies an active union of opposed moments which will proceed to a further process of separation and reunification, with the new-born child as its result, in which the original 'union has become unsundered'.

All of Hegel's obscure language here results from his struggle to find his own authentic expression for all those concepts of law, punishment, sin and forgiveness which Storr had once expounded in traditional theological form in his Tübingen lectures. And this leads him to think everything anew 'from the ground up'. One can easily perceive here the lonely writer seeking to develop his own conceptual language in order to transform and translate this ancient Lutheran heritage into philosophical terms. Although his progress is laboured and only half-formed, the writer who is only gradually finding an appropriate path to pursue is already acquiring solid insights of his own. His conviction that 'all suffering is guilt' can be brought into relation to the Pauline doctrine of death as 'the wages of sin'. But the sudden appearance of the idea of 'fate' is unexpected. The Christian traditionally believes in Christ as the crucified and resurrected one but he certainly does not believe in 'fate'. That is something that must be left to the Greeks and their experience of fate in the realm of 'tragedy'. In Christianity all belief in fate is regarded rather as a characteristic of a much lower, 'pagan' level of religious thought. It is 're-demption' that overcomes and abolishes all evil without residue. But something astonishing now announces itself in Hegel's thought, for in his essay on *The Spirit of Christianity and its Fate* it is precisely fate which appears to produce reconciliation: 'fate on the other hand is as incorruptible and un-bounded as life itself'; it is an idea that cannot be captured within the con-fines of a *doctrina christiana*, and indeed is something powerful that can draw 'Christianity' into its own orbit. Almost imperceptibly we can see how Hegel is beginning theoretically to shake the entire edifice of Christian dog-matics. The tentative theological investigations of the Berne house tutor are not so harmless for theology after all. It is true that the 'unbounded' charac-ter of fate seems to confirm the traditional theological idea of our human limited knowledge of things, but Hegel's notion of fate soon seems to lose itself again in groundless philosophical speculation: 'In fate punishment ap-pears as a hostile power', punishment as fate is 'something individual in which the universal and the particular are united in such a way that what ought to be and the realization of what ought to be are not separated from one another'. He writes further that 'fate appears to have arisen only through an alien act'. That means that in resisting fate we only evoke a further 'con-test of power with power'. The struggle is not yet lost and the final decision results from the character of fate itself which cannot be avoided either way. The one who enters the lists for his rights bravely challenges the other, and thereby enters the sphere of right and power. 'But bravery is greater than painful submission'; and it is superior because it is prepared to assume the burden of guilt. In itself the 'struggle for rights' is a contradiction. For 'the right' cannot be divided – as is presupposed here – unless right as the universal has dissolved itself into two universal rights. As soon as the one who is challenged defends himself, the attacker himself is placed in the position of defending himself likewise, and both have right on their side. Both of them find themselves in a conflict which bestows on each the right to defend himself. The decision about the right is therefore consigned to the realm of strength which itself has nothing to do with right and possesses a quite different character. There is of course another possibility: both opponents subject themselves to a judge. They repudiate their own power, offer themselves up defenceless as if dead, and allow an alien third party to decide the case. We can always consider the possibility of reconciliation with fate. And why? 'Because enmity is also felt as life.'

With *The Spirit of Christianity and its Fate* Hegel has already clearly distanced himself from the theological domain in the narrower sense in the direction of pre-Christian antiquity. The one God of the tradition who reveals himself in his only Son is already very close indeed to the single 'Substance' of Spinoza, another author whose works were well represented in the library of the von Steigers at Tschugg. Everything that exists participates in this one substance, or 'Nature' as Spinoza calls it. This is also true in a negative sense for transgression: 'Transgression or crime is a destruction of nature; and since nature is essentially one, it is as equally destroyed in the destroyer as it is in the destroyed.' What is intrinsically opposed must constantly remain present all the same. A further destructive agent arises out of destruction and creates further destruction in turn in its transgression of life. The process Hegel here describes is naturally also subject to 'dichotomy' in turn. Hegel speaks from his own experience, from the felt experience of someone periodically subject to profound depressions, someone who saw the acute experience of alienation develop with his own sister into a kind of schizophrenia and mental derangement and consciously reflected in productive and dialectical fashion upon the experience. It is impossible in life simply to ignore the 'terrible actuality of evil' for a moment, just as it is equally impossible to ignore 'the unchangeableness of the law'. In view of such powers, to which the human being is constantly subject, we can only 'flee to the gift of grace'.

Once again we see the Lutheran theologian at work, severely testing out his theology and his Church and realizing that he can only grasp the phenomenon of religion, whether Judaic or Christian, by elaborating a philosophy that is systematically framed in terms of a sequence of 'oppositions'. What has simply been 'posited' must also be overcome and transcended. The result which should never be lost sight of here is the 'immorality' of a human life caught up in positive beliefs or, more fundamentally the 'immorality of positivity itself'. Authentic religion is something quite different from this:

'when a god acts it is only from spirit to spirit', a truth that has never properly been allowed effectively to penetrate to the heart of the 'Christian Church'. It is a thought which came to grief upon 'the fate that Church and state, the worship of God and the realm of everyday life, piety and virtue, spiritual and worldly activity have never been able to coalesce as one'.

One should not give credence to everything that Christians say about themselves. In the beginnings of Christianity in the Roman world, in the face of powerful opposition, they may well have sought hope and consolation in their religion in the desire to see their oppressors finally vanquished and punished. But how will they behave in turn when the faithful themselves have acquired despotic political power, when the prelates exploit 'the sweat of the poor' and 'the rentiers' attend the same ceremonies? Under the Roman emperors the Christian religion proved quite incapable of preventing or reversing the process of moral decline, the subjugation of freedom and rights, or the tyranny of their rulers. And why? Because Christianity too was infected and 'consumed by the same universal plague', functioning merely as a tool of despotism and encouraging the decline of the arts and the sciences. It even became, says Hegel, 'the most ardent advocate of crimes which cried to the heavens themselves'.

This provisional settling of accounts with the tradition will eventually be entered in the books of Hegel's later philosophy of religion and philosophy of history. The windmills of world history grind slowly, but they grind nevertheless. All of this will be made explicit later on and the cunning of reason at work here will be examined in terms of the 'crimes' and 'passions' that motivate historical events. Partial anticipations of an as yet undeveloped 'method' already make their appearance here and there, flashing forth from the obscure depths of Hegel's penetrating observations, although it cannot be said that they are operating in any intelligible connection with one another. What is already hovering indistinctly before Hegel's eyes, although he cannot clearly grasp it properly since his knowledge of Kant is still insufficient, is the necessity of articulating an alternative, and objectively methodical, approach to the so-called 'subjective idealism' of the Critical Philosophy.

9

A Stuttgart Romance

Hegel's move to Frankfurt helps to provide a small insight into his relationship with the dressmaker Nanette Endel, who was clearly not just a friend of
Hegel's sister and actually lived for a while in his father's house. When in
1841 David Friedrich Strauss came across five letters from Hegel to Nanette
Endel, he inferred an originally romantic attachment between the two of
them which subsequently developed into a more settled friendship after his
move to Frankfurt. This could be true, especially if we provide a very literal
interpretation of certain passages which are written in the somewhat effu-
sive style of the period, but it seems more likely that the latter simply represent rather high-flown epistolary sentiments on Hegel's part.

It is obvious, however, that at least during the few weeks of Hegel's stay in
Stuttgart after returning from Berne their relationship was quite a close and
familiar one. There is much to suggest that these letters are essentially a
continuation of conversations they had had in Stuttgart. Thus they were
hardly laden with matters of grave philosophical import or intellectual discussions of any kind. He talks, for example, of the urgent need to improve
his pronunciation, that is, to leave behind his local German accent and dialect. The friend who had entreated him on his departure to send her news of
his new situation now learns of his numerous efforts to accustom himself to
the worldly atmosphere of Frankfurt. After a short time there Hegel began
to frequent the theatre a couple of times a week and mentions seeing Mozart's
Magic Flute as well as his *Don Juan* (as he calls it after the Spanish title).
Now he is in Frankfurt, after his years of isolation in Berne, he understandably makes his first attempts to participate in a far more challenging and
interesting social scene. He even goes to local dances, as he tells his friend
back in the Swabian heartland. But above all he is exposing himself to fresh
impressions of the people around him and decides that 'it is impossible to
want to improve such people and we must simply go and howl with the

wolves'; they are as they are, and only if one day 'my star should lead me to Kamchatka or amongst the Eskimos', he writes, could he hope to provide 'an example that would help protect these nations from the most various kinds of luxury, the taffeta underclothes, the quantities of rings, and suchlike things'.

These are of course allusions to the new social environment of Frankfurt, where the commercial class endeavoured to live in accordance with the style they thought fit, and whose conspicuous consumption and sense of display contrasted dramatically with the typically Swabian virtues of modest simplicity and contented thrift. This is also something that Hölderlin was forced to endure from the master of the Gontard household and which only encouraged further irresolvable conflict with his situation. Hegel's initial response to Frankfurt society seems to have been a kind of Rousseauian flight into the arms of nature. 'I must confess that it has taken me quite some time to get over the temptations offered by society, town life, the attendant love of distraction and entertainment which feeds on boredom', he wrote on 2 July. And suddenly he even finds himself recalling his Berne years with a certain pleasure. He writes that

> the memory of days spent out in the country now constantly drives me out of Frankfurt [he is thinking of Tschugg on the Bielersee] and just as I could then feel reconciled to myself and to other men in the arms of nature, so here I often seek refuge with this faithful mother in order to separate myself from the people with whom I live in peace, in order beneath her aegis to protect myself from their influence or from the dangers of associating too closely with them.

This Rousseauism of 1797, expressed in Hegel's lines to Nanette, is a late flowering of sentiment on the part of a young man from a backward agricultural community with a recently vanquished absolutist system of government; now finding himself suddenly cast from Switzerland into the busy social life of an important commercial centre, he turns emphatically to the consolations of 'nature'. It is noticeable that, without becoming explicitly philosophical about it, he also introduces his own personal ideas of separation and dichotomy into these Rousseauian reflections.

But Hegel's principal interest was not directed towards praising the virtues of a pastoral life in epistolary form. The inexhaustible source and subject of their earlier conversations in Stuttgart would seem to have been Nanette's own confessional commitments. She was a Catholic and, during the few weeks that they daily spent together, had tried to explain something of the character of her faith to Hegel. The remarks in Hegel's letters from Frankfurt rather suggest that he was genuinely interested in exploring the implications of the situation to the full. Hegel was a Lutheran and Catholicism in Württemberg was the religion of a distinct minority which he could study first hand in the Rottenburg diaspora only ten kilometres away from

Tübingen. It appeared in his eyes as an authentic religion with certain exotic attractions of its own. This much is clearly evident to us now from Hegel's correspondence. In the case of Catholicism Hegel encountered a religion with aspects which were unknown or only appeared in a highly diluted form in the Protestant faith he knew: the cult of saints, the practice of the confessional, the rosary, and the Capuchins. If Nanette had enthusiastically instructed him in this new subject at Stuttgart, Hegel now presents himself as a well-informed and eager student who has mastered the curriculum. 'As soon as I find the chance to attend High Mass', he writes to his friend a few weeks after his arrival in Frankfurt, 'I shall dutifully go and worship, and raise my soul in veneration before some beautiful effigy of the Virgin.' He attempts to employ her own language when he points out that amongst the people he is acquainted with the virtues of Saint Alexis are but ill represented and that Saint Anthony of Padua enjoyed greater success in preaching to the fishes than he ever would in Frankfurt. In comparison with a figure like Saint Alexis he cannot avoid feeling unworthy, but rejoices in the good fortune of having a correspondent like Nanette 'to act as a mediator between Saints and mere mortals, who can represent my cause before the Saint and through whom I may become the recipient of his grace'. For the sake of one gift from her hands he is prepared 'to attend Mass and to count rosaries' as often as she requires. He also feels it necessary to add that he has noticed 'many a dirty Capuchin running around the place'.

The tenor of his letters must actually have pleased the recipient considerably and we can only surmise that she tried strongly to encourage Hegel in his new interest. She may have felt that he understood her attitudes and she played her part with vigour and enthusiasm: the devout young Catholic girl in full intellectual possession of her creed who is eager to share this knowledge with her interested adept. For his part Hegel was happy to allow Nanette to play the role of a gentle and attractive guide in such theological matters. He also enjoyed and slightly played up his student role, although he could equally reveal a deep and genuine interest in what she had to teach. For Hegel the Protestant Württembergian the Catholic religion resembled something from another world. But that was precisely the point, and he was determined to exploit the opportunity. As he had with Schelling earlier, Hegel here presents himself as the learner and recipient of knowledge and that is what he was; but at the same time he raises his objections, makes ironic reservations of his own, exaggerates a little here and there, occasionally offers a few critical observations which hardly fit with the image of a genuine believer. The view he has already expressed concerning the 'positivity of religion' – albeit as unpublished reflections – reveals his own real opinions in these matters. But even these are still provisional. Everything is still in flux and there are no certain positions as yet.

Although the prevailing tone of his correspondence with Nanette Endel is non-committal and gently ironic, there was nevertheless a more serious aspect to this for Hegel. It is clearly revealed when, still in Frankfurt himself, he turned to Schelling on 2 November 1800 to enquire after suitable contacts in Bamberg, which he was then considering visiting. He explains the reasons why he is so interested in Bamberg, although he had no acquaintances there at all: 'I am looking for inexpensive board, the opportunity of good beer for my physical constitution, the chance of meeting a few people', and then significantly adds: 'I should prefer to live in a Catholic rather than a Protestant town; I should very much like to observe that religion at first hand.' What he was looking for, and later avowedly found, in Bamberg was 'Catholicism' as an unadulterated expression of the 'mediaeval world', as one particular stage in the course of 'world history'. He was willing to expose himself directly to the phenomenon in order to experience it for himself as a still living and experienced reality.

In this sense, Hegel must have viewed his relationship with Nanette Endel, which was otherwise so unmarked by intellectual 'reflections', as a sort of introduction to the Middle Ages. Life and thought coincide for him here. It was a question of finding an entry into and becoming directly acquainted with a world that was otherwise closed off to him by virtue of his immediate cultural background.

Shortly after Hegel left Stuttgart the circumstances of his friend Nanette were to change significantly. Within a few weeks, in March 1797, she entered the service of the Baroness von Bobenhausen in Schweinfurt. Hegel, who had originally hoped that her chosen route would take her through Frankfurt, soon found himself without any contact address for her and was forced to write to her via Stuttgart where his sister could forward his letters. Later Hegel observed that they were only separated by a twenty-four-hour journey, a trip of two or three days, and expressed the possibility of visiting her perhaps in the coming summer or the following year. Or alternatively, as he put it on 2 July: 'Might it be possible for Madame to consider undertaking a journey to Swabia through Frankfurt on occasion?' Thus speaks a man in educational service to the household of the businessman J. N. Gogel at the Rossmarkt in Frankfurt to the still unmarried young lady Nanette in Schweinfurt: correspondence from the perspective of the humble valet, something which he could still remember in later years when, in his *Philosophy of History*, the role of emperors, queens and mighty rulers would stand at his disposal.

10

Farewell to Frankfurt

Towards the end of 1800 Hegel had made up his mind to give up his current job in Frankfurt. He had spent almost four years there as a house tutor. By means of a small inheritance which he had received on his father's death he was finally in a position, at least for a time, to pursue an independent life quite free of external obligations. But that fact alone had not exclusively • determined his decision to leave Frankfurt. After all, his father had died two years before and all the legal details concerning the inheritance had long been settled.

This delay may have been due to Hegel's characteristic lethargy, his tendency to wait and see how things generally were developing, although a sense of consideration for the Gogel family and the child in his charge might also have played a part, together with the current state of his own researches. The composition of the so-called *Systemfragment* falls in the year 1800 if the editor of Hegel's early manuscripts, Herman Nohl, is to be believed (and his dating has been called in doubt). On the 29th of the same month Hegel completed a new introduction to the essay on *The Positivity of the Christian Religion*. There were still a number of fundamental questions to be clarified in his mind. The careful process of revision corresponds entirely with Hegel's character and general approach, which always gives an external impression of extremely laborious and protracted development. This tendency to wait until he has taken stock of the terrain, his caution about drawing first and decisive conclusions from anything, seems appropriate to the difficult subjects which constituted the first stage of Hegel's developing thought.

But then it seemed he had had enough. Even in Tübingen we saw that he had contemplated the prospect of going to Jena where Schelling had already established himself in the meantime. The correspondence between Hegel and Schelling seems to have become much more infrequent, certainly on Schelling's part, after the latter accepted his new position in Jena where he was busily occupied with his own work, with social life in the city, and not least with his many travels.

We have a fairly good idea of the more precise reasons why Hegel now began to seek Schelling's assistance since Hegel enumerates a number of them in a letter to his friend of 2 November 1800. He does not broach the matter of Jena directly, but initially communicates his idea of staying in Bamberg for a while, where Schelling had also spent some time to explore his interests in natural science at the Faculty of Medicine there. Hegel had thought to meet Schelling on that occasion, although the plan was abandoned after the latter returned to Jena. And as we have seen, the idea of a stay in Bamberg also corresponded with the intentions he had expressed to Nanette about getting to know something about the Catholic world.

But the reason why Hegel had thought of Bamberg in this connection had a different motivation. Hegel clearly saw the place as a suitable preparatory residence for him. It probably did not seem advisable at this stage to entrust himself to Jena, a veritable hive of literary activity with the two Schlegel brothers, not to mention Schelling's future wife Caroline who had done so much to poison life for Schiller. He must have been apprehensive about leaving the comfortably modest life style at the Rossmarkt in Frankfurt and plunging immediately into such difficult and challenging new territory. 'Before I dare to entrust myself to the literary commotion of Jena I would like to strengthen myself by spending a little time somewhere else beforehand', he wrote to Schelling, the only person to whom he could dare to entrust himself and from whom he could expect any real assistance at this time. But since Schelling had long since left Bamberg to return to Jena the possibility of their meeting there evaporated. He therefore left it up to Schelling to suggest how and where else they could meet up together.

For all the convolutedness of its style, Hegel's letter clearly amounted to a request to share a modest place in the protective shade of his already celebrated and successful friend. He expressed his willingness to consider doing anything suitable that Schelling can suggest. As he put it in his own way: 'For I look to you, in my own case as well, with sentiments of great confidence, in the hope that you will be able to recognize my own disinterested aspirations, even if my sphere is a less elevated one than your own, and find something of value there.'

11

The Frankfurt Writings

Apart from a small number of everyday and useful items he took with him from Berne to Frankfurt Hegel's baggage also contained his manuscripts on the 'positivity' of religion. These constituted the incipient form of Hegel's understanding of religion in general and would eventually provide certain fundamental elements of his later philosophy of religion proper.

He already possesses the idea of a system organized in stages, although the exact conceptual character of the latter can only be theoretically reconstructed now with some difficulty. The fundamental thought here is supplied by the doctrine of different epochs succeeding one another according to some intelligible order, an idea he could certainly find in Rousseau and which he had begun directly to pursue when he was in Tschugg. But Herder's philosophy of history was also based upon the idea of a sequence of 'epochs' as so many 'stages' through which 'humanity' was destined to pass. Applied to religion, this would signify in Hegel's eyes the following: the religion of nature as the earliest stage would itself emerge from the world of Greek mythology in which reality and beauty, nature and history, poetry and art were all indissolubly fused with one another. The second level is constituted by the Judaic religion, a faith characterized alike by sublimity and a bifurcated consciousness. This in turn would give rise to the third stage, that of Christianity with its central doctrine of the incarnation of God. Christianity itself also passes through a process of development leading from Catholicism as an aesthetically 'beautiful' form of faith to Protestantism as its highest form. This process reaches its outer limit with philosophy itself which finally represents the highest stage of human development.

The *Systemfragment* normally ascribed to 1800 (and even if this dating is too early) presents a kind of comprehensive but concentrated manifesto of Hegel's thought. Without a knowledge of Hegel's Berne sketches and his surviving Frankfurt notes and manuscripts, and especially the Positivity essay, the *Systemfragment* would be impossible to interpret. The 'positivity of religion' for Hegel always signifies an essentially two-sided phenomenon, and Hegel is always concerned to articulate the opposed poles involved in such a phenomenon. The 'self-understanding' of one party and the alternative understanding of another must always be thought together, in accordance with the insight expressed in Lessing's *Nathan the Wise*: 'What makes me a Christian in your eyes, makes you a Jew in mine!' If the Christians can emphasize 'how much Christ was concerned in his teaching to secure the cultivation and perfection of the individual human being', then the opponents of Christianity can bitterly cite 'the most scathing examples of the moral corruption of Christians, and particularly of their spiritual leaders in the Church as a counter-proof to the alleged truth of this religion and its supposed benefits'. In order to identify the persistence of 'positivity' within it, Hegel questions the Christian religion directly: 'Did it ever attempt to oppose despotism? – and for how long has it opposed the slave-trade?'

To Hegel the theologian, as he still was in Frankfurt, religion appears to him as the fundamental problem, although his reflections are constantly couched in a language of unparalleled awkwardness. In his Berne and Frankfurt manuscripts his language and thought appear strikingly incongruent with one another. Where his thought calls on a particular language of his own to assist its expression, this only too often results in further obscurity and misunderstanding. Language itself sometimes seems inadequate fully to express the thought, and the writer entangles himself in difficulties precisely when he tries to make himself most intelligible.

This is a fundamental feature of Hegel's work which must be recognized: thought as such cannot simply and straightforwardly be communicated. In contrast to Lessing, and indeed even to Kant, Hegel wields a blunted rather than a sharpened pen which loves to write in awkward and ungainly capitals. He never possessed any of the literary virtues of Schopenhauer, the opponent whom he would emphatically overshadow for so long in terms of public influence. Schopenhauer's thought finds immediate and perfect expression in his writing. Hegel the theologian seems to think in terms of things and processes which lie at the foundation of being and which require all the symbolic resources of religion if they are to be brought to light at all. The Eucharistic sacrament – the communion of bread and wine – is an immediate presence for Hegel as it was for Hölderlin. It was impossible to ignore the daily influence and significance of such things for Hegel, even though he is equally aware that the rational understanding cannot help resisting the sacramental idea of the Host. A mystical aspect is involved here since meaning is only bestowed on the object through the accompanying act of worship. To make his thought intelligible Hegel draws a comparison with the act of reading: the reader only has these dead letters before his eyes which remain even when they are read and their sense is grasped, but in the Eucharist the bread and the wine disappear as they are actually consumed. They pass over into the very life of the communicant. Bread and wine represent eating and drinking as indispensable elements of life. The Eucharist affects to bestow on man a kind of unification with the divine, but all that is actually communicated is a material substance that immediately dissolves in the mouth. The feeling of elevation produced rests upon a kind of deception. Although during communion the external thing, the Host, stands for what it signifies, there is a persistent remainder for the believer which is not absorbed, a feeling which does not correspond to the felicity expected. After the Last Supper the disciples of Jesus were filled with grief.

Form and matter fall apart here. They also fall apart in the experience of the Greek who beholds a statue of Apollo and is inspired with elevated feelings of joy in immortal youthfulness and beauty. But if he were to grind the sculpted marble into dust, then he would immediately lose the intuition of the statue. It was not the substance of the marble but the form which inspired him.

This brings us back to a powerful Hegelian idea drawn from the immediate experience of life and one which will constantly recur now and in the future: the opposition between a visible and an invisible Church. The 'invisible Church' is untouched either by the unity of Church and state or by the separation between them that Kant demanded and Hegel contested. The idea of the 'invisible Church', quite independently of Hegel who adopted it, was widely disseminated in the second half of the eighteenth century. Hölderlin and Schelling themselves inherited an idea which had been employed by Lessing, Herder and Jean Paul to suggest a non-confessional union of free spirits without reference to the ecclesiastical sacraments. For Hegel the idea no longer had any connection with the Church as an established institution and essentially belonged to philosophy as something quite beyond that sphere altogether. In this spiritual brotherhood there were no distinctions of rank or status and no need to preach or proselytize, there was no alliance with force or despotism. The glory of God was not to be promoted by external means and there would be no question of excluding citizens from their rights if they failed to belong to the Church or religion of the state. It cannot be disturbed by the conflict into which Church and state can always fall historically, because its essential content is utterly different. In this invisible Church there are no officials, no sanctified objects or special places of worship, no cults or ceremonies and no tithes or offerings.

Schelling unambiguously announced his membership in this 'Church' in his letter to Hegel of 4 February 1795, where he explains that he has now 'become a Spinozist' for whom there is no divine 'object' as such. Schelling also draws the necessary conclusion from this: 'Therefore there can be no personal God.'

For a trained Tübingen 'theologian' to challenge the existence of a personal God in this way would naturally produce conflict with the Church of Württemberg. But Schelling's correspondence with Hegel clearly reveals that

Schelling had no intention of avoiding such conflict, and indeed actively courted it. In his reply of 16 April Hegel likewise openly expresses his distance from the 'religion' of the 'visible Church' when he writes: 'Religion and politics have played the same game behind a single curtain, the former taught what the latter wanted, namely contempt for the human race.' He was sure to have Schelling's hearty agreement in this. For when Schelling presented himself as prospective house tutor for the young baronets of the Riedesel family, he was thoroughly questioned to find out whether he was a 'democrat', a partisan of 'Enlightenment', or a radical 'freethinker'.

Schelling was the more intellectually agile spirit of the two men. And in his letter of February 1795 he already anticipated something of Hegel's *Systemfragment* of 1800, when he describes the movement of spirit as a 'highest striving' which is directed towards 'the destruction of our personality' as 'a transition into the absolute sphere of being, a transition which however must remain impossible for all eternity'. But this incapacity is the point. Because the 'transition' is impossible for us here in this life, where we can only attempt 'a practical approximation to the absolute', we are guaranteed a kind of 'immortality'.

This explanation of 'immortality' is one of the most brilliant notions of the 21-year-old Schelling. The 'ego' is immortal because it is denied entry into the very sphere it must strive to attain. This idea will return, heavily laden with further intellectual content, in Hegel to form a fundamental aspect of his thought when he later speaks so often of 'the return of spirit to itself'. In the Frankfurt *Systemfragment* he writes: 'The partial character of the living being is taken up and transformed in religion, the limited life elevates itself to the infinite; and it is only because the finite is itself life that it bears within it the possibility of elevating itself to infinite life.' But this is not so much an insight of 'religion' as one that is explicitly obtained by philosophy.

Hegel's thought has begun to move and quicken, tracing patterns and circles that are difficult to decipher. What Fichte said of Kant, according to Schelling, namely that 'the genius of a Socrates' was required in order to understand him, can equally, and indeed later with even greater justice, be said of Hegel himself. His Berne and Frankfurt writings contain certain fundamental themes which will recur again and again later in his thinking, themes which are rooted in equally fundamental experiences of life, like the idea of 'love' as 'union' and as 'duplication of itself', an idea based upon the experience of propinquity as well as of distance and separation. 'Love proper can only transpire amongst equals' but it also stands in an indissoluble connection with death: 'There is no mere matter involved between lovers . . .; to say that loving individuals are independent, or possess an autonomous principle of life entirely their own, is only to say that they can die.' Between life and death there is none the less a kind of 'immortality'. If Schelling had provided such a surprising explanation for the idea of immortality, Hegel now presents an alternative interpretation of his own which he had not explicitly communicated to Schelling. 'Love strives . . . to unify even what is mortal, to render it immortal' and represents the 'destruction of what is opposed in the act of unification'.

Hegel's manuscripts here show his first and still provisional response to the questions addressed by Schelling, and it certainly does not coincide with the traditional views of what the German mystic Jakob Böhme once called 'the external Church' built by hands. In Berne we saw how Hegel, left to his own devices, tried to find his own intellectual bearings by putting down his tentative ideas on paper. He was testing out the field step by step, developing his thought from the ground up, his own reflections relatively unencumbered by a mass of erudition. At the beginning we encounter 'life' and 'death', 'love' as a means of 'immortality', 'bread and wine', 'movement' as 'approximation' and 'separation', an incipient principle of something resembling thesis and opposed antithesis. Hegel's initial reflections seem to be at home with simple unified concepts, but once his thought begins to move, and the concepts he deploys begin to combine with one another and then to repel one another, there arises a turbulent network of ideas which seems to disintegrate even as it is being fashioned. 'The elevation of the finite to the infinite can be characterized as an elevation of finite life to infinite life.' Thus he writes in the Frankfurt *Systemfragment*, providing a foretaste of what is to follow when his thought comes to fruition after a long and protracted process. The *Systemfragment* contains the developing seed, the first embryonic form of what will eventually be called 'the Hegelian philosophy': the end of religion (as it formerly existed) and the transition to philosophy proper, namely Hegel's own.

The principle of opposition is already contained in the *Systemfragment* as a central element of Hegel's method. He is *underway* to his authentic and versatile conception of the dialectic which will mediate the abruptness of these oppositions of living experience and dead objectivity, of spirit and positivity, of the finite and the infinite, by exploring an array of possible transitions between them. Hegel gradually loosens these concepts of their apparent rigidity and one-sidedness and relativizes their absoluteness by attempting to locate them in an organic series of stages. Given the fragmentary state of this manuscript of 1800 we cannot of course accurately or precisely construct the already systematic structure of Hegel's thought at this time. But that does nothing to disguise the fact that there is a persistent inner continuity between Hegel's Berne, Frankfurt and indeed his Jena manuscripts, in spite of all his numerous improvements and revisions. The acute emphasis upon the philosophical moment in religious experience, along with an analysis of the subject–object relationship clearly based upon religious images and ideas, is maintained throughout:

Philosophy therefore has to stop short of religion precisely because it is itself a process of thinking and, as such a process, still implies an opposition to non-thinking processes as well as the opposition between the thinking mind and the object of thought. Philosophy has to reveal the finiteness in all finite things and promote their integration by means of reason. In particular it has to recognize the illusions generated by its own infinite and thus to place the true infinite outside of these confines.

The attempt to articulate thought in terms of a kind of objective idealism or intrinsic and independent thought must reckon with the sphere of religion as the opposite of thought. Philosophy must construct itself both in relation to and in opposition to religion, must develop its own distinctive conceptual resources which are not at the disposal of religion as a form of being 'external to reflection'. The 'elevation of man' which transpires here is not, as Hegel insists, an elevation from 'the finite to the infinite' as such, since this would only represent another structure of opposition, but is an elevation of 'finite life to infinite life'. It is an intrinsic part of the developing dialectic process that new dialectics are constantly produced along the way as means of further advance. At this level of knowledge the relationship with religion is indispensable to philosophy since it hereby identifies and recognizes the relevant divisions within the sphere of life. In so far as Hegel describes religion in the *Systemfragment* as the 'non-thinking process' it none the less becomes, even in its opposition to philosophy, a continuing source of knowledge, albeit one whose authoritatively self-evident truth has been forfeited along the way. Philosophy will engage productively with religion and learn from it, but it will also be delimited in its scope, interrogated and examined with respect to its place in the autonomous and all-embracing system of philosophy. The well-known traditional oppositions between the finite and the infinite, the limited and the unlimited, the mortal and the immortal, cannot be expected to avail very much in the light of a philosophy that is capable of recognizing 'the illusions generated by its own infinite' and replacing the abstract infinite with the 'true infinite outside of these confines'. Philosophy, i.e. the *Systemfragment* of 1800, is based upon a different opposition, that between 'spirit' and 'law'. It is obvious that this opposition is also drawn from the language of religion and clearly recalls the idea of the New Covenant, the 'spirit' of which liberates from the 'law' of the Old Covenant. And that means that philosophy cannot articulate its message at this stage of its historical development without recourse to the means of religion. But it means equally that philosophy is also free to reject the former understanding of ancient theological ideas: 'One can describe this infinite life as a spirit', or: 'Spirit is the living unity of the manifold.' In opposition to the latter stands the 'mere unity which is called law, something merely thought which is itself lifeless'. Hegel proposes a synthesis: 'Spirit is the enlivening law which is unified with the manifold and thus exists as something living.'

The dialectic here, although this term is not yet used, is concerned with 'infinite opposition'. Hegel is attempting to elaborate a system in which 'an infinite multiplicity of organized forms, of individuals, constitute a unity, a single organized whole that is at once separated and united', where everything can potentially enter into relationship with everything else, namely 'Nature'. Hegel was writing this under the influence of Schelling's very first writings on the philosophy of nature. Nature understood in this way, according to Hegel, is 'a positing of life itself', a life that has been made into Nature through such positing. The ego 'posits' nature as something it appears to have produced itself. The positing ego is thus forced to determine what is to be understood as separation and what as union, what as individual and what as objective reality. With the Fichtean ego in the background it is possible to see how the subject–object relation, initially grasped in terms of rigid and mutually exclusive opposition, can be raised to an ultimate identity of subject and object.

As far as Fichte's thought was concerned, Hölderlin had already played a significant role for Hegel. He had written to Hegel from Jena on 26 February 1795 to say that 'Fichte is desirous of moving beyond the fact of consciousness in the theoretical sphere.' This was a path that Hölderlin was then prepared to follow too, as in fact he showed in some of his great poetry. His verse drama *Empedocles*, for example, presents the tragedy of the self-conscious individual who casts himself down into the crater of Mount Etna in a self-destructive process that simultaneously represents a process of becoming, a kind of union with Spinoza's all-embracing 'Nature'. This is a path that will lead us from Fichte's concept of 'consciousness' and his philosophy of the ego to Hegel's concept of 'self-consciousness' in the *Phenomenology of Spirit*, to 'the truth of self-certainty' where we shall enter 'the native land of truth'. It is clear that Hölderlin's remarks about Fichte's philosophy, as he then understood it, provide the first suggestions of themes that Hegel elaborates in a comprehensive manner. In the same letter we learn that Fichte's 'absolute ego' (which Hölderlin identifies with Spinoza's 'Substance')

> contains all of reality; it is everything and outside of it is nothing. For this absolute ego therefore there is no object, for otherwise it would not contain all reality; but consciousness without an object is inconceivable, and if I am myself this object, then I am necessarily limited. ... Thus no consciousness is conceivable for the absolute ego, and as absolute ego I have no consciousness, and in so far as I have no consciousness, then I am (for myself) nothing, and thus the absolute ego is (for me) nothing.

If it seems difficult to determine the precise sense of these lines and one requires intuitive illustration of these motifs, one should look immediately to the poet's *Hyperion* and *Empedocles*, to the great hymns inspired by Greek models, which presuppose this experience of the absolute ego, this ego without consciousness or object, which dissolves into nothingness. They document an autobiographical moment on Hölderlin's part, the romantic feeling of the infinite that was stimulated in Jena under the impact of Fichte's thought. In a piece published in Beissner's edition of the poet's works under the title *Coming to be and Passing Away*, which he composed around 1799 as he was beginning work on *Empedocles*, Hölderlin reveals the impact of Fichte's Doctrine of Science on his mind: 'Out of this tragic union of the infinitely new with the finite there develops something individual, in so far as the infinitely new individualizes itself in its own shape through taking on the shape of the finite moment.' This already corresponds with the way in which Hegel describes the wanderings of 'Spirit' as a threefold process of externalization, differentiation and reintegration. 'This idealistic process of dissolution is fearless', we read in Hölderlin,

> the beginning and the end are already posited, as something bolder and more irresistible, and the process presents itself as what it actually is, as a reproductive act whereby life passes through all its moments, and in order to attain the final result comes to rest with none of them, but dissolves itself in each, in order to produce itself in the next.

In this dialectic of coming to be and passing away, unexplicated as it is here, nothing is utterly lost in the process. 'Dissolution' is grasped as a reproductive act which attempts to 'produce' itself, to 'sublate' itself as Hegel would say. It is difficult to ignore the accents of Hegel's language in this prose fragment of Hölderlin's.

If Hegel had long since felt himself trapped within the limits of subjective idealism, once he had discovered the lived experience of contradiction as the principle of being in the fragmentary Frankfurt manuscripts he strove vigorously to attain a higher standpoint altogether. Contradiction is objectively grasped as the moving principle in general, something that cannot be eliminated from the organization of reality and continues rather to produce itself in newer and newer forms and ramifications. Contradiction is everything and everything is contradiction: 'Death, opposition and the divisive understanding is simultaneously posited with the living whole, namely as a manifold that is alive, as a living being that can posit itself as a totality that at the same time is also a moment, i.e. a part for which something is dead, and which itself is dead for others.'

On his return from Switzerland Hegel once again encountered the current social reality in the German states. In his essay *On the Recent Affairs of Württemberg*, which Hegel composed in Frankfurt in 1788, he presented a bitter critical analysis of the situation. In view of the wretched conditions in his home state he is forced to confess his inability to make any positive proposals for improvement. The situation is so corrupt that any attempt to encourage reform is doomed to failure.

In view of this hopeless state of affairs Hegel also considered in an unfinished manuscript whether 'the magistrates should be elected by the people', or by 'the citizens' as he put it in a revised version of the piece. That would inevitably lead to the urgently required reorganization of the system of Estates Assembly. At the opening of the manuscript Hegel says:

> It is high time that the people of Württemberg ceased wavering between fear and hope, and advanced instead from this alteration of expectation and disillusion towards the former. . . . How blind are those who allow themselves to imagine that arrangements, constitutions and laws which no longer correspond to the customs, the needs and the views of the people, and from which the spirit has flown, can possibly continue to survive; that forms of life in which neither the understanding nor the sentiments take any further interest are powerful enough to sustain the bond of a people any longer.

It must have been obvious to him, and it was soon pointed out to him anyway, that his views would find little resonance in the princely capital of Stuttgart. He had hereby unmistakably revealed himself as 'a friend of change', something not to be taken lightly in such a place, and thus only confirmed the earlier image of sympathizer with the Revolution and planter of 'freedom trees'.

But his notes and contributions were not simply concerned with the situation in Württemberg alone. When he says that 'A people, the Germans, should not permit themselves the spectacle of such weakness' he is certainly thinking of change far beyond the borders of his own state. It was a claim which mercilessly repudiated the provincialism and the cult of the small state at the end of the eighteenth century. And he openly suggests unmistakably revolutionary conclusions when he goes on to say: 'according to the sober conviction that change is necessary people must not be afraid to examine the situation carefully and in detail; and when they find cases of injustice the disadvantaged party must demand redress, and the party in unjust possession of advantage must be prepared to relinquish it'.

The Hegel of the Frankfurt years is as given to collecting excerpts of material as he was before. He reads books and journals pen in hand, always ready to mark interesting passages and transform them later into notes or quotations. His interest in English newspapers is particularly striking. England was not merely the country of parliament and property, but was already about to become the land of commerce and world trade, the exporter and importer of enormous quantities of goods between the continents, without that centralized 'statist' approach which characterized the Prussian economy and confined commerce and trade in a straight-jacket of complicated rules and regulations from above.

What fascinated Hegel about Britain ever since the years in Berne was above all the parliamentary process and the institution of the poor tax as a measure undertaken by the ruling classes to pacify the dispossessed, as Hegel had observed in his commentary and notes on Steuart's *Political Economy*. As far as the German social conditions were concerned it was now the 'General Prussian Law' which occupied the centre of Hegel's attention. This system, in contrast with the 'liberal' regime in England, insisted on the inalienable character of feudal property and strengthened the existing socio-political order. What Hegel was particularly concerned to criticize with respect to the 'General Prussian Law' was the penal system. Hegel remarks on the institution of punishment exemplified here:

> Is it not more like the Iroquois to meditate on the pains to be devised for enemy prisoners, and take pleasure in exercising every new kind of judicial torture? . . . To treat and order people around now as labouring and productive beings, now as raw material for improvement simply becomes the most offensive form of tyranny because the good of the whole remains an alien end as far as they are concerned under conditions of injustice.

In the Frankfurt period Hegel largely remains what he was in Berne: an independently minded writer who does not compose for the reading public in general. In the only piece he actually published at this time his name does not even appear on the title page. This was his edition of *Confidential Letters Concerning the former Legal Status of the Pays de Vaud in the State of Berne. Translated from the French of a Deceased Swiss Citizen and further Annotated*. The little book appeared at the Frankfurt book fair in Easter 1798. It was originally written by the lawyer Jean-Jacques Cart who was not yet dead, as the title suggested, but lived another fifteen years. In view of the political situation in Switzerland it looks as if the author thought it advisable for the authorities to believe he had indeed died. It is now assumed that Hegel was the translator of the text, though this is not certain beyond all doubt. He probably got to know the manuscript while he was in Berne and then wrote a commentary on it himself.

As far as his attitudes to the ruling oligarchy of Berne are concerned, Hegel had already made these abundantly clear in his correspondence with Schelling. His letter to Schelling of 16 April 1795 agrees fairly literally with Cart's remarks. Hegel refers to the various 'intrigues' and 'alliances', the general nepotism that was involved in securing election as a member of the Grand Council of Berne. This was a subject Hegel had thought about in detail since it touched so closely on his own experience in Berne, and it gained a certain European significance during these months when the French, with La Harpe at the head, marched into the Pays de Vaud and forcibly liberated the region from the control of Berne.

What was often enthusiastically described as typical 'Swiss Freedom' was hardly in evidence in the Pays de Vaud, as Hegel's commentary on Cart goes out of its way to show. It is not based on a theory of revolution but called rather for the re-establishment of the traditional 'old law' of the region which had been destroyed by the tyrannical behaviour of the Berne oligarchy. The judicial system operated by the Berne government was the precise opposite of what it claimed to be. Arbitrary power ruled here instead of rights and the legal defence offered to those inhabitants of the Pays de Vaud who were officially accused of harbouring seditious sentiments against the government was purely formal and nominal. Hegel is closer to Montesquieu than to Rousseau when he compares the political system against its own principles, 'l'ésprit des lois', and finds the Berne aristocracy wanting in this respect. As a commentator and translator Hegel agrees wholeheartedly with Cart's convictions when the latter observes that 'in no other country that I know that is comparable in size is there so much hanging, breaking on the wheel, beheading and burning as there is here in this Canton'. This produces the distinct impression that things are far worse in the Swiss Republic than they are in the hereditary monarchy of Württemberg in the time of Karl Eugen. In view of the power of the Berne government it is not difficult to understand why the publishers who advertised the book, the Jägersche Buchhandlung in Frankfurt, took the precaution of declaring the author dead and suppressing the name of his translator Hegel.

12

The Unpaid Lecturer

In January 1801 Hegel arrived in Jena without making a detour through Bamberg as he had originally planned. He initially took up lodgings with Schelling, his protector and chief support in seeking academic employment. He was still sharing this apartment with Schelling on 10 December, as we learn from Hegel's letter of that date to the theologian and teacher Friedrich Hufnagel in Frankfurt. Schelling's busy social life at this time must have generally kept him away from the house in the evenings, especially now that his friendship with Caroline, who was still married to August Wilhelm Schlegel, had become an increasingly close one. When we consider Schelling's new friend, shortly to become his wife, and her entire romantic circle in the Jena salons, then it is not surprising that Schelling required more than Hegel himself for constant company. And the anti-romantic Hegel was in any case far too busy with his files and papers to socialize. And a short time later Hegel was giving his address in Jena as Löbdergraben at the Klipstein Garden.

The Jena which now received Hegel was certainly no longer the same Jena which had received Schelling before him, and which had originally caused Hegel some apprehension. The celebrated Jena of the romantic writers was now entering upon a period of gradual decline. The Schlegel brothers had already left the city, along with Ludwig Tieck, who with them can be counted as one of the founding fathers of the romantic German school. Fichte had been driven out and forced to take refuge in Berlin, Schiller had now moved to Weimar, and Novalis died in nearby Weissenfels not long after Hegel's arrival. After a short but vigorous moment of flourishing the romantic movement was visibly wilting. At least as he prepared to become a university lecturer in Jena Hegel was spared the physical proximity of Friedrich Schlegel, who had previously lectured there for one semester on aesthetics.

Schelling's star, on the other hand, was still very much in the ascendant.

This was particularly favourable to Hegel who had followed his friend's intellectual development and sought out his company and counsel in order that he too might be born aloft with his successes. There was nothing unseemly in this and Hegel did not need to steel himself to the task. After all, he had been observing Schelling's career with the closest interest ever since he was in Berne, had watched the emergence of the new Fichtean philosophy in opposition to Kant, and had seen the latter almost immediately challenged in turn by the young Schelling. Hegel had reflected carefully on Fichte and had already communicated some thoughts on this subject in his letters to Schelling. By the time Hegel turned explicitly to his successful young friend for assistance he had already quietly consolidated a distinctive position of his own with respect to the principal issues involved. Hegel was thus peculiarly competent in the subject he had chosen to write about in order to inaugurate an academic career: *The Difference between Fichte's and Schelling's System of Philosophy*.

This essay was published in July 1801, but the work with which Hegel formally acquired his *Habilitation*, the qualification required to offer lectures at any university, was a treatise called *De Orbitis Planetarum* ('On the Orbits of the Planets'). In addition Hegel had to 'defend' twelve pre-announced theses before an appropriate academic panel. The actual oral examination took place on 27 August, Hegel's thirty-first birthday. The part of the defence, together with the author himself, was shared by Karl Schelling, the philosopher's brother, while the official 'opponents' were Schelling himself, despite his implicit support for Hegel's cause, Friedrich Niethammer and a student called Thomas Schwarzott. In accordance with the regulations Hegel also had to pay a fee of around 2 thalers and convince the members of the philosophy faculty that he had sufficient resources to support himself as a lecturer. Once he had done all this and successfully passed his 'defence' examination Hegel was duly authorized to give philosophical lectures at the University of Jena from the next winter semester onwards. The faculty had agreed to this authorization on the understanding that Hegel's as yet unfinished written dissertation on the planets would be handed in shortly. In fact Hegel only submitted the dissertation about seven weeks later on 18 October. For a while it looked as though serious problems were brewing as a result. Those university members who were generally rather hostile to the incoming Swabians saw their chance. There was muttering about the extraordinary speed with which Hegel had been granted the *Habilitation*, and in the middle of the academic vacation when other lecturers were difficult to contact, and some talk about preferential treatment being given to the candidate. And when Hegel delayed such a long time in submitting the dissertation, this too gave rise to suspicious rumours. The logician and metaphysician Henning, whose chosen domain Hegel would later revolutionize, claimed to have uncovered serious irregularities and expressly demanded the immediate withdrawal of Hegel's teaching licence 'because there has been deception involved'. In fact Hegel's dissertation was officially handed in to the authorities the very same day.

The value of Hegel's dissertation from a scientific point of view has been fundamentally questioned ever since it was submitted in 1801. But it has also often been regarded, as it was by its first reviewer, F. X. von Zach, as an actual intellectual scandal of the first degree. And there was little change in this regard until the recent publication of a new edition of the work with accompanying commentary by Wolfgang Neuser.

The prevailing negative judgement may well be justified as far as the mathematics and physics involved are concerned and is unlikely to be revised in the future, but there are few of Hegel's early manuscripts which reveal the fundamental philosophical structures of his thought in such a pregnant and abbreviated manner. As his first complete and independent published essay it represents a clear statement of Hegel's initial philosophical position in Jena. It also reveals the quite indeterminate boundary separating the 'philosophy of nature' from the newly emergent natural sciences and their empirical and experimental methods. At the same time the dissertation documents Hegel's attempt at producing a provisional system and elaborating an appropriate methodology for it.

The work itself was preceded by the theses which were supposed to indicate the content of the 'science' of philosophy represented in the following text and to invite further academic discussion. The first thesis claimed: 'Contradiction is the rule for truth, non-contradiction for the false', and the second: 'The Idea is the unity of the finite and the infinite, and the whole of philosophy lies in the ideas.' Both theses present the fundamental maxims of the logic which Hegel was then attempting to develop and announce his central methodological claim that logic should constitute the original discipline, the 'first science', from which all others are to be derived. Hegel confronts his main philosophical antagonist in the seventh thesis: 'The critical philosophy is lacking in these ideas and represents an imperfect form of scepticism.' This is aimed at that limited rationalism defended by Kant's followers but which contains more than it realizes. As the eighth thesis spells out: 'The material content of the postulate of reason, erected by the critical philosophy, actually destroys this philosophy and represents the principle of Spinozism.'

Hegel's distance from Kant's critical philosophy could hardly be greater than it is here where he implicitly declares it 'finished', and that by its own hand, so to speak through the postulate of reason. This philosophical prelude in the form of theses strongly suggests that the following treatise on 'celestial mechanics' will not have very much to add to our scientific knowledge of the field in physical and mathematical terms.

Hegel's work was essentially concerned to articulate a critique of Newtonian physics, concentrating on two central issues: the question concerning the actual reality of mathematically postulated lines that are then identified with forces, and the role played by the concept of centrifugal force in Newton's physics. Hegel took offence at Newton's attempt to deal with the concepts of physics in terms of purely mathematical argumentation. Hegel regarded this approach as impossible and proposed that the empirical concepts be derived philosophically in order to produce an appropriate concept of the solar system as a whole.

We realize today without a doubt that Hegel's attempt to produce a physics of his own was clearly destined to failure, not to mention his particular critique of Newtonian physics with philosophical methods of his own. None the less, it would be premature simply to ignore Hegel's dissertation on the planets entirely. Hegel had objected to the philosophical pretensions of Newton's 'mathematical principles as applied to the philosophy of nature' and alluded to the lack of (Hegelian) logic in the Newtonian approach. But if logical-conceptual considerations of this kind were simply ignored, then nature itself was robbed of its own genuinely rational character in Hegel's eyes. Nor was Hegel alone at the time in believing that Newton had encouraged a number of fundamental errors in the understanding of nature. It had become something of a fashion to make such critical observations about Newton. The most prominent of Newton's critics was Goethe himself, the very man who formally nominated the professors at the University of Jena. From this perspective, Hegel's choice of the theme itself, as well as its actual treatment, is easily understandable. Newton of course survived this Hegelian 'refutation' in the spirit of Goethe. As far as mathematical physics is concerned Hegel's dissertation remained nothing but an academic curiosity from the dubious field of nature philosophy.

If one consults the official university records one can see that Hegel's rather hasty *Habilitation* process had caused considerable resentment in faculty circles. For the way in which Hegel's teaching certification was obtained rather flew in the face of the seniority of two other colleagues. On 26 August 1801 the Faculty Senate reprimanded the 'presumption' of Herr Dr Hegel in believing he enjoyed academic precedence over the two other current candidates Schwabe and Danz, even though both of them had submitted their dissertations on time before Hegel had finally handed over his. It was obvious that Hegel, after years spent on the margins, was very keen to catch up and make his mark in academic circles. Problems with the faculty continued when it emerged that Hegel had already announced his intention to offer a lecture at the university gratis (something normally permitted only to regular professors). Opinion in the faculty was divided, as some saw their own sinecures threatened, while others counselled toleration. The seeds of opposition to Hegel in Jena, a problem he would have to contend with until his final departure from the University, seem to have been sown very early on.

With his *Habilitation* Hegel officially increased the already fairly substantial number of *Privatdozenten*, or unpaid university lecturers, in Jena. Their income from teaching was generally slender, based as it was on standard fees paid by the students who attended their lectures, and was certainly insufficient to live on by itself. Under these circumstances there was considerable concern over the increasing number of such non-official and non-salaried teachers – by 1803 there were seven of them, including Fries and Krause, in addition to three regular and two non-regular professors. But the main bone of contention was the fact that so many of these new people were from Württemberg. We remember how Schiller had originally suggested his fellow-countryman Hegel, whom he had not even met at the time, as a house tutor in the household of Frau von Kalb. Since Hegel had already decided to leave for Berne, the post was then offered to Hölderlin instead; and it was Hölderlin who had first secured some kind of footing in Weimar and Jena where he supported Schelling's philosophical cause even before the latter arrived. And now Schelling had called his old Tübingen student friend to Jena too.

All this could hardly go unnoticed amongst Hegel's new university colleagues. But the final insult was certainly the way Hegel's *Habilitation* had been handled. The process had involved two former graduates of the Tübingen Stift. For the second official 'opponent', alongside Schelling, had been Immanuel Niethammer, Hegel's oldest friend from the Württemberg period, and the one who would remain his most loyal friend in future as well. There was now also another graduate of the Tübingen Stift who had recently gained a foothold in Jena: Heinrich Eberhard Gottlob Paulus, a rationalist theologian who had given evidence of his own lack of orthodoxy by publishing the first complete edition of Spinoza's writings.

This evident solidarity on the part of the native Württemberg contingent was revealed not only now when Hegel arrived in Jena but equally later when Niethammer, Schelling and Paulus left Jena one by one in the shared purpose of seeking alternative employment in Bavaria, with Bamberg or Würzburg as their first stop.

As soon as Hegel received his licence to lecture he began to prepare for the next stage of his academic career, and with a dedicated purposefulness that had hardly been obvious in him before. Two days after the *Habilitation* was formally ratified on 18 October 1801, Hegel arranged, through his friend Schelling, to be received by Minister Goethe in Weimar. Goethe noted in his diary under 21 October: '11 o'clock Dr Hegel'.

This first meeting, about which nothing precise is known, must have proceeded in a very formal manner. Goethe himself was already the poet of *Faust*, in a fragmentary form at least, but he cannot have imagined then, any more than Hegel himself could have done, that this inconspicuous visitor, a teacher still in search of secure employment, would one day present an interpretation of world history that might have been inspired by *Faust* and translate the images and forms of the poet into the philosophical 'Idea'. This was an encounter of fundamentally different character-types: on the one hand a poet who relied upon a keen visual sense and distrusted all abstract speculation, a man for whom experience signified tangible contact and an immediate empathy with things, a natural scientist and a man of the world in the broadest sense, an individual in whom nature and art seemed to combine in perfect harmony. On the other hand a man of abstraction who sought to reduce objects and forms to theoretical explanation, to discover the regularity of law behind the underlying forces of nature and to calculate their effects. On the one side the impetuous man of exceptional nature, the original romantic exponent of 'Storm and Stress' and prime mover in the German aesthetic cult of genius. On the other side the cautious man of painstaking reflection, for whom every positive claim also involved a qualified retraction in turn. Here the bearing of an artist and connoisseur, there the clumsy behaviour of the schoolroom scholar. Such is surely the scene of their initial encounter.

Although we know nothing of what was said on that occasion, something quite remarkable seems to have happened, given their profound dissimilarities of character and especially given Goethe's courtly appreciation of respectful distance. For the Minister was clearly taken with the rather awkward thirty-something in front of him. This seems quite incomprehensible since Hegel's typically abstract mode of thought and speech represented everything that Goethe disliked and distrusted. Yet this must have been far more than simply a case of Goethe's usual benevolent tolerance towards others. For the friendly relationship between Goethe and Hegel that began on this October morning of 1801 was to last another thirty years, quite undisturbed by the often considerable physical distances between them. But Hegel had not come to Goethe entirely with empty hands on this first visit. In the dissertation he had just completed Hegel supports Kepler in order to prove the absurdity of Newton's theory of gravitation. The celebrated case of the apple with which Newton defended his doctrine of gravitational force merely struck Hegel as an appropriate symbol for the failures of the experimental method. The theologian in him recalled the apple of Eve which had originally plunged mankind into its fallen state, not to mention that other apple chosen by Paris which eventually led the Trojans to their destruction. This was naturally music to Goethe's ears. In several writings of his own the poet had already undertaken to criticize Newton's theory concerning the refraction of light. Newton's errors seemed incontestable to Goethe for the poet had been unable to produce a refracted ray of light in his own experiments.

Goethe saw Hegel as a potentially worthy ally in the struggle against Newton, especially since he came expressly recommended by Schelling. And after some initial hesitation Goethe had come to recognize the latter's early views concerning nature as highly congenial to his own. Nothing could have rendered the new young lecturer, whom Goethe would soon be calling his 'dear friend Hegel', more acceptable to the Weimar minister than his shared sympathy with Goethe's own theory of colour. For Goethe was nowhere more sensitive to criticism than in this domain. Anyone who even remotely questioned his theory of nature, and in particular his theory of colour, or who gave the slightest suspicion of doing so, was instantly dropped for good. Thus the first steps of Hegel's academic career, which itself had taken a conspicuously long time to commence, were not inauspicious ones. Hegel would soon find further occasion to call upon the support of his ministerial patron, and would not be disappointed in the result.

Hegel was unable to bring one project to satisfactory completion during this period, and that was his extended essay on *The Constitution of Germany*. The piece probably remained unfinished in the first place on account of the composition of his dissertation for the *Habilitation*, and in the second place on account of his preparations for the lectures he was to give in the winter semester of 1801/2. He had already announced a series of special lectures on the subject of logic and metaphysics, as well as an introduction to philosophy in collaboration with Schelling. Hegel's work on *The Constitution of Germany* had apparently continued until the summer of 1801. We cannot exclude the possibility that the beginnings of this essay go back to Hegel's Frankfurt period. As far as the overall theoretical conception of the piece is concerned there is in fact no doubt about this since in respect of content the piece clearly connects with Hegel's earlier essay on the constitution of Württemberg and the notes he supplied to his anonymous translation of Cart's *Confidential Letters* on the Pays de Vaud.

These two earlier works, as well as his running commentary on Steuart's *Investigations into the Principles of Political Economy*, appear in the light of the essay on *The Constitution of Germany* as fundamental and detailed preparatory studies, as an initial exploration and gradual penetration of a complex thematic problem. Hegel had already remarked with regard to Steuart's work that 'one has perhaps done the system of the *sansculottes* in France an injustice by simply identifying avarice as the cause of their concern to establish a greater equality of property'. But in Hegel's essay on *The Constitution of Germany* we see that Württemberg, Switzerland and France alike have receded into the distance.

Hegel's question here is: what are the current prospects for the German 'Empire', for its internal constitution and its external circumstances alike? The philosopher who laboriously undertakes to find an answer to this question is very different from Kant, Fichte or Schelling. Right down to the smallest stylistic details of the text we cannot find the slightest similarity with those thinkers. The ensuing analysis of what is called the 'Empire' is quite without illusions. Germany has lost its most precious character: 'There is no longer any state.' And the reason for this lies in the anarchy sanctioned by traditional constitutional rights. The old enfeebled Empire immediately prior to its final collapse is characterized precisely by that 'stateless' character which results directly from the fundamental lack of centralized power in the system. Political impotence and an intrinsic incapacity to defend itself against its enemies are the fundamental evils which have brought Germany to the edge of destruction. And this is grounded not in the character of the people as such but in the nature of the existing constitutional arrangements. The prevailing political impotence is rooted in the constitutional system itself.

On account of this 'constitutional anarchy' Hegel describes the Empire as nothing but an 'imaginary state'. It cannot possibly be saved from itself by yet more imperial decrees. For even when they are issued they are never effectively put into practice anyway. If Hegel would later project an elaborate philosophy of the state which went far beyond Fichte, he would conceive it in direct contrast with all the salient characteristics of the present political system, this 'non-state' as he called the Empire after the Treaty of Lunéville. Anyone who has no desire for a proper 'state' will find himself well served by the so-called 'Holy Roman Empire of the German Nation' as constituted immediately prior to its demise. When the Empire in fact collapsed in August 1806 with the abdication of Emperor Francis II, Goethe, who was staying in Bohemia at the time, seemed according to his own account less concerned about the new political situation than he was about the violent argument which the news provoked between his manservant and his coachman.

Things had not yet reached this pass when Hegel was working on his essay on the German constitution, but his manuscript anticipated the imminent destruction of the Empire. The system was already in its final throes and Hegel regarded it as good as dead. What had originally moved Hegel to compose this piece was the desire to understand just why the imperial forces had fared so wretchedly in comparison with the soldiers of the French Republic. How on earth had it come to this catastrophic conflict which threatened to overturn the forces of the old order, and the traditional God to whom they made appeal? We know the early history of these reflections in the mind of the young Tübingen student who went out to plant freedom trees in enthusiastic support of the French Republic. In Switzerland we saw him forced to recognize that the Bernese Republic was in fact nothing but an oppressive oligarchy which continued to exercise its glorious power unchecked. With the expansion of French influence under the leadership of Napoleon the political question assumed a new form in Hegel's eyes. The reasons for the declining military fortunes of the Empire, as Goethe himself had seen it at the battle of Valmy, were to be sought in its excessive decentralization, in the contractual freedom of the individual German member states, which could even enter into alliances with the enemies of the Empire itself, and in the poor organization of the imperial army. Hegel witnessed how the imperial forces had been routed by the French. This was hardly surprising in Hegel's eyes on account of the irregular and unreliable fashion in which the soldiers themselves were recruited. People of one social standing would be responsible for the drummers themselves, while people of another would be expected to supply the necessary drums, some abbot would supply the imperial bodyguard, one part of the country would look after the city defence forces, while another would provide the guards for ceremonial parades. But no one supplied soldiers with any military self-confidence of their own. An army like this was a joy to its enemies, just as a decentralized Germany in general was a joy to its ambitious neighbours. Hegel draws his own conclusions:

> In the war against the French Republic Germany had come to experience for itself that it is not a state at all; and Germany has been made fully aware of its political condition both in the war itself and in the peace which has concluded it with the following results: the loss of some of the fairest German lands, of some millions of its own former inhabitants, a reparations bill which weighs heavier upon the southern half of the country than upon the north and which only extends the hardships of war into the peace; and apart from those who have passed under the domination of their conquerors and their alien laws and customs, there are also many states which will soon forfeit their own highest good, namely that of being *autonomous* states at all.

Hegel was merely describing the actual consequences of something which should surely never have come about in the first place: that a God-given monarchy should be roundly defeated by the forces of a godless republic. Something unheard of had been accomplished, and that through the process of world history itself. This was a 'phenomenon' of history which required investigation and would in time become the object of Hegel's 'phenomenology'.

With his essay *On the Difference between Fichte's and Schelling's System of Philosophy* Hegel had expressly attracted the attention of all the philosophically interested parties then active in Jena. The title alone spelled out the topical and local nature of a comparison between two of the professional philosophers most intimately associated with Jena and simultaneously indicated the final culmination of the most advanced form of contemporary philosophy which appealed to Kant as its original inspiration.

When one considers the matter more closely the 'difference' between Fichte and Schelling, as articulated here, lay essentially in Schelling's recent self-distantiation from Fichte. Schelling himself had once appealed to Fichte's 'objective idealism' precisely in order to help him to escape from Kant's 'subjective idealism', although there was a sense in which the latter had only inwardly been transformed by Fichte into another typically 'German and idealistically exaggerated form of subjectivism' (Lukács).

Without some preliminary study and understanding Hegel's language in the *Difference* essay is hard to fathom. It requires a veritable labour of decipherment which only serves to reconfirm just how profoundly sybilline the original really is. In a sense the essay was supposed to represent a neutral examination of the differences between Fichte and Schelling, but it was also clear that the two parties involved could draw their own different conclusions from the discussion. Fichte had certainly been highly praised in the piece, but it was none the less Schelling who appeared as the philosopher destined to surpass the Fichtean standpoint. As Hegel put it in terms Schelling could have used himself: 'the identity involved in the Fichtean system is constituted as a merely subjective subject-object'. This was Hegel's essential and explicit criticism. Schelling thus found it necessary to write somewhat apologetically to Fichte on 3 October 1801 and disclaim 'any contribution' on his part to Hegel's essay.

The nuanced preference which Hegel revealed for Schelling over against Fichte in the *Difference* essay certainly resulted in part from his own philosophical considerations. Hegel's clear affinity with Schelling's overall philosophical outlook also encouraged the plan for a jointly edited *Critical Journal of Philosophy*. The idea for such a journal had come from the Cotta publishing house and had originally envisaged the explicit collaboration of Fichte and Schelling in the project. There had also been some talk of inviting the Schlegel brothers to participate. But since they had departed Jena now only Schelling and Hegel were left behind.

Hegel assumed this new task with a vigorous zeal that had hardly been seen in him before. The watchword the collaborators had chosen for their enterprise was mentioned by Hegel in a letter to Caroline Hufnagel on 30 December 1801: 'To put paid to the current unphilosophical nonsense' and to employ 'whips, scourges and cudgels' in the struggle if it should prove necessary. All this for 'the intrinsic good of the cause and the greater glory of God'.

The collaborators clearly agreed about the highly polemical character of the undertaking from the very beginning. Any compromise with the enemy, and that meant the enemy of true philosophy, was emphatically rejected in advance. According to Hegel and Schelling the principal contemporary problem with regard to philosophy lay in the complacent cultivation of a multiplicity of systems. Everyone had to think out his own particular 'system'. Hegel and Schelling took the emphatic claim of truth seriously and could not contemplate with equanimity the spectacle of mutually opposed and rival positions continuing to flourish unabated. In their eyes 'Reason is only ever one and the same Reason.' The principal opponent in this respect was what they dubbed 'crude empiricism', which liked in times of freedom and equality simply to appeal to 'the healthy common sense' of people. One of those singled out here by Hegel was Wilhelm Traugott Krug. The fact that Hegel regarded him merely as an idle babbler did not prevent the University of Königsberg from nominating him as Kant's successor in 1804. Another explicit target was one Gottlob Ernst Schulze who had quite falsely presumed, in Hegel's view, to appeal to ancient scepticism against the new speculative philosophy. Popularization was certainly not one of the aims of the *Critical Journal*. In the 'Introduction' it was expressly stated: 'No sooner has the true idea of philosophy or art revealed itself to view than the packaging starts at once, until the subject has been duly prepared for the pulpit, the compendium, or the domestic requirements of the public eager for all the latest news.' In his essay on scepticism directed principally against Schulze Hegel admits that the sceptical position has a justified place in philosophy. But genuine scepticism for Hegel has a positive as well as a negative side: 'for even Diogenes Laertius himself points out that some have called Homer the first protagonist of scepticism'.

That remark is clearly aimed at theological dogmatism, Hegel's principal target of criticism ever since his Tübingen days. The reservations that had been expressed about Kant both in Hegel's correspondence with Schelling and in the so-called 'Earliest System programme of German Idealism' are taken up again here. Hegel writes, for example, that Kant actually delivered 'a critique of the understanding rather than of reason'.

Hegel's philosophical engagement with Kant, which had begun so late and was only cautiously articulated for so long, as Hegel attempted to test out his own objections, is now carried to a decisive conclusion in the fourth contribution to the *Critical Journal*, entitled 'Faith and Knowledge or the Reflective Philosophy of Subjectivity in the Complete Range of its Forms in Kant, Fichte and Jacobi'. The rather long-winded title states accurately enough that a close comparison of different philosophies is being undertaken here. Hegel writes:

> According to Kant it is impossible for the supersensible to be known by reason ... According to Jacobi reason is ashamed to go begging and has neither hands nor feet with which to dig – man is vouchsafed nothing but the feeling and consciousness of his own ignorance of the truth, and reason contains merely a presentiment of the truth ... According to Fichte God is something quite incomprehensible and inconceivable, while knowledge knows only that it knows nothing and must take refuge in faith.

But the old oppositional relation between faith and knowledge has already begun to change in the work of all these thinkers according to Hegel: reason is curiously coming to resemble faith or has actually already become a species of faith. The difference between the three philosophers considered in Hegel's essay lies solely in the different manner in which this process has been accomplished in each case.

With these thinkers the movement of the Enlightenment in Germany had also reached a certain culmination, in which the Enlightenment began to reflect critically upon itself, and indeed in Jacobi's case turned into a kind of anti-Enlightenment outlook. In this essay Hegel presents his first somewhat tentative views of three important systems of thought which would continue to occupy his mind for the rest of his life. If Kant had removed metaphysics from the realm of secure and well-founded philosophical knowledge, Hegel had expressly reversed this decision once he began developing his own metaphysical reflections in Jena. There was a sense in which he wished to reintegrate metaphysics back into the body of philosophy proper. Even as an unpaid lecturer Hegel was already addressing the fields of metaphysics and logic at the same time. This is not merely true of his later thought as expressed in the *Science of Logic* where Hegel famously identifies logic and metaphysics with one another. The unparalleled character of this enormous intellectual undertaking is only fully appreciated for what it is when we reverse the equation: Logic = Metaphysics. From a Kantian perspective such an identification could only appear abstrusely implausible, however powerful an exponent of this view Hegel turned out to be. But the years immediately after the turn of the new century had not yet brought Hegel that far. Or at least he was not yet willing to commit such views to paper. Unless of course one expressly emphasizes the sense in which Hegel's notion of 'dichotomy' in Jena already testifies to an equally emphatic concept of implied 'unity'.

Hegel's early intellectual history plays a crucial role in this development. The prospective theologian of Tübingen had left Berne and Frankfurt for Jena with the idea that 'religion' represents the highest expression of the spirit. Any 'philosophy' which wishes to approach this sphere and to explain its significance in the process of world history will sooner or later engage directly with the religious claims themselves and judge them accordingly. In this case philosophy cannot but assume a superior position with regard to religion itself. Schelling would hold a rather similar position on religion one day, but the young Schelling was quite convinced that art and not religion was the most sublime manifestation of human life.

Schelling's reflections on art belong amongst the greatest things which have ever been said on the subject, and have retained their living significance to the present day. These fundamental changes of orientation would fatefully shape the future of both thinkers in different ways. While Hegel in a sense exchanged religion for philosophy, Schelling would later abandon the priority of art in favour of religion. When the religious issue became a burning question again in the 1840s after the death of Hegel, Schelling came to be regarded as an obscurantist by the post-Hegelian revolutionary left, and not only by them but also by the Berlin university scene where the memory of Hegel's memory was still fresh.

That is all a matter for the future. But the various contributions to the *Critical Journal* already reveal certain potential difficulties in the relationship between the two editors. As a writer Hegel's style at this time seems the more vigorous, dictates the general tone of the articles and indicates the principal intellectual thrust of the journal. This is particularly clear in the case of Hegel's essay *On the Scientific Treatment of Natural Law, its Place in Practical Philosophy and its Relationship to the Positive Sciences of Law*.

If Hegel as a theologian had long since emancipated himself from the kind of Lutheran orthodoxy staunchly maintained in Tübingen, his turning to the question of natural law took him even further away from Lutheranism with regard to the nature of the state. Hegel repudiated the apolitical outlook associated with the Lutheran position and developed a political philosophy which was marked by more western European attitudes rather than by the conservatism of the German Lutheran east. From the very beginnings of his political reflections Hegel's idea of the 'state' has nothing to do with Fichte's idea of the 'closed commercial state', which was effectively envisaged as a police state. The Hegelian state is an ethical organism which rests upon the harmony between a people and its inherited ethical life.

'State' and 'non-state', 'war' and 'peace', 'freedom' and 'slavery' are presented here as the continually recurrent shapes of 'natural law'. In good scholastic tradition Hegel treats these subjects with reference to the ancient world. The classic spectacle of the decline and fall of the Greek and Roman civilizations naturally provoked fundamental questions about the ultimate causes of this process. If there was a sense in which Greece stood for the decline of art, there was a sense in which Rome stood for the degeneration of the state. The fate of Rome was even more significant for those with strong political interests than that of Greece. Gibbon's *Decline and Fall of the Roman Empire* had provided a masterly narration of that process as a political story turning into a story of disease and corruption. Hegel draws the following conclusion: 'the long period of peace and the homogeneous domination of the Romans merely introduced a slow and secret poison into the living body of the Empire. The attitudes of the people were gradually reduced to a level of uniformity, the ardour and inspiration of genius was extinguished, and even the old military spirit languished.' There was soon visible evidence of the approaching end: 'the several countries [of the Empire], robbed of their political strength or their unity, sank down imperceptibly into the dull indifference of private life'. For the Hegel of the natural law essay in the *Critical Journal* the decline of the Roman Empire was indissolubly connected with the end of the system of slavery which essentially supported it. The elimination of social differences through formal equality before the law eventually deprived the Empire of its own substantial foundation. With the end of slavery, political freedom came to an end as well. Hegel underlines the dialectical nature of the process by reversing the proposition: 'with the loss of freedom, slavery also necessarily ceased to be'. The Hegel who gave his Jena lectures in 1804–5 was already well aware that 'Factories, manufacturing industries, base their survival precisely upon the misery of a class.' They cannot eliminate this misery which they intrinsically produce, and in a sense intend to produce.

These were insights that had been dialectically developed. It is always necessary to take account of the various meanings of dialectic in Hegel's Jena period and the process of transformation to which it is constantly subjected. In Hegel the respective spheres of logic, metaphysics and dialectics are extremely difficult to disentangle. There is a sense in which metaphysics itself should be regarded as philosophy proper. But philosophy as the doctrine of the Idea 'as such' simultaneously involves both metaphysics and logic, which seem to represent a certain division of intellectual labour here. Metaphysics is the 'science' of the 'pure Idea' in its autonomous formal character. Both subjects are complimentary sides of the philosophy of idealism. But it is equally true that logic can only serve as an introduction to metaphysics as philosophy in the true sense.

This is true only with regard to Hegel's Jena version of logic as the embryonic form of the later *Science of Logic* where all 'sciences', including therefore metaphysics, are subsumed under 'logic' as the fundamental and primary science. Spheres which might otherwise appear to be identical with one another here change their respective places and positions. In Hegel's Jena logic, on the other hand, the dialectic is still very much a background presence and awaits its full emergence in the new metaphysics which has been resurrected despite Kant's critique of the tradition. And the same is true for logic, the discipline which had long been associated with the medieval idea of the liberal arts. If logic successfully maintains its traditional status as the art of truth, then it also represses the sphere of dialectic and treats it merely as a logic of error. But when logic itself is suspected as a means of encouraging purely spurious conclusions, then it too comes into the perilous proximity of dialectic. Although Kant thinks in a quite traditional manner in some respects, he does recognize dialectical reasoning as a kind of perverted logic. Goethe would later describe dialectic in conversation with Hegel as something 'diseased'. Hegel responded by consciously distinguishing his own understanding of dialectic as a mode of thought uncontaminated by such intellectual degeneration.

In Hegel's lecture notes for 1804–5 logic and metaphysics are also brought into direct relation with the philosophy of nature. In fact there is a continuous transition between these realms in Hegel's exposition. This was nothing new in itself, for Hegel had done the same in some of his earlier papers and was to do so again in his fairly rounded exposition in the *Phenomenology of Spirit*. This combination of logical-metaphysical reflection with the dimension of nature is an extraordinarily significant step that is worth considering more closely, however difficult it is to appreciate its importance today in the age of the natural sciences. The philosophy of spirit (logic and metaphysics) cannot be separated from the philosophy of nature in Hegel's thought. They are merely regarded as two aspects of the same reality.

In his manuscripts of 1804–5 Hegel distinguished between a 'metaphysics of objectivity' and a 'metaphysics of subjectivity', a distinction which he also applies to logic. The 'soul', the 'world', the 'highest being' belong to the 'metaphysics of objectivity', while the 'theoretical ego' or 'consciousness', the 'practical ego' and 'absolute spirit' belong to the 'metaphysics of subjectivity'. These ideas are not difficult to bring into harmony with the metaphysics of Fichtean or Schellingian idealism. But Hegel already projects a peculiar and characteristic tendency to rearticulate the boundaries and transitions which they had generally assumed. The principle of identity or of non-contradiction the principle of sufficient reason, the law of the excluded middle, all of them traditional themes of logic since antiquity, are now treated within metaphysics itself on the assumption that logic and metaphysics can be regarded as identical, as opposed to the earlier view that they represent essentially different disciplines. What lies between logic and metaphysics, according to Hegel, is the process of cognition itself: 'In so far as it passes over into metaphysics cognition is the sublation of logic itself, as dialectic, or is idealism.'

Hegel cannot tear himself away from this idea of the ultimate identity of logic and metaphysics, and he will never abandon it in future. It forms the methodological foundation stone of the *Science of Logic* later composed in Nuremberg. On this view all the regional competencies of the disciplines included within the philosophy of nature and spirit are subordinated to logic. This is equally true of history, which as political history and the history of spirit belongs in part to the process of natural history as well, as the backdrop of its development. History is subject to the same dialectic which logic intrinsically involves. Metaphysics naturally makes its claim in the sphere of history no less than in that of nature. History and its movement towards an end, namely 'freedom', do not simply depend upon themselves, but are oriented towards fixed points beyond themselves, although the latter are not immediately visible to the eye or perceptible to the agents or participants in the process. The same is true of the philosophy of nature in relation to logic and metaphysics. 'The sun as light becomes fire in the earth' – this proposition from Hegel's Jena manuscripts of 1803–4 is not exactly perspicuous with regard to our knowledge of nature. It is an insight based on the philosophy of nature, on metaphysical considerations, but seems to reveal a certain truth about the laws concerning the preservation of energy in nature. These in turn reveal something like a logic of nature, and of nature's dialectic. This path would later be followed of course by the Left Hegelian Friedrich Engels in his work *The Dialectics of Nature*. Engels attempted to grasp the interactive processes, the inner metabolism as it were, of society in accordance with the internal and external logic of its natural history. In Hegelian terms this approach is still very much a form of metaphysics in so far as it seeks to understand the metabolism of nature, the processes of birth and death for example, as a necessary factor in the preservation of the species as a whole, even though the exact nature of the governing process may be extremely difficult to discover.

Hegel's early Jena versions of his system are generally characterized by a certain rough-hewn quality, by a rawness of form which had been considerably smoothed out by the time he wrote the *Phenomenology of Spirit*. Hegel struggles tirelessly with language here to articulate how 'consciousness' develops its dualistic character in the context of the subject–object relation. Hegel writes: 'It has been shown that the highest essence is the one and only being, is the In-Itself.' Over against it there stands the 'evil principle' in its 'equality with itself'. Hegel concludes that this darkness does not exist in its pure clarity; for the darkness is a nothing for the light, while the darkness is equal to the light as to itself; but equally the light does not exist without the darkness, just as the darkness does not exist without the light. The highest essence or being has created the world, and the world exists for it in ethereal transparency and clarity; but the latter is dark with respect to itself.

This is esoteric enough. The elements that will go to make up Hegel's later *Science of Logic* are here displayed in a state of separation and juxtaposition. They are conceived in terms of the logic of negation and logic by its very nature is not affirmative but negative in Hegel's view: 'But negation, the nothing, is not at all something merely empty, but is the nothing of a specific determinacy and has genuine significance as opposed by way of negation to other determinacies.' We sense here something of the difficult and obscure path of thought to which Heraclitus has made a decisive and fully acknowledged contribution. For him too darkness exists in the light and light in the darkness. But the way the elements are combined with one another here also suggests the influence of Böhme's theosophical reflections on Hegel. There are also some oracular and archaic-sounding remarks in Hegel's 1803–4 manuscripts on 'consciousness' and 'recognition' (in the context of the family). The logic of these relations is interpreted in terms of the dialectic between being and non-being:

I can only recognize myself as this individual totality in the consciousness of the other, in so far as I posit myself in his consciousness, as an exclusive being in my own right, as a totality of exclusion, as one who aims at his life; in so far as I aim at his death I simultaneously expose myself to death, and put my own life at risk.

Hegel's interpretation of human labour in his Jena manuscripts effectively incorporates these interrelated themes directly into philosophy at an elevated level of reflection. Hegel here pushes beyond the previous development of idealistic thought, even beyond Herder who had explicitly discussed these subjects in important passages in his *Ideas on the History of Humanity* and his essay *On the Origin of Language*. Hegel pursues the development of labour from the primitive tool to the factory machine as described by Adam Smith. The 'tool' is absolutely necessary for man. It protects the human being from 'material destruction' and preserves him from death. But the activity of the tool remains a purely 'formal' one. 'In the machine man overcomes and sublates this formal activity and allows it to work independently for himself.' But for Hegel this also means that man loses his more original natural relationship to things.

But every deceit which he inflicts upon nature, and with which he still remains in the particularity of nature, avenges itself upon him, and the more he wrests from nature, the more he subjugates her to himself, the more humiliated he becomes himself. In so far as he belabours nature with all kinds of machines, he does not eliminate the necessity of his labour, but merely postpones it, removes it further from nature; he does not engage in this labour for a lifetime as a living activity, but sees this negative activity vanish and the labour he is left to perform becomes all the more machine-like in turn; he merely reduces the labour necessary for the whole, but not for the individual. He produces more only for the whole, but not for the individual, and the more machine-like his labour becomes the less value it possesses, and the more he must continue working in this manner.

The introduction of the machine as a productive force does not place people in a position where they have to work less than before or where their circumstances are less harsh than they were. The 'deceit' involved in machine labour penetrates all the relations of life. Man no longer works on what he needs, and he no longer needs what he works to produce. The machine creates products which are superfluous for the direct satisfaction of human needs. They are not produced for the 'actuality of satisfaction' but rather for the 'possibility' of satisfaction. Man can make use of such products, or he can ignore them. His labour is therefore directed to the sphere of need as a possibility, as an 'abstraction'. Labour in and for itself is directed to the possible satisfaction of all human needs. With the specialization of labour, its 'particularization' as Hegel calls it, the worker's skill or aptitude is certainly further developed with regard to a particular task, and the product of such labour is also correspondingly improved. But as the quantity of the produced goods rises, the value of the labour itself falls. The particular skill of the individual cannot be maintained for long and eventually declines to produce negative consequences:

> the consciousness of the factory worker becomes reduced to a level of utmost dullness, while the relationship between the individual kind of labour expended and the entire infinite mass of needs that are to be satisfied can no longer be recognized; thus a blind dependency arises so that some distant economic enterprise can suddenly affect the labour of an entire class of people, who met their own needs thereby, thus making these people superfluous or useless.

In these Jena papers, unknown and unpublished for a long time as they were, Hegel was developing his notion of the factory-worker, the worker under the economic conditions of industrial capitalism, which in the *Phenomenology* he would apply to the abstract relation of 'master and slave' against a feudal background in order to expose the contradictory character of this dialectic. For in their relationship with one another a point is eventually reached at which the master becomes the slave of the slave precisely through his own dependency on the labour of the slave without which he could not be master in the first place.

We can see from the Jena manuscripts that it belongs to the way the system is constructed, and to its very method, that all the individual details and moments of Hegel's analysis are sublated into a totality. They find their respective places within the whole, but they can only be isolated and separated, and explicitly experienced as such, in relation to this whole. What Hegel understands by 'science' here is already on its way to becoming an 'encyclopaedia', literally a 'circle of sciences', in which every subject will be covered. Hegel's so-called *Realphilosophie* of 1805–6 already contains many detailed and advanced contributions in this respect.

Hegel expounds the basic outlines of the Lutheran doctrine of the social estates and their respective functions, but simultaneously expands and loosens up this tradition by reference to the beginnings of the Industrial Revolution in England: 'The peasant class thus represents this immediate state of social trust without further individualization, which possesses its own individuality in the earth itself.' Peasant life can only really be understood in relation to the earth: 'he tills, and he sows, but it is God who gives the harvest – the turning of the seasons and the faithful trust that what he sows in the earth will emerge in and of itself'. The completion of his labour does not essentially lie in his own hands and 'the relationship between his purpose and its actualization resides in the unconscious life of the earth'. This attachment of the peasant to the earth as his own 'unconscious' element is what accounts for the irresistibly stubborn resistance displayed by peasant armies in time of war, as Hegel notes in another connection. It is almost as if the earth itself moved with them as an indissoluble factor of their life. The 'social estate' in question finds its appropriate expression in its own peculiar set of attitudes and sentiments. Peasants and citizens 'know how to get on with one another more easily – they can come to blows and subsequently make up again'. This contrasts with the attitudes of the 'higher social estates': 'the more deeply rooted sentiments of these classes are concentrated within them; they can neither forget an injury nor establish subsequent reconciliation', and that is comparatively speaking the more 'malignant' attitude. The characteristic labour of the businessman lies in the sphere of 'pure exchange', a process which involves 'dichotomy' since it consists both in a 'particular' dimension, namely the commodity itself, and an 'abstract' dimension, namely that of money as the medium of exchange. The soldier on the other hand finds his function in 'war' as a 'genuine form of self-sacrifice'. Here Hegel stands firmly upon the ground of natural law. Transgression or 'crime' in war is 'transgression on behalf of the universal'. In so far as it is oriented towards the preservation of the whole, it is directed against the 'enemy' and the potential 'destruction' of the latter. Hegel exposes the full significance of this 'transgression' by pursuing it right back to its origins: the 'concept' of 'transgression' is already implied in that of 'right' and the 'non-violent exercise of law'. In war the enemy is not directly attacked in person and 'death is dealt out and received in an empty fashion'.

The lectures on *Realphilosophie* of 1805–6 go beyond Kant in their treatment of socio-political reality with regard to questions concerning the family, marriage, personal property, capital, rights of inheritance, and so on. For they essentially reflect the transformation of the social world which was effected by Napoleon and the Revolution and felt throughout all the German territories. Hegel himself had witnessed these developments in person. Hegel presents a completely different conception of 'marriage' from that of Kant. For Hegel, unlike Kant, marriage is not to be grasped on the model of a 'contract' alone. The 'law must take due regard of the living individuality of the participants here'. Thus 'a marriage is not concluded by virtue of the marital promise, nor through sexual union, but through the explicitly *declared will* of the parties'. Whether the ultimate 'purpose' of marriage is 'positively fulfilled', is consummated through coitus for example, is no concern of legislation itself. The indissolubility of the marriage relation can only be claimed by an 'empty law' which judges abstractly and one-sidedly without regard for the 'living individuality' of the partners. Equally a marriage cannot simply be broken through 'adultery, malicious neglect, personal incompatibility, inadequate financial support, but only if and when both partners expressly *regard* it as broken or *wish* it be so regarded'.

The principal maxim at work in Hegel's *Realphilosophie* is that of unity in dichotomy: a process which manifests itself in the phenomena of 'nature' and 'spirit' alike, whether in the creation of electricity or in the realization of sexual life. It is not so difficult to understand why Hegel should appeal to the Platonic idea of the hermaphrodite nature as an image of the union and the division of the sexes.

13

Domestic Affairs

~∞~

The quarters that this unsalaried lecturer had taken up 'auf dem alten Fechtboden' ('At the ancient Duelling Ground') were modest enough. The move had certainly taken place sometime between the beginning of January and May 1802 since Schelling already sent his letter to Hegel of 24 May from Leipzig to the new address, which Hegel would not subsequently change again until he actually left Jena for good in the autumn of 1806. Goethe also records it in his own Jena list of addresses after 18 October. The little household and slender possessions which now stood at Hegel's disposal were easily looked after by a suitable housekeeper or landlady. Hegel's needs were also modest as far as food was concerned, although he did expect a reasonable quality of wine, which he ordered in small barrels from the Ramann family, Erfurt wine merchants. He naturally had to be careful about suddenly spending any of the money he had just inherited, which had to last him for general expenses for as long as he remained in Jena under his present circumstances. Hegel could not consider major purchases unless he could realistically expect a reliable salaried position of some kind. And for him there was little prospect of that in Jena.

During Hegel's years at Jena the number of students attending his lectures increased steadily but it never went beyond thirty. In itself that was fairly encouraging but was decidedly meagre in relation to the crowds who flocked to hear Fichte. As far as external form was concerned, Hegel's lectures were not particularly enticing: his delivery was awkward and the content obscure to the point of unintelligibility. From the reminiscences of the philologist Abeken, who taught Schiller's sons but at this time was a student at Jena, we learn that the motto under which Hegel then presented his lectures was drawn from the inscription over Hell Gate in Dante's *Inferno*: 'Abandon hope all ye who enter here.' But word none the less got about that it was worth making the effort to understand him. Thus over the semesters there formed a small circle of devoted students whom no amount of oracular pronouncements could deter from attending Hegel's lectures.

Hegel's chief rival at Jena was Jakob Friedrich Fries, three years his younger and whose theological origins were rooted in the pietistic sect of the Herrnhut brethren. Fries would certainly have acquired a more thorough knowledge of Kant before Hegel did. As it was, parties soon emerged for and against. The members of the university administration were not unaware of the academic competition between the two lecturers but they generally, as will soon be seen, tended to support Fries rather than Hegel. Fries had actually obtained his *Habilitation*, the formal qualification required for offering lectures at the university, some time after Hegel, but he was already being proposed, unlike Hegel, for the position of 'extraordinary professor' at the university. Hegel was understandably dissatisfied with this and on 29 September 1804 penned a letter of complaint to his famous patron in Weimar concerning this act of obvious injustice as he saw it. Goethe read the following:

> Since I hear report that some of my colleagues are hoping for the most gracious nomination as Professor of Philosophy, and am thereby reminded that I am myself the most long-standing of the independent lecturers at this university I would therefore be so bold as to submit to the judgement of Your Excellency whether such a decision made with respect to others on the part of the highest authorities might not lead me justifiably to fear that my own efforts to contribute to the university would be severely disadvantaged thereby.

Hegel knew he could reckon with Goethe's sympathy and with his added support he managed to obtain a similar nomination, although it is clear that the university authorities had initially been unwilling to treat him as an equal with Fries. Goethe exerted his influence and successfully obtained the agreement of the governments of Saxony-Coburg and Gotha, Altenberg, Meiningen and Hildburgshausen, for all of which Jena was the principal university centre. At the beginning of 1805 Hegel officially became a professor, along with Fries, although he still remained without an academic salary to go with it.

This meant of course that Hegel would have to keep looking for suitable opportunities elsewhere, hoping to abandon the increasingly unpromising Jena and follow in the footsteps of his other Swabian colleagues Schelling, Niethammer and Paulus. And most of all he hoped to follow them to Bavaria.

Just why Bavaria was to prove so advantageous to them all would soon be revealed in a quite unexpected manner. Though it was an electorate, Bavaria feared annexation through the territorial ambitions of Austria and decided to support the Napoleonic cause. Bavaria thus swung in line with the current policy of the Rhineland League and soon belonged amongst its firmest supporters in favour of Napoleon against Prussia and the Habsburgs. Bavaria felt it was on the winning side here. The feeling of hopelessness which Hegel experienced whenever he thought about the German 'Empire' was profound, and it would very soon prove to be well grounded when ensuing events fundamentally affected his own life in a dramatic way. Saxony and Thuringia quickly became the arena where the French army and its hapless opponents came to blows. Hegel could feel the signs of approaching disaster in the rancorous atmosphere of the university at Jena and the serious financial cuts imposed by the various state governments. The future chronicler of world history sensed the imminent collapse from the manifest social symptoms and he was not mistaken.

During these years in Jena Hegel had clearly also shown an unmistakable desire to get closer to the seat of real power and to establish a positive relationship with it. In this case it was the all-powerful minister Goethe. When Goethe visited Jena from nearby Weimar and stayed there for months on official business, Hegel revealed an exceptional keenness to maintain contact with him. As far as Goethe was concerned, he showed his usual conventional liberality with a certain distance and his general tendency to live and let live. He would ask guests to tea, especially officials and officers from the Jena administration, people who enjoyed his personal trust and belonged to his broader circle. Amongst a list of 'Jena friends' which Goethe himself wrote out later (18 October 1806), we also find Hegel's name – at the very bottom in accordance with his social status. Schiller had noticed Goethe's increasingly benevolent interest in Hegel at first hand. 'I see with pleasure that you are getting better acquainted with Hegel', he wrote to Goethe on 30 November 1803. But his correspondence with Goethe is chiefly concerned with Hegel's difficulties in making himself understood amongst people generally. Goethe himself had remarked on the same question, only a few days earlier: 'As far as Hegel is concerned, the thought has occurred to me whether we might not be able to do him a considerable favour in terms of rhetorical technique.' In other words: he finds it extremely difficult to express himself in language. Goethe was not referring here to Hegel's public delivery in front of students but rather to Hegel as he appeared in more intimate social gatherings. Goethe clearly believed it was possible to alleviate Hegel's problems in this area. Schiller, however, expressed his doubts: 'What he lacks here is certainly no easy thing to procure for him, but this defective manner of expression of his is generally a national German failing, and it is compensated for, at least as far as a German listener is concerned, through the German virtues of thoroughness and genuine seriousness.'

In other respects Goethe had every reason to be satisfied with Hegel. Hegel felt he enjoyed Goethe's trust and was happy to communicate pieces of news, small harmless items of information, to Goethe and thereby prove his general worth to the minister, however unsuccessful he may have seemed to be as a teacher of philosophy.

But Hegel had equally good reason to be concerned about his immediate prospects. As the year 1806 approached, the circumstances began to look increasingly threatening. Schelling had long since left the country. On 11

July 1803 from Cannstatt he had informed Hegel of his recent marriage with Caroline, who had eventually got a divorce from August Wilhelm Schlegel. But Schelling also had another, more disheartening piece of news for Hegel: 'The most grievous sight which I have endured here during this present stay was that of Hölderlin.' Memories of a happy past turn, at a stroke, into oppressive feelings of burden: 'The sight of him was shocking to me: he neglects his personal appearance to an appalling degree.' Schelling wonders whether Hegel can see any hope for his wretched friend, whether he might be able to take him on himself. Hegel responds by saying that he will do his best if Hölderlin should come to Jena, but adds that his damaged friend could expect little from Jena itself. It was singularly fortunate for Hölderlin that in fact Sinclair undertook to look after him during these years and took him back home with him to Homburg.

If Hegel hardly expected much from Jena for Hölderlin, this was also because he had exactly the same reservations about the place himself. Hegel would soon be drawing Goethe's attention to the imminent departure threatened by other notable academics like Hufeland, Paulus and Thibaut. At the same time he began to make specific enquiries on his own behalf through Gries in Heidelberg. In the draft of a letter to the famous translator of Homer, Johann Heinrich Voss, he writes explicitly: 'I would wish to be included amongst the teaching body in Heidelberg.' The response he got was a negative one, allegedly because the financial resources of the university were in a wretched state. With the support of Niethammer, who had moved to Bamberg in the meantime, Hegel now considered the idea of going to Altdorf. At the same time he realized that the university there would have to be completely 'reorganized' since it was now little more than a phantom of its former self after a long period of sad decline.

All these negative responses did nothing to dampen Hegel's determination to leave Jena. It is clear from the letters to Niethammer that Hegel was filled with apprehension at the thought of war breaking out, and was certain he could not endure the quartering provisions that would immediately ensue. Hence he would do almost anything to escape from his current situation and the threatening future. As regards his own work, he did not feel bound to any particular place and was now sure his time in Jena was fast running out. He considered the idea of trying to set up a philosophical journal in southern Germany, seeing an opportunity in the fact that as yet there was nothing of the kind being published there.

As matters drew to a head for Hegel, it was Niethammer who increasingly became his principal ally and source of support for the future. He told Hegel that if war should indeed break out then he must immediately find alternative employment elsewhere. Once again, as six years before, Hegel turned his thoughts to Bamberg. It was not simply that Niethammer himself could promote his academic interests there; there was also a major academic publishing house based in the town: Joseph Anton Goebhardt. In connection with a prospective move to Bamberg, Hegel had already set his eyes on this celebrated institution for the publication of his most recent manuscript. The publisher showed positive interest, and he gave Hegel, then in some considerable debt, large advance payments on regular receipt of substantial portions of the said manuscript. But Goebhardt's payments began to falter as he developed the distinct impression that Hegel had not yet completed the work and he started to fear for the established publication deadline. Niethammer intervened immediately and promised to guarantee the delivery and stand surety for it himself. But Niethammer, along with Hegel, soon found himself in a difficult situation as a result. Troop movements between Saxony and Bavaria had seriously interrupted the postal service and it was feared that the final part of the manuscript might have been lost in transit. That was not the publisher's problem, for Niethammer had agreed to pay for the 21 gatherings at 12 gulden a piece if the manuscript were to arrive after the date stipulated in the contract agreement. The finished manuscript would have to be at the printer's by 18 October 1806 at the latest.

However, on 13 October the French army occupied the city of Jena, and with it, as Hegel wrote to Niethammer the very same day, the 'world soul on horseback'. The impression which Napoleon made on the population was dramatic. After the departure of the Prussian troops many of the people were openly sympathetic to the French. Hegel, fascinated by this expression of power, was caught up in similar sentiments: 'Indeed it is a wonderful feeling to see an individual like this, concentrated as it were in a single point, sitting on his horse, reaching out over the world and mastering it.'

In fact Hegel too was fortunate in one respect at least. The final manuscript did actually reach the publishers in time to meet the deadline. But his situation in Jena itself was plagued with difficulties. French soldiers had forcibly taken over his lodgings and he was forced to move into the home of Prorector Gabler as a result. Hegel was both the witness and victim of some harrowing scenes. There had been many casualties in the fighting and he had felt something of the resulting anarchy himself. 'I have been quite plundered here', as he wrote to Niethammer on 18 October. Death itself had almost touched him and the future analyst of world history had experienced something of the realities of war at first hand.

The entire circle of his Württemberg friends who had been living in Jena had got out in time and Hegel alone was left behind as the fateful events overtook him. The most difficult thing of all for him was that while he had seen the disaster approaching, he had been quite unable to avoid it himself. The question of a future career in Jena was now clearly settled in the negative.

The university had closed down. Hegel was now without any official position and his financial resources had long since shrunk to a one-off discretionary payment of 100 thalers for the year, which he had only obtained from the Duke through the personal intervention of Goethe. 'Look upon the contents of this letter, my dear Doctor, at least as an indication that I have not ceased discreetly to promote your cause.' Thus Goethe wrote to Hegel, enclosing the tactful payment, on 27 July 1806. Only four months later Hegel found himself more or less dispossessed of everything he had by the depredations of the soldiery. Once again it was Goethe who stepped in after enquiring with concern after Hegel's predicament. On being informed by Knebel on 24 October that 'Hegel is quite without money', Goethe responded the same day and declared: 'If Hegel needs some money, then give him up to about 10 thalers.'

There was now nothing to keep Hegel in Jena any longer. But it was equally obvious that Hegel was not going to find it at all easy to find the kind of position he was looking for elsewhere, i.e. suitable employment at one of the German universities. All his previous attempts had, one by one, eventually fallen through. Niethammer was certainly successful in solving Hegel's problems with his publisher, but he was unable to find him the desired academic position in Bamberg. Nor did Schelling seem to have exerted much real influence on his behalf. Was the main reason for Hegel's failure here simply the wretched financial state of affairs in the relevant states? Perhaps the question goes deeper than this, touching upon aspects of Hegel's personality that were not without a certain influence on his philosophy itself. Certainly there was that characteristic element of caution and even at times lethargy which had already seemed to hold him back, at least from a career perspective, in Berne, in Frankfurt and in Jena. But this aspect was only the complementary feature of his particular gift for searching out the innermost grounds of things and painstakingly analysing them. His comprehensive and conciliatory nature also compensated for that quality in turn, allowing him to explore things from within in all their materiality and givenness, to look at them in different ways and disclose their internal ambiguities and ambivalences. This did not make Hegel the easiest of people to work with for any extended period of time. Schelling would soon encounter an example of this which he would never forget for the rest of his life.

In November Hegel had set out to Bamberg to sort out the remaining contractual issues with his publisher and oversee the printing of his manuscript of the *Phenomenology of Spirit*, a work written under extreme conditions of indigence, debt and general anxiety for the future and which only arrived at the publishers section by section. Hegel actually departed Jena in a cart loaded with money-barrels but he was fortunate none the less. In spite of the dangerous times they managed to reach their destination without disturbance. For a while Hegel lived in a little room in the Niethhammer household, who were all delighted to see him. The business with Goebhardt seems to have been settled quickly and the friends were now able to give themselves over to the pleasures of beer-drinking and card-playing. The money Hegel had just received from the publisher allowed him to spend a pleasant few weeks.

Thus, much seemed calculated to make Bamberg an attractive place for him from the start. There was no comparison with Jena, for in Bamberg there were also plenty of ladies sitting around the card tables, as Hegel explicitly notes. And this emigrant had long since come to support the French cause in Germany. His old fears about the collapse of the 'Empire' had now been amply confirmed in his eyes. He was very struck by the way in which the French appeared to bring effective organization into the sluggish and corrupt arrangements of the old order. He expressed his thought on the causes of this transformation a couple of weeks later in a letter of 23 January 1807 to his former student Zellmann:

> Thanks to the bath of its revolution, the French nation has liberated itself from many of the institutions which the spirit has long outgrown like children's shoes, institutions which weighed oppressively upon the French as upon other nations and held them bound in spiritless fetters. What is more, however, is that the individual as well has cast off the fear of death and shed that old-accustomed life of habit which can no longer sustain itself now that the scene has changed.

Everything which once held undiminished sway has lost its power to convince: 'The fatherland, princes, constitutions, no longer seem to be the lever with which the German people can be roused.'

Even if Hegel was able to enjoy his first few weeks in Bamberg, the various soundings he made with Niethammer's assistance in order to find an academic post had been fruitless. So although Hegel had inwardly and decisively rejected the University of Jena, he was nevertheless forced to return there after all. He attempted to score a small success by appealing to his patron Goethe once again, asking if he might receive the remuneration formerly paid to Schelver, who had now been called to the University of Heidelberg, and move into his now vacant official apartment in the Botanical Garden since he was more than willing to perform the appropriate services there himself.

Goethe did not explicitly reject Hegel's epistolary attempt to secure a reliable position in Jena but he did not respond to it directly. For he had already long since decided on a different course of action. The doctor Siegmund Friedrich Voigt, also a botanist, had been chosen for the post. Hegel's declaration that he would resume his own botanical studies and even give lectures on the subject did nothing to alter Goethe's decision. Once again Hegel's attempts to find a firm footing had failed.

Then in Jena he received a letter from Niethammer on 16 February which offered him the now vacant position of editor at the local newspaper, the *Bamberger Zeitung*. The offer was a not unfavourable one at a salary of 540 gulden a year. In Jena Hegel had been essentially an unpaid lecturer, and the payment he received from the Duke on Goethe's request was a temporary and entirely discretionary one which had not prevented Hegel from having to borrow more money after his inheritance had finally been used up. But Hegel cavilled again. The proposed salary appeared to be too low. Hegel was still thinking about Heidelberg where Schelver had promised to promote his case for a second academic post which had become vacant there. He was also considering the idea of editing a new journal in Heidelberg if nothing else turned up. But what he really desired, now as earlier, was a university position or at least close proximity to a university. The thought of taking over the editorship of a daily newspaper could hardly have held much appeal to him in the circumstances. Hence the reservations he expressed to Niethammer on 20 February, warning him that he could not consider 'this engagement as something absolutely binding' on him. His friend had enjoined him from Bamberg to 'come at once without delay', since the position in question had to be taken up before 1 March. Hegel had already decided to accept the offer for, after all, what other options did he have under the enormous pressure of his present circumstances? But he still requested a short postponement. He clearly did not wish the authorities in Jena to believe he had committed himself to leaving for good and he explicitly intended to give the impression that he would soon be returning.

Hegel's caution in these matters was not without reason. Something else had recently transpired which made a hasty departure from the city particularly welcome to Hegel. He had just become the father of an illegitimate son. The mother was his chambermaid and housekeeper Christiane Charlotte Burkhardt, who had clearly required no elaborate or ardent courtship on Hegel's part before becoming involved. The baptismal register in Jena noted, accurately enough, that this was 'the third time the mother has borne an illegitimate son', already preceded by 'one daughter' and 'two sons out of wedlock'. In the milieu of a place like Jena this sort of thing could hardly be concealed from public knowledge. For Hegel, who had already encountered opposition from some of the university authorities against his appointment as a professor there, the social situation could not have seemed less promising. What was more, this 'Burkhardt person' as he called her, was obviously insisting on a pledge of marriage on Hegel's part. Hegel appears to have agreed to this in order to avoid more unpleasant publicity if he should refuse to do so. There is a different version of events in the ecclesiastical records, according to which Christiane Burkhardt was already legally married at the time of her relationship with Hegel and was thinking of marrying Hegel only if her husband were to die before her. On 4 July 1844 Varnhagen von Ense wrote down what he had heard from Hegel's student Leo, material later published for the first time by Lasson:

> Hegel used to live with a family of tailors at the time and he formed a relationship with the wife; the husband died soon after the son was born and Hegel thereupon promised he would marry the widow ... Once he had left Jena he didn't give much further thought to the whole matter. But when he came to marry Marie von Tucher the tailor's widow suddenly reappeared to remind Hegel of his pledge of marriage to her ... She had to be pacified and the affair had to be settled for good.

The fact of this illegitimate child would continue to embarrass the philo-sophical advocate of legitimacy in future. The birth of Ludwig Fischer, as he was later called after his mother's maiden name, marked the beginning of a regrettable human tale which was never fully acknowledged by his father.

The offer of the position as newspaper editor allowed Hegel to escape from this rather uncomfortable situation. He was so secretive about his com-ing departure from Jena to Bamberg that he not only failed to apply for official leave of absence from the relevant authority – in this case Goethe – but also announced his lectures for the summer semester in the event that the university were to be reopened. Only once he was in Bamberg did he make the appropriate formal application to the minister, who must himself have already been well aware of Hegel's personal circumstances and seems to have been quite undisturbed by them. On the contrary, Goethe appeared to be extremely pleased on hearing of the reasons for Hegel's trip to Bamberg. Hegel told him – which was certainly half of the truth – that he was going there to oversee the publication of his manuscript at first hand. Goethe's letter to Knebel seems to betray a certain impatience about the tardy progress of his protégé, like that of the Theatre Director in his own *Faust*: 'Plenty of words have been exchanged, for sure, / But now it's time to see you act'. Goethe responded to Hegel's intentions by exclaiming: 'At last I am anxious to see a careful presentation of your manner of thinking.' It was certainly not due to any lack of encouragement on Goethe's part if nothing substantial appeared to have come from the almost 37-year-old Hegel's stay in Jena over the last six years. Goethe certainly expected him to make the effort to develop an intelligible prose style: 'He has such an excellent mind but it is so difficult for him to communicate.'

As we shall see, Hegel did not in the event even remotely fulfil Goethe's hopes in this regard. The work in question was none other than the *Phenom-enology of Spirit*. The book appeared in March 1807, shortly after Hegel's arrival in Bamberg. There are many things that can be said about the author of this work, but a capacity for the lucid expression of ideas is certainly not one of them.

14

A Difference with Schelling

If Schelling was soon to discover that Hegel had now departed from what they had both formerly understood under the term 'Idea', this was only appropriate. For what had united them both since the later Berne period was their shared hostility to a philosophy of 'subjective idealism'. But this common perspective in philosophy was only possible because Hegel was himself still working essentially in terms of Schelling's own systematic thought. And it only fully remained in force as long as Hegel himself made no attempt to free himself from his 'Father-Octopus Schelling', as Jean Paul put it in a letter to Jacobi on 6 September 1807.

That process began in earnest with Schelling's departure from Jena to Würzburg in 1803, but there are also a number of clear anticipations of the break even before then. For during the intervening period Hegel had quietly been developing a conceptual approach of his own. There were certainly some aspects of Hegel's writings in Frankfurt and the Jena period which could clearly be compared with Schelling's work. And on the other hand, one could also say that in his *Exposition of My System of Philosophy* in 1801 Schelling also came closer than he ever would again to a specifically Hegelian approach to philosophy, one that would later emerge in mature form as the dialectic.

Hegel's growing distance from Schelling, about which the early written sources remain so obstinately silent, was originally largely methodological in character. That meant that Hegel's own early work could not effectively aspire to the heights of Schelling's *Philosophy of Art* (1802–3), that he remained far behind Schelling in the development of original ideas and was well aware of the fact. But it is also clear that Hegel considered Schelling's brilliant facility in this regard as a great potential danger as far as the systematic development of philosophy was concerned and explicitly communicated as much to his audience in Jena. When Hegel spoke of adepts merely repeating the thoughts of others, and the source of the problem was not named as such, Schelling was under no illusion about who was being referred to by implication.

It is obvious that a marked distance between the two of them had begun to develop after Schelling's departure for Bavaria, but it was also naturally the consequence of their radically different personalities and natures, something which could easily manifest itself openly and unreservedly now that the two of them were no longer in such close personal contact with one another. It can also be seen in the diminishing interest they took in one another's affairs, particularly during the months in Bamberg when Hegel sought the assistance of Niethammer and Paulus in his search for suitable employment and Schelling seemed to offer little relevant help. From the remarks made by Schelling during this period it looks as though he was merely waiting to see what his old student friend would make of himself in his own right. But for his own part Schelling was now increasingly getting embroiled in difficulties with the Catholic ecclesiastical circles in Würzburg and he was doubtless fully occupied as a result.

The difference between Hegel and Schelling touched directly upon the immediate conditions of life of the two men, or rather, proceeded from those conditions and simultaneously reflected itself in the philosophical sphere. For this reason one should not merely think in one-sided terms of Hegel distancing himself from Schelling. For Schelling himself was also changing, and moving away from positions he had long been able to think of as common ground with Hegel. Take the dialogue *Bruno*, for example, composed in 1802 while Schelling was still working in Jena and written in the Platonic and mystical vein which had become popular amongst the romantic writers of the time, or his piece entitled *Philosophy and Religion* which already contained the kernel of Schelling's later philosophical reflections. Schelling increasingly revealed a certain aristocratic attitude which would seem to reserve the true cognition of the absolute for a select circle of the initiated. This was accompanied by a related concentration upon questions of the aesthetic sphere, whereas Hegel even before the composition of the *Phenomenology of Spirit* had displayed a vigorous interest in political history and the philosophy of government, areas that would always remain secondary in Schelling's eyes and would never inspire his philosophical imagination to the full.

In his private notes from the Jena period Hegel had already begun to articulate the imminent crisis of Schelling's thought: 'What Schellingian philosophy is in its innermost essence will shortly be revealed. The judgement upon it already stands at the door since many now understand it.' For Hegel the growing influence and intelligibility of a philosophy will finally reveal to its supporters just how far one can advance with it. Hegel sees Schelling falling victim to the same fate as Kant and Fichte before him and places them all together in terms of the central issues of 'transcendental philosophy' precisely in order to delimit his own alternative perspective. He admits that the transcendental philosophy of Kant, Fichte and Schelling treats the problems of logic (and dialectic) but holds it incapable of comprehending this domain as an integral part of itself. Hegel, on the contrary, wishes to undertake the task of uniting transcendental philosophy as metaphysics with logic itself and producing from this union a new 'science' altogether. If Kant pointed out in the Preface to the second edition of the *Critique of Pure Reason* that the science of logic had made no real advance since the time of Aristotle, then Hegel believes now that the same is true of Kant as well. But if Hegel could succeed in uniting so-called transcendental philosophy and logic, something still to be achieved but clearly envisaged as the programmatic core of the *Phenomenology of Spirit*, and eventually realized in Hegel's *Science of Logic*, then logic will finally have made a genuine advance for the first time in more than two thousand years.

All of this implied 'differences', explicit or implicit, which would sooner or later lead to a rupture of the existing philosophical communication between Hegel and Schelling. Part of the emerging problem was also the different approaches both thinkers took to the understanding of history. While Schelling's interest in historical questions was beginning to ebb, Hegel's fascination with the field was growing. This eventually led Hegel to a conception of 'world history' as a process which advanced not continuously but by detours, contradictions, mutually opposed developments, by the obstruction or even defeat of the progressive cause, by wars and conflicts, all of which challenged the idea of smooth historical transitions. Hegel's philosophy of history was still embryonic at this stage but he was already developing the idea of a kind of variable pace of historical progress in which contradictions within a 'unity of continuity and discontinuity' (as Georg Lukács described it) are repeated on higher levels of historical development.

Hegel's increasing distance from the philosophy he had previously shared with Schelling was thus directly connected with the changing direction of their respective thematic interests and their own continuing concentration on different areas of research. Of course, this alone would not have prevented them from continuing to make common cause in the overall perspective they had once pursued together. In view of the development of an anti-dogmatic, quasi-pantheistic doctrine of spirit, and the repudiation of the established Church as the appropriate spiritual authority for man, all of which Schelling had articulated in his early Tübingen dissertation on the Gnostic Marcion, Hegel did not for a moment challenge the importance of Schelling's pioneering role. And indeed Schelling's place in the history of philosophy, and the part he played in the development of the dialectic, can hardly be over-emphasized. And when he moved away from Hegel, it cannot plausibly be said that Schelling became untrue to himself either; he merely continued on his intellectual path, admittedly with ever more extreme emphases of his own. The dialogue *Bruno* was already one entrance into the realm of 'The Mysteries'. Here Schelling understood philosophy as religion transposed onto a higher plane, as a continuation of religion by other means: 'But the pure subject-object, that absolute form of cognition, the absolute ego, the form of all forms, is itself the inborn son of the absolute, of equal eternity with the absolute, unseparated from its essence and one with it.'

But philosophy, as the highest level of knowing which renders dogmatic religion superfluous for the knower, now runs the danger, in taking the place of such religion, of falling back into the same forms that it had tried to repudiate. This can be seen in the style of language which Schelling likes to invoke in his essay on *Philosophy and Religion*: 'Apart from the doctrine of the absolute, the true mysteries of philosophy are concerned with the doctrine of the eternal birth of all things and their relationship to God as their pre-eminent and indeed single content.'

With his talk of 'the mysteries of philosophy' and the 'eternal birth of all things', Schelling is spelling out what will become the principal object of his later thought and indicating the manner and tone in which he will henceforth discuss it. The 'secret mystery of religion' against which he had polemicized in his youth with the weapons drawn from Kant and Fichte, and which had for him once constituted the heart of scholasticism, dogmatism, orthodoxy, the Tübingen theology he had been taught, now finds itself transformed into 'the secret mystery of philosophy'. The traditional resistance of reason to the mystical and the occult dimension dissolves away. This was also Schelling's tribute to the German Romantic movement which found such an exemplary representative in his own wife Caroline, this 'masterpiece of the spirit' which he called her, who was torn away from him by death in 1809.

When Schelling remarks with considerable surprise, in his letter to Hegel of 2 November 1807, that his friend seems to have abandoned the notion of 'intuition' which they formerly shared, he was merely touching the tip of the iceberg. In his Jena lectures Hegel had already discussed, and without any polemical emphasis, themes which simply by virtue of their content and manner of presentation were leading him away from Schelling's preoccupations. This was true of Hegel's interest in the economics of bourgeois society, in questions concerning labour, money, property and possessions, world trade, and so on. Over against Kant's and Fichte's 'subjective idealism', Hegel undertook the sober and rigorous analysis of the alienation of factory-workers in the manufacturing industries of England as the most advanced form of capitalist production at the time:

Need and labour raise themselves to the form of consciousness; they simplify the process but the resulting simplification is formally universal and abstract, the dissolution of the concrete which thereby becomes an empirical infinitude of particularities; and in so far as the worker subjugates nature to his purposes in this false and formal manner, the individual merely increases his dependence upon it, and the specialization of labour increases the quantity of the produced object; in an English factory eighteen human beings work at the production of a single needle; each one is occupied with a particular aspect of labour, and only this aspect; an individual on his own might not be able to make twenty, or even one such needle. . . . But as the quantity of the objects produced increases, so the value of the labour decreases accordingly; the labour involved becomes all the more absolutely deadened as it is turned into mechanical labour, and the skill of the individual worker all the more infinitely restricted.

This passage belongs to a largely unfinished and unpolished text from the stylistic point of view, essentially notes for a lecture which were not intended for publication as such. Marx, who developed his own theory of labour in the light of Hegel's analyses of the subject in the *Phenomenology of Spirit*, never knew these texts. This is all the more significant in that they touch directly on the question of the factory-worker's exploitation and his alienation from the product of his labour through mechanical forms of production, and do so in a way that goes much further, and approaches Marx much more closely, than the passages Marx could read in the *Phenomenology*. For us their significance principally lies in revealing how far Hegel had transcended the horizons of Schelling's interests. Here again we encounter Hegel's cumbrous and archaic mode of expression as he seeks to find a 'universal concept' for the need of labour and formulates it as follows: 'Money is this material existing concept.' He asks after the causes behind the bourgeois proliferation of needs: 'the activity of labour' find its 'resting side in property'.

With these questions concerning the nature of property Hegel enters territory which the previous tradition of German idealist philosophy, in Kant, Fichte or Schelling, had never seriously examined. And indeed Hegel himself did not immediately pursue this material further himself. He never succeeded in bringing his reflections on this subject into a definitive form, although he kept coming back to it later on. But the general approach which he initiated in his Jena lectures certainly led him beyond and away from Schelling.

Hegel and Schelling had both agreed that philosophy as such must take a 'speculative' form. But in his early essay on *The Difference between Fichte's and Schelling's System of Philosophy* Hegel had already implicitly criticized the fact that Schelling had not properly demonstrated the speculative Idea in its development and had placed the philosophy of nature at the beginning of his system instead. This insistence on the development of the speculative Idea already forms a central part of Hegel's later attack on Schelling. For Hegel it is logic and metaphysics that must stand at the very beginning of the system. Metaphysics, phenomenology as the doctrine of knowledge, and logic proper are all speculative disciplines, as Hegel attempted to show in practice as a philosophical author. This is equally true for the philosophical treatment of religion and history, and even of nature. Speculation involves the need for a bold and initial hypothesis: this is a danger which must be faced and dealt with dialectically. The philosophy of nature, a particular domain of Schelling's where Hegel never achieved comparable insight, would eventually have to face challenges in the later nineteenth century which were never envisaged at the beginning, as its claims and conclusions failed to stand up before the methods of the newly emerging empirical natural sciences.

The victory of the natural sciences sealed the fate of the 'philosophy of nature' in general. It also marked a decisive rupture with the idea of philosophy as pre-eminently 'science', as a privileged body of systematic knowledge, a conception which appeared valid for Hegel and Schelling alike. Henceforth anything that could not be conclusively demonstrated in an empirical and experimental manner, however plausible it seemed from the perspective of a philosophy of nature, could not be regarded as properly 'scientific' in character. In this respect Schelling was more vulnerable to attack than Hegel was. The realms of metaphysics, phenomenology, logic and history could clearly never become the objects of an empirical-experimental method in the way that a scientifically interrogated nature can. On his own journey from 'system' to 'method' Hegel explicitly attempted, from the time of the *Phenomenology* onwards, to protect his speculative position from possible objections. This is precisely what the method of dialectic would successfully accomplish in Hegel's eyes. The revision and reorganization of the Fichtean doctrine of knowledge in the *Phenomenology* was intended to demonstrate what Hegel had announced to his students from the lectern in Jena: in the new system of science the inspired brilliance which Schelling and his followers were convinced they possessed would cease to be brilliance.

Schelling's response to Hegel after receiving a copy of the *Phenomenology* hardly reveals much of the true feelings and thoughts which must have been provoked by study of the book. But it none the less marked a fundamental, and irrevocable, break between the two men. The former friends were never to have very much to say to one another afterwards. For a while this fact was tactfully ignored and was not immediately obvious to the outside world either. In Schelling's eyes Hegel would henceforth appear, as he put it in a letter of 27 May 1809 to G. H. Schubert with an allusion to Goethe's *Faust*, as nothing but 'a spirit of denial'. From his own point of view he may have been correct, for Hegel had indeed now risen up against him.

15

The Phenomenology of Spirit

The drastically problematic character of Hegel's *Phenomenology* can probably best be appreciated when we consider the range of interpretations of it that have been attempted. If in the search for understanding here we compare the works that have been dedicated to this text – those of Rosenkranz, Haym, Hoffmeister, Haering, Hartmann, Lukács, Bloch, Heidegger, Kojève, Hyppolite and Pöggeler, to name but a few of the most important commentators – it is difficult to avoid the distinct impression that we are dealing here not with *one* book at all, but rather with several quite different ones. Rosenkranz felt certain he was only following his teacher's own understanding of the matter when he considered the *Phenomenology* as *one* moment of the entire system: namely a specific analysis of consciousness, detached momentarily from the system and initially treated in its own right as the *experience* which consciousness makes with itself. He argued that Kant's philosophy was not properly constructed from the exclusive standpoint of consciousness and its experience, and that it further required Fichte's Copernican discovery of the ego as the sole point of certainty in the phenomenon of self-consciousness as a distinctively new achievement before Hegel could pursue the thought of the 'truth of self-certainty' as he does in the *Phenomenology*.

But was the book really an application of Hegel's logical method? Did the work actually emerge in accordance with Hegel's original intention, that is, as the first part of 'the system of science'? Or did it perhaps merely represent a kind of experiment which was destined rather to remain in some sense *independent* of the later system? Pöggeler, for example, is firmly convinced that 'Hegel never unambiguously clarified the significance of the *Phenomenology*'. For otherwise it would be impossible to understand why different commentators have produced such directly contradictory but apparently equally plausible interpretations of its relation to the system, stressing now the alleged indispensability and now the supposed superfluousness of the text in this regard. The experience of *consciousness* as constitutive 'subject' would seem to account for some of these differences and is perhaps the simplest way of describing the underlying project. But Hegel does not even keep rigorously to this theme, but goes on to introduce apparently quite different questions concerning 'Reason', 'Spirit', 'Religion', 'The Work of Art', and 'Absolute Knowledge', all the while revealing his own role directly by constantly stressing the importance of 'the relationship of the writer to his public'. He pursues the various experiences of consciousness through the manifold phenomena that are traversed and observes the resulting encounters by 'positing that through which science [the systematic knowledge of philosophy] exists within the self-movement of the concept'. What is 'reason' after it has experienced its relationship to the 'Enlightenment', what is 'Enlightenment' after it has been subjected to the Critical Philosophy of Kant? What are the stages in which spirit makes its appearance as 'true spirit', as 'spirit alienated from itself', as 'spirit certain of itself'?

Quite independently of the question whether the *Phenomenology* should be read in relation to the development of the 'system' or simply as a largely provisional conception later modified or abandoned, one can assert that with this work Hegel went beyond Kant and Fichte precisely by emphasizing the role of negativity and the 'nothing' as a principal constitutive feature of genuine thought. This 'nothing' cannot be ignored in Hegel's work: 'Nature is, through its very essence, the nothing; but this nothing itself equally exists.' The nihilistic element that contradicts the thought of being is constantly present in Hegel's ontological conception. 'But the first task of philosophy is to comprehend the *absolute* nothing', as Hegel had already written in his essay *Faith and Knowledge*, published in the *Critical Journal*, and explicitly adopted as the maxim of his own thought. And he also provided the reasons why he thought Fichte had failed to appreciate the significance of this principle. It was the latter which supplied Hegel with his concept of a presuppositionless beginning, with its constant recourse to the identity of being and nothing.

As a form of thinking governed by the idea of the nothing the *Phenomenology* is certainly, amongst all Hegel's works, the one with the strongest autobiographical resonance. This results in part from the precise circumstances of its composition. It was written in the culminating crisis of Hegel's life in Jena, when he was directly exposed to the gravest threats of extreme poverty, imminent unemployment, emotional disorientation and uncertainty about the immediate future, the personal problems involved with the birth of his illegitimate son. We have seen how all of these things contributed to his decision to abandon Jena, but it is surely the image of Hegel despoiled even of his personal possessions which really completes the dismal picture of this wretched period of his life. For a moment he had also stared death itself in the face. On 14 October 1806 Hegel was alerted to the battle of Jena and Auerstadt, where the war began to reveal its cruellest side, as the clamour of battle penetrated into the nearby town.

When Hegel heard the sounds of gunfire his manuscript was essentially finished. Hegel's claim that the composition of his *Phenomenology* was accompanied by the noise of artillery can only really be true of its final concluding pages. When the plundering French soldiers finally 'brought his papers into a state of disorder', as he wrote four days later to Niethammer, the manuscript of the book had already been dispatched to the printer in Bamberg.

The principal question addressed by the *Phenomenology* is the same as Kant's in the *Critique of Pure Reason*, the question concerning the nature of knowledge. Hegel, however, does not ask directly about its supposed 'limits' but rather about its range and character, questioning the notion of knowledge as 'an instrument by means of which one could take possession of the absolute'. The 'critical' question in the Kantian sense does not have to determine the philosophical beginning, in Hegel's view, and cannot be treated preferentially or independently in its own right; rather it must emerge, in accordance with the new method, in the process of application 'along the way'. In the 'Introduction' Hegel analyses certain hindrances which seem to stand in the way of his approach, particularly the idea that there may be 'different kinds of truth' or the fear that we might be misled into grasping 'clouds of error' instead of attaining the 'heaven of truth'. The approach to the absolute must initially appear nonsensical to abstract reflection until the very notion of knowing as an 'instrument', which supposedly stands *between* the knowledge and the absolute like a 'dividing wall', is finally discarded as inappropriate. To 'distrust' this new approach in advance, as Critical Philosophy would naturally tend to do, would not lead us any further and Hegel asks 'why on the other hand, we should not rather place mistrust in this mistrust' since the fear of error may already be the error itself. It is a consequence of Hegel's programmatic claim that 'the absolute alone is the true, or the truth alone is absolute' that he can reject the 'distinction between ourselves and the process of knowing', and repudiate the associated idea that 'the absolute stands, as it were, on one side, while knowledge stands on the other, independently in its own right and essentially separated from the absolute'. Nicolai Hartmann summed up Hegel's position: 'The central core of Hegel's philosophy lies in his truly comprehensive concept of the absolute and its categories.'

Any attempt at interpretation soon runs the risk of shipwreck on the perilous reefs of this particular text. For any understanding of the book one has to proceed one step at a time, and even then the path is quickly lost from view amongst the rationally incomprehensible intervening sections. The *Phenomenology* has rightly been described as a 'Faustian book'. And indeed it gradually emerged in the vicinity of Goethe himself and his own question concerning 'what it is that holds the world most inwardly together'. We are presented here with the entire world of man and spirit, life and death, freedom, aspiration and destruction, the realm of work, master and slave, self-consciousness, objectification, art and religion, all of it subjected to order through the 'system of science'. In his book Hegel omitted nothing that essentially belonged, as he saw it, to the newly emerging world of the early nineteenth century.

The *Phenomenology* was Hegel's first work to present the incipient form of the dialectic and already contains the entire future programme of the Hegelian philosophy, and without the suggestion of any contradiction between system and method, a problem that would only emerge later on. There were specific reasons for this. The Hegelian system was intimately connected with its immediate historical-philosophical situation as represented particularly by Kant, Fichte and Schelling, and it was thereby inevitably exposed to the historical process which would overcome it in turn. Everything here depends upon the idea of spirit and its own internal dynamic. Spirit has nothing but itself to rely on as it now enters upon the final stage of idealism. As Heidegger writes: 'In Hegel's idea of the phenomenology of spirit it is not spirit which is the object of a phenomenological approach . . . ; but rather the way and manner in which spirit exists.' In dialectical thought, as thought proper, spirit comes to itself and is finally capable of comprehending the significance of God and the actuality of his purpose in the world. As Hegel says: 'Spirit is thereby the absolute real essence which bears itself within itself.'

But it should be noted here that the dialectic is not really a matter of the 'world-historical individual' as such. The Napoleon whom the Hegel of the *Phenomenology* so much admired is clearly no dialectician himself and explicit dialectical insight would only weaken his impulse to action. But the acting individual is none the less still subjected to the law of dialectic in history, as we shall see, and indeed after the battle of Jena, which Hegel witnessed and indeed welcomed, the apparently irresistible victor himself soon came to experience defeat in turn and eventual military and political destruction. Here Hegel sees the 'world spirit' immediately at work, the spirit which, as he says in the *Phenomenology*, has had 'the patience to take upon itself the monstrous labour of world history'. Nothing is left to mere chance, and when its hour approaches the spirit irresistibly pursues its course and shapes the path of world history. Such is the case with Napoleon, the 'world spirit on horseback' for Goethe, the 'world soul' as Hegel calls him. We can sense something of the autobiographical dimension of Hegel's sympathetic relation to the French Revolution and the subsequent Napoleonic period when he writes in the 'Preface' to the *Phenomenology*: 'The spirit has broken with the previous world of its existence and its thought, and is now preparing to submerge it into the past.'

Following Heidegger, it is possible to read the *Phenomenology of Spirit* as Hegel's version of the Fichtean 'Doctrine of Science'. Hegel was quite aware of this continuity with Fichte's thought, even as he strove to overcome it and incorporate it into his own. Its influence is directly reflected in Hegel's claim that there can be no genuine philosophy that is without 'the form of science'.

'The true shape in which the truth exists can only be the scientific system of the same. To work towards this goal, so that philosophy may approach more closely to the form of science, is what I have undertaken to do in this work.' A philosophy that was completely detached from the other sciences, or a body of sciences completely detached from philosophy through the process of specialization, would only produce 'alienation' in Hegel's view of things. 'The goal is insight on the part of spirit into what knowing is.' Any attempt to split the two moments apart would destroy the purpose and cause us to lose our grasp of the 'totality': 'For the method is nothing other than the structure of the whole, expounded in its pure and essential character.' Hegel's 'Preface' clearly expresses his dialectical method as the only one appropriate to thought in its proper nature.

The emphatic announcement of this project, with a concomitant emphasis upon its exclusive character, is surely one of the boldest intellectual strokes of the new century, and there will be a great deal more to say about it in due course. But there is another and equally bold step involved, one which will eventually implicate the 'Hegelians' and their opponents in a ruthless struggle. And this is Hegel's recommendation 'to avoid the name "God" since this word is not immediately and simultaneously identical with the concept, and merely presents a name in the static form of an underlying and unchanging subject; whereas, for example, terms like "Being" or "the One", singularity or the subject, immediately and of themselves serve to denote concepts'. The former Tübingen student of theology was here enjoining a cautious use of language which seemed to turn the personal and spiritual object of traditional theological reflection into something resembling an essentially neutral concept of an impersonal absolute. This looked like trying to square the intellectual circle, transforming theology into anti-theology while yet remaining an esoteric form of crypto-theology. This is the beginning of a problem which will later lead to consternation in some quarters and a plethora of dissenting voices amongst the next generation. One should not merely think of the various Hegelian schools in this context, such as Bruno Bauer who openly claimed Hegel for atheism, or Marx and Engels who were the most influential defenders of Hegel's 'method'. One should also consider Schopenhauer, Hegel's least sympathetic reader, who saw him as the ardent advocate of a Judaeo-Christian monotheism merely expressed in the latest philosophical garb.

The 'Preface' to the *Phenomenology* represented Hegel's first vivid and grandiose attempt to develop a method for reconciling the apparently unreconcilable. And the writing was not lacking in conspicuous examples of linguistic barbarousness in the actual execution of the plan. Hegel sometimes seemed here to be spinning out and recombining threads of thought in a playful and bewildering tapestry of his own. The *Phenomenology* can easily produce the impression of the dialectical method as some obscure kind of 'infernal device'. If Adorno found the dialectical heart of the book to lie in the sudden eruption of Napoleon and scenes from the French Revolution into the story, one could surely say the same of the unexpected appearance of Gall's 'phrenology' or Lavater's 'physionomics'.

The difficulties attendant on understanding the *Phenomenology* also arise from the way in which a concrete historical mode of thought is simultaneously combined with a highly systematic and abstract one. This corresponds to Hegel's assumption that the latest stage of the theoretical and intellectual development of humanity must be directly related to the appropriate historical context of material culture as well. This reflects the insight that history generally must also be understood in the light of the 'natural history' of humanity (as Lukács calls it). This constant shifting between different levels of reflection, the way in which extremely abstract categories are immediately connected with historical phenomena like art, religion, natural science and philosophy, only adds to that intrinsic complexity of the work which has proved so fateful for all subsequent interpretations. Friedrich Engels, in his essay on Feuerbach, saw the *Phenomenology* as a sort of 'parallel example of an embryology and palaeology of the spirit', depicting 'the development of the individual consciousness through its various stages, and grasped as the abbreviated reproduction of the stages which human consciousness as a whole has already traversed historically'. Engels is alluding here to the inner relationship in Hegel between the realms of spirit and nature, between historical development and the existing natural environment that is progressively developed by human labour and intelligence. The general impression which the *Phenomenology* leaves behind in the mind of the reader is almost invariably one of baffling obscurity. Rudolph Haym expressed something of this irritation in the predominantly negative tones of his own interpretation of Hegel when he famously described the *Phenomenology* as 'psychology brought to confusion and disorder by history, and history brought down by psychology'.

As a result of the preliminary philosophical labours of Descartes and Fichte the concept of 'self-consciousness' had become the crucial new element in the boldest forms of contemporary philosophy. Hegel accordingly presents it as 'the new shape of knowledge', as a form of 'self-knowledge' as opposed to the earlier sections of the *Phenomenology* on 'consciousness', which was essentially related to an object 'other' than itself. That knowledge has 'disappeared' and 'passed away with self-consciousness', but its moments have also been sublated (i.e. transcended and preserved) and the loss consists in the fact that they are now present as they are *in themselves*. 'Self-consciousness' is essentially 'the return to itself out of otherness', that is, like Fichte's opposition between the ego and the non-ego, it also requires the 'other' of itself if it is to attain to the 'truth of its own self-certainty'. And this is where 'self-consciousness' coincides with a 'certainty' that has developed into its 'truth'. According to Hegel 'certainty' in its initial rudimentary form, or 'in itself' as he says, is inherently limited. Immediate sense-certainty, the very first stage of the *Phenomenology*, can 'say of what it knows only that it *is*'. The so-called 'truth' of sense-certainty contains only 'the *being* of the matter'. The object is because it is. The 'consciousness' that is 'certain', for its part, simply brings the *pure ego* into play in order to institute the subject–object relation. We now have the ego as a pure This and the object as a pure This. As Hegel puts it: 'I have the certainty I have by virtue of another, namely the object; and the object is also certain *through* another, namely through the ego.' Thus in 'self-consciousness' we find the point of union between subject and object, certainty and truth, where *consciousness* has become 'for itself the true'. Hegel's preliminary exposition here is intended to clarify the further advance of spirit, the progressive self-movement of the concept, and to present the concept of self-consciousness, in contrast to Fichte's conception, as a process of self-becoming (Otto Pöggeler).

Although Fichte could be considered as the original father of the 'philosophy of identity' developed by Hegel and Schelling, he had failed to grasp that the various forms in which the subject appears must coincide with the various forms in which the object appears as well. The process of 'appearance' or manifestation, according to Hegel, belongs intrinsically to the object itself, although it must also be distinguished from it in turn. The object as it 'appears' is experienced by the subject, but this does not guarantee its 'truth' since the appearance in question may involve deception or illusion of one kind or another. The individual as subject, or more carefully expressed, the human individuality which culminates in modern civil society, an area to which Hegel will dedicate particular attention in his *Encyclopaedia* and his *Philosophy of Right*, has a lengthy process of maturation behind it. The progressive development of individual consciousness has led to an opposition between the subjective ego and objective actuality in which a process of dialectic reversal provokes a tragic collision. The thought of 'self-externalization' produced through the labour of the entire human species can only gradually come to dawn on the consciousness involved. And even then it has still to become a matter of developed and explicit knowledge.

In his celebrated dialectic of master and slave in the *Phenomenology* Hegel has succeeded in shedding some light on the initially obscure and dialectic essence of labour. The attitude which the master demonstrated towards the slave in the 'struggle' for recognition, as Hegel calls it, has kept the slave in the state of dependency that is necessary if he is to fulfil the wishes and desires of the master. All the work is consigned to the slave, while the master himself reaps the benefits of his labour. But in the course of this process, where labour and benefit, working and consumption are separated from one another, the produced 'thing' now emerges between the master and the slave. Thus the master finds himself 'relating simply to the dependent thing . . . and [finds that] that he has conceded independence to the slave who has worked on the thing'. Thus the self-consciousness of the master, who sees the slave simply as a means of labour for his benefit, culminates here; whereas through labouring on the physical object the consciousness of the slave has come to develop a sense of independence. The dialectical nature of their mutual relationship intrinsically results in a changed, and indeed reversed, relationship between slave and master. The master who forces the slave to labour has become dependent on the slave through the labour he requires of him. The slave who obeyed out of need or fear the demand to work acquires power over the master as he successfully labours on the object, and the worker comes to attain that self-consciousness which the master, in accordance with his nature as master, could not acknowledge.

The systematic character of spirit in all its characteristic manifestations as observed by Hegel always finds its phenomenological expression and effect in history. After the significant labours of Herder and Kant in the field of the philosophy of history this could not be disputed or ignored. In Herder, and especially in his *Ideas towards a Philosophy of History*, we can already perceive all the elements of Hegel's later philosophy of history, including the idea of dialectical development. Herder was already well acquainted with the great turning points of world history, the decline of the ancient world through the rise of Christianity, the feudal system which grew up out of the institutions of Roman slavery to become the economic basis of the Catholic Middle Ages, the degeneration of the priesthood and the loss of true religious spirit, and the beginnings of the new bourgeois epoch and its so-called 'civil society'. What distinguished Hegel from Herder was not so much a different perspective on history itself as the way in which he interpreted the same historical material in the light of his own systematic conception of philosophy, which was conceived of independently of the historical process. For Hegel always and emphatically *insisted* (as Jean Hyppolite points out) upon the system itself as the repository of truth. The abstract master–slave relation as articulated by Hegel can be concretely applied to the real history which extends from the ancient slave societies to contemporary bourgeois society; for in the latter, just as in the former, we can also recognize the exercise of violent power as explicitly described by Hobbes: the bourgeois economy of Adam Smith, with its more sublimated forms of selfishness, as a 'society of wolves' . These were crises which have been absorbed into the development of consciousness through the transition from the ancient to the Christian world and the emergence of bourgeois society, and have come to shape the foundations of the modern age. According to Hegel bourgeois society is based upon the social character of labour itself, that is, of labour which the individual performs not merely for his or her own interest, but for everyone else as well, a process in which the achievements of past labour are also involved: 'The labour of the individual for his needs is just as much a satisfaction of the needs of others as it is of his own, and the satisfaction of his own needs can only be met through the labour of others.' This phenomenon essentially belongs to the interaction between the individual and the social world, and forms part of its dialectic between them. The moment of alienation consists in the fact that the antagonistic forces involved cannot be recognized by each other or clearly deciphered for what they are. According to Lukács, it is this characteristic perspective which makes Hegel the *only* philosopher 'in the period after Kant who seriously addressed the problems of the epoch in a truly original sense'. The significance that lies in the 'power of universality' is invisible to the individual who finds his own needs and purposes misunderstood and can only face *destruction* at the hands of 'abstract necessity' if he should attempt to resist. In such a collision of forces the helpless individual finds himself an object of tragedy. His downfall teaches the individual of civil society that he is, like that society itself, no 'raw natural product' but rather the provisional result of a long process of natural and social history.

In order to reach the domain of 'objective spirit' the individual must already have liberated himself from the sphere of 'subjective spirit', and this is one reason why Pöggeler believes that the *Phenomenology* must be understood as 'part of the philosophy of subjective spirit'. But it is only from the higher standpoint of objective consciousness that the individual consciousness is properly in a position to comprehend itself and the path which has already been taken in the history of human development. In its encounter with the 'objective' dimension the subject experiences the 'externalization' of individual consciousness. This externalization in the process of labour leads the subject to the union of different social interests, where the paths of subjectivity and objectivity encounter and subsequently combine with one another as they develop further along the way.

The path which is taken by 'absolute spirit' leads from art and religion to philosophy, culminating in an 'absolute knowing' where philosophy as the highest expression of spirit naturally *sublates* the earlier stages of art and religion and spiritualizes them in the most perfect manner. What Hegel calls 'absolute spirit' has cast off all alien objectivity. It harbours nothing but spirit itself, without the material forms of art or the devices of religion. It would appear that with this conception of 'absolute spirit' the idealist development which leads from Kant to Fichte has reached its final culmination. The relinquishing of everything purely material is accomplished.

But for Hegel the active culmination of absolute spirit in philosophy certainly does not mean the end of the story, does not relieve him from the task of returning again and again to examine the earlier stages of art and religion. Hegel's encounter with Goethe had taught him that there is a domain of art in its own right which speculative philosophy must acknowledge as material for its own reflection. And this is what Hegel will later address in his *Lectures on Aesthetics* where he investigates the idea of 'objective art' (in Homer, Sophocles and Shakespeare). Hegel's treatment of religion as an intermediate domain between art and philosophy reveals not only the ambivalent and problematic character of the phenomenon itself but of Hegel's own analysis as well. It is not entirely clear whether it is 'the religion of art' which was characteristic of classical antiquity which is providing the criterion against which religion is properly measured, or whether it is the Christianity that has emerged from Judaism with a profoundly influential conception of salvation history which is being posited as the central axis of development.

The concept of 'externalization' reveals the manifold ambivalence of Hegel's whole understanding of religion. In a sense Hegel's approach already anticipates the path of thought which leads to Feuerbach's critique of religion, but Hegel himself did not directly pursue the latter's idea of religion as a subjective product of human consciousness in a quest of 'egoistic blessedness'. He left the origins of the various religions in their own mythical obscurity and merely subjected their subsequent history to a threefold dialectical analysis which culminates in the 'reconciliation of consciousness with self-consciousness'. First the immediate state of nature – then the fall into externalization – and finally reunification. And it is this dialectical process which Hegel claims to discover in the historical domain of religion itself.

The path of thought which has gradually led Hegel from his first reflections on the 'positivity of religion' has culminated with the *Phenomenology* in an idealistic system which formally recognizes the phenomenon of religion while simultaneously preparing its grave. The actual historical religion which, in its highest monotheistic form, appeals to 'heaven and earth', to the 'creation' and the 'beginning', finds that its own self-understanding evaporates when it is interpreted as a transitional stage of the dialectic. Such a religion must draw a distinction between the truly *divine God* and the *dialectically mediated God* of speculative philosophy (as Dieter Sinn puts it). A religion which does not take absolute precedence over everything else is no longer religion, and a God who is no longer conceived as Creator but rather as a process of dialectical self-production has lost the decisive characteristics of the One God, is no longer what he must be if he is indeed to be God at all. The 'feeling of grief expressed in the harsh saying that *God is dead*' remains behind after all.

It is a defining feature of Hegel's theoretical 'sublation' or 'overcoming of the Christian religion' (as Karl Löwith calls it) that it is accomplished at the highest stage in the development of objective idealism. It has incorporated the earlier phase of subjective idealism, the Spinozistic dissolution of the individual in spirit, and the final assimilation of the object to the 'Concept'. It was no accident that Hegel took such pains later to reject the identification of Spinoza's philosophy with 'atheism', for he was well aware how closely such criticisms could touch his thought as well. According to Schopenhauer, speaking specifically as a disciple of the Indian doctrine of salvation, the philosophy of pantheism ultimately represents nothing but a more elevated form of atheism. Here God is politely 'shown the door' as far as the world is concerned. In view of the importance of Spinoza for the entire movement of German idealism and for the Weimar tradition of Schiller and Goethe, it is crucial not to overlook the question of pantheism in Hegel. Where the object, the body and thinghood in general are transfigured into 'spirit' as they tend to be in such an idealistic theological and philosophical approach, then the pantheistic consequences are extremely difficult to avoid and it soon becomes impossible to think of the Judaeo-Christian God effectively as a *person*. A Christian philosophy of essentially pantheistic inspiration was doomed to eventual failure. It was no surprise that when Friedrich Wilhelm IV later ascended the Prussian throne he expressly announced his desire to see the 'dragon-seed of Hegelianism' stamped out in Berlin and the country at large.

It was obviously part of Hegel's self-understanding in the *Phenomenology* that no intellectual quarter could be given and that trenchant criticism all round was the order of the day. Now 'reason' is defended against the claims of 'faith', and now the claims of 'faith' are defended against the assaults of 'reason'. By 1806 the main tide of the Enlightenment had ebbed away and its protagonists found themselves in retreat on almost every front. Of course the consequences of the Enlightenment cannot simply be wished away; nor indeed should they. Hegel himself is a good witness here. But the originally unquestioned power of the great movement had been broken and it would henceforth have to fight with all means available to maintain itself. This too has an autobiographical dimension in Hegel's case for the torch-bearer of a now barely flickering 'Illumination' into the new century was none other than Paulus, Hegel's countryman and former colleague in Jena. But Hegel's principal criticisms were aimed at Schelling, although they were carefully camouflaged so that their target could continue to regard himself as above them and untouched by them. When Hegel wrote things like: 'When the formalism of the philosophy of nature teaches that understanding is electricity, for example, or that the animal is oxygen . . . , then the inexperienced may be overcome with feelings of astonishment and even venerate such things as a profound species of brilliant insight', Schelling could hardly ignore the affinity of his own ideas with the object of such scorn. Hegel is pointing here to the intellectual degeneration of the philosophy of nature, it is true, but the degeneration itself inevitably points back to the source from which it all originated, to the credulous faith in the 'dowsing rod', the experiments with the 'pendulum', the fascination with magnetism and siderism, the depths of the inorganic, and above all the cult of 'intimated spiritual affinity' and inspired genius.

But there was also another rival position which Hegel wished ruthlessly to destroy as publicly as possible: the position of so-called 'healthy common sense' or 'natural philosophizing' which was so eager to emphasize the 'blameless heart' and the 'pure conscience', which prided itself on the wisdom of the 'catechism' and the ultimate truths exhibited in the common 'sayings of the people'. At the same time proponents of this view would generally appeal to their 'feelings' as an infallible 'inner oracle'. Even before he explicitly engaged with Schleiermacher's 'religion of feeling' Hegel was aware of the attendant dangers here. Anyone who simply appeals to the oracle of feeling is 'finished and done with anyone who disagrees; he must proclaim that he has nothing more to say to anyone who fails to feel and find the same things in himself as he does. In other words he simply tramples underfoot the roots of our common humanity.' Trusting to immediate feeling as the first and last court of appeal is to repudiate any attempt 'to strive towards agreement with others'. And, as Hegel adds: 'The inhuman, the merely animal consists in simply staying with one's feelings and communicating through these alone.'

The determined opponent of 'healthy common sense' here accuses the faculty of 'feeling' of being a very poor source of philosophical insight. Naturally he is not simply aiming at Schelling here, although Schelling had allowed himself to be guided by feelings of 'presentiment' in his philosophy of nature, but also at Fichte's subjectivism of the ego which appealed so strongly to the ideology of the romantics and the creed of 'Feeling is all' which Goethe had put in Faust's mouth and thereby made him into a harbinger of the romantic spirit. Hegel wishes rather to insist that the Enlightenment, even if it has been superseded, cannot be reversed.

The priority of spirit always remains an a priori principle of Hegel's thought since, as he put in the 'Preface' and in the later *Encyclopaedia,* 'The absolute is spirit.' This is equally true for all philosophy, religion and knowledge in Hegel's view: 'world history can only be comprehended in accordance with this impulse' to spiritual self-knowledge. The *Phenomenology* enquires after the 'appearing' of spirit, enquires in literal accordance with the German word *Erscheinung* after its 'self-showing' character. In the 'Difference' essay Hegel had already written in 1801 that 'appearing and self-dichotomy are one'. The 'self-consciousness' in which 'consciousness' has become *other* to itself in the process of experience and thereby returned to itself has also necessarily passed through the condition of 'dichotomy' that belongs to 'appearance'.

The future would show that Hegelian 'speculation' continues to exercise its effect even amongst those who believe they have finally 'overcome' Hegel, something which has often enough been proclaimed. What the Hegelian philosophy did not accomplish, and what it was incapable of accomplishing – as is surely clear already from the *Phenomenology* – was a fundamental clarification of the relationship between 'spirit' and the realm of the 'material'. Hegel did indeed make a number of various and rather contradictory attempts to resolve this question, particularly in his Greater Logic where he analyses the concept of matter in relation to Platonic thought and Aristotle's distinction between form and matter, but in the last analysis the material seems to be sublated and effectively dissolved in the 'concept'. Matter cannot be encountered, Hegel thinks, as an 'actually existing thing' but is merely 'being' in its pure universality. One can easily comprehend Goethe's reservations with respect to the *Phenomenology* and appreciate why a man so steeped in solid objectivity could not understand this apparent transformation of matter into the abstract concept.

16

Journalist in Bamberg

The *Phenomenology* appeared in May 1807, the very month in which he took up his new post as newspaper editor. Even if Hegel's departure from Jena had essentially been precipitated by external events, and in particular the closing of the university because of the war, Hegel seems to have reconciled himself to the idea of his new practical career in Bamberg with remarkable speed. And indeed, he soon found it was a welcome opportunity for him to pursue interests which had been rather neglected during his time as an academic teacher. If we think back to the years in Berne when he successfully combined his official pedagogical obligations in the Steiger household with all the other administrative and financial tasks entrusted to him, then this lively desire for some practical employment after years of philosophical reflection seems to betoken something of a new man. Hegel appears to have regarded his editorial position as a natural point of entry into the world of politics.

But as we shall see, this soon proved to be a rather exaggerated expectation. The *Bamberger Zeitung* had been founded by one Gérard Gley, a French priest who had been forced to leave his country in 1791. It had subsequently passed into the hands of an official church coachman by the name of Schneiderbanger and was naturally subject to the censor's control, in accordance with the uncontested principle vigorously maintained throughout those parts of Germany which were deferential towards the established authorities: newspapers as such are useless things, but if they do exist they must certainly be censored if necessary.

When Hegel entered the newspaper's premises in March 1807 to start overseeing publication he was taking up an activity which at that time required little preliminary technical or professional expertise. The daily paper in question certainly enjoyed no great national reputation. It was printed on absorbent paper in quarto format and consisted simply of two sheets with eight columns, the last and occasionally the penultimate of which contained all the local news in smaller print. There was also no official imprint to indicate the publisher's or the editor's name.

Basically, therefore, we are talking about a very modest news-sheet and no more. And this made a leading editorial column quite superfluous. We are merely deceiving ourselves if we imagine it is possible to discover Hegel as an author in these pages. His principal task was to edit and assemble the news in a form that was acceptable to the censoring authorities. This actually required some skill and the kind of cautious eye which Hegel abundantly possessed. But Hegel did not have to do any violence to his own conscience in order to follow the appropriate pro-Napoleonic line. And it was immediately obvious to Hegel, as the son of a state official himself, that there was no question of allowing any explicit criticism of the Bavarian government to appear in the paper. Nor did Hegel himself doubt for a moment that the press generally was an institution essentially intended, and rightly so, to serve the needs of its country and its government. The idea of the press as a quite independent source of influential critical comment on the state was naturally alien to Hegel by virtue of his background and education, of the existing system of government and all the political arrangements of Germany in either the immediate pre-Napoleonic period or the Napoleonic period itself. If Hegel had in any way thought otherwise, he would not have been a suitable candidate for the job as editor in the first place, and he would certainly never have been able to apply for a government subvention to assist with publication costs.

This does not mean, however, that Hegel performed his allotted role without any friction whatsoever. The balance he wanted to establish in the newspaper between the proportions of news and comment would already go far beyond the usual press regulations then prevailing in Bavaria. And that in itself was naturally a matter for caution. As an editor, and as a philosopher, Hegel was particularly skilled in successfully pursuing his aims by indirect means, in discovering suitable detours and alternative approaches that would bring him closer to his ultimate purpose in the end. He soon introduced private correspondents and well-briefed sources for particularly reliable reports, something which immediately aroused suspicion with the censoring authorities. In the period when Montgelas was in power, the Bavarian government explicitly distinguished between 'official' and 'irresponsible' sources of news, i.e. between favourable news that would be published and unfavourable news that would not. By employing these 'private correspondents' to write their own special 'reports', Hegel contrived to bring some colour into a paper that was otherwise dominated by reprints of already published material. And in this way Hegel did successfully avoid becoming merely an official mouthpiece for the government on everything. It was precisely the unrestrained and interminable supply of already printed material which drove Hegel so doggedly to pursue other alternatives. But in the last analysis it cannot really be said that Hegel was ever able to emancipate himself as a journalist from the fetters of government control in the name of intellectual freedom as we understand it.

In fact all of Hegel's caution not to arouse the slightest suspicion on the part of the authorities of harbouring oppositional sympathies proved to be insufficient in the end. The censors were very vigilant and on one occasion Hegel was temporarily forced to suspend publication of the newspaper on account of a particular article that had just appeared there. The authorities, as usual in such a situation, made strenuous efforts to extract further information from him about the exact source of the piece. Hegel thereby found himself in a rather difficult position and asked for Niethammer's advice on the matter. He even thought that he might have to present himself personally in Munich and sue for leniency. On 9 November 1808 he finally revealed his sources, with 'the deepest devotion', as the *Allgemeine Deutsche Staatszeitung*, a newspaper published in Erfurt, and the *Nationalzeitung der Deutschen*, published in Gotha. To his great relief the whole matter was finally forgotten or ignored and his paper was allowed to resume publication.

All in all, Hegel's activities as an editor had turned out to be quite advantageous to him in a number of ways. While it is true that he still remained financially dependent, the situation marked a considerable improvement on his predicament in Jena where he was forced to rely on the temporary largesse of the Duke of Weimar to survive at all. He now lived in doubtless very comfortable surroundings in the so-called 'Haus zum Krebs' and found his own maxims of life being amply fulfilled. On 30 August 1807 he writes to Knebel: 'Experience has confirmed me in the truth of the biblical saying which has now become my guiding light: Seek ye first after food and clothing, and the Kingdom of God will fall to you also.' Hegel had indeed rejected the idea when Schneiderbanger offered him the opportunity to buy the newspaper himself, because, quite apart from the fact that he lacked the money, Hegel had never considered spending more time in the newspaper business than he had to; but also because this kind of work, as he wrote to Niethammer on 30 May 1807, 'can hardly be regarded as a reliable établissement', and more specifically because 'however tempting such a state of independent isolation may appear, one must maintain a connection to the state and work on its behalf'. Although his editorial labours could be considered as a way of serving the state, they were not enough to relieve his dissatisfactions with a purely private life of 'independent isolation'. And even the fact that he probably enjoyed more time to pursue his scholarly and scientific interests in Bamberg than he ever had in Jena was quite insufficient to keep him there indefinitely.

By 15 September 1808 we find him writing to Niethammer with reference to his aforementioned difficulties with the censor in the following terms: 'I am now all the more anxious to quit slaving in this galley of a newspaper since we have once again recently had to put up with a veritable Inquisition which only brought my current situation vividly home to me.' Hegel's hopes had already been raised considerably when Niethammer was called to Munich in 1807 to serve on the central commission for educational reform. We know that Hegel had often looked to Niethammer for help and support from early on. In a letter of 6 August 1806 Hegel had written to his friend in extravagant terms: 'Lord, when you enter into your Kingdom, forget me not and I shall praise thee!' Hegel owed his Bamberg position to Niethammer and now that the latter had firmly established himself in the Bavarian capital Hegel could expect him to use his influence to help him find a much-desired post in the state administration.

Niethammer's 'General Recommendation for the Establishment of Public Educational Institutions', the so-called 'Niethammer School Plan', certainly exerted an influence upon the history of Bavaria's educational system. It very much reflected the era of Montgelas, a period of enthusiastic reform throughout Bavaria. When he was later established in Berlin, Hegel explicitly praised the 'reorganization' undertaken by Montgelas, in which Niethammer himself had played a significant part. Hegel's admiration for the Bavarian minister was well grounded. Montgelas had certainly introduced some powerful rays of Enlightenment into an intellectually darkened country still dominated by ultramontanist sympathies. Without the efforts of Montgelas, who in Catholic Bavaria lay under the terrible and accurate suspicion of being a Freemason and had suffered persecution because of it in his youth, the political situation in the country would probably have been much worse. Hegel's favourable judgement of Montgelas in this respect seems to be more than justified. The basic educational system in Bavaria, which was directly under the control of the Church, was in a parlous condition. The Order of Jesuits, who liked to regard themselves, and were often enough regarded by others, as friends of progress, had been a principal stronghold of reaction in education. With the Catholic Church as the established religious confession of the state, it was extremely difficult to find any trace of an independent intellectual or cultural life. That is why Hegel could only regard Bavaria, as he wrote to Niethammer on 22 January 1808, 'a real blot on the luminous picture of Germany'.

But the reform programme of the period did do something to confirm his favourable judgement of Montgelas. After Max Joseph acceded to power a determined attempt was made to attract outside teachers and scholars to Bavaria. Schelling, Paulus and Niethammer himself were numbered amongst them. They all enjoyed the reputation of being 'free spirits' from the intellectual point of view and the government of the country must have expected to receive much 'enlightened' criticism from them. And we can therefore understand why Hegel was so keen to find a professional academic or teaching position in a country he is otherwise so scathing about in his letters.

By the end of October 1808 part of Hegel's wish was finally fulfilled. On the 26th of that month Niethammer wrote to Hegel, informing him that he had been appointed as Professor of Philosophical Propaedeutics and Rector of the *Gymnasium* of Nuremberg. It was obviously Niethammer himself who had secured this appointment for his long-standing friend and fellow-countryman, his good companion and drinking partner from the Jena days. In his letter Niethammer asks Hegel to arrive promptly the following week and gives an interesting reason for this: 'so that you can begin organizing the new curriculum with regard to the *Gymnasium* under the direction of the Regional School Inspector Paulus'. The three Swabian friends and former students of the Tübingen Stift, who had all been so uncomfortable in their former positions in Jena, had now been reunited on Bavarian soil thanks to the diligent efforts of Niethammer. The Principal School Inspector in Munich, the Regional School Inspector of the Province of Franconia, and the *Gymnasium* headmaster in Nuremberg prepare together to pursue the reorganization of the educational system in the newly expanded Kingdom of Bavaria.

17

A Turning Point

What Hegel had sought and indeed found in Bamberg, apart from the necessary means of earning a living in his capacity as a newspaper editor, was direct contact with an unspoilt example of almost medieval Catholic culture (not to mention an experience of the local beer). He had long expatiated on this prospect with Schelling. But he had also settled in a country which in many respects represented everything obsolete and intellectually backward in his eyes. And in one of his letters to Niethammer he would promptly transform the name of Bavaria into that of 'Barbaria'.

And indeed the Enlightenment had been particularly tardy in reaching Bavaria. Under the government of Montgelas the movement had certainly produced certain necessary changes in the field of political administration, but the opposition it otherwise encountered from the country at large and its largely agricultural population with their priests and prelates, from the monasteries and the landed nobility, prevented it from exercising a truly deep or lasting influence. The habits and customs of the country were long established and essentially alien to the new ways: extravagant processions, ceremonies with the participants in brightly coloured chasubles, the enthusiastic observance of saints' days, and an irrepressible tendency to Mariology, all of it combined with a need for a kind of enjoyment of everyday life which resented any attempt at administrative control from above. This naturally fitted in both with the grandiose sacred architecture in the cities and the smaller rural towns alike and with the outstanding artisanal skills of the inhabitants of the Alpine regions; but as far as the spirit of the critical philologist, or the sons of Saxon scholars, or thinkers like Kant and Fichte, or the classical German poets of Weimar were concerned the state of Bavaria was then pretty much barren ground. It was therefore quite surprising when the Bavarian government demonstrated some desire for a renewal of learning by inviting men like Friedrich Thiersch and Friedrich Jacob (who both came from Saxony) to take up academic posts there, and when the Bavarian Academy of Sciences appointed the Rhinelander Friedrich Heinrich Jacobi as its president. And in every case these moves were strongly opposed by the local academic establishment, who jealously resisted any perceived intrusion upon their own preserve.

It is hardly surprising therefore if Hegel the German southerner, who experienced all this in Bamberg and was himself directly affected by it, should support the political cause of northern Germany. He had been forced to admit that there was no prospect of finding a suitable position as a professor of philosophy in the ecclesiastical academy there. And a single glance at the Bavarian register of educational institutions would rapidly reveal that philosophy was taught in neither Altdorf, nor Landshut, nor Innsbruck. Hegel must have wondered about the country he had ended up living in.

Niethammer had been Hegel's greatest hope and in a sense he did not disappoint him. For it was Niethammer who personally got Hegel involved in the process of school reform that was currently being undertaken throughout Bavaria. Hegel would often refer somewhat satirically to his part in this 'reorganization' of the educational system. Hegel could certainly appreciate the necessity for this in a country like Bavaria but he did not conceal his concern about the considerable administrative work that it would inevitably involve him in as well. When he was offered the position of headmaster at a major school in Nuremberg Hegel at least realized that his precarious period of professional insecurity in Bamberg was certainly at an end.

The opportunity clearly revealed Hegel's attitude to his employment in Bamberg as a purely provisional arrangement. His great tendency to caution explained his insistence on keeping the Jena connection open as a future option. Technically speaking he had only received permission for temporary leave from his academic duties there. But in November, after he was officially offered the post in Nuremberg, he formally and obediently requested Duke Karl August to relieve him of his position in Jena as extraordinary professor.

Hegel was now clearly hoping for a fundamental improvement in his work and quality of life. His income as an editor of the newspaper had not been insignificant but the post was associated with a general feeling of material insecurity, and this must have been particularly depressing for the Swabian side of his character. He was naturally constantly reminded of the awkward situation every time he had to haggle with the government censorship system that was in force there. And whether in fact his income was also sufficient for him to support his son is difficult to assess. One passage in a letter to his friend Fromann on 9 July 1808 suggests that he had a bad conscience about the whole affair: 'I must constantly and painfully regret the fact that I have still not been able properly to extricate from her current situation the woman who is the mother of my child and who therefore has a right to expect the fulfilment of all my obligations.' Whatever the significance of the remark,

Hegel clearly felt that he was not in a position to do more to help at the time.

Hegel was able to contribute directly to the Bavarian school reforms by obtaining a contract through Niethammer to compose the obligatory logic textbook for all the universities in the country. Hegel had not completed any independent philosophical work in Bamberg, but he had been able to dedicate any free time he enjoyed between the editor's office and the printing shop to further reflections on the subject of logic in the broadest sense. What he had understood by 'logic' in Jena was only gradually revealing its full significance for him and he was now beginning to envisage the subject as an entirely 'new science'. He regarded what appeared traditionally under this name as hopelessly corrupted by 'fruitless scholastic ingenuity'. He wrote to Niethammer on 20 May 1808 claiming that 'nothing could be more desirable to me (both from the financial perspective and in respect of such a book itself, and indirectly of further writings too) than to elevate one's philosophy in this way to a predominant position in a kingdom'. The last remark here is striking: Hegel not only expresses his current wishes and intentions, but also announces and anticipates a comprehensive claim on behalf of logic as a science which he will undeniably make good later.

From the surviving Bamberg correspondence we can infer that Hegel's life had come in the meantime to acquire a certain measure of stability. He now enjoyed the personal company of Gries, a literary man who hailed from Hamburg and had also spent some considerable time in Jena. Gries had made a name for himself as a translator of Tasso and he was highly regarded by Goethe and Schiller as an interesting conversationalist.

By this time Hegel had become a committed partisan for the Napoleonic cause and was ardently hoping that the French troops would reach Munich before the Austrians did. Indeed the prospect of renewed conflict was only likely to further his own ambitions at the time. Writing to Niethammer on 20 August 1808, Hegel himself suggests as much and points out that 'the possibility of imminent war might well accelerate the reorganization programme', that is, Niethammer's educational reforms, and thus also accelerate his own emancipation from the editorial drudgery of his current work.

It is undeniable that all of this essentially reflects small-scale domestic concerns on Hegel's part. There is little here to recall the 'greater world' of Jena and Weimar or the significant developments which he had even directly witnessed there in the proximity of Goethe himself. The rise of Napoleon can only have increased his desire to return to this broader world. Goethe and Napoleon had represented the most important contemporary figures in his life to date and they would continue to shape his ideas about art and politics and influence the way he would articulate them in his later lectures on aesthetics and the philosophy of history. Towards the end of the Bamberg period Hegel appears in many ways as just another ordinary citizen, but within he essentially feels himself to be an oppressed one, an obedient subject who is forced to tread carefully with the police and the political authorities, who must struggle to maintain a fairly precarious and modest living. All of the stages in his life to date had merely served to underline his material dependency: whether he thought back on his father who had hardly bestowed sufficient financial support on his wife and son, or on his time as a scholarship student in Tübingen, as a private tutor in Berne and Frankfurt, as an unpaid lecturer in philosophy at Jena, or finally as a slave in the 'journalistic galley'. And he was now thirty-seven years old. He had written his first book, the *Phenomenology*, where he found some temporary refuge in the idea of 'spirit' if not that of 'God', under the most desperate financial conditions and without any visible prospects for the future.

It would also be the *Phenomenology* which, during these Bamberg months, finally precipitated the long-delayed break in his relationship with Schelling. Goethe was actually the first person to be sent a copy by Hegel. With Schelling, on the other hand, Hegel took his time, although along with Goethe he had previously done most to promote Hegel's career and was therefore the most important potential recipient of the work. And it must have been Schelling who largely occupied Hegel's thoughts when he came to finish the text for publication.

Given Hegel's delay, Schelling's response was correspondingly slow in coming. Though he had nothing more urgent to do which might prevent his starting Hegel's book at once, Schelling writes to Hegel on 2 November 1807 that he will look at it in due course. He suggests that the difficulty of the subject naturally demands a long and careful study of the text. But it looks as though Schelling had in fact immediately understood the significance of Hegel's argument:

> Up till now I have only had time to read the 'Preface'. Inasmuch as you yourself mention its polemical part, I must say that, having as I believe an appropriate estimate of myself, I should have to think too little of myself if I were to relate this polemic to me. Thus the latter may well strike home, as you say in your letter, at the misuse of babbling imitators, although in the book itself this distinction is not drawn.

Schelling is hedging his own disappointment with all the appropriate qualifications. He suggests that he gives greater credence to the remarks in Hegel's letter than to those he can read in the book. But he clearly realizes that if they no longer share a common perspective, then a clear distinction between their respective philosophical views will have to be made urgently.

If there had indeed been a break with the ideas they used to share, then it had clearly come from Hegel's side. Thus Schelling writes: 'I must confess that I do not understand the sense in which you oppose the concept to intuition. For by the former you can hardly mean anything other than what we both used to call the Idea, whose nature is to have one side on which it is concept and another on which it is intuition.'

Schelling was not mistaken when he interpreted the *Phenomenology* as a retreat from the fundamental convictions they had once shared, a retreat which only appears in a very abbreviated form in the new concept of 'intuition' that Hegel is now using. Schelling immediately grasped that the whole intellectual situation had changed significantly. Even if Schelling was not entirely unprepared for the break when it came, he was certainly surprised by its intensity: with the *Phenomenology* Hegel had exhibited, at a single powerful stroke, his own quite different philosophical nature compared with that of Schelling. Schelling had probably not anticipated that and it certainly ended the long-established and peaceful coexistence they had hitherto enjoyed.

18

Headmaster in Nuremberg

On 6 December 1808 Hegel formally assumed his position as Rector of the Nuremberg *Gymnasium* with all due solemnity. His keenest desire had thereby been fulfilled: he had, after considerable delay it is true, become a *Beamter* or official employee of the state.

This was a position of some influence. The self-conscious city of Nuremberg, with an eminent tradition behind it as a former 'Imperial City' and major centre of humanistic learning, had only recently become part of the Kingdom of Bavaria after the collapse of the Empire. The city was prepared to offer the new professor an annual salary of 900 gulden, with free lodgings above the school and another 100 gulden for the rectorship. This was actually far less money than Hegel was getting in Bamberg. The finances of the school were severely stretched, as the Rector soon discovered when his salary was repeatedly paid late. The school itself, founded by Melanchthon in 1526 right alongside the Ägidienkirche, was in very poor physical shape. All in all, Hegel found there was constantly plenty to complain about.

But Niethammer had expressly called Hegel to Nuremberg because he knew the Bavarian government also fully understood the urgent need for serious school reform. Niethammer's authoritative 'General Recommendation for the Establishment of Public Educational Institutions' envisaged the reorganization of the Protestant schools of the Franconia region rather along the lines of the Württemberg model. In his eyes, as a Swabian teacher himself, this naturally seemed the only way any fundamental improvement could be effected.

Niethammer's plan intended to separate the *Gymnasium* type of school from the more vocationally oriented *Realschule*. At the time both kinds of school were still combined and drew their teaching staff from the primary and elementary school system. Both kinds of school were essentially similar as regards the basic philosophical and classical studies. The difference lay in the fact that the *Gymnasium* curriculum was effectively aimed at developing the study of Latin and Greek, whereas the *Realschule* emphasized the more practical areas of study. The new curriculum proposed an 'Introduction to Speculative Thinking' and Niethammer could not have have found anyone more suitable than Hegel in this respect. The instruction envisaged here was to be graded in levels: 'Psychology' for the lower class, 'Phenomenology' and 'Logic' for the intermediate class, and 'Encyclopaedia' together with 'Transcendental and Subjective Logic' for the senior class. The details were not entirely fixed, however, and Hegel could exercise some freedom in how he chose to organize the different subjects. In Niethammer's plan the philosophical disciplines were all linked together in an organic fashion, something which actually deviated completely from the established Württemberg system. It was natural that Hegel decided to teach most of this material himself, and indeed the curriculum here seemed tailor-made for his interests and purposes. When Hegel became Rector the lower class numbered eleven students, the intermediate class fifteen and the senior class twelve. A further eight students would also join the classes during the course of the year.

Hegel found the amount of administration involved in the Rectorship to be an oppressive burden. He was obliged to deal directly with school essays, reports, certificates and testimonials and to draw up the necessary class-lists by hand. He regarded it as unfair to delegate some of these things to the students: as a result we soon find him urgently applying to Niethammer to see if he can employ a janitor at the school to lighten the load.

But there was little immediate help forthcoming from Munich. In the section of the Education Ministry specifically concerned with Protestant schooling one was thankful enough to escape obstructive administrative interference. For a short period, in the autumn of 1810, there was even talk of closing down the *Gymnasium* in Nuremberg or at least moving it to Ansbach, although this came to nothing in the end. That would indeed have been a serious personal blow for Hegel. He felt that there was no easier way of seriously harming and directly offending the sensibilities of Protestant citizens than by attacking their educational institutions. 'Protestantism consists not so much in a particular religious confession as in the general spirit of reflection and higher rational education', as he wrote to Niethammer on 3 November 1810.

But for all the difficulties involved in his rectorship at Nuremberg Hegel could count himself fortunate. Matters could have turned out a great deal worse after his more or less enforced departure from Jena. In the meantime word had got around amongst some former acquaintances with whom he had now lost touch that Hegel was still sunk in penury. Hegel suddenly heard from his early student van Ghert, who had heard the stories and wrote to him offering to find him an academic position in Holland. Ghert was currently employed in the official service of the Dutch Ministry of the Interior and certainly believed he could assist his old teacher. Hegel reacted with some interest to the proposal. After all, he only saw Nuremberg, like Bamberg before it, as an intermediate station in his career until he could return to academic life. He now heard that there might be prospects of a teaching position at the university in Leiden, especially if he did not actually get called to Erlangen first where Niethammer was also agitating on his behalf.

The question of Erlangen became increasingly urgent over the next few months since it was closely bound up with his own personal life. There were certainly obstacles to overcome: Niethammer's limited influence in the ministry, competition from Schelling, and the lethargy of the Erlangen authorities themselves. If Hegel was now particularly keen on exchanging his rectorship for a professorship at a university as quickly as possible, it was above all because he wished to get married.

The intention itself was not that new. Shortly after Hegel had been appointed Rector at the *Gymnasium*, his friends Paulus and his wife Caroline had already offered to help him find 'a slow and loyal Nuremberg wife'. If it is another two and a half years later before we find Hegel talking about the idea of marriage again, this only reveals once again his customary caution and characteristic circumspection.

But once he began to take steps in this direction he suddenly showed a surprising sense of determination, something that was often to be observed with him when his plans were finally settled in his mind. We do not know very much in detail about how Hegel actually came to be acquainted with Marie von Tucher, who belonged to an ancient patrician family in Nuremberg. It would also appear from Hegel's personal correspondence that their relationship developed very gradually. Hegel adopted a distinctly formal approach when he wrote in early April 1811 to Frau Sophia Maria Grundherr von Altenhamm, requesting Herr von Tucher's permission to ask for his daughter's hand in marriage. A few days later, on 8 April, Hegel asked the father to make his permission conditional upon the daughter's personal decision in the matter and further requested an appropriate opportunity to come and visit his chosen bride-to-be.

In this way Hegel had initiated a relationship with no great danger of losing face if Marie von Tucher should actually turn down his suit. In all probability the family would not have looked unfavourably on the Rector of the most important school in Nuremberg asking the hand of their daughter in marriage. On the other hand, Hegel's financial situation, with no capital of his own and a rather irregular professional salary, was anything but secure. And Hegel himself could hardly expect a significant dowry from the family of the prospective bride since they already had another seven children to provide for. In fact worries on the financial side continued to haunt Hegel right up to the eventual marriage, for he feared creating more economic problems for the future. His current position did not seem adequate if he was to present himself comfortably, according to the strict social conventions, within the family of the bride. There was some expectation in the von

Tucher household that Hegel would attempt to find a somewhat 'higher position'. Hence Hegel's letter to Niethammer on 18 April 1811: 'My happiness is partly conditional upon the possibility of finding a university position.' The reservations of the family were not particularly strong in this respect but they were sufficient to make Hegel hesitate. He wished therefore to postpone the marriage and particularly any formal announcement about it for a while longer. In his detailed response to Hegel's letters Niethammer attempted to dispel these prevarications. On 5 May 1811 he wrote: 'Do you not then feel yourself, as a professor and Rector of the *Gymnasium* in Nuremberg, well-regarded or worthy enough to be solemnly and officially admitted into a family which itself formerly enjoyed considerable standing in the heyday of the Imperial City of Nuremberg?' And Niethammer, knowing Hegel's personality as he did, added: 'In short, I regard all this as an unfortunate and quite ungrounded fear on your part.'

In the meantime Hegel had been busily engaged in convincing the Tucher family that there was a good prospect of his finding imminent academic employment at the University of Erlangen. In fact there were problems here too. For Erlangen itself was at a very low ebb, as Hegel's current correspondence with Niethammer reveals. Hegel was vigorously urging Niethammer both to verify the credibility of these academic hopes with the von Tucher family and to intensify his promotion of Hegel's cause in Erlangen at the same time. It seems that Hegel was successful in convincing the Tucher family about his excellent chances of soon becoming a professor in Erlangen and thus in dispelling any lingering doubts about his financial state. On 30 May 1811, Hegel wrote to Niethammer: 'We have already talked about the Erlangen business so much, that in the imagination our union and Erlangen itself have become indissolubly fused together, just like man and wife.'

But why was Erlangen so important in Hegel's mind, and in the eyes of the von Tucher family? Partly because the 'widow's allowances' there were said to be more generous for university professors than for *Gymnasium* professors, something which mattered just as much to this traditional Nuremberg family as it did to this Swabian teacher with a still uncertain future. Niethammer's letters were written in such a way that Hegel could read them out as credible evidence of an imminent call to Erlangen, or at least of an improvement in his current station. Thus Niethammer wrote on 5 May 1811: 'According to my reading of the situation your promotion is so little in doubt that I cannot now conceive otherwise, even if I myself should leave my current position.'

Hegel most probably received these gentle encouragements from the von Tuchers to find a 'higher station' for himself (as he put it to Niethammer on 30 May 1811) as a welcome endorsement of his own ambitions. He did not relish the thought of permanently remaining a *Gymnasium* teacher any more than that of surviving as a freelance writer without an institutional position.

But suddenly new possibilities emerged with the departure of Paulus to the

University of Heidelberg where he had now been appointed Professor of Church History. Hegel immediately pursued his old friendship with his Swabian compatriot Paulus, and in particular with his wife Caroline. Hegel's letter to her of 13 July 1811, further supplied with personal addenda from his bride-to-be, is nothing but an expression of his urgent wish to obtain a professorship in Heidelberg: 'How happy I should be, if I might find my ultimate destination in that place! Is it not true? But you will not fail to answer my hopes.' Marie von Tucher herself added between the lines: 'Please, please, let it be soon!' In fact during the last few months before his impending marriage Hegel appears to have fallen into one of his depressed phases. Even as the workmen were busy producing chairs and seats for the future couple's home, Hegel was looking on the dark side once more and seriously considering postponing the wedding again because his pay was now five months in arrears. Hegel did not radiate faith in the future to his wife. On the contrary, in an undated letter of summer 1811 he begged Marie von Tucher to be the 'saviour' of his 'downcast heart'.

Hegel's hesitation and anxiety about the prospect of getting married under conditions of economic hardship surely proceeds from much deeper levels of his own personality and reveals a certain insecurity in his character. However, once the official permission for the marriage, as formally required by his position, had been granted there was no question of any further delay. In one of Hegel's letters to Caroline Paulus the bride Marie von Tucher inserted an interesting remark about her 41-year-old bridegroom: 'Hegel also belongs to those hopeless people who expect nothing, who desire nothing.'

If Hegel appeared to undertake his marriage without the slightest evidence of exuberance, there were other very real grounds for this than his supposedly innate lack of expectations. For the question of his illegitimate son by Frau Burkhardt in Jena would soon painfully be brought back to him. The son in effect became the victim demanded by Hegel's social elevation into the circles of the patrician Nuremberg class. The boy had been ill for a long time and Hegel was relieved to hear that, under the care of Frau Fromann, his 'bloatedness', 'torpor', and 'mental dullness', which Hegel ascribed to his previous style of education, had now disappeared. He had obviously been taken out of the hands of the mother, who had seemed incapable of bringing him up properly, and accepted into the educational institute of Betty Wesselhoft, the sister-in-law of Hegel's friend Fromann.

Hegel's marriage was set for 16 September 1811. Niethammer had offered to advance the necessary credit to Hegel, who was still in a parlous financial position because of his delayed salary. As it turned out, Hegel could refuse the offer because he had already borrowed from Merkel, a friend of Hegel's and member of the town council who was also actively involved with him in the work of the school commission.

The actual marriage and the ensuing 'honeymoon' apparently did little to interfere with Hegel's work on his *Logic*. On 1 February 1812 we find him writing in hindsight to Niethammer: 'It is no small thing during the first semester of married life to produce a thirty-quarto-sized book of the most abstruse content' – something which is indeed hard to deny. But it is equally interesting to note another remark he made in this connection concerning the formal deficiencies of his new book: 'I am no academic scholar; I would really need another year to bring the thing into proper shape, but I need the money in order to live.'

As a teacher of philosophy at the *Gymnasium* Hegel began to relax the pace somewhat. His educational labours in this field did not produce the success he had originally hoped for. He even came round to thinking that there was actually too much philosophy being taught at the school. He confesses that he has long been wondering whether or not 'perhaps all philosophical instruction at *Gymnasium* level might well seem superfluous', as he writes to the educational authorities in the shape of Niethammer on 23 October 1812, suggesting instead that 'the study of the ancients is probably the most appropriate and intrinsically the most authentic introduction to philosophy for students of *Gymnasium* age'.

Hegel soon came to experience his married state as a more or less complete transformation of his way of life, although it naturally did nothing to alleviate his immediate economic position since his wife was quite without independent means of her own. No significant financial assistance was forthcoming from Marie's father because the paternal grandfather exercised exclusive rights over the disposition of the family inheritance. So Hegel was now solely responsible for the upkeep of the new family. After the birth of a daughter who died shortly afterwards, Marie was successfully delivered of a son in June 1813, an event that brought considerable happiness to Hegel. His father-in-law died only a few days later.

The same year also witnessed significant events on the social and historical front. The Bavarian professor he now was could hardly be described as an avid supporter of king and country. As an editor of the *Bamberger Zeitung* he had of course already served his adopted country loyally enough, but his real admiration and sympathy went to Napoleon. Nor did Hegel have to do any violence to his own conscience in this, since Bavaria was an ally of Napoleon in the war against Austria and Russia, and had also been joined by Prussia after the Treaty of Tauroggen in 1812.

None the less the 'world soul on horseback' had long since passed the zenith of his power. By 1813 even his long-established supporters had come to feel that Napoleon's time was nearing its end. The military operations in Bavaria revealed a man on the retreat. Hegel himself was able to observe on the spot how the Bavarian army had initially advanced with Napoleon against the Austrians, only to change sides and join the Allied powers after all. According to his own account Hegel personally benefited from the political crisis in the short term since, in order to secure the continued loyalty of its officials and employees during this period, the Bavarian administration made sure it properly paid all outstanding and, in Hegel's case long overdue, official salaries. As a result of these events the French withdrew from Nuremberg and the Austrian and Russian 'liberators', as Hegel sarcastically called them, occupied the town instead. Hegel was now forced to repeat the painful experience he had already had in Jena as the new troops set about requisitioning materials, confiscating possessions and plundering property. There was no doubt about it: the old admirer of Napoleon suddenly found himself serving quite new masters. Elements of his future conception of historical dialectic were being formed under the pressure of such events. It seems to him irrational to put faith in forces doomed to historical defeat and their fate is not to be lamented. The birth of the new already 'carries within it the seed of its destruction'. After the depredations of the French who plundered his modest possessions in Jena, Hegel is now forced to witness the depredations of the Austrians and the Russians as well. The question was naturally whether these new masters would prove worse than the old ones. Better to be quartered with six French soldiers than two Russian ones was the general opinion in Nuremberg, and Hegel himself could not disagree – not to mention the Austrians, whom Hegel accused of stealing his personal property. In Hegel's eyes the defeat of Napoleon produced not 'floods of joy' but simply 'a turbid brew of that ultra-patriotic coffee' which Hegel had so little time for, as he put it in an image repeated several times in his correspondence.

As he observed the scenes before him Hegel was already applying a dialectical method of historical understanding, one that was constantly alert to sudden changes of circumstance and reacted promptly to every new impression, which corrected itself and revised earlier over-hasty conclusions, and oriented itself to new aspects of the situation with regard to new and different possibilities.

Hegel's domestic life during the Nuremberg period was firmly rooted in everyday experience without a trace of external eccentricity. Significant deviation from a settled bourgeois life style was quite alien to Hegel's temperament in so far as it would only court unpredictable risks. In the family he played an undisputed patriarchal role, taking full charge of all domestic expenditures and recording all ingoings and outgoings in his own hand. In his correspondence Hegel habitually refers to his 'dear little wife' and invariably compliments Niethammer's wife stereotypically as the 'best of women' – typical expressions in comfortable middle-class family life at the time. Marriage had now furnished Hegel with that characteristic middle-class sentiment of stability and security. There was no obvious evidence of any conflict although there must have been certain domestic problems. These would almost inevitably arise from the existence of young Ludwig Fischer who was still living in care in Jena, more often ill than well, and a long way from his real father and mother. Hegel regularly paid some maintenance costs from Nuremberg but it went no further than this. It appears that his attempts to introduce the child into his household on periodic visits were discouraged by his wife. There were delays in sending clothes to the boy in Jena and Hegel had to apologize to Frau Fromann about the situation. Hegel's wife probably felt that there was more than enough to do at home with their own two sons, Karl and his younger brother Immanuel, the latter named in honour of Hegel's Munich friend and patron Niethammer.

Hegel had been hoping, as we saw, that his 'saviour' Niethammer would soon be able to find a professorship for him at Erlangen, or perhaps that Paulus or Schelver would facilitate his employment at the University of Heidelberg. But now a remarkable new academic possibility appeared on the horizon and revealed something of Hegel's renewed and considerable self-confidence as a philosopher. For Fichte himself had died in Berlin on 27 January 1814. And there was now talk of calling the author of the *Logic*, the first volume of which had appeared in 1812, to Berlin as professor. From now on Hegel's eyes were to be firmly fixed on this possibility, in accordance with his principle that any possible sign of God's will was earnestly to be assisted by his own and his friends' efforts to fulfil it.

Now that his hopes in this respect had been kindled by the publication of the *Logic*, it was an urgent necessity for him to define his own position carefully. Paulus had registered distinct opposition to Hegel in Heidelberg on the part of Fries. With his own logic, which was based on an 'anthropological foundation', Fries felt justified in appealing amongst others to the philosophical example of Kant, although he also drew on the deliverances of 'feeling'. Writing to Niethammer on 10 October 1811 Hegel referred to this position as the kind of 'utterly disorganized dirty linen that only a fool sitting on his toilet could possibly produce' and repudiated its appeal to 'the very shallowest aspect' of Kantian philosophy. Even if this strange combination of 'anthropology' and the fashionable ultra-romantic notion of inspired 'feeling' indeed seems highly dubious, Hegel's judgement on Kant here was a decidedly 'unofficial' one. Although it certainly indicated the principal thrust of Hegel's objections to Kant, he still played his intellectual cards rather close to his chest in the *Logic* itself. Something similar had also been true in his earlier relation to Schelling. In the *Phenomenology* Hegel had only partially revealed his critique of Schelling's standpoint, although it was quite enough for Schelling to perceive the fundamental nature of this attack. In remarks that were not intended for print Hegel's judgements were often much harsher. Then he speaks of the 'trickery of nature philosophy', as if the acknowledged field of Schelling's expertise was essentially a matter of empty chatter.

Schelling can hardly have been unaware that Hegel now represented a rival as far as possible future professorships were concerned. While he was living in Munich unburdened by any teaching obligations Schelling received a professorial call from Jena. He decided against accepting because the salary appeared too low. When Hegel learnt about the position he immediately wrote to Fromann on 14 April 1816 suggesting himself as a possible candidate, though he admits concern that his poor presentation of course material in his lectures at Jena will still be remembered there. He confesses that he was at that time 'still bound entirely to my notes when giving lectures' but tells Fromann that his experience as a teacher in Nuremberg has since given him a much better and freer technique in this respect. He clearly hoped Fromann might be able to do something in Jena to dispel such 'prejudice' about his earlier reputation. But Hegel also made it quite clear that he would not leave his relatively comfortable situation in Nuremberg for the usual professorial salary on offer. In fact the situation was soon decided anyway, when the faculty at Jena accepted his old antagonist Fries for the position.

But the imminent departure of Fries from Heidelberg now naturally raised Hegel's hopes with regard to that university. He informed his supportive friend Paulus that he would even be prepared to forgo a higher salary than he was currently receiving in Nuremberg if he was offered the professorial chair vacated by Fries. The Heidelberg theologian Karl Friedrich Daub, who was also sympathetic to Hegel's candidature, enquired whether he would be happy with 1,300 gulden in addition to material perks in the form of spelt and corn. Although that would actually constitute less than he was getting in Nuremberg, Hegel was told there was no question of being offered anything higher. He was advised to follow the example of Fries and negotiate for free lodgings estimated at the value of 150 gulden. Hegel told Paulus on 8 August 1816 that he was indeed willing to accept this proposal in order to escape what he called the 'pandemonium of school life'. And for his own part Hegel could draw some further comfort from the fact that he had also been considered amongst the candidates to succeed Fichte in Berlin.

There were a number of objective as well as quite personal reasons for Hegel's decision to abandon Nuremberg. The Württemberg emigrants who had formerly been so enthusiastic to leave Jena for positions in Bavaria were now equally keen to move on. Their expectations there had been disappointed and Paulus had only been the first to take the opportunity of leaving by going to Heidelberg. In Munich Schelling was also ready to depart for almost anywhere else in Germany. And Niethammer was now encountering formidable obstacles himself in the Bavarian capital and was beginning to feel the displeasure of the King. The representatives of the old Bavarian Catholic culture were no longer prepared to be instructed by 'foreigners' and were doing everything possible to get them to leave. Niethammer was forced to confess that the Protestants in Bavaria were still disadvantaged before the law and considered that their best option now was to depart as quickly as possible and find alternative livings elsewhere. In turn Hegel himself would now try and comfort the friend who had exerted himself so much on his behalf and on whom he had depended so much before. In view of the deteriorating situation in Bavaria he communicated his own historico-philosophical maxims to Niethammer in a letter of 16 July 1816: 'I remain convinced that the world spirit has issued the age with a command to advance. But there is still resistance.' A year after Napoleon's defeat the full political consequences were now beginning to show themselves in Europe. In the light of the emerging 'Reaction' against the immediate past Hegel stood more firmly than ever on the side of Napoleon's achievement. The Reaction was in truth nothing but the expected response to the man of action around whom world-historical events revolve.

In the meantime certain difficulties had developed in the course of Hegel's written negotiations over Heidelberg. His request for free lodgings was rejected in the end, although Hegel was able to negotiate an increase of a further 200 gulden in compensation. Thus Hegel eventually secured a salary that almost corresponded with what he was living on in Nuremberg, and openly expressed his expectations to the university authorities that he would earn more through the zealous performance of his academic duties in the future.

With his nomination as regular professor at Heidelberg Hegel may well have felt himself at last born aloft on the breath of the 'world spirit'. This was the first time in its history that Heidelberg could count a major philosopher amongst its teaching body, given that Spinoza himself had once famously refused a call to the university. Hegel's letters henceforth reveal a new tone of self-confidence. In contrast to Nuremberg, Hegel now occupied an incontestable position of academic authority from which he could bring his philosophy to the attention of the country and seek to extend its intellectual influence. And as we know, this had always been Hegel's wish.

The dream of finding a post in Erlangen had not been fulfilled. It was in fact Hegel's apparently much more fortunate former friend Schelling who eventually assumed the professorship there. Hegel had actually been called to Erlangen after all, but, as happened to Kant some decades before, the official call arrived a few days too late. Hegel had already formally accepted the position in Heidelberg. That there was some method behind the delay in Erlangen has been surmised, and perhaps plausibly enough. But it was impossible to prove and Hegel now had no further reason to investigate the matter.

19

The Science of Logic

~∞~

When Hegel's *Science of Logic* appeared between the years 1812 and 1816 it found no reviewers apart from Fries, who criticized it very severely. There seemed to be no one willing to offer a considered judgement or assessment of the work. This was essentially because, then as now, Hegel's *Logic* can only be properly explained by recourse to Hegelian logic itself. Any attempt at external interpretation soon encounters a fundamental obstacle in the very semantics of Hegel's thought, and one which cannot quickly (if indeed ever) be wholly overcome. This is effectively true of Hegel's philosophical language in general, and accounts for why the *Phenomenology* in particular has remained such a mysterious text from the beginning. The work which the *Phenomenology* was expressly designed to introduce represents the accomplishment of Hegel's original aim in the fields traditionally described as logic and metaphysics: a single 'science of logic' in which 'system' and 'method' were to be united.

From a Kantian point of view there was something fundamentally problematic about the very attempt. For the Kantians, as numerous in the nineteenth century as they were to be in the twentieth, endorsed the perfectly clear and to them incontestable claim that 'pure reason' and its 'critique' has fundamentally put the entire metaphysical tradition in doubt. If there was any post-Kantian philosopher who was bold enough to oppose a new system with its own distinctive method to that of Kant, then it was the Hegel of the *Science of Logic*. At the beginning of the 'Preface' to the original 1812 edition of his work Hegel described the gulf which separated him from Kant:

> The total transformation which the philosophical perspective has undergone in our midst during the last twenty-five years, the higher standpoint which the self-consciousness of spirit has successfully attained during this period, has so far exerted little influence on the sphere of logic. And what was formerly called

metaphysics has been so thoroughly rooted out that it has disappeared from the realm of the sciences altogether.

Logic itself had been spared the fate of metaphysics. But if Kant believed that logic had made no significant advance since Aristotle, Hegel was convinced that it had certainly made no further progress after Kant. The task Hegel has set himself, and here announces, is nothing less than the reconstruction of the entire subject from the ground up. In the *Science of Logic* Hegel understands his subject matter as 'the science of thought in general', articulated in a number of absolutely fundamental concepts like 'being' and 'nothing', 'becoming', 'determinate being', 'reality', 'determinacy', 'change', 'negation', 'quality' and 'quantity', 'being-for-self', and so on. In logic as Hegel understands it, unlike the other disciplines (or particular 'sciences' in the plural), there is no distinction to be drawn between method and object. The method is the subject matter itself, and the subject matter is the method. For the method is intrinsically dialectical. Hegel claims, with a backward reference to Kant, that the dialectic 'which has been previously treated only as a specific part of logic and whose point and purpose has been thoroughly neglected, here assumes a quite different position'. For him the dialectic is no purely 'negative approach', no 'tissue of illusions', and no sophistical game, as its opponents constantly allege. Even Kant had already protected the term from that charge. Logic is rather the reason which is immanent in things themselves, or as we would put it today, 'the methodical unfolding of the fundamental determinations of being and thought alike' (R. P. Horstmann). There is therefore no reflection that could itself be prior to logic and no real preliminary introduction to logic. It can only begin directly with the subject matter itself.

The *Science of Logic* slowly and deliberately sets in motion an enormous conceptual apparatus that is quite unparalleled in the history of philosophy, either in Aristotle or in Kant. Perhaps something analogous can be found in the kind of mystical and speculative thought which Jakob Böhme applied to the phenomena of nature and the spirit, but it hardly figured as 'logic' in his work. We certainly know that Hegel was reading Böhme at the time he was composing his *Logic* since he expressly arranged for the Amsterdam edition of Böhme's writings to be sent to him through his Dutch friend van Ghert.

Böhme's influence and that of the rationalist tradition of Aristotelian, Wolfian and Kantian logic leave their stylistic mark on every aspect of Hegel's ontological language. In the last analysis there is no obvious effectively separate treatment of 'being' or 'essence' in Hegel's text: he is only interested in the dialectical distinction of the unfolding determinations within an ultimately all-encompassing unity. 'Being' here corresponds to the Old High German verbal form 'Wesan'. For the German terms 'Sein' and 'Wesen' French often uses the same word 'être', reserving the term 'essence' for the latter term only, although it is hardly identical with the range of meanings in the

German word. And the same is more or less true for the distinction in English between 'being' and 'essence'. For Hegel it is 'pure being' that forms the starting point: 'being and nothing else, without further content or definition'. 'Essence' on the other hand contains intrinsic determinations within itself. For Hegel the Latin term 'ens' includes both senses.

The expressive power of language itself does not suffice to articulate the distinction between being and essence clearly. The question concerning being and essence belongs to the 'objective logic' which takes the place of the former metaphysics and corresponds to 'transcendental logic' in Kant's sense. What Hegel calls 'subjective logic' deals with the explicit forms of the thinking process. But given the identity of thought and being which Hegel presupposes throughout, this final section also ultimately forms part of the section on ontology as the doctrine of being.

The doctrine of being includes that of non-being. Hypothetically speaking, non-being or the nothing precedes the category of being. The third term of comparison between being and nothing is the 'beginning': the 'beginning' is a

non-being which is related to being as to an other; that which begins is not yet, and is only approaching being. But at the same time the beginning includes being, but as being which distinguishes itself from non-being and as something opposed sublates it. But further that which begins already *is*, although it is also *not yet*. Being or non-being therefore are contained within the beginning in an immediate unity.

As far as the significance of this 'beginning' for the relationship between being and nothing is concerned, it is necessary to emphasize the 'analysis of the beginning' in Hegelian 'thought' which reveals the result in the method and the method in the result. The analysis in question produces the 'concept of the unity of being and non-being' or the 'identity of identity and non-identity'. Hegel adds a further remark which proved particularly important for the later interpretation of his thought: 'This concept could be regarded as the first and purest definition of the absolute.'

But it remains the case that the explanation of this logic can only take place in its own conceptual terms. Hegel struggled hard to try and describe the actual process of thought and find an appropriate language in which to render it intelligible. But given the difficulties which have bedevilled the interpretation of his work ever since, it can hardly be claimed that he was particularly successful in this.

Hegel's speculations on 'being' and 'nothing' prepare the way for his understanding of the 'absolute'. Hegel's conception of the absolute, despite or even because of one's reservations about hazarding an interpretation of it, has acted as something of a lighted fuse in the subsequent history of philosophy. The 'absolute' cannot but appear as a kind of substitute for God, as a supreme but impersonal principle offered in place of the living God of the

Jews and the Christians. Reflecting on this threatened disappearance of Yahweh in the nameless abstraction of the 'absolute', Schopenhauer considered it one of Hegel's most astonishing feats that the theologians could believe their God had been rescued and legitimated by the Hegelian 'absolute'.

But was there really any room in Hegel's philosophy of the absolute for the idea of God, when the philosopher carefully avoided saying anything more precise about the 'name of the absolute'? The later post-Hegelian exponents of philosophical atheism did not hesitate to find the original theoretical seeds of their own position in Hegel's thought. The 'non-being' of God could also be counterposed to the 'being' of God, in accordance with the formula that 'pure being and the pure nothing are the same'. This allowed Hegel to maintain a certain neutrality on the question. And even if it seemed a difficult undertaking to denominate the absolute as God and God as the absolute, there was at least *one* certainty – that which Fichte had introduced into philosophy and which now reappeared in Hegel's logic as 'the most concrete' of all certainties: there is no doubt that the ego is identical with itself. The ego as the 'simple certainty of itself', as the 'beginning and ground of philosophy', remains untouched by sceptical doubt of any kind. It was not so surprising that Hegel later expressed the wish to be buried alongside Fichte in Berlin.

If 'being' stands opposed to 'non-being', they in turn form a 'unity' over against the category of 'becoming'. Neither being nor nothing can simply be identified with becoming. Becoming lies between nothing and being and belongs to 'the analysis of the beginning'. It points to the beginning of the world, in theological terms to the creation, and in specifically Judaeo-Christian terms to the original 'creation out of nothing' as the established dogmatic interpretation the Genesis story. Hegel's logic effectively denounces the intrinsic absurdity of this mythological conception as it has been handed down in accordance with traditional belief: 'Nothing can begin, neither in so far as something is, nor in so far as something is not; for in so far as it is, it does not begin, and in so far as it is not, it does not begin either.' This amounts to a decisive repudiation of the Judaeo-Christian notion of the creation from nothing in so far as it is intended as a real explanation of the beginning of the world: 'If the world or something is supposed to have begun, it would have begun from the nothing, but in the nothing or as the nothing there is no beginning.'

It was Heraclitus on the other hand who had emphasized the centrality of 'becoming'. His claim that 'Everything flows' underlined the fact that everything constantly finds itself already caught up in an unoriginated movement, that everything is indeed 'becoming'. 'Neither being nor nothing can hold out against becoming.' The process of 'becoming' governs the entirety of life from birth to death. It grounds the dialectic of life and death in general and demonstrates 'that everything that is bears the seed of its destruction in its own birth, and death on the other hand is the entry to new life'.

That everything 'bears the seed of its destruction in its own birth' already contains the central idea of Hegel's dialectical conception of history. He was already collecting material on this subject in Nuremberg, although it was only later that he methodically organized and expanded it in the *Philosophy of History*. What is true for every 'ego' is equally true for all the dynamic processes of history which prepare their advance, experience their growing power, attain their culmination, and finally undergo the experience of decline and eventual destruction. And this is just as true of those movements and developments which believe themselves exempted from this law. They turn into their opposites in a dialectical reversal, they experience the implicit law of the infinite which is precisely the act of self-sublation. Hegel attempted to demonstrate this principle in his logic with his usual exhausting thoroughness:

> The finite only exists as its own self-transcendence; the infinite is already contained within it as its own opposite. Equally the infinite is only the self-transcending of the finite, it essentially contains its own other, and is the other of itself in that respect. The finite is not sublated by the infinite as by something existing outside of itself; rather its infinitude consists in its self-sublation.

In the strict sense logic cannot properly treat its various objects in a simple sequence. The introduction to logic is already itself a logical operation. Like a fugue, the logical operation contains both a mathematical kind of rigour and an element of intuition; a theme is speculatively posited and allows a certain play of the imagination in its subsequent development. 'Being' is not just 'being', the 'being' of Parmenides can be seen to correspond to the 'becoming' of Heraclitus. This combination of rational inference with an initially hypothetical and freely developed intuition is what truly makes Hegel's *Logic*, in Hegel's own words, 'a book of the most abstruse content'.

This remark of Hegel's is not to be found in the book itself, but refers unerringly to its central theme. For to approach thought in itself, as well as its subsequent objects of nature, religion and history, we must simultaneously begin from opposite ends, as it were: from the two electric poles, from the opposition of good and evil, from the relationship between reason and the passions. On the high sea of speculation pure thought can travel on indefinitely from its starting point in pure being. In the phase of *Dasein* or determinate being we can already see 'etymologically' that being has now acquired further determination: 'In being for self qualitative being is completed; it is infinite being . . . Being for self, as the negation of other being, is a relation to self; equality with itself. This constitutes the moment of its being in itself.' It is clear, as Dieter Henrich expresses it, that Hegel's logic is, above all, an 'ontological theory'.

This points far ahead to the somewhat mannered and playful linguistic speculations of Heidegger. But Hegel is also a philosophical descendant of

Jakob Böhme and something of the mystical gravity of the latter's *German Philosophy* also characterizes Hegel's language and intellectual style. If, according to Hegel, the infinite possesses the finite within itself and the finite constitutes the inner 'essence' of the infinite to the point of ultimate coincidence, then we can see that the mystical has a rational root and rationalism a mystical conclusion. What radically separates Hegel from Böhme and Heidegger alike is the fact that he also remains an Enlightenment thinker at the same time.

In his *Science of Logic* Hegel treated all the themes of the classical philosophical discipline of logic and rejected the supposed certainties of this tradition from Aristotle through to Kant. Hegel discovered intrinsic characteristics of thought which were not at all obvious at first sight. The fundamental and uncontested proposition for every logical system is the principle of non-contradiction: A cannot simultaneously = non-A. The identical judgement A = A is an empty tautology which indicates that the 'result simply contains that from which it resulted'. There is nothing here to express the kind of identity involved in the 'movement of reflection' as Hegel calls it. That comes about only with the formula: a = b, b = c, ergo a = c as the conventional logical sequence of propositions. The profound claim of Hegel's logic leads to the apparently monstrous assertion that the principle of non-contradiction as an identical proposition represents merely a 'formal, abstract and incomplete truth' because 'the truth is only complete in the unity of identity and variety, and thus only exists in this unity'. Applied to the formula A = B, that means that an A that is B also contains non-A within itself, for otherwise it could never advance beyond the tautology of A = A to become B and despite its internal moment of non-A would never cease to be A which, according to the principle of non-contradiction, cannot be non-A. Hegel had already offered an explanation of this view in the *Phenomenology* when he wrote: 'determinacy has its other-being within itself and is a self-movement . . . this is contained in the simple operation of thinking itself'. As spirit and thought *par excellence* logic is not some persisting or static self-identity but is essentially an intellectual act, a 'self-movement' of internal division and self-reconstitution, the 'movement of reflection' whereby identity disappears in other-being and other-being in identity. After Hegel logic can no longer simply be organized in terms of the principle of non-contradiction. If it is true, as Hegel says, that 'all things are in themselves contradictory', then the principle of non-contradiction is itself logically contradicted, and the sublation of contradiction as a logical operation becomes in turn a contradiction of the contradicted contradiction or a case of double negation (as Nicolai Hartmann saw). All previous conventions are thus turned upside down: 'in the possible A the possible non-A is also included and it is this relation which determines both of them as possible' in accordance with the thought that 'the negative is equally the positive'. What was previously considered inconceivable is intellectually articulated as conceivable after all. Here the *Logic* reveals itself as the natural continuation of the *Phenomenology*. The latter was to constitute an introduction to the dynamics to which nature, spirit and history are subjected: movements like the growth of a plant, where the bud is 'refuted' by the blossom that results from it and the fruit reveals the blossom as 'a false existence on the part of the plant'; but also movements of a historical kind, which turn into their opposites precisely when they reach a point of culmination.

Dialectic as the logic of illusion in Kant's sense or dialectic as the intrinsic nature of thought in and for itself is the central point at issue here. The dialectic of course can easily appear as a diabolical intellectual conjuring trick which merely appeals to the name of logic. One is reminded of the lines which Goethe puts in the mouth of Mephistopheles when he recommends the infernal complexities of the *Collegium logicum* to the enthusiastic student:

> Truly the fabric of mental fleece
> Resembles a weaver's masterpiece,
> Where a thousand threads one treadle throws,
> Where fly the shuttles hither and thither,
> Unseen the threads are knit together,
> And an infinite combination grows.
> Then, the philosopher steps in
> And shows, no otherwise it could have been:
> The first was so, the second so,
> Therefore the third and fourth are so,
> Were not the first and second, then
> The third had likewise never been.
> *(Faust I, lines 1922 ff; Barnard's translation)*

It is difficult to suppress the feeling that Goethe's lines about the endless shuttle of concepts were not simply directed against the Kantian notion of dialectic as a logic of illusion. They rather suggest that Hegel's own dialectic is the target here. Compared with the traditional logic of the schools Hegel's conception of the subject appears an elevated one. And there can be no straightforward retreat back to the stage of Aristotelian and Kantian logic after Hegel's work. None the less, Hegel leaves the reader with the impression that something quite unheard of, something almost impossible, has been accomplished in this book, even though we cannot properly explain precisely how it has actually been done.

That A (preserved in B) = non-A, and that the infinite should become the infinite through the power of the negative, is something that before Hegel perhaps only Heraclitus could have claimed with equal boldness. What was new about the self-confessedly abstruse treatment characteristic of Hegel's book was that such a formula and all its implications would henceforth belong amongst the indubitable first principles of logic itself. From now on the idea of 'intrinsic contradiction' could not be banished from the manifestations of reality in general, from the experience of subject and object, life and death, war and peace, the phenomena of religion, politics and history. The Hegelian logic thus becomes a site where the most contradictory concepts are fully articulated as such and simultaneously reunited with one another.

It is obvious that for Hegel 'being' is not an exhaustive concept. In a sense it is already the absolute, but the latter seems to reveal features that distinguish it from mere being. Although the terms 'Sein' (being) and 'Wesen' (essence) have commonly been used synonymously in the history of the German language, the latter term goes further and deeper than the former. Being rests upon essence as its original ground. But the ultimate ground in turn is also to be distinguished from essence. Ground is that upon which everything ultimately depends, represents the deepest level of all in the sense of commencement and cause. In his speculations concerning being, essence and ground Hegel once again approaches the mystical domain of Böhme and integrates its contents into the intellectualized system of cause and effect. The ramifying connections which can arise here are infinitely various in character. The concept of ground involves that of consequence, and the concept of consequence refers us back to ground. There is no escaping this circular relation. Since Aristotle it had been an established philosophical insight that the ground (or essence) of things lay in their form. That meant that the real is not itself form, but that it owed its essence to form. Form, on the other hand, is not something that can simply exist in its own right but requires a content, something to be formed in the first place. 'There is absolutely no matter without form and no form without matter', Hegel writes in the notes to his *Propaedeutics*. That does not mean that Hegel philosophically posits matter as the first principle of things. Any philosophy essentially governed by the 'Idea' inevitably encounters a fundamental difficulty with matter and cannot possibly acknowledge its ontological priority. Hegel claimed that Kant 'constituted' the concept of matter from the twin concepts of repulsion and attraction. Hegel's difficulties with the realm of the material continue to plague him in the *Logic*. Pure matter is not the first or primary reality at all but merely 'what remains after we have abstracted from feeling, seeing, tasting, and so forth'. In the larger perspective matter thus enjoys no priority over spirit. In the hierarchy of concepts it belongs on the lowest level, something essentially negative which draws its energy dialectically from the negative. According to the *Phenomenology of Spirit* matter was 'not to be regarded as an existing thing in its own right, but was being as a universal or being in the form of the concept'. Furthermore, matter is essentially *passive* with respect to the activity of form. It responds to this activity of form with its own 'inertia'. As the counterpart of form, matter plays a necessary role for form, which only realizes itself as form in so far as it actually materializes itself.

Once again then: matter and form reveal themselves to be a 'unity' precisely in their mutual 'otherness'. This unity in turn reveals itself in the 'content' of reality. Each in its own being-for-self is already the totality, since each can only appear in identity with the other. Or as Hegel puts it: 'What appears as the activity of form . . . is the authentic movement of matter itself'; and this in accordance with the principle of sufficient reason: 'There is nothing in the original ground which is not equally in the grounded.' The one is not possible without the other, form and matter presuppose one another in their mutual relationship just as ground and consequence, cause and effect likewise do in a different categorial context.

This line of thought can naturally be applied dialectically to other relationships as well which transcend such circular patterns of derivation. Hegel enriches the play of possibilities here by introducing new conceptual cards, as it were. Thus the category of actuality presupposes that of possibility. Considered amongst the originally unlimited array of possibilities, the actual initially appears as something contingent. As one commentator on Hegel's *Logic* puts it with regard to the complex relation between actuality, possibility and contingency: 'Not only is the actual something possible, but the possible is equally something actual or contingent' (Bernard Lakebrink). But contingency alone cannot decide whether the possible turns into the actual. For that additional content is required on the part of the possible. The content itself belongs to the conditions which are also involved in the transformation of the possible into the actual. The sequence of conditions must be completely given if *one* of the existing possibilities is to qualify as the one which shall become actual. And here contingency finds itself replaced by necessity. Once the content reveals its possibility under all the attendant conditions it can now become actual: indeed must now become actual with necessity. One and only one of the many possibilities must now be actualized: like the little ball which, in contrast to the finer particles of powder for example, fails to pass through the sieve on account of its size. In the last analysis Hegel's conception of necessity is a teleological one which is oriented to the Idea of the world itself as a purposive totality.

Classically speaking the concept of necessity is the opposite and counterpart to that of freedom. The latter figures as the fundamental principle of the philosophy of spirit, as the ultimate end and fulfilling purpose of the world. But freedom itself necessarily presupposes its opposite. In its dialectical reversal necessity also turns into freedom, and freedom is transformed into necessity. Necessity here is not an external compulsion but rather represents 'the truth of substance' as the 'concept'. This must first be recognized if Hegel's philosophy of spirit is properly to be understood, and belongs as it were to the algebra of the system and its method. The truth of being is to be found in essence, the truth of essence is to be found in the concept. The transformation of 'representations' into the form of the concept, as an identity which contains contradiction within itself, ultimately leads us to the ground and origin of things. The latter do not depend upon any conditions external to themselves, but on the true objectivity of substance which itself coincides with subjectivity in the absolute subject-object.

Over against Kant's subjective epistemology, according to which the world is subjectively posited, is our 'representation', an image variously caught and reflected in our own retina as it were, Hegel affirms the objectivity of being as intrinsically accessible to the powers of reflection. For Kant there can only be a subject where there is an object, and the latter only deserves the name of object if it is an object for a subject. Ernst Bloch has identified the central problem of Hegel's philosophy in the question of the subject–object relation and the ultimate realization of their identity. One could also call this the ultimate fundamental question of logic in the broadest sense. Hegel can justly maintain his own position against Kant only on the supposition of the absolute or the infinite totality. Of course, in the prose of everyday life, as far as the identity of thought and being is concerned, we cannot question the validity of Kant's rule that a merely imaginary house is not an actual case of property, that a hundred thalers in the mind is by no means the same as a hundred thalers in one's pocket.

Thus the attempt which has sometimes been made on the part of later bourgeois idealism to construct something like a comprehensive 'national' German philosophy, including Kant, Fichte, Schelling and Hegel alike, is doomed to failure. The supposed harmony here is entirely forced and is intrinsically incapable of being demonstrated if only because of the completely different meanings given by the different thinkers to otherwise semantically identical terms. Kant's conceptual language, obscure as it is, differs from that of Hegel precisely because his entire thought is quite differently structured and affirms the unattainability of metaphysical truth in the first place. Hegel's intent is to reach the absolute and this governs the advance of his *Logic* from the very beginning. The unity of system and method predetermines the conceptual path of the *self-unfolding Idea* until the absolute standpoint is attained in which self-knowledge coincides with and simultaneously realizes the absolute itself. And here the busy shuttling of concepts back and forth can clearly be heard once more. For the 'Idea' in Hegel's language signifies both the 'subject' as 'being-for-self' and the 'object' as 'being-in-itself', and unites two sides of one and the same reality grasped as the comprehensive 'subject-object'. This is what effectively reveals Hegel's peculiar and systematic achievement in relation to his other idealist predecessors. The subjective dimension represents life, the individual, the self, while the objective dimension represents the totality with all its reciprocal transitions and interconnections. The objective dimension is borne along upon the stream of becoming, while the subjective dimension is a part of the totality. For the end which is to be attained by the 'Idea' through all the way-stations of the system as an ultimate subject-object identity in the absolute, is not really an end or purpose at all. It is merely the totality of life maintained dynamically as a beginning – the beginning of a constantly renewed dialectical process and not that simple beginning which according to the *Logic* itself is impossible.

Goethe dedicated his lines about the *Collegium Logicum* in his *Faust* to the diabolical play of false dialectic. The true and genuine dialectic which Hegel tried to articulate in his *Phenomenology of Spirit* doubtless left the first reader to whom it was sent, namely Goethe himself, in a state of considerable bewilderment. None the less, there was certainly a sense in which he was prepared to recognize its significance. But confronted with the fully developed dialectic of the *Science of Logic*, which Hegel once attempted to explain to the poet on a visit to Weimar as he returned from Paris to Berlin, even Goethe himself must have been lost for words.

20

Professor in Heidelberg

Hegel travelled to Heidelberg alone when he departed to take up his new responsibilities. His wife had to remain behind in Nuremberg for a while because she had suffered a miscarriage amidst all the busy travel preparations and the work of packing up their modest possessions and household goods. We owe what insights we have about the first beginnings of Hegel's time in Heidelberg to the correspondence between husband and wife that ensued as a result of this situation.

Hegel was initially rather disappointed at the small number of students who attended his lectures. For his lectures on the philosophical encyclopaedia, five hours a week, he was limited to an audience of four. He had certainly imagined something better than this. 'The students have yet to warm to us', he wrote to Nuremberg on 29 October 1816, just after the commencement of his lectures.

There were a number of other unexpected circumstances as well. His academic duties actually claimed a good deal more of his time than he had originally anticipated. He was forced to confront his own slowness in dealing with administrative affairs, for what we would today call 'flexibility' was not exactly one of Hegel's principal virtues. This was not something that had been particularly expected of him either at Jena or in Bamberg, or even later in Nuremberg. He found it extremely difficult to deal with two or three matters at the same time. He wrote to Niethammer on 19 April 1817: 'There is something so laborious in my nature so that even if it only requires half an hour to write a letter, I cannot do it until all my other business has been dealt with first.' As Rector in Nuremberg he had constantly complained about the numerous impediments to work caused by aspects of school administration, but he had at least been master in his own house. The sphere of his activities was well defined and therefore manageable. In Heidelberg he now had to accustom himself to a new situation and to set about establishing contacts with colleagues whose professional relations with one another were far from clear. Apart from the theologian Daub, the principal support for his call to Heidelberg had come from his old friend Paulus. But Hegel's relationship to Paulus had never been as close as that with Niethammer. In his correspondence with other friends Hegel does not seem to have expressed a very positive opinion of Paulus and was not above criticizing the 'busybodyness' of this foremost editor of Spinoza's works. And the fact that some conflict soon developed between them is perhaps less surprising than it would at first appear. Hegel certainly offered the first opportunity for such problems when he refused to publish an essay by Paulus ('Wangenheim's Conception of the Constitution') in the *Heidelberg Yearbooks*, a journal that was being co-edited by Hegel. He complained, with the agreement of Wilken and Thibaut, that the essay was simply too long.

That may well have been true but it was certainly not the entire story. For in fact there were some very serious differences of opinion between Hegel and Paulus concerning the future of the constitution of Württemberg. At least Paulus could not help interpreting the situation in this light, suspecting an intrigue against him on Hegel's part and naturally enough resenting it as an expression of profound ingratitude. Hegel was not prepared to see his authority questioned in the matter and Paulus broke off relations with him as a result.

When he first moved to Heidelberg Hegel and family resided at no. 300 in the Friedrichstrasse, now no. 10. His domestic situation here appeared almost idyllic. The owner of the house was a farmer, and Hegel could observe from his window the farmhouse itself with its horses and cows, or watch the harvest being collected in the summer. The picture as Hegel himself describes it evokes something of the agricultural, pre-capitalist origins of his own thought. As an employee of the government, a *Beamter*, Hegel also received a quantity of agricultural produce as part of his 'salary' and he was able to sell off any surplus remaining after his personal use, something which significantly increased his income as the price of grain began to rise, as he noted with satisfaction. In January 1817 he changed address and moved into a house about a hundred metres away, which is today a new building at no. 48. Hegel lived here until his departure from Heidelberg in September 1818.

Once he was installed in Heidelberg Hegel finally felt himself in a suitable position to take his illegitimate son Ludwig into his household. The natural mother had died in the meantime and Hegel did not conceal a certain feeling of relief from his friend Fromann about being liberated from a formerly rather embarrassing and difficult situation. At first things seemed to go fairly well. Ludwig attended the *Gymnasium* in Heidelberg and Hegel was delighted with the boy's intelligence.

The Hegel family was certainly not short of interesting diversions in Heidelberg. The immediate and more distant environs of the place positively encouraged excursions of one kind or another, long walks along the river

Neckar or trips to the surrounding mountains. Hegel was particularly fond of the Bergstrasse quarter, but Mannheim and Speyer were also visited and he was particularly impressed by Schwetzingen.

In July 1817 Hegel received in Heidelberg a letter from Goethe dated the 8th of the month. Goethe had learned through his friend Sulpiz Boisserée that in his *Encyclopaedia of Philosophical Sciences* Hegel had openly criticized Newton's theory of colour. Goethe always reacted very sensitively to objections to his own rival theory, although he generally liked to emphasize his 'naivety' in philosophical matters and preferred to appeal to a direct intuition of nature. He thanked Hegel for his remarks on the subject. We know that Hegel's conception of the 'nature of light' in his Jena period had already attracted Goethe's sympathetic attention. The poet now felt himself confirmed and justified by the insights of a 'higher philosophy' which was in a position to 'vindicate the independence, purity, and indivisibility of light'. Goethe wrote in this vein to Boisserée on 1 July, emphatically adding that 'this pure light now comes from Heidelberg'. And it was hardly to Hegel's disadvantage that his old antagonist Fries had proclaimed the following in a review of Hegel's *Logic* that had already appeared in the *Heidelberg Yearbooks of Literature*: 'It is risible to behold how tireless pedantry and lacklustre presumption simply continue to parrot Goethe's own mistakes.' Hegel thus inevitably appeared before all eyes as an express supporter of Goethe's theory of colour. Professor Hegel now responded on 20 July from Heidelberg to Goethe's brief remarks by enclosing a little treatise on colour theory and contemporary experiments with mirrors which can only have delighted the poet. One can see how easily Hegel's own personal admiration for the man Goethe effortlessly combines with the philosophical conclusions of nature philosophy.

Hegel's first year in Heidelberg also saw the arrival of the writer Jean Paul who certainly enlivened the atmosphere amongst the professors and their students. Heinrich Voss, philologist and son of the famous translator of Homer, had encouraged the university to bestow an honorary doctorate upon Jean Paul. No one could resist the fascinating appeal of the writer's *Flegeljahre* ('Adolescent Years'), not even Hegel with that detached coolness of his that always needed closer personal acquaintance before it began to thaw. And indeed Jean Paul would seem to have exercised a surprisingly uninhibiting effect upon Hegel. There was even a punch evening arranged in honour of Jean Paul in the home of Heinrich Voss which revealed Hegel in unusually relaxed mood. A letter from Voss to a friend of 18 July 1817 reports that 'tongues were increasingly loosened' as the evening wore on. At the party one cleric asked Hegel if he would be willing to compose 'a philosophy for young ladies'. Hegel responded with some hilarity to this suggestion and excused his reluctance to do so with reference to the obscurity of his philosophical language. When the guests finally stood up to go around midnight, after four strong bowls of punch, they were distinctly unsure on their feet.

And just as he was about to leave, Hegel is said to have pointed a finger in Jean Paul's direction with the words: 'That man must certainly become a doctor of philosophy.'

Although this suggestion was made in the later hours of a successful party, Hegel seriously stood up for Jean Paul in the official faculty meetings of the university as well. When Hegel's colleague Langsdorf had objected that Jean Paul could not be regarded as a 'proper Christian', Hegel had responded with quite uncommon eloquence, arguing that Jean Paul was indeed a 'splendid Christian' with moral views that no one could rightfully impugn. A day later Jean Paul duly received the scroll with his honorary degree in a leather binding from the very hands of Hegel and Creuzer.

In August 1817 the writer and philosopher Victor Cousin travelled from France to Heidelberg. The principal intention of his German trip had originally been to meet Schelling. He had sought out Schelling and found Hegel, as he put it himself in his essay *On French and German Philosophy*. From the very first moment they met the two men seemed to have established an extremely strong and mutually sympathetic relationship. There were some problems at first, for Hegel's French was not significantly better than Cousin's German. Yet both soon developed a feeling for what essentially linked them despite all differences. Indeed this was even more so in the case of Cousin.

This fact is interesting in its own right. Hegel's reputation in Heidelberg was still very far from being established. At the time he certainly headed no philosophical school and was still widely regarded as a 'Schellingian'. That was one reason why he seemed to recommend himself as a possible successor to Fichte when the philosophy faculty in Berlin made their preliminary soundings about Hegel before he went to Heidelberg. And Cousin expected to meet just such a follower of Schelling when he first encountered Hegel personally. But he would very quickly learn otherwise.

Cousin actually met the Hegel who had just completed the *Encyclopaedia of the Philosophical Sciences*. The work both filled Cousin with enormous admiration and also provoked a certain bemusement in him. He found it to be 'rather scholastic in appearance' and certainly written in 'an insufficiently clear language'. Cousin's personal impressions of Hegel correspond closely with those of many other witnesses: 'It costs Hegel enormous effort to produce a few profound but very enigmatic words; his powerful though somewhat clumsily expressed diction, his concentrated countenance, his brooding brows – they are the very picture of thought wholly wrapped up within itself.'

Cousin later claimed that he had predicted the eventual victory of the Hegelian philosophy. There was some truth in this for this Frenchman was certainly amongst the first to recognize Hegel's significance. This casts an interesting light upon the great influence which Hegel would subsequently exercise upon a culture and a language which might naturally have been expected to resist his truly sphinx-like speech, but which actually seems to have felt itself strangely attracted instead.

Hegel only began to gather a wider audience in Heidelberg with his lectures on logic which now attracted seventy listeners. The hesitant character which so many people had remarked in Hegel, and which indeed he never entirely lost, was being increasingly countered by a self-assertive confidence. After his break with Paulus, Hegel associated within the university most closely with Daub, the jurist Thibaut, the theologian Schwarz, and the philosopher and historian Creuzer.

Johann Heinrich Voss, associated with the university but not obliged to give lectures there, belonged to the more democratic faction in Heidelberg. Hegel's good relationship with the revolutionary sympathizer Voss the elder, as well as with his son Heinrich, the classical philologist who had encouraged Hegel's nomination in Heidelberg, was neither helped nor hindered by this fact. Hegel certainly kept his distance from the classical philologist Welker, who was a German democratic constitutionalist and hardly his kind of chosen company. On a boat trip which the Heidelberg professors once took along the Neckar towards the little town of Hirschhorn, the two factions began to argue violently with one another. The occasion for the dispute seems to have been a toast which Hegel had made to the health of the Crown Prince of Sweden. Welker protested about this to Daub. Sulpiz Boisserée noted the incident in his diary under 13 July 1817: 'A revolutionary and respectless bunch of people: prof. Welcker, Kropp etc.' But he revealed a striking objectivity on his own part when he also made a critical observation about Hegel's 'absolutism'. Hegel represented in his eyes 'the philosopher of everything the same, the philosophy of yes on the one hand, and no on the other'.

Boisserée seems to have caught an important element of Hegel's philosophy here, although he expresses it reductively, in the form of a slogan. He was referring to an 'absolutism' in the political realm which seemed to slip out of serious difficulties by appealing 'on the one hand' to this aspect and 'on the other hand' to that aspect of the issue. At the same time it appeared to proceed quite autocratically in refusing to relinquish its decisive reservations about questions of 'the constitution' and of 'German freedom' which Welcker was so keen to champion. This could be seen particularly clearly during these weeks as the city was preparing for the imminent Wartburg Festival and addressing the question of who precisely would be participating in it. On 18 October 1817 the *Burschenschaften* or student fraternities expressed their desire to gather at the festival in express commemoration of the Reformation and the German war of national liberation against Napoleon. The debate even penetrated within Hegel's family, although he strongly opposed the idea and soon enforced his own view. Hegel tacitly followed the official line of the Heidelberg authorities which wished to avoid the dangers of such a gathering. It is easy to claim that Hegel's lack of interest and participation in the great patriotic festivities had serious consequences of its own, but it cannot be said that Hegel underestimated the power soon ruthlessly brought to bear on the democratic-constitutionalist movement by the legitimist state authorities. Hegel felt he had good reason to distrust the participation of the student fraternities in a festival to mark the 400th anniversary of the German Reformation and the idea of attending the festival himself went against all his instincts. The fact that Fries, the old antagonist from Jena who had so harshly criticized his *Science of Logic* on the basis of his own 'anthropological' logic, was himself one of the invited patriotic speakers at the Wartburg could only give him further satisfaction and amply confirm his original judgement of the man.

Two years after the great victory of Waterloo, the widely discussed question of who would or would not officially participate in the Wartburg Festival, itself reflected the beginning of a new stage in the post-Napoleonic political situation. The governing powers no longer seemed willing to share the fruits of victory with the people as they had once promised to do. In the eyes of the authorities the Wartburg Festival was the sign of unwanted things to come, shortly to be followed by the assassination of the playwright Kotzebue at the hands of the student Sand in Mannheim. The ruling powers responded to these threats by joining with Austria and Russia in the so-called 'Holy Alliance', which was itself largely the work of Tsar Alexander I and the Austrian statesman Prince Metternich. The members of the alliance regarded it as the natural response and a necessary reaction to the powerful challenge of dissension and disorder which they saw all around them.

In this context must we then call Hegel himself the philosopher of 'reaction', of the age of restoration that was already on the threshold, of autocratic state intervention? These were all things which Hegel in Heidelberg had sensed in advance and to which the 'absolutism' critically noted by Sulpiz Boisserée would seem peculiarly appropriate. It certainly looks rather like this in the Heidelberg summer of 1817. For the Tübingen student of revolutionary sympathies who had once gone out with his friends to plant 'freedom trees' seemed to have successfully shed his skin on the way to becoming a political legitimist and advocate of monarchy, admittedly with a number of intermediate anti-feudal and constitutional qualifications of one kind or another.

21

Feudalism or Monarchy?

Hegel's essay on *The States Assembly of the State of Württemberg in 1815 and 1816* was largely written in Nuremberg but only appeared during the first year of Hegel's university teaching in the *Heidelberg Yearbooks for Literature* in 1817. It is a brilliant piece of writing from the stylistic point of view, something that one rarely enough encounters in Hegel's authorship.

The most remarkable thing about the piece, essentially concerned with the question of the constitution in the monarchy of Württemberg, is that he seems now to be defending the very reverse of the position which he originally articulated in his 1798 essay *On the Recent Internal Situation in the State of Württemberg*. There he had spoken of elected representatives of the people. Hegel considers the 'constitution' the King of Württemberg is willing to give his subjects to be of no great significance in itself. For the old 'Empire' which had since disintegrated also had its 'constitutions' alongside its 'imperial assemblies'. As Hegel writes:

> The political nullity to which the German people has been reduced by its constitution, and the incapacity of the numerous smaller totalities, the greater part of the Imperial Estates, to forge a decision or will of their own, inevitably produced a spirit which was quite submerged in the sphere of its own private interests, a spirit of indifference and even enmity towards the thought of national honour and the idea of sacrificing something for the latter.'

This is a decidedly unfavourable judgement of what might be expected of a 'constitution' that was so urgently desired and which the former King of Württemberg had been willing to grant. The question remains: do those to whom the new constitution has now been offered really want it? Since the new constitution was designed for the 'subjects' of the state the nobility objects because it does not consider itself to belong in that category, the Counts of the House of Limburg appeal to ancient documents proving that they do not belong to Württemberg in the first place, while the Protestant prelates come forth with special petitions of their own. In the end the Estates Assembly ends up rejecting the constitution which has been offered by the King. They thereby challenge, as it were, their own right of assembly, although they here make use of that right precisely to reject the constitution. This was nothing unusual in Hegel's eyes and he ascribes such behaviour to the traditional 'querelles allemandes' which had regularly contributed to the political helplessness of the old 'Empire'.

Why do the Estates Assembly now reject the new constitution? Simply because it is not the ancient one. What they want returned to them is 'the good old law', the familiar Württemberg constitution of old. They hesitate to move forward because the old moribund mentality is unable to rouse itself to new life. Württemberg has slept throughout while the other German countries were transforming themselves from imperial fiefdoms into sovereign communities, i.e. independent states. As for the old constitution itself, Hegel considered it remote from the 'people' it was supposed to serve and a prey to lawyers by virtue of its own complexity.

Hegel was well aware that the Estates Assembly was an ancient institution in Württemberg. But he is not slow to point out that when the Estates Assembly was at its strongest, the state was at its weakest. And the reason for this situation lay in the fact that the Estates Assembly controlled the finances of the country. It was only a small step from that to maintaining one's own troops and forming alliances with foreign powers as one saw fit. And control of finances here meant: 'employment of the country's money for personal matters' or 'private plunder' in short. The situation offered a natural opportunity to decree various kinds of special payments for oneself, to offer rewards and enticements to one's own supporters and executives of the treasury for real or imagined services of one kind or another.

These objections which Hegel raised against the Estates Assembly had some substance. Hegel draws express attention to the extraordinary tendency of the Estates Assembly to confiscate land and property for the purpose of subsequent private enrichment. The 'old law', the 'old constitution' – these are all so many hollow-sounding words which in all good conscience could equally be used to justify traditional practices like human sacrifice, slavery, and feudal despotism in general. They say as little as the often-invoked 'will of the people'. 'When the Swabians possess free will, nothing whatsoever happens.' The incapacity to decide anything appears characteristic of 'the people'.

Hegel had here delivered a crushing blow to all the factions of post-Napoleonic Germany which had been striving to establish a 'constitution', and what is more had done so with an extraordinary display of personal passion. Although in one sense the essay concerned a regional issue, nevertheless its execution also embodied Hegel's own principles with regard to historical development in general: fundamental principles of a universal politics in which feudalism represented 'violence', 'caprice' and 'despotism', while 'monarchy' on the other hand played the historical role of bringing all oppressive feudal institutions to an end, something which had already been accomplished in countries like England and France but had yet to occur amongst the German states. At this stage of historical development 'monarchy' for Hegel essentially signified an element of political progress. It was not to be disturbed in this task by other forms of self-proclaimed progress which only flatter the contemporary age while simultaneously appealing loudly to supposedly ancient freedoms.

Hegel had presented a drastic picture of the past history of the Württemberg Estates Assembly with all its failures and misdemeanours. If these were the social forces with which monarchs after 1815 would have to share power, then Hegel felt that he had to issue an urgent warning. If Hegel's analysis was valid for Württemberg, however sharply it contested the views of the constitutionalists, it clearly harboured a more far-reaching political perspective which suggested a strong future career as a philosophical servant of the Crown. The author of the essay on *The Estates Assembly of Württemberg* had publicly revealed himself admirably fitted for such a role. Hegel regarded his position as professor of philosophy at this time, we now know, merely as a transitional stage on the way to other and potentially higher things.

At present the professorial chair in Berlin vacated after Fichte's death was still unavailable. None the less the Prussian authorities had already cast an interested eye upon the logician and metaphysician then employed in the service of the Bavarian government. With his essay on *The Estates Assembly of Württemberg* Hegel had shown himself a defender of legitimist monarchism who could hardly fail to appeal to the government in Berlin. And the Prussia now entering upon a period of Restoration was undoubtedly looking for an appropriate philosopher.

22

From Baden to Prussia

In Berlin it had not been forgotten that Heidelberg had only just succeeded in appointing Hegel to his position by closely anticipating the Prussian capital itself. Hegel would certainly have preferred to move from Nuremberg to Berlin if the Prussian offer had arrived first. The Prussian minister Freiherr von Stein zum Altenstein had not forgotten these events. As head of the new Prussian Ministry for Education and the Arts, recently created by order of King Friedrich Wilhelm III, one of Altenstein's first acts in government was to write personally to Hegel on 26 December 1817. Altenstein wanted to encourage Hegel to accept the imminent offer of a chair in Berlin which the minister was already planning. The minister suggested a salary of 2,000 Prussian thalers, which when converted to gulden represented almost double the sum Hegel was currently receiving in Heidelberg. Moreover Altenstein was offering Hegel a much broader sphere of potential influence in a city which was rapidly becoming a significant European metropolis – in Prussia of all places, with its exemplary administration in matters military, political and cultural alike, the same country which had joined forces with the old hegemonic powers of Russia and Austria in order to defeat Napoleon. The new University of Berlin, as established by Wilhelm von Humboldt, by virtue of its official statutes, its model organization and its guarantee of academic freedom, and its impressive circle of teaching staff, had become the leading centre of learning on the soil of the vanished Empire. In this context a call to Berlin certainly represented a singular honour for anyone.

Hegel asked for four weeks in which to consider the offer before officially accepting the position on 24 January 1818. The minister had been quite prepared to grant everything that Hegel had asked for (apart from the offer of free accommodation, something that was only granted to professors in certain select institutions). Given the 'exorbitant cost of rented accommodation' in Berlin, Hegel also requested part-payment in terms of natural produce, something that was still common in Baden and Württemberg at the time. The Prussian ministry overcame any final problems or reservations on Hegel's part by agreeing to start paying his salary immediately, even before he had made any financial arrangements for moving and travelling.

Hegel actually left Nuremberg for Berlin with his wife and family in the middle of September. The precise information about his current property and financial situation, which Hegel was officially required to submit to Berlin, revealed his extremely modest circumstances at the time. His 'effects' which were granted excise-free admittance to Prussia amounted to one barrel full of bedding and household goods, two crates of books, and a single case of clothing. Hegel expected to arrive in Berlin on 29 September, where Minister Altenstein's sister had already rented an appropriate apartment for the family. There is no doubt Hegel was in a hurry to arrive in the Prussian capital, but he was also constantly anxious throughout the trip lest his luggage be opened in his absence and then charged with extra border tariffs.

It must have been particularly gratifying to Hegel to pass *en route* through Jena, the place that had caused him so many terrible problems in the past and which he had been forced to leave so ignominiously because of both external and extremely personal circumstances. At least he did not have to encounter the mother of his son Ludwig since she had died some time before. He was of course delighted to see his old friend Fromman. The day before this Hegel and his wife had taken the opportunity of visiting and lunching with Goethe in nearby Weimar. Given his recent account of refraction in the *Encyclopaedia* Hegel could certainly be sure of a warm reception. Goethe writes in his diary that he would indeed have liked longer to discuss matters of mutual interest with his guest. The Hegel the poet encountered now was much changed and had lost much of that cramped and heavy quality that Goethe had once associated with him. From amongst Goethe's own circle, Knebel expressly remarked that Hegel had acquired a new 'freedom in his social manner'. Hegel certainly knew how to entertain his Weimar hosts and left a very favourable impression upon them. Hegel finally reached the Prussian capital after travelling on through Weissenfels, Leipzig and Wittenberg.

In the eyes of the general public Hegel's arrival was very far from representing the grand triumphal entry of a great philosopher into his new domain of intellectual influence. He confided in his first letter from Berlin to his friend Niethammer in Munich that he felt a chill wind blowing at first. Hegel and his friends alike must already have wondered before his departure from Heidelberg just how his new colleagues at the university in Berlin would respond to him.

Other members of Humboldt's generation who were then active in the university included the jurist Savigny, and the theologians de Wette, Marheineke and above all Schleiermacher. Schleiermacher represented a rather sensitive point. How would the relationship with Hegel actually develop and work out in practice? Schleiermacher was widely regarded as the most important Protestant theologian since Luther himself. He was a Christian and a Platonist at the same time, a man who had expressly attempted to reconcile Christianity with the contemporary age. As a preacher with his impeccable German Schleiermacher exercised considerable influence in the best society circles, and he was well acquainted with the latest literary movements of the time without exhibiting any of the usual Christian vices of prudery or hypocrisy in this respect. He combined a refined philosophical sophistication with worldly cultivation, and above all with a genuine patriotic sensibility. As an orator during the Napoleonic Wars he had demonstrated himself to be as effective as Fichte in respect of his patriotism. He felt himself naturally allied with the forces of contemporary youth and was gifted with an almost irresistible sense of paedagogic fervour. If Hegel believed that the authentic religion of Protestantism found its essential expression in the realm of culture generally, then Schleiermacher was the perfect living example of this ideal. Schleiermacher combined in himself the kind of gifts and virtues which the ever laborious Hegel, always struggling to find the right expression for his ideas, could never hope to emulate. And then there was the marked difference in their political backgrounds as well, given Hegel's past enthusiasm for the revolutionary and Napoleonic cause. The rhetorical elegance of the Prussian royal preacher contrasted sharply with the awkward manner and ponderous delivery of Hegel.

But Hegel had hardly been called to Berlin solely on his own account. With the casual worldly insight of the courtier Goethe had already noticed what was going on here. On hearing of Hegel's call to Berlin Goethe expressed his suspicions to Sulpiz Boisserée on 1 May 1818: 'Minister Altenstein would seem to want to provide himself with a learned bodyguard.' Hence the minister's efforts on behalf of the author of the *Science of Logic*, all the express manifestations of his particular favour, and especially the manner in which he earned Hegel's personal loyalty by suggesting his own sister as a conscientious adviser to Hegel's wife in all things.

There was nothing intrinsically unworthy about all this as far as Hegel was concerned. Altenstein was not a radical reorganizer, as Humboldt and Süvern had been, but he was still a firm supporter of moderate reform. There is no reason to identify his position straightforwardly with the emerging forces of 'reaction'. Any doubts in this regard could quickly be allayed by looking by contrast at Austria or the Kingdom of Bavaria that had already drawn so much scorn from Hegel in the past. If there was *one* single state in the Europe of 1818 which could plausibly claim to represent both the conscious idea and actuality of real progress in the field of administration, military organization or cultural life in general it was certainly Prussia. The state had risen like the legendary phoenix from the ashes of the Napoleonic Wars to establish its pre-eminent position on the political scene. The southerner Hegel was forced to reconsider some of his old-fashioned attitudes when he entered Prussian service. And with Hegel called to the new university

Altenstein thought he could hold his own against the King. In his essay on the Estates Assembly Hegel had revealed himself as an apparent friend of non-constitutional monarchy, and this was just the kind of person urgently required in the University in Berlin after the king had rescinded his pledge to offer the country an independent constitution. Hegel could be counted upon both vigorously and forcefully to oppose the contemporary currents of west European liberalism and to depict the Catholic faith as a religion of obscurantism in comparison with the Protestantism of the Prussian ruling house.

On 22 October 1818 Hegel opened his inaugural address as newly appointed professor in Berlin with the same words he had used in an analogous situation two years previously before the assembled students in Heidelberg. The professor hereby 'honoured with this position as a teacher of philosophy through the grace of His Majesty the King' appeals to the nation to embrace the cause of philosophy as its own. In recent times philosophy has merely borne the name of 'science' in other countries, so Hegel tells his audience, while in effect the subject itself has largely wilted and vanished. Philosophy has therefore 'taken flight to the Germans and now properly survives only amongst them'. And it is they who are now 'called upon to preserve this sacred flame'. The new aspect of Hegel's address was to emphasize the crucial role which Prussia was playing in post-Napoleonic Germany and to stress the absolute centrality of philosophy in particular within this state. For here 'alongside the actual political world the free realm of independent thought would also come to flourish'.

In spite of Hegel's exalted words on this occasion, immediate academic success still eluded the new professor. Solger, a younger colleague of Hegel's who had supported his nomination amongst the Berlin faculty, noted Hegel's initial failure to attract many students to his courses. In the winter semester of 1818 Hegel lectured five times a week between the hours of 4 and 5 (on 'Natural Law') and between 5 and 6 (on his *Encyclopaedia*). In the following summer semester he started to lecture on logic and the history of philosophy. In his letter to Niethammer on 26 March 1819 Hegel himself admits that he is still 'at the periphery or even beyond it' as far as his teaching activities are concerned and consequently is not currently in much of a position to further Niethammer's own hopes of getting to Berlin himself. At this time Hegel's only strong personal connection amongst his professional colleagues was with the young theologian Philipp Marheineke, who was already attempting to bring the Hegelian philosophy into suitable concordance with Protestant dogmatics.

But there was now another possible source of anxiety for Hegel, on top of those he had already brought with him from Heidelberg, when he suddenly found himself caught up in the Prussian government's attempts to discourage the activities of the lively student fraternities. The authorities in Berlin had become particularly defensive after the assassination of the German playwright Kotzebue who was a counsellor for the Russian government and was widely regarded as little but an agent of the Tsar. The new attempts to regulate political activity were directed above all at the young student groups from which the idealist extremist and assassin Sand himself had emerged. In the course of the many measures taken against any potentially suspicious elements, and particularly the student fraternities as the alleged source of such plots, the police arrested a student by the name of Asverus at his lodgings and took him into armed custody. Asverus was one of the students who attended Hegel's lectures, although at this time he does not seem to have felt particularly close to Hegel philosophically speaking. His father, an important judicial officer who had once assisted Hegel in some legal matters in Jena, now turned to the philosopher for help when his son was sentenced to a term of imprisonment for his alleged political activities. Hegel responded immediately and issued a written testimonial in favour of the incriminated student, confirming that the latter had long since 'renounced' membership in the said student fraternity and certainly posed no further threat whatsoever to the government. But as matters turned out, Hegel's assurances in this respect were somewhat premature. For during his incarceration Asverus had written letters which were intercepted and interpreted as an expression of open sympathy for Sand and his actions. Hegel now found himself in a rather awkward situation. He had offered 500 thalers from his own pocket as bail for the student, something which itself played a role during the long-drawn out proceedings, and he genuinely regarded Asverus simply as a formerly misguided and now repentant young man. Hegel now ran the risk of appearing in the eyes of the criminal authorities and even the ministry as a sympathizer with the very 'enthusiasm for liberty' which in fact he regarded as thoroughly misguided and remote from political reality.

The case of Asverus, which was finally only legally closed in 1826 through a ministerial order without officially clearing the defendant of suspicions of treason against the state, was what reluctantly brought Hegel into direct contact with the so-called demagogues and their movement for the first time. In the second such case, involving the student Carové, Hegel had also unwittingly played a significant role. Carové had been a student of Hegel's in Heidelberg and one who felt close enough to the philosopher to address him in correspondence as 'Friend'. But Carové was not merely a Hegelian, he was also definitely a member of one of the offending student fraternities. As a Catholic Rheinlander Carové belonged not to the extreme radical patriotic wing associated with Giessen but to the more moderate wing which unlike the other was quite prepared to admit foreigners and Jews into its ranks. As a leader in one of the fraternities Carové had only recently made any political impression or exerted any influence on the movement. When he came to Berlin Carové already imagined that his career as a political activist was largely behind him and he had recently been attempting to find a teaching position as a *Repetent*. Hegel had proposed him in this regard although the university Senate rejected his application. The cautious Altenstein instituted further enquiries into the matter and was alerted to a speech which the candidate had made at the Wartburg Festival, allegedly defending Sand's reasons for murdering Kotzebue. With that the case was decided immediately. All further attempts to support or justify the candidate, including Hegel's testimony, were now hopelessly dashed. The authorities came away from the affair convinced at least that Carové was not the sort of individual who should be employed giving academic lectures in Prussia.

The list of cases similar to those of Asverus and Carové was soon extended with the names of Förster, von Henning, Gans and many others. From the perspective of the conservative factions of the administration all these individuals appeared, for a variety of reasons, to be less than reliable subjects, even if they could not exactly be regarded as an immediate danger to the state. The government did not know what to expect of such people in future and was determined to keep a careful eye on their activities.

And what of Hegel in all this? He was certainly opposed in all conscience to the intrigues of the demagogues and the student fraternities, and all such similar organizations, and constantly warned against their dangers. And yet he now found himself advising and assisting members of the persecuted party as he had before in Heidelberg. But there was nothing cynical about Hegel's ambivalent role in the matter. For Hegel not only defended them as best he could, he also did everything possible to encourage such young men to enter the service of state and its institutions where they could exert a positive influence on society.

But there was never any doubt about Hegel's loyalty to the state itself. He explicitly took every opportunity to express as much. As he wrote in a copy of his *Philosophy of Right* personally dedicated to Prussian Chancellor von Hardenberg on 10 October 1820, Hegel desired above all

> to demonstrate the harmony of philosophy with those principles which are generally required by the nature of the state, but most immediately with the principle which the Prussian state – belonging to which is a source of the greatest satisfaction to me – has had the good fortune of having upheld and continuing to uphold under the enlightened government of His Majesty the King and the sagacious leadership of Your Highness.

One can certainly object to the style of such things, but the cumbrous syntax in no way invalidates the sincerity of Hegel's supportive and respectful attitude to the Chancellor. These words would naturally have revolted Fries who had since become the leading spokesman of the Jena student fraternities, the most extreme patriotic wing of the 'freedom-loving Germans', and had recently lost his teaching post as a result. In a letter to a like-minded student leader called Ludwig Rödiger on 6 January 1821 Fries commented that 'Hegel's metaphysical mushrooms have grown not in the gardens of knowledge and learning but upon the dung-heap of sycophancy. Until the end of 1813 his metaphysics had given succour to the French, then it became royalist in the best Württemberg manner, and is now kissing the riding-whip of Herr von Kamptz [Head of the Berlin Police]'. The external impression of Hegel's frequent changes of political course and all the signs of a loyal and devoted defender of the authorities generally might seem to justify some of this harsh judgement. But Fries's catalogue of Hegel's political commitments was still incomplete. The student Friedrich Förster, who belonged amongst Hegel's closest circle, noted down one interesting incident from this period in his personal diary. In July 1820 Hegel undertook a short trip to Dresden, the principal purpose of which was to see Raphael's Sixtine Madonna in the art gallery there. Amongst a small circle of friends one evening in the tavern The Blue Star Hegel refused a glass of the best Meissner wine that had been offered him and ordered a number of bottles of champagne instead. Hegel did the honours and then encouraged them all to raise their glasses 'in memory of this very day'. Outside of Prussia itself he was toasting the anniversary of 14 July 1789 and the storming of the Bastille.

If Hegel himself had become on occasion the object of secret police investigations, something he thought he could easily counter through his public activities and academic teaching, he could not fail to recognize evidence of irritating and persistent opposition to his influence within the university. He had only gradually, and even then only incompletely, emancipated himself from his original sense of intellectual isolation in general. In part, of course, this was due to the almost impenetrable wall of obscurity with which he surrounded himself, and which could only be breached to some extent after the most sustained and stubborn efforts of study. But it was also due to the presence of Schleiermacher whose constant opponent he was destined to remain for a long time, not least through Altenstein's express designs. Schleiermacher defended a theology of 'noble simplicity and quiet grandeur', to borrow Winckelmann's expression, and very much in the manner of Schinkel's classicism, something which only recommended him all the more to the important circles of Berlin society. He attempted to respond to the disturbing depths of the human heart by an appeal to dialectics. In this he resembled Hegel, but his immediate model for dialectical thinking was derived from the Platonic dialogue. He was animated by the hope of eventually attaining a reliable harmony of opinion through a process of mutual discussion, one which was equally compatible with the faith in the crucified and resurrected Son of God.

In this context conflict between the two of them was inevitable. Schleiermacher had originally been amongst the supporters of Hegel's nomination for a professorship in Berlin and had regretted the fact that Heidelberg had secured his loyalty first. In contrast to Hegel's own earlier opinion of him, he had expressed a certain incomprehension with regard to Hegel rather than animosity, and he can surely hardly be blamed for that. But when Hegel went to Berlin to encounter Schleiermacher for the first time in person he already appeared in Daub's eyes as a 'cuirassier armed to the teeth cutting his way through the battle with his sabre'. Schleiermacher on the other hand resembled 'an agile lancer skilfully managing his slender little horse'. This image which Rosenkranz passed on to us seems a particularly well-chosen one.

Hegel's attitude to Schleiermacher had never really been positive. To some extent he was already an object of criticism in Hegel's early theological writings. Without knowing Hegel's writings at the time Schleiermacher had repudiated 'speculative philosophy' in the first speech he delivered before the Prussian Academy of Sciences on 29 January 1811. As a theologian he could not seriously regard it as a form of systematic or scientific knowledge at all. The major living exponent of speculative philosophy as a science must already have felt personally slighted in his endeavours. If Schleiermacher had indeed supported Hegel's call to Berlin, this was only because Hegel appeared the lesser evil compared with Fries. The whole procedure was essentially a formal one and it was more or less Schleiermacher's duty as Rector of the university to second Hegel for the position which Altenstein had long since destined for him. But as the threat of Hegel's speculative philosophy began to approach, and Schleiermacher felt largely powerless to prevent it, the sophisticated Christian thinker and subtle tactician took certain steps to weaken its influence. He suggested dissolving the Philosophical Section at the Academy. He knew where Hegel would soon be directing his critical attention. But here Schleiermacher inevitably encountered the resistance of Altenstein who opposed Schleiermacher's scepticism concerning the ultimately scientific character of philosophy with the conclusive argument that Leibniz himself had been the original president of the Academy of Sciences.

If Schleiermacher was unsuccessful in decisively eliminating this possible power base for the philosopher, he now set about ensuring that if the Philosophical Section were to continue, then at least Hegel would be kept out of it. And after some subtle diplomatic manoeuvres Schleiermacher was successful in his efforts. Schleiermacher had correctly anticipated that there would never be any real chance of agreement between Hegel and himself. And indeed the basic opposition between the two men soon surfaced in a very personal way as a result of the measures which the Prussian government felt forced to take after the Sand affair.

In the philosophical field Schleiermacher as defender of morality was also one of the first to object to Hegel's attempt to 'demote' the status of religion in general, if not actually of Christianity. He had every reason to oppose his own theological perspective to that of Hegel. In the Preface to the essay *Religion in its Inner Relation to Science*, a piece written by Hegel's pupil Hinrichs, the philosopher himself had tilted at Schleiermacher's now celebrated definition of religion as 'the feeling of absolute dependency'. Hegel remarked that this would make 'a dog into the best Christian of all' since it surely revealed 'this feeling in its strongest form'. That was a savage blow which effectively seemed to accuse Schleiermacher of a literally 'bestial ignorance of God', as he put it himself in a letter to K. H. Sack on 28 December 1822. Hegel was equally unimpressed by the appearance of Schleiermacher's *Dogmatics*, comparing it to a very large money bag which on being opened revealed nothing but a pile of tiny IOUs.

During the years in Berlin Hegel's relationship to Goethe in Weimar continued largely unaffected. In his eyes Goethe represented a powerful reinforcement of his own views without whom his philosophy would not have assumed the form it did. Although essentially unphilosophical in the technical sense, Goethe did in fact like to keep himself generally informed about the latest developments in philosophy, and particularly Hegel's philosophy. He presented himself as a curious student who was willing to receive peripatetic instruction in such matters. Thus Hegel's student Henning used to visit him in Weimar and report in some detail about Hegel and the general situation in Berlin. The Court at Weimar did not involve itself in the persecution of the student fraternities and thanks to Goethe himself the Dukedom was run in a highly constitutional manner. Weimar even served, alongside Jena and Wartburg, as something of a refuge for such people. Goethe regarded himself as a 'pagan' and, in contrast to Schleiermacher, rather presented the living image of a 'Greek' soul who disdained the typical Christian denial of 'nature'. This is also how Hegel regarded Goethe as the author of *Faust* and as a natural scientist. He was well aware that the poet had full confidence in him by virtue of their shared views on the theory of colour. Hegel once described Goethe in the poet's own words as a 'primal phenomenon' and 'demonic nature'. Goethe thanked him accordingly and responded from Weimar in the summer of 1821 with a memorable dedication of his own: 'The primal phenomenon happily commends itself to a friendly reception on the part of the absolute.'

Goethe and Hegel, the primal phenomenon and the absolute respectively: they could certainly feel some solidarity with one another in virtue of their related views of nature. The yellow-tinted wine glass which Goethe sent Hegel as a gift was intended to reveal the colours produced by the refraction of light and thus visibly to confirm the correctness of the poet's theory of colours. In his reply of thanks Hegel suggested that the wine that would fill the glass likewise be regarded as a sign that 'spirit dwells in nature' too.

This was something more than a merely theoretical agreement about fundamental attitudes to 'nature' that lay close to the hearts of both men. If we remember Goethe's former bond with Schiller, it looks as though he later formed another such bond with Hegel as well, something which would also have enormous consequences for Hegel's own thought in the future.

23

The Prussian State Philosopher?

After a couple of years Hegel's position at the University of Berlin had begun to be firmly established at last. But his position was certainly not an uncontested one and remained a controversial issue among his university colleagues. It was quite impossible to deny the growing appeal of his lectures amongst the students and the emergence of an opposed party only served of course to increase Hegel's profile and influence generally. Independently of what people knew about Hegel in particular, it began to seem an attractive idea in Germany to go and attend some of his celebrated lectures in Berlin. Apart from his growing reputation and general usefulness to the state, Hegel's most important source of strength was the unstinting support he continued to receive from Minister Altenstein. And then there was also Hegel's warm personal relationship with another authorized representative of the Prussian government, Johannes Schulze, who was both pupil and friend of Hegel. After listening to Hegel's lectures, Schulze would often accompany Hegel on walks where the philosophical issues that had been raised in the class would be discussed at further length.

Hegel's friendship with a man like Schulze, employed as he was in the Ministry of Education and therefore capable of officially exercising at least some political influence in the affairs of the university, was not exactly an encouraging sign in the eyes of many other members of the university. Schleiermacher soon felt he could detect new evidence of Hegel's influence. But Hegel's principal antagonist, or at least the one with the highest academic standing, was the noted historian of law, Friedrich Carl von Savigny. He still represented the original founding idea of the university as this had been articulated by Humboldt and Süvern. He regarded Altenstein with suspicion and feared that he was encouraging the turn to a more and more centralized cultural policy on the part of the Prussian government. The government seemed about to reclaim something of the power and influence it had earlier freely relinquished, and Hegel appeared at the side of the less than popular Schulze as the very embodiment of the new system.

Minister Altenstein for his part had good reason to be content with his trusted philosopher. Yet Hegel constantly had to confront further problems and complications on the professional as well as on the domestic front. The opposition to Hegel was naturally at its strongest where he lacked outright supporters or any potential backing from the ministry, and that meant in the Berlin Academy of Sciences. At home Hegel was anxiously preoccupied by an extended illness his wife had contracted. The cost of living proved much higher than he had originally anticipated and he was paying a lot for the education of his children. His sister back in Württemberg also constantly required some financial support. Hegel found himself carefully entering every item of expense into his household accounts book in his own hand.

On 6 July 1822 Hegel finally decided to reveal his somewhat precarious financial position to the minister and tactfully to remind him of the good service he had already given. And in fact it was true that his general financial state had not essentially improved in comparison with his time in Bamberg. Hegel pointed out in his letter to the minister that in Berlin he had suffered 'a number of unfortunate domestic difficulties'. Hegel now felt he had to secure a widow's pension for his wife and this required a yearly contribution of 170 thalers on his part if the family were to receive 300 thalers a year on his death. Altenstein responded on 25 July in an attempt to calm Hegel's worries about the future. He apologized for not having procured Hegel an official increase in salary by explaining the delicate nature of such decisions, but said he was in a position to offer Hegel further renumeration of '300 thalers not merely for last year, but for this year as well'. The 600 thalers thus relieved Hegel of his most pressing financial worries and on 3 July 1825 he expressly thanked the minister for his encouraging show of support for a man in his 'difficult profession'. He also discreetly but explicitly assured Altenstein that any

> troubling concerns which the highest government authorities might entertain concerning philosophy, and the manner in which certain misguided opinions can easily be provoked through study of the same, have been quite unrelated to my own official activity as a teacher; on the contrary I have not been without some recognition or success in attempting to instil proper concepts in the students here and to render myself worthy of the trust which Your Excellency and the Royal Government have seen fit to bestow upon me.

Hegel himself explicitly reminds the government here that he has defended the state from the embarrassment which philosophy could have caused it. He had brought the students back on the right path, protected them from possible errors, and thereby done his best to strengthen the monarchical system. The Prussian state philosopher almost inevitably appears here in the role of a philosopher king. Schopenhauer, who certainly saw Hegel as the classic representative of a philosophy essentially nourished on the accomplishments of the ruling political class, would surely have been quite delighted to read the correspondence between 'faculty philosopher' Hegel and the influential minister of state. It could only have confirmed the suspicions he already had. But he was right and wrong at the same time. He failed to appreciate, perhaps as much as the minister himself, the profoundly ambivalent character of Hegel's thought, the oracular obscurity of his language which was capable of implying the opposite of what it appeared to say. In this respect it was post-Hegelian philosophy, which was in part no longer Hegelian or no longer wished to be Hegelian, which effectively clarified this curious situation. In a sense the minister was certainly well advised to rely upon the philosopher of monarchical government in the name of the Prussian king and state, but in another sense he was deluded if he believed that the intrinsically unlimited power of philosophy could effectively be brought into permanent harmony with the ultimately limited means of state power.

When Hegel's philosophy began in the 1820s to be universally recognized as a prevailing intellectual influence in Berlin, it was inevitable that amongst the older generation of the Fichte era Hegel would eventually find himself compared with the latter. Hegel had already been honoured simply by being called to take up Fichte's former chair in the Prussian capital. He had thereby scored an advantage over his rival Schelling, who might well have seemed to enjoy much greater seniority as an original 'follower of Fichte' than Hegel himself. Without Fichte the whole development of the 'new' post-Kantian philosophy would have been inconceivable. And for all the criticisms they made of Fichte themselves, his central role in the intellectual biography of both philosophers is impossible to deny.

Fichte had after all been called to Berlin – clear evidence of an enlightened cultural policy – even though he had once lost his academic position in Jena, and not entirely without Goethe's involvement, through the so-called 'atheism controversy' of the time. One could even say that the Prussian government had called a noted 'atheist' to occupy the chair of philosophy. If Hegel now prided himself in some respects on being an appropriate successor to Fichte, this alone was sufficient to raise doubts in some quarters about the old spirit of Berlin philosophy now apparently clad in Hegelian dress. As the most prominent and penetrating member of the anti-Hegelian party at the university Savigny had a clear eye for the influence the philosopher was now wielding in Berlin. In a letter to Georg Friedrich Creuzer on 6 April 1822 Savigny wrote that 'his enthusiastic students are abandoning any relationship to religion and in this respect Hegel has even gone beyond Fichte'. The Prussian state philosopher thus appeared to some as another intensified form of Fichte, similarly intent upon further undermining the existing religious institutions of the time. That was one possible view of the matter. On the other hand the Munich theosophist Franz von Baader, who had fundamentally undertaken to oppose any and every form of contemporary 'atheistic thinking', could not see Hegel as anything but 'a castrated Fichte', as he wrote to Schelling on 28 August 1821. What was the reason for such different views of Hegel? One answer to this question was provided by Hegel's pupil Michelet who interpreted the Hegelian philosophy as an ambivalent balancing act between pantheism and monotheism, between idealism and materialism. The single body of Hegel's thought as it were incorporated various members which could be independently adopted to express different views of the world as a whole. This only seems to confirm Savigny's opinion that Hegel lacked Fichte's activist zeal and that his philosophy effectively neutralized the internally conflicting forces it absorbed. Savigny wrote to Creuzer on 6 February 1821 that 'Fichte harboured and revealed no less presumption than Hegel, but there was none the less a fresher and more vital spirit alive in the man and his work'.

This remark was doubtless the product of long and careful observation of the university scene in Berlin, which had undergone an enormous change since Hegel's arrival. Hegel's dominance had now become so great, Savigny claims in a letter to the Marburg Lutheran theologian Christoph Andreas Leonhard Creuzer on 16 December 1822, 'that even the most vigorous teachers of philosophy cannot find employment if they do not belong to Hegel's school'. Savigny was particularly anxious about the 'contempt for Christianity' which seemed to emanate from Hegel and his circle, and which Schleiermacher had already claimed to have witnessed as well. Above all, Hegel seemed to neglect the national-patriotic dimension in comparison with Fichte. Savigny wrote explicitly in this vein to Christoph Creuzer on 26 November 1821, suggesting that this was surely the reason why Hegel was so 'enthusiastically venerated' amongst the many foreigners studying in Berlin (and especially amongst 'the Poles who can neither speak German nor properly understand anything'). This is clear enough evidence that Hegel and his philosophy were on the advance at this time despite all the opposition mounted by some of his academic colleagues. The days in which some of his immediate students could be persecuted and incarcerated on account of harbouring suspected sentiments against the state belonged to the past.

Thus the beginning of the 1820s saw Hegel's philosophy increasingly establishing itself in Prussia as something like the official philosophy of state, with a monopoly on influence essentially guaranteed by the continued favour and support of the government. And this process only consolidated itself further with the passing years. Hegel's students were preparing to assume official posts or indeed already occupying them in significant numbers. In the winter semester of 1823 the young Ludwig Feuerbach came to Berlin to pursue his academic studies. He had originally trained as a theologian and had already been introduced to Hegel's thought at Heidelberg by Hegel's old friend Daub. None the less, Feuerbach was not particularly disposed to adopt a Hegelian style of thought straight away. In his eyes it was essentially Schleiermacher, the recognized leader of the Berlin theologians, who best represented the 'essence of religion' at this time. Feuerbach experienced both Schleiermacher and Hegel as classical exponents of theological and philosophical thought in their heyday at Berlin. Similarly Hegel's future biographer Karl Rosenkranz deliberately attended the lectures of both men, comparing Schleiermacher's smooth and elegant delivery with the dragging paragraphs of Hegel's lectures, constantly interrupted as they were by the philosopher's coughing and regular snuff-taking.

If Hegel gave the impression of someone prematurely old, it must be said that he was never really young. His pupil Hotho sketched a vivid portrait of Hegel during the Berlin years: already hunched up in posture, 'his features hung pale and loosely upon him as if he was already dead'. His style of lecturing corresponded to this impression: 'He sat there morosely with his head wearily bowed down in front of him, constantly leafing back and forth, this way and that, through his compendious notes even as he was continuing to speak.' Yet this man who had always found it so difficult to express his thoughts aloud from the lectern was already well on the way to becoming the absolute and undisputed leader in his subject who would exercise an appeal far beyond the borders of his own country. In Hegel's thought philosophy came to conceive itself as a rounded totality. This philosophy was truly comprehensive and the man who propounded it so vigorously appeared to have penetrated the very secrets of God and the creation. He had openly claimed to have disclosed the inner secret of being itself. God as the founding source of Mosaic Law, the Christian incarnation, the Caesars and the Roman Empire, with its medieval continuation in the German concept of the Empire, Luther's purification of the Church, Prussia as the exemplary rational state, all of this was taken up and conceptually organized within Hegel's idea of the 'absolute'. And Hegel teaching in Berlin was now the sole authorized representative of this same all-encompassing absolute. The Judaeo-Christian God who had been successfully dissolved into the fundamental philosophical principle of Hegel's absolute was satirized by Schopenhauer as 'The Lord Absolute', which was also his name for Hegel himself. But the charge reflected the indisputable fact that Hegel had indeed disconcertingly identified philosophy and with theology. Barthold Georg Niebuhr, the diplomat and historian, wrote anxiously to his wife on 18 March 1825 that Hegel, according to the circle around Victor Cousin, had claimed that 'Christ himself actually knew very little concerning Christianity'.

As far as his external dress and behaviour were concerned Hegel at no time made any serious effort to adapt himself to the expectations of Berlin society. To one visitor from Stuttgart he appeared to be just another typical product of the Tübingen Stift. One had to wonder just how this man with his dark unkempt locks, and with that same careless style of dress that had been noted in Württemberg when he was still a student, could possibly come to 'impress the fastidious Berliners'. The visitor encountered a rather morose-looking character in a worn-out dressing gown, with jaundiced features and evident shortsightedness, and given to making rapid but awkward physical movements. In the course of their discussion they touched briefly on the recent political situation in Württemberg, whereupon Hegel expressed his considerable irritation at the thought that 'any ordinary person these days can aspire to become a minister', folded his hands and closed his eyes as if he were about to go to sleep. The same visitor also recounts his impression of Hegel's personal manservant who interrupted their conversation on another occasion: 'an ancient Franconian character, a withered and powdered old greybeard who looked even older than his master'.

According to his own testimony Hegel kept himself largely to himself in his academic activities at the university. He did not really take part in any social faction or circle, unless of course it was at Schleiermacher's expense, but he certainly enjoyed participating in regular whist parties amongst friends. Hegel never forgave the theologian, whom he occasionally dubbed 'Herr Schläuermacher' (i.e. Slymaker) amongst his students in class, from successfully obstructing his entrance into the highest intellectual circles, i.e. the Prussian Academy of Sciences.

Despite this significant blemish on his Berlin career, Hegel managed to enjoy an extended and very comfortable domestic life firmly rooted in his family. With time he also became more and more the academic teacher and less of a philosophical author. The lectures he regularly held between twelve and one o'clock belonged to the major Berlin events, along with the appearances of the actor Ludwig Devrient in the principal theatre, and the elegant and sincere sermons which Schleiermacher confidently delivered from the pulpit of the Church of the Holy Trinity. Hegel's lectures could command an audience of two hundred listeners, and he used to give special cards to other visitors travelling through so they could obtain a particularly good place to see and hear the ensuing performance. Hegel's audience included Prussian civil servants and government officials, diplomats, military officers, Muslim visitors and Catholic priests, foreigners and businessmen, not to mention numerous young men of the Polish nobility. It is more than doubtful whether many of them even remotely understood anything of the notes they were conscientiously taking down at Hegel's celebrated lectures. They would observe how the master would permit himself a pinch of snuff at the lectern and then begin to speak with few notes in his hand. He would often begin his sentences with 'Thus', one of his favourite words. The delivery itself was not particularly dramatic and his speech was strongly coloured by dialect. Opinions about the precise character and effectiveness of the lectures vary. Some spoke of a laboured and even intolerable delivery which only served to conceal its own excellent content, while others praised a deliberate clarity of presentation which avoided unnecessary dialectical subtleties or external effects and never simply sought to impress the listener. It would seem that everything here depended essentially on one's own attitude to Hegel's thought in the first place, so that some were simply irritated by the formal defects of

Hegel's manner, while others quickly perceived the conscientious serious-ness of Hegel's engagement with difficult issues which resisted easy formula-tions or facile solutions.

There are also other reasons for feelings of irritation, some of which have persisted to the present day. For in lecturing Hegel would often abandon the precise letter of his manuscript and extemporize freely on his theme. De-pending on circumstances he would sometimes incline to a very pointed for-mulation, or again sometimes to a weaker expression of his thought. Thus we must always remember that Hegel's listeners probably heard things which are not identical with the written manuscripts that are all we possess now. Thus on one occasion a number of Catholic students made an official com-plaint to the education ministry that Hegel had impugned the Catholic reli-gion in his lectures. This turned out to be true, but the remarks were made in the course of one of his improvisations during lectures and are not to be found in Hegel's manuscript. Hegel's student Hotho reports the incident in a letter to Cousin of 1 April 1826: Hegel 'had said that in the Catholic cer-emony [of the Eucharist] God is conceived as existing as a material thing, and that if therefore a mouse should consume this thing [the Host], then God would exist in the mouse and even in its excrement'. The offended stu-dents claimed Hegel had been guilty of blasphemy. In the response he was asked to make to the ministry in justification of his remarks Hegel appealed to Humboldt's principle of academic freedom and claimed that 'as a Protes-tant teacher and professor of philosophy he had the right to speak as he had in investigating the nature of Catholicism, and that Catholics who did not like to hear such things were under no obligation to attend his lectures'.

Hegel had long been convinced of the pressing need for a journal which could serve as an organ of his own ideas and as an exemplary periodical of philosophical 'science' in general. As an editor in Bamberg Hegel had al-ready entertained the idea, and had become particularly interested in the prospect by the time he went to Heidelberg. His growing and by now unpar-alleled influence in Berlin made it appear more urgent than ever in his eyes to take decisive action in this direction. Such a journal would also provide a useful sphere of activity for many of his students and Hegel set about finding suitable collaborators for the enterprise. Hegel's student Leo could assume the role of secretary. The first and most trusted student to be directly in-volved in the project was Eduard Gans, who undertook a special journey in order to sound out possible contributors and reviewers at other German universities. The reports he sent back to Hegel gave precise information about the course of his characteristically enthusiastic enquiries in the academic world. The first task was to establish suitable contact with the premier German publishing house of Cotta in Stuttgart. Cotta seems to have been convinced of the advantages of such a project more or less immediately. Delighted with his success Gans wrote to Hegel once the agreement had been signed and told him that there was also a possibility of combining their own proposed journal with a literary periodical which Cotta were planning to bring out in Munich. Gans could count on Hegel's support for the idea given that the philosopher had always wanted to elevate the German 'South' to the higher cultural and philosophical level of the German 'North'. When Niethammer heard of the plan, however, he advised against it, holding that it was far easier for a camel to pass through the eye of a needle than successfully to marry the spirit of Munich with that of Berlin. Hegel addressed an elaborate letter with all the considerable formality at his disposal to Goethe and Varnhagen von Ense, inviting them both to offer contributions of their own to the new journal. Goethe replied promptly, informing Hegel that he would like to see the first issues of the new Berlin publication and observe its general direction in order later to 'communicate something worthy as the circumstances may be'. But he also added a little later that there were already some suitable manuscripts to be published from Weimar if required. For Goethe had made enquiries amongst his friends about possible collaborators for Hegel's projected journal.

Goethe must have studied the first issue with great attention although, as he says himself, with certain misgivings. The emphasis on self-knowledge revealed too much evidence of the kind of self-torturing and self-destructive tendencies which now ran quite counter to his personality. Goethe must have appreciated very quickly the possible future moderating effect of Hegel's thought on the alienated mood of those romantics who all too easily despaired of the world. He recognized the dangers of such a mood, which he had once had to resist in himself and which had already taken hold of spirits like the poet Lenau (for whom Hegel's philosophy indeed represented for a while a single ray of hope in a dark period of his sad life). Goethe's unshakeable sympathy for Hegel allowed him here to close his eyes to certain currents of thought and feeling which he would otherwise have surely treated with severity. The letter which Goethe wrote to his friend in Berlin on 17 August 1827 expresses a spirit of friendly reconciliation without any concessions on his part to an alien point of view: 'I keep my mind as open as possible for the gifts to be obtained from philosophers, and I am delighted whenever I can truly appropriate what has been discovered along a road which nature has not apparently wished me to travel myself.'

In contrast to Kant Hegel had enjoyed the extraordinary opportunity of close social contact with a number of significant poets, quite apart from Goethe. As far as the true significance of Hölderlin was concerned Hegel was probably never very clear about just how he stood with him, and perhaps in the nature of the case never could have been. The young poet had certainly attached himself to Hegel in the early years and although he seems to have vanished from Hegel's consciousness later on, we cannot really imagine that to be the case. Hegel's contact with Schiller in the Jena years was characterized by a certain mutual aloofness and there was never much of a personal relationship between them. Jean Paul had proved stimulating company for

Hegel in Heidelberg, although the philosopher did later make some derogatory remarks about him. When in September 1806 the writer and playwright Franz Grillparzer visited Berlin, Hegel invited him into his home. Grillparzer explained his failure to visit Hegel any earlier by appealing to the philosophical backwardness of the Austrian territories where people 'had only just got as far as old Kant' and Hegel's system was still totally unknown. Hegel was rather amused to hear this, but his own reply revealed a certain knowledge on his part of Grillparzer's own *The Golden Fleece*. As the conversation developed the two men learned more about each other and began to get on very well. As a result Hegel invited Grillparzer to visit him at home again where the poet came to meet a Viennese compatriot whom Hegel regarded as diverting company, the satirical writer Saphir who then edited the *Berlin Messenger for Literature, Theatre and Society*. Hegel's judgement on Grillparzer (that he was 'an honest, intelligent and enthusiastic person') was more or less reciprocated by Grillparzer who described Hegel as 'agreeable, intelligent and conciliatory in manner'. Grillparzer was rather repelled by the 'abstruseness' of Hegel's system when he later attempted to penetrate his philosophy.

The Austrian writer had met Hegel when the latter was already exercising considerable social influence. At this time Hegel was indeed at the height of his contemporary fame, something even reflected in his dress for once (a blue frock coat with yellow breeches and even boots). But nothing was more alien to Hegel than the idea of holding forth on theoretical subjects of an abstract philosophical nature in the course of his personal conversations. The theatre was the most natural point of contact in discussions with his wife, and they would often exchange opinions about prominent actors, singers or dancers. One of Hegel's frequent guests in Berlin was the singer Henriette Sontag. Hegel himself would lend a hand at these musical evenings if more chairs needed to be brought in from the neighbouring street or whatever. Music for Hegel did not represent the very first amongst the arts, as it did for Schopenhauer, but it was certainly an inspiring and indispensable element in his life. After his lectures in the late afternoon Hegel would often walk directly to the Opera House situated just opposite the university buildings.

As a native of Württemberg Hegel was just one of the many 'foreigners' who had been attracted to the increasingly powerful Prussian state by the prospect of exercising greater influence. And the country certainly offered uniquely good opportunities in this respect if we consider only the aristocratic Stein from Hess, Hardenberg and Scharnhorst from Hanover, Savigny from Frankfurt, and many others from the Reform period of Prussian politics. Hegel's early correspondence with Schelling shows that this Swabian of Lutheran background originally left his country not because of any direct political pressure but on account of his profound antipathy to the prevailing theological orthodoxy and its constricting intellectual horizons. He had lived in a Swiss republic, and then a German one, before ending up in a tiny Saxon-

Thuringian monarchy. From there he moved on to Bavaria where he was not spectacularly comfortable, although he did succeed in marrying into a very respectable family there. His patriarchal domestic life was henceforth characterized by largely undisturbed happiness. It is true that his wife was extremely ill for a period and there continued to be financial worries of one kind or another which were not entirely resolved even when Hegel moved to Berlin. But the most difficult burden still proved to be his son from Jena, Ludwig Fischer, who had been taken into Hegel's household after the death of his natural mother. There was obviously some resistance to this arrangement on the part of Hegel's wife from the start, but it only intensified as Hegel's other two sons began to grow up. This eventually resulted in the stepmother's rejection of this intelligent but rather difficult child, something in which Hegel acquiesced. The parents both agreed in the end that the young man had to leave. Hence Hegel turned once again to his friend Fromann in Jena for assistance and asked if he could possibly find Ludwig an appropriate apprenticeship there. Hegel was thinking of commerce rather than a training apprenticeship which would require 'substantial fees'.

The old problems with Hegel's sister also continued to plague him in Berlin. Indeed matters became even worse and he felt obliged to write her long strongly worded letters of advice about her behaviour. Christiane Hegel had shown a very intense dependence on Hegel ever since her youth, to which he had responded as solicitously as he could. With advancing years the 'demoiselle' from Stuttgart proved increasingly difficult to help out of her problems. Since the time of her employment with the Berlichingen family she had developed certain extravagant traits of character which suggested the social station of a countess, and undoubtedly went far beyond her means and standing, not to mention those of her brother in Berlin who had no independent wealth of his own to rely upon. When she finally left patrician service she originally hoped above all to become a domestic housekeeper in a parsonage somewhere. But this actually required a service she now felt below her station and all kinds of difficulties resulted. Beset by disappointment and a profound inner insecurity, she had started travelling through one Swabian town after another seeking suitable employment and somewhere to settle. Hegel originally thought the problems might be explained by the menopause, but then recognized that his sister was already beyond this stage. He had done what he could to relieve her difficult predicament by sending her a couple of substantial payments, the last one amounting to 300 gulden, and had ended up in 'straitened' financial circumstances himself as a result.

Hegel's letter to Christiane of 12 August 1821 is essentially one long admonition: 'you must make a real effort with yourself and your present state of mind, and your relationship to others'. He does not deny that she has suffered certain injustices and slights at the hands of other people, but advises her to banish these from her memory if she really wishes to regain her health and strength. On the other hand he recognizes, as one of those directly involved himself, that 'you have a very imperfect idea, as is only natural, of the effect which your behaviour and illness have had upon other people'. This seems to allude to certain unpleasantnesses in relation to Hegel's wife, something which was absolutely bound to affect him for good or ill. Perhaps these problems were also directly related to the predicament of young Ludwig Fischer, which she could behold with her own eyes whenever she visited the Hegel household.

In the particularly difficult months of 1821 Hegel had stood by her in brotherly support. He renewed his earlier counsel: 'You must raise your thoughts to God in order to find strength and consolation for your heart in this higher love.' In addition he explicitly recommends her to regain her physical health through 'appropriate advice' and try and follow his own example: 'I have managed to earn my bread and done so with a good conscience.' And in the end Christiane did seem to have followed Hegel's advice. After she had settled in Stuttgart she opened an embroidery school and offered tuition in French.

Hegel's wife, twenty-two years younger than her husband, was apparently a beautiful and elegant woman. Their social life was generally restricted to the bourgeois world of Berlin, the circles associated with contemporary art, the new sciences, the learned and literary journals, the commercial and manufacturing class, and the salons. This is also the Berlin of Beer, Saphir and Mendelssohn, with that 'emancipated' bourgeois culture which the Prussian state philosopher himself admired. In his social life Hegel had never sought any contact with the Prussian aristocracy. That was something that appealed more to Schleiermacher and Savigny. Savigny's rather exceptional situation at the University of Berlin was essentially based upon the fact that he was the first person since its recent foundation to overcome the aristocratic resistance to becoming an academic professor in a sphere that generally remained a monopoly of the middle classes. In this Savigny formed an interesting contrast with Wilhelm von Humboldt.

Hegel had also been invited to Berlin by Altenstein because the professors closely associated with the arrogant upper classes in Prussia had begun to threaten the position of the minister himself. As Hegel's student Heinrich Leo wrote to the publicist Wolfgang Menzel on 31 December 1854, Altenstein had wanted 'to free himself from the truly tyrannical cliques of the learned aristocracy of the time'. From his personal observation of the situation Leo concluded that Hegel was not entirely clear about the real purposes which had prompted the call from Altenstein in the first place. Leo ascribed Hegel's belief that scholarly and academic considerations played the major role to his master's 'naive nature'. It is certainly true that Altenstein did not call Hegel to the chair in Berlin simply on account of the *Science of Logic* or his essay *On the Württemberg Estates Assembly*. The manner in which some made fun of him and offered spiteful criticisms of his work must soon have taught Hegel that he had entered something of a wasps' nest at Berlin and he saw no other possibility than holding all the more firmly to the central monarchical line. Hegel made sure that his position was secure from external threats but there were plenty of difficult problems and situations along the way. On the one hand the awkward Swabian from Tübingen faced the contempt of the aristocratic party, and on the other he was easily embarrassed by 'Gans and his consorts', as Leo described Hegel's more liberal-minded followers. Hegel's natural tendency to depressive moods, the grimness he would often display in the Berlin period, all of this had real external as well as imaginary causes. It was only the power of Hegel's own personality that managed to conceal the enormous gulf which lay between the contradictory interests he was expected to serve, something also exacerbated by the contradiction between the claims of scholarship and those of the state. This situation helped to produce a permanent system of compromises that was maintained right up to Hegel's death. After that, as the example of his students and the fate of his school clearly demonstrates, this carefully constructed system fell apart.

24

The Philosophy of Right

Hegel was only too well aware of what was expected of him in the official position which he owed to the gracious favour of the King, as he put it himself in his inaugural lecture at the university: support for the monarchy against any further unwelcome constitutional changes and support for the religion of state in the Christian form currently recognized in Prussia, endorsed by the Crown and broadly shared by the people. The great care which Hegel took in fulfilling these tasks, and the emphatic style in which he did so, can hardly be overlooked. With the elevation of his 'Logic' to the status of the primary science of philosophy from which all other disciplines were to be derived, he was the right man in Altenstein's eyes to provide the current outlook of the state with the aura of uncontestable truth. Hegel thus found himself to be an intellectual representative of the general government policy in a difficult transitional phase between the Reform era, to which the university owed its very existence, and the Restoration period, that is, in a phase of somewhat arrested development.

That is how matters look at first sight. But appearances are fairly deceptive here in a number of respects. It should not be forgotten that the general ideological turn in which Hegel found himself caught up resulted from a much greater rupture in the process of German history, one which has many different levels and aspects that are difficult to grasp all at once. The form of Christian religion endorsed by the Hohenzollern dynasty in Berlin and supported by the preponderant majority of the population was that of historical Protestantism. This Protestant doctrine tended to consolidate the political principle of the unity of Church and throne and, despite its formal tolerance of other perspectives in law, encouraged general opposition to alternative forms of faith in the state, i.e. attempted to reduce their significance and relativize their claims.

As a Württemberg Lutheran, of course, Hegel could support his minister and the Crown in this without violating his own conscience in any way. His early theological writings and his polemic against Schleiermacher reveal Hegel's sustained struggle to find a way of articulating a new orthodoxy that maintained the appropriate balance between Church and state. Hegel's idea was based on the old Lutheran doctrine of the 'two realms' but also recognized the overall controlling function of the state necessitated by the plight of its citizens in this world. The state could not simply be expected to give entirely free rein to the official representatives of the Church who were themselves quite capable of secret political 'scheming' and sometimes even of 'deceiving' the people at large.

Hegel thus clothed himself with a large and impressive mantle of loyalty to the state and it was this which allowed him to grapple openly with Schleiermacher as a representative theologian of the Berlin Court. But it was also this same protective mantle beneath which Hegel in his *Philosophy of Right* would fracture the pillars supporting the official Prussian view of politics and religion, a view he was supposed to be defending on behalf of the state. The state authorities were largely unaware at the time of the full nature or the possible consequences of Hegel's perspective on the matter. Hegel's philosophy of right is essentially a philosophy in the tradition of 'natural law'. That fact alone should have alerted the Berlin authorities and prompted a certain caution on their part. For the orthodox Lutheranism which was the principal religious confession in Prussia had never developed a serious philosophical doctrine of natural law, and in so far as it appealed to Luther himself it is difficult to see how it could ever successfully have done so. Luther and his closest followers would be quite unable to comprehend the idea of a set of inviolable 'eternal' rights, what would later be called human rights, that were supposedly derived from nature. It was unthinkable for them that man should presume to claim 'rights' for himself rather than simply faithfully relying upon God's promises. This would be like trying to put a man who is by 'nature' nothing but 'a drunken peasant' on horseback and inevitably seeing him fall off the other side. Man should rather recognize his proper place in God's eyes: 'You shall take pleasure in My grace.' Luther's attitude to 'natural rights' can easily and convincingly be deduced from his demand that the rebellious peasants be cut down like savage dogs, that the faithless Jews should have their synagogues burnt down and their property confiscated, and be driven out of the country for good.

Hegel's very different interpretation of the Lutheran doctrine of the 'two realms', which was willing to abandon the degenerate and wholly evil worldly state simply to the justice of God, should have raised some suspicion amongst the conservatives. For the idea of natural law introduces a further and very dangerous criterion of judgement in relation to that of a personal God. If one were to grant the legitimacy of such a criterion in all spheres then very uncertain and unwelcome results for the established order would be likely to ensue. Early Christian and medieval theology, with Augustine and Thomas

Aquinas, had found it necessary to appeal to a doctrine of natural law as a further source of knowledge in addition to the supra-natural truth of revealed religion. And some versions of Protestantism, especially that building on Calvin, had helped to develop the idea of a legal codex independent of the Judaeo-Christian notion of God. Hugo de Groot and the other jurists of the Low Countries represented the fruit of this tradition. But as far as the orthodox Lutherans were concerned all such talk of human rights and natural law was anathema.

If Lutheranism as the prevailing confession in most of the German princely territories largely abandoned the idea of natural law, it merely left the field open to others: to the forces of humanism and the Enlightenment, and to the philosophy which emerged from these movements (even as it laboriously continued to maintain certain important theological commitments at the same time). In this respect there is a striking continuity to be seen in the philosophies of Leibniz, Kant, Fichte, Schelling and Hegel.

The Hegel who expounded a political philosophy also based upon the idea of natural law played it very safe, and began work only after taking the most careful steps to advertise his loyal devotion to the state. For the essence of reason also includes the cunning knowledge of its proper use. Hegel had to anticipate any possible suspicion of seeming to endorse those who clamoured for change on the basis of the doctrine of 'abstract right'. The speculative philosopher in Berlin knew which way the political wind was blowing and also understood how the idea of natural law could easily be used as an argument for reform. Hence Hegel explicitly focuses in his 'Introduction' and 'Preface' to the *Philosophy of Right* upon Fries, this 'champion of superficiality'. As Hegel writes: 'Herr Fries did not blush, on the occasion of a public festival which has since become notorious, to express the following ideas in a speech on "The State and the Constitution": "In a people ruled by a genuine communal spirit, life for the discharge of all public business would come from below, from the people itself".' Hegel's remarks sounded like something from the mouth of an official of the ruling Prussian class, and indeed there is a sense in which that is how Hegel not unjustifiably regarded himself.

Hegel himself certainly had nothing to do with and scant sympathy for the Wartburg Festival and the speeches associated with it, with the idea of dissolving the 'articulated structure' of the state in all this 'broth of the heart, of friendship, of inspiration' etc. He regarded the German patriotic movement of 1820 as nothing but a misguided form of enthusiasm fatal to reason. The appeal to the freedom of the individual, which Hegel originally traced back to the Christianity of the fourth century, must not be interpreted simply as a freedom from the state, or even as a freedom against the state. The free ownership of property has only 'recently' been recognized as a 'principle' and represents an achievement of modern civil society and the bourgeois revolution. The principle is essentially characterized by the possibility of relinquishment or alienation in the legal sense of the term. But the individual person as such is inalienable and that is what constitutes the consciousness of freedom. Our physical and psychological capacities and the things we thereby produce can certainly be alienated, i.e. sold, to others for their use. Concrete labour time, for example, can be alienated in this way so that its substantial element becomes the property of another. Property can involve direct physical intervention as it is produced and increased, as well as the particular means that are used to accomplish this. As Hegel says: 'mechanical forces, weapons, instruments – all these increase the range and extent of my power'.

Hegel's philosophy of right falls into three parts: 'abstract right', 'morality' and 'ethical life'. The different significance of the German terms 'Moralität' and 'Sittlichkeit', standardly translated in English as 'morality' and 'ethical life' respectively, has now largely disappeared from linguistic consciousness. The former indicates the moral dimension of subjective self-determination, while the latter indicates rather the ethical dimension of reason as the codified life of a society in its laws and customs. In his philosophical doctrine of right Hegel brought his 'method' and 'system' to bear upon a particular discipline for the first time. The 'content' of the discipline is determined and articulated by the 'dialectic' as the 'dynamic principle of the concept'. The dialectic here is not regarded as some 'external operation' on our part but represents the very 'soul of the content'. Dialectic and material subject matter coincide with one another. The traditional bourgeois institutions like marriage and family life, and the phenomenon of courtship on which they are based, rest upon an enormous contradiction. For Hegel, unlike Kant, marriage is no longer a civil contract, but nor is it simply to be regarded simply as a matter of sentiment, for then it would be variably and contingently dependent upon a mood of the moment without any prospect of permanence. It is rather to be understood as a lawfully grounded condition. It cannot therefore be regarded as something intrinsically superfluous, as it is for example in Schlegel's novel *Lucinde*, where true love grounded in a union of hearts no longer requires any legal status or confirmation. Hegel's judgement reflects his anti-romantic outlook. The key to understanding the essence of real love, in Hegel's view, lies in the experience 'that I win myself in the other person, that I count as something for that person, just as that person in turn counts for something in me'. Love as such cannot simply replace marriage as an institution in which this mutual relationship perpetuates the process of human life through the family. Hegel expressed himself at length about the institution of marriage in his lecture notes on political philosophy. The student Peter Wannemann recorded what Hegel had to say on the subject in his 1817-18 lectures in Heidelberg: 'Marriage is the union between two persons of the opposite sex who decide to constitute *one* person in love and trust, a union which is formally and publicly recognized and thus explicitly established as a lawful relationship.' The ethics of marriage and an enlightened moral outlook are harmoniously combined in Hegel's account: 'The two sexes have natural differences, but these differences are reconstructed in the partners through the exercise of rationality.' Hegel goes on: 'The husband is directed towards universal interests in abstraction from the sphere of subjectivity; to him belong the role of practical life in the state, the realms of science and art . . . There have indeed been women who have applied themselves to the sciences; but they never penetrated very deeply into the subject or made significant discoveries.' In a military state like Prussia the traditional conviction taken over by Hegel from Plato was hardly to be challenged: 'If women count for something in the state, this is a sure sign that the state is on the wane' (as Wannemann duly noted down and went home to contemplate after Hegel's lectures).

With the phenomenon of marriage Hegel also comes into direct contact with what he calls the sphere of 'civil society', a crucial and new characteristic of the modern age. It was somewhat suspect to concentrate so much attention on this area of life in the Prussia of the Holy Alliance. For civil society is not identical with the state but actually represents a rather unpredictable quantity, so to speak, something with regard to which the state must exercise caution in so far as civil society itself appeals to the loyalty of the citizens and is guided by other interests of its own. *One* principle which is recognized by civil society is the 'concrete person' who regards himself as a particular individual and posits himself as his own end, while the *other* principle is precisely the *relationship* of *one* such 'concrete person' to *another*. And that is something which the state as such is loath to recognize. Every 'concrete person' in his 'being-for-self' constitutes his particular end and purpose, and everything else is 'nothing' to that person. But since the individual cannot realize his ends without any relationship to others, he posits these others as a means to the fulfilment of his own particular ends. The particular end that is sought thus comes to appear as a universal end, one in which the other is also fulfilled in his purpose likewise. Thus the realization of selfish purposes is constantly conditioned by universality and grounds a state of comprehensive mutual dependency. The resulting system is based upon 'need' and the exercise of the 'understanding' in Hegel's sense of the term.

The ends which the 'concrete person' envisages represent a combination of 'natural necessity' and 'arbitrary choice'. And without these two elements things could not be set in motion as they must be in order to satisfy given ends. As long as the overall balance of the system is not disturbed the functioning mechanism will work for the satisfaction of universal needs. On the other hand, where purely arbitrary will and subjective preference become predominant, whenever the 'being-for-self' or subjectivity of the particular individual abandons itself solely to its own needs and satisfactions, then the community is destined for decline. The perfect example for this can be seen in the fate of the ancient states which were eventually corrupted and destroyed by moral decline from within.

Hegel's concentration upon the question of 'civil society' reveals how far social relations had changed even in a state like Prussia which had never undergone a revolution. In the older Prussia of Frederick the Great civil society in this sense was still hard to imagine. The phenomenon had only properly shown itself, as something that now had to be comprehended theoretically, with the French Revolution and the newly emergent bourgeoisie oriented to the rights of private property, and with the British economists like Adam Smith and David Ricardo whose thought reflected the Industrial Revolution and the vast expansion of the maritime economy. Civil society is based upon the institution of private property and is principally directed at the protection and preservation of the same. Property in turn is based upon contract and the legal rules and regulations formally governing agreements of this kind. Civil society dedicated to the rights of property thus reveals itself as an immensely powerful force which irresistibly attracts people to itself and produces on them the distinct impression that nothing can be achieved by them independently. Civil society demands that the individual work for its own sake, although it also provides him with rights which he can use in opposition to that society. It can give him the possibility of acquiring great wealth, for example, which can function as a means of further economic protection in future. But every individual is naturally exposed to the threat of poverty as well. One can fall into penury through accident of birth, through extravagance, or through various other contingencies. If a large number of people sink beneath a certain 'level of subsistence' and are no longer guaranteed even the necessities of life, this produces the phenomenon of social exclusion. Hegel was thinking here particularly of the situation that was produced in Britain by the Industrial Revolution and draws his own conclusions: that the generation of a poverty-stricken 'rabble' and the possibility of amassing enormous wealth in a few hands actually belong together. The one case mutually presupposes the other.

It is not material poverty alone which produces such an outcast group, but rather an attitude of resentment, produced by such poverty, against those who do possess sufficient property and security, against society, the government and the state as such. The danger here is that civil society merely perpetuates the misery of one part of society. As Hegel puts it, civil society for all its riches is not rich enough to control excess poverty and prevent the emergence of a disaffected class within its midst.

Hegel cannot be shaken in his central conviction that wealth and poverty alike have their sources in contingent physical and external circumstances. The extension of the problem of 'need', in both directions, knows no natural boundary and can continue indefinitely. Thus the basic needs for food, drink, clothing and accommodation can be extended beyond any given measure and their satisfaction can lead to the production of entirely new needs as well. In order to reach the stage of life which the English describe as 'comfortable', new measures are constantly required every day. Thus the phenomenon of luxury as an 'infinite increase of dependency and need' only corresponds the more closely to poverty itself. Luxury can go even further and penetrate the domain of philosophical thought itself, as with Diogenes whose cynical withdrawal from the social life of Athens reveals itself as a product of that same social luxury.

As far as the question concerning the best kind of political constitution is concerned, Hegel finds himself in something of a quandary. His wavering political judgement had taken him from a short-lived endorsement of the revolutionary principle to the explicit condemnation of the Jacobins who had followed Robespierre; this led him to sympathize with liberal constitutional aspirations, although he also abandoned this position in his Heidelberg period and embraced the monarchical principle instead; and then there was the Napoleonic period which had seen him supporting the French Emperor's cause. Hegel now described the formation of the system of constitutional monarchy as a specific 'accomplishment of the modern world' in which the 'substantial idea has assumed its infinite form'. That was certainly a positive recommendation in Hegel's eyes, though not exactly of the Prussian state whose monarch opposed any further change with all the means at his disposal. The philosopher himself harboured considerable reservations about the constitutional monarchy since he expressly says in relation to the systems of monarchy, aristocracy and democracy that the basis has not yet attained its 'full depth and concrete rationality'. In the system of constitutional monarchy the other forms are demoted to the status of 'moments'. Aristocracy and democracy are incapable of offering a sufficient counterweight to the monarchy. The idea of constitutional monarchy arouses the impression that one, or many, or all could stand at the head of the state. Hegel finds further foolish talk of a 'constitution' to be particularly harmful and refuses to have anything to do with it. 'Democracy' is dependent upon the virtue of its leaders, but what happens when the latter is lacking, as Montesquieu pointed out with regard to seventeenth-century England? 'Aristocracy' with its characteristic principle of 'moderation' reveals the separation into the spheres of 'public power' and 'private interest'; this is a constitutional system likely to produce either tyranny or anarchy and thereby destroy itself as in the famous examples from Roman history.

Perhaps these considerations are what finally led Hegel to justify the monarchical system as superior to the others and one which apparently required no constitutional guarantees of any kind. This system alone seems to Hegel to realize the three necessary moments within itself: the universality of the constitution, the relation of the particular to the universal, and self-determination in the form of the monarch's final decision. Hegel's project for a system of constitutional monarchy for large states like Prussia does not detract from the reservations he still has about such an arrangement.

25

The Philosophy of History

Hegel delivered his first lectures on the philosophy of history in the academic year 1822–3, and he would subsequently repeat them before the public in more extensive form many times before his death. When he treated this theme he did not essentially do so with the prospect of a published book in mind, but rather as a direct exercise in thinking about historical actuality. Our sources for reconstructing Hegel's thought here are a number of substantial drafts and manuscripts (sometimes worked out in detail word for word for his lectures, sometimes concentrating on essential points, and sometimes consisting of little more than jottings and headings) and a number of student transcriptions of the lectures by various hands. As a result any precise philological-hermeneutic analysis of the sources remains a highly problematic enterprise on account of the differences and discrepancies between the various texts. There is therefore really no such thing as an undisputed 'Hegel-philology' (as Theodor Adorno has pointed out), and the necessary limits of any such attempt soon quickly reveal themselves.

This of course is true only for the precise systematic shape of Hegel's philosophy of history, rather than for the general method. 'The sole thought which philosophy imports to the subject is the simple one that reason governs the world, that things have proceeded rationally in the course of world history.' This clearly enunciated presupposition of philosophical-historical enquiry certainly appears to be unambiguous enough. And anyone tempted to doubt that Hegel still stands in the great tradition of the Enlightenment, which posits the thought of reason emerging through all the apparent chaos of the world, should be convinced by this emphatic claim alone.

Logic and spirit as the mighty elementary factors in Hegel's thought continue to conspire here to render the process of history, in and through and beyond all of its passions, intelligible precisely as a progressive movement intrinsically oriented towards a final end or purpose. Naturally further logical and metaphysical moves are required in order fully to understand the 'spirit' that is involved here. Spirit is presented as something independent of contingent and essentially external purposes. The self has returned to itself in spirit: the latter is a form of 'being at home with itself' which does not simply remain wrapped up in itself but goes forth to find its full realization in the state. Nothing can come to pass without the formative agency of this spirit. But Hegel also knows that this spirit possesses an internal and essential character of its own, a substance with a special name: 'Just as weight is the substance of matter, . . . so too freedom is the substance, the essence, of spirit.'

Hegel thus explicitly states his claim: spirit is a progressive force with freedom as its substantial content and represents the essential purpose in all authentic historical advance. This insight is predicated upon Hegel's philosophical logic and can therefore claim the same necessity as the *Logic* itself: 'World history is the progress of the consciousness of freedom – a progress which it is our task to grasp in its necessity.' And all reflection upon the course of world history must therefore be governed by this principle according to Hegel. In every case freedom is continually being advanced by spirit in the historical process, freedom ultimately reveals itself as the true final purpose of history, and freedom functions as a demonstration of the reason in that history. The movement of history proceeds according to immutable principles just as as the solar system itself proceeds according to own laws. Hegel permits no doubt concerning the ultimate logic of history or nature, any more than he does concerning the realms of law or of art.

Hegel presented his thought of freedom, progressively and ineluctably unfolding its substance through the initially obscure medium of human history in spite of all obstacles and difficulties, according to the explicit pattern of successive 'epochs'. The 'Orientals' knew only that *one* is free – the despot; the Greek and Roman worlds knew that *some* are free; but the modern or Germanic world has learned through Christianity that in principle *all* are free, something that neither Plato nor Aristotle had been capable of grasping. The world spirit has worked continuously to realize freedom and the consciousness of freedom more and more through the historical process in spite of various temporary setbacks and regressions of one kind or another.

Freedom as the final purpose of history is really a discovery of Hegel's. Neither Kant, nor Fichte, nor Schelling had done so with such unmistakable explicitness in any of their writings. Schiller's Elysian thought of a reconciliation of all human beings in a single community of freedom arose from a personal mood of his own, but found no systematic or methodical development and never became a philosophical and speculative perspective in Hegel's sense. The speculative philosopher also recognizes that: 'This final purpose is what God intends with the world.' The means which freedom employs on its path towards self-realization can certainly obscure the divine contribution to this process. For it could quite naturally appear that the hand of God was the very last thing likely to reveal itself at work in history. It is surely the drives and passions, the immediate interests and vital needs of human beings which furnish the principal 'moving cause' here, while the exercise of virtue and good intentions must appear insignificant by contrast. And indeed the 'passions' and the satisfaction of our selfish desires are the most powerful factors in the course of history. The crimes and transgressions of the great historical actors also have their part to play here. It is they who possess the power and who refuse to recognize any of the limits otherwise imposed by law or morality. Above all it is the passions which most intimately move human beings to action. Where the passions exercise their influence, there is nothing that can oppose them. As Hegel says: 'Nothing great in the world has ever been accomplished without passion.' On the other hand, it is also the unchaining of the human passions which has brought about the destruction of flourishing civilizations through cruelty, violence and and 'evil'. And of course, in the end, all the great cultures and peoples of the ancient world have gone down into ruin. This is history as a 'slaughter bench upon which the happiness of peoples, the wisdom of governments and the personal virtue of individuals have been offered up as a sacrifice'.

In the advance of the idea of freedom in history we cannot ask what victims have been claimed in the process. As the progressive agency of historical change the world spirit finds itself confronted with 'an immense mass of human desires, interests and activities' as the very 'instruments and means' at its own disposal. This also includes the great actors and doers, the 'world-historical individuals' as Hegel calls them, who seem to be pursuing their own ends but unwittingly appear as 'executants' who essentially serve the world spirit itself. They do not recognize their function in the service of reason since their entire nature is shaped and constituted by the passions. They know not what they do. Once they have served the purpose for which the world spirit has, as it were, chosen them, then there is no further necessity for their continued existence: 'They die young as with Alexander, they are murdered like Caesar, or they are banished to Saint Helena like Napoleon.' It is all part of the so-called 'cunning of reason' that they 'let their passions work on their own account'. For without the passions nothing can actually be brought to pass in the course of history.

The claim that reason rules and will continue to rule the world also rests, according to Hegel, upon faith as the counterpart to logic. The great realms of the state, religion, art, science and philosophy all belong to the field of 'philosophical history' as Hegel understands it, and all receive their appropriate articulation there in speculative terms. This permits Hegel's fundamental claim that the state is the site where freedom finds its realization. This abstract truth must be illustrated concretely with respect to the various systems of government which Hegel examines from the Oriental world right through to the Germanic world shaped by the impact of Christianity. The political systems and constitutions developed by the various 'world-historical peoples' belong to them and to them alone. Consequently there is nothing to be learned from them with regard to the historical present. The Greek and Roman constitutions, for example, cannot simply be transferred to this present. For all their other differences, however, these systems are still marked by the separation between 'the ruler' and 'the ruled'. From the monarchist standpoint which he defended himself, or at least the one to which he felt closest, Hegel did not share the widespread conviction that a 'republic' was the only just form of constitutional government. He had seen in Berne how a republican constitution can easily prove the equal of other constitutional systems as regards corruption or political oppression. Nor can a democracy continue to remain true to itself for all time. When a people decides to go to war, it requires a general to lead it. And when the will of the majority is realized, the will of the minority cannot be realized and will only feel itself infringed as a result. But freedom itself, with all the ambiguities inherent in the concept, can prove highly problematic for the state. In the Polish parliament individual freedom was so highly prized that unanimity in voting was absolutely required for all political measures. As a result Poland ultimately perished at the hands of its own freedom.

And then in Hegel we also encounter the Goethean thought that the ancient Greek world is essentially superior to every other. This belongs to Hegel's fundamental experience of world history, and is only partly qualified by the recognition of the emergence of a higher kind of freedom in the Germanic world as introduced through the agency of Christianity. Hegel's perspective is thus thoroughly Eurocentric. For in Hegel's systematic philosophy of history every other continent falls necessarily behind that of Europe itself. The latter appears as the focal point of the world as a whole; the Mediterranean, or 'Middle Sea' as the name implies, is the central and 'middle point of world history'; and Greece by virtue of its geographical position is the 'illuminated point of history'. Without the Mediterranean the whole course of history would be inconceivable. That is the reason why East Asia remains essentially excluded from the process of world history. Hegel cannot be shaken in his belief that countries like India, for example, 'lack the slightest glimmer of historical consciousness with historiographical records that are purely fantastical and magical' (as Georg Lasson puts it). East Asia plays no role in world history. Nor for a very long time does northern Europe make an entrance into world history in this perspective.

For world history must always be understood with reference to the overall geographical conditions which ground it. From a climatic point of view the more moderate zones provide the most suitable stage for the process of world history. Africa remains shut up in itself and appears untouched by the advances of world history, while its inhabitants are merely ascribed great physical prowess and characteristics of untamable wildness. It is described as a 'land of gold' and a 'land of children'. It only reveals any real movement in those parts where Islam has penetrated and exerted an influence. None the less, in contrast to the dominant opinion of the time, Hegel entertains no doubts about the potential educability of its native peoples.

America is presented as the land of the future, especially for all those for whom Europe has lost its former historical attraction. It is a land of independence which no longer has to bear the burden of the past and thus recommends itself to strong new possibilities. Its peculiar weakness, on the other hand, is always shown when it is fighting for something other than its own independence. The origins of history, according to Hegel, certainly lie in the Orient, but China and India on his account still stand essentially outside the world-historical process proper. It is only with the Persian Empire that a direct connection with the latter process is first really established. And while the civilizations of China and India still remain to this day, that of the Persians has long since disappeared. Hegel sees the beginnings of monotheism amongst the Jews: 'The Jews possess whatever they possess through the 'One God.' The exclusive 'One' belongs essentially to the inner character of Judaic monotheism. There are those who worship and obey the Lord God and those who have no knowledge of Him altogether. This constitutes an enormous difference which separates the Jews from the Greeks. Hegel talks of the 'elementary character of the Greek spirit', which is marked by a 'beautiful individuality' and the typical features of a more advanced sense of freedom. It was Homer and Hesiod who bequeathed to the Greeks their gods. The Greeks were characterized by the idea of formative culture in a way quite unmatched by any other civilization. The particularly rich and manifold nature of this culture also rested upon the rich geographical variety of the country itself.

This immediately throws up the problem of the opposition between Greek culture and historical Christianity, something which Hölderlin felt so deeply within himself and expressed so powerfully in his own hymnic poetry. The Greeks understood their gods to be anthropomorphic, endowed them with human form and thus made men appear more divine themselves. That is what seemed crucial in Hegel's eyes. The Greek god has come to visible manifestation in the marble statue and appears there as a transfigured image of the imagination. Of course, it is true that the Christian religion also represents the incarnation of the divine in human form since no other form is thought capable of becoming the proper vessel for the spirit. The actual manifestation of God in the world is essentially necessary. For only what actually appears (*erscheint*) can be properly 'essential' (*wesentlich*). The difference between Greek and Christian religion consists in the fact that with the former visible manifestation or 'appearance' represents 'the highest form' of the god and 'the entirety of the divine', while in the latter appearance as such is only grasped as 'a moment of the divine life'.

Was the path which led from the Greek religion to the Christian a movement from a lower to a higher level, as the Christians themselves have always believed? We know that Goethe was never really able to accept this view himself. Hegel does appear to share it, but he also rejects it in another sense. The view is true with respect to the 'freedom' which the Greeks were never capable of grasping in its 'abstraction', but then again is not true with respect to the 'beautiful individuality' realized paradigmatically by Greek culture. But Hegel does not simply subscribe to Winckelmann's idealization of 'the Greeks' in terms of their supposed 'noble simplicity and restful grandeur'. This is also true for the political constitutions represented amongst the Greeks, which of course included a form of 'democracy'. The democratic equality of the citizens presupposed the exclusion of other people. Slavery was an essential condition of Greek democracy. This institution was necessary in order that each citizen could make full use of his rights and live up to his obligations, which included giving and hearing public speeches on good government in open discussion, as well as exercising his prowess in the gymnasia and participating in the political and religious festivals of the city. The citizens of the city-state could not be expected to perform manual labour or share any of the mundane activities necessary for daily life. The others, who had no real share in political equality, were there for that.

The ancient democracy of which Hegel speaks in this connection was only possible in small states, typically in the Greek city-state where all human relations could be seen and comprehended at a glance, where in times of danger the citizens could withdraw into the city itself and entrench themselves within its walls. In Greece the entire community was not yet penetrated by the idea of freedom. The principle itself can be known in part, as something that accrues to man himself, without the institution of slavery ceasing to exist immediately. 'Slavery only comes to an end when the will is infinitely reflected within itself, when the principle of right is recognized as belonging to every free person as such.'

The Greeks had not advanced so far as that. But the advance of freedom certainly involved Greece and Greek culture as it came into world-historical conflict with the despotic principle of the Persian Empire. The Greek victory over the Persians at Marathon and Salamis represented the salvation of 'reflective culture' and 'spiritual power' from 'the Asiatic principle'. World history certainly knows of bloodier battles than these, but none in which more was essentially at stake. The victory of the Greeks over Oriental despotism inaugurated the most brilliant epoch in the history of Greece. It also marks the beginning of the opposition between Athens and Sparta. Athens was a state which essentially lived for beauty and actively pursued the great interests of the human spirit. Sparta was a state of abstract virtue in which life was dedicated entirely to the security of the collective with little regard for individual freedom. The one represented the arts, which presented such beautiful forms for contemplation, the place where tragic theatre experienced its first beginnings and its glorious consummation. The other represented a culture of rigid discipline which maintained the equal division of inalienable landed property in order to preserve proper equality amongst the citizens.

What was it, then, that led to the eventual decline of the Greek world? All the contributory factors can ultimately be condensed into a single one: the emerging principle of corruption. The Athenian city-state was destroyed in the end by its own 'frivolity', while Sparta, where the system of democracy gave way in time to aristocracy and oligarchy, eventually fell victim to 'universal selfishness'. But Athens in decline and in failure has lost nothing of its original beauty and attractiveness as far as our human historical memory is concerned. Those subjugated by Athenian power still recognized that such domination was easier to bear than that of Sparta would ever be. The sphere of its customary religion, an institution originally 'without need of further reflection', was eventually penetrated by the power of 'thought' as represented by the Socratic-Platonic dialogues. That is to say that religion gradually lost much of its former power. The constitutions of the Greek states were also shattered by arbitrary human passions and desires. According to Hegel, the Greece that had begun with Achilles came to an end with Alexander the Great. With him the Macedonians absorbed Greek culture and subjected it, or at least appended it, to the exercise of military domination. Alexander the Great, a born conqueror and military genius, was fortunate enough to receive Aristotle, 'the most profound and comprehensive thinker of antiquity', as his own personal tutor. One cannot do justice to Alexander by simply applying moral criteria to him. He introduced the final act of Greek political history in so far as he extended Greek power into Asia through his military campaigns and thereby fundamentally opened up the East to the Europeans for the first time. But the decline of the Greek world was a fate that had long since been sealed by the general conditions of prevailing corruption and nothing could be done to prevent it now. Once this stage of decline is reached the 'great individuals' are powerless to reverse it. They still struggle against the evils but are incapable of eliminating them and they themselves go under in turn. If a world is indeed caught up in a decline like this, there are only three possibilities left for such a 'beautiful individuality': to despair, to seek refuge in philosophy, or to die fighting. From this world-historical perspective Alexander's early death proved nothing less than a stroke of fortune. He left historical memory with a beautiful image of youthful death to seal the very moment when Greece as a political power departed the stage of world history. The role of world-historical people had now passed to Rome.

This brings about a total change of scene. The world forfeits all of its former character and is plunged into the deepest grief. The heart of the world is broken, as Hegel says. It must now continue to live without the ancient splendour of Greece, for the natural life of the spirit belongs to the past. Instead of that, we must now behold the rule of 'abstract freedom', of an 'abstract state' that lacks all 'individuality', albeit according to a new historical necessity. For this is how the world must be fashioned if Christianity and its 'free' spirit is to arise from its soil.

In contrast to the systems of Oriental despotism and of Greek democracy, Rome represents that of aristocracy. This system originally defended itself against the institution of kingship and later found itself opposing the demands of the common people for political participation. In this process the democratic party initially gained the upper hand only to encourage the phenomenon of factionalism, which in turn helped to produce the great individuals of the Roman aristocracy. The Roman policies which were about to go forth and conquer the world rested upon this oscillating and dualistic system of government.

According to Hegel this Roman world is 'spiritless' and 'heartless' in comparison with the Greek world that had preceded it. And this character infects its law and its religion alike. The Romans took over the former Greek gods but their veneration of the same remained cold and external in nature. Whereas the Greeks participated in their own games and festivals, the Romans remained nothing but spectators at the arenas where the spectacles gradually degenerated into bloody gladiatorial conflict and finally into the mass destruction of animal and human life. A certain inflexible harshness was a fundamental element of Roman politics from the very beginning and was not something introduced from outside later on. It went back to the emergence of a kind of robber culture with Romulus and Remus. The individual experiences only despotism in the state and acts equally despotically towards everyone else. The ancient quarrel between the patricians and the plebeians eventually developed through the course of Roman history into a sort of balance of power and finally to a political union to the advantage of the public good and the private citizen. The state thus attained its greatest strength, uniting its various factions against external enemies in contrast with its former civil conflicts. This is what permitted the state to prosecute its mighty wars, deploying its troops in massed phalanx formations on an entirely different scale from the military arrangements of the Greeks and the Macedonians before them. Increasing power always naturally presupposes or results in the concomitant decline of other rivals: 'The fall of Carthage and the subjugation of Greece were the decisive factors which permitted the Romans to extend their power even further.' But Roman power was essentially based on military might, and this was also where 'the Roman principle' found its exemplary expression. And this only reveals that Rome lacked a real spiritual focus altogether. That is why the Republic was also doomed to fail. It collapsed not through 'the contingent fact of Caesar' but through 'necessity'. Hence its end is irrevocable. Rome in its period of decline did not, as in the case of Greece, produce great works of art or exercise any significant influence on the development of philosophy. The works of art that were displayed in Rome were all trophies pillaged and stolen from Greece. The Romans could only receive the elegance and culture they desired to possess at the hands of their Greek slaves. It was the latter who represented poetry and the education of children as far as the Romans were concerned. And Greek philosophy itself could no longer satisfy the needs of a living spirit. What philosophy offers now is rather a 'counsel of despair' for it recognizes nothing but 'the negativity of all content' in a world that is quite without any reliable foundations in itself.

In this Rome represents a preparation for something that is essentially new. The pain and godforsakenness of the Roman world constitute the birth pangs of a higher spirit altogether. Hence it becomes the very birthplace of Christianity, of a religion that will lead to the 'reconciliation of the world'. Rome supplied the underlying conditions for this event. In the Roman world, where 'the spirit of the Orient' had already entered the lands of the Occident, we find East and West alike united with one another. The religious cults of Isis and Mithras were celebrated in every corner of the Roman Empire but what they essentially lacked, according to the Hegelian perspective, was the 'yearning for that deeper and purely inward universality' which Christianity not only aroused but was also capable of satisfying. There now emerges for the first time something that the ancient world had not recognized and which would constitute the very postulate of the future: 'the principle of absolute freedom in God'. Man no longer finds himself caught up in a position of sheer 'dependency' but appears as an object of divine 'love'. With Christianity mankind suddenly finds itself endowed with a new 'consciousness' that will eventually come to penetrate its entire being. But in Rome and the ancient Roman world itself Christianity cannot find its true ground nor can it transform that world into a new kingdom. According to Hegel, it is the Germanic peoples who are called to this task.

This is an impressive conception, and one which hardly fits in with the concept of religion which developed on Roman soil and accordingly understood itself as essentially 'Roman' in character and ultimate validity. Hegel holds, on the other hand, that: 'The Germanic spirit is the spirit of the modern world, whose final purpose is the realization of the absolute truth as the infinite self-determination of freedom, that freedom which has the absolute form itself as its very content.' Rome itself is incapable of establishing what the Germanic peoples who overran and conquered it were destined to accomplish as the privileged historical bearers of the 'Christian principle' in the service of the 'world spirit'. But the Roman world was necessary in order to grant the Germans a role of their own in relation to another world-historical people. This presents us with the idea of a kind of historical succession as something that bears the spirit further onwards, something without which the spiritual heritage itself could not be essentially preserved. Where newly emergent Christianity returns the spirit to itself, there we also perceive the coming 'world of fulfilment' articulated through the message of 'reconciliation'.

This all corresponds comfortably with the self-conception of the Prussian state between 1820 and 1830 where the Hohenzollern dynasty was avidly preparing to assume part of the heritage of the now defunct 'Holy Roman Empire of the German Nation'. Byzantium, on the other hand, the obvious alternative path that leads from Rome, is clearly regarded here as nothing but a false trail. In the Byzantine Empire where the new religion was officially founded by Constantine and a constant succession of crimes, including intrigue, murder and the poisoning of emperors by their sons and wives, proved the order of the day, until the assertive Turks destroyed it in the middle of the fifteenth century, Christianity merely remained something purely 'abstract', as Hegel puts it. But the very same dangers accompanied the Papacy in the Western Empire as well and thus prepared the predicament into which it too would eventually fall. In so far as Christianity represents the cause of the 'spirit' the Hegel who writes the philosophy of history can express himself as well as any devout preacher from the Württemberg pulpit: it is the Church itself founded on the Holy Trinity and continuously active in the world. But that does not nearly exhaust the full historical actuality of the phenomenon. For that also involves the ecclesiastical theocracy with its fundamental distinction between the priesthood and the laity, with the holy sacraments which the Church dispenses, together with the medieval and feudal-monarchical state essentially allied to the Church. A historical fate overtook the Church as it entered the Middle Ages and rendered them 'Christian' in character. Hegel was deeply familiar with this story. According to his own report he had originally moved to Bamberg to observe the Christian Middle Ages at close quarters directly for himself and see to what extent it had made itself a reality in everyday life. Hegel describes the ramifications and significance of the Christian 'Middle Ages' with an unflinching realism. It is dominated by the 'contradiction of the infinite lie' which infects the entire process. The feudal political circumstances which attend it only reveal an intrinsic 'bond of injustice, a relationship which attempts to realize what is just but which has what is equally unjust as its very content'. It is characteristic of the system of feudalism to establish a relationship of loyalty towards the prevailing political power, to encourage the weaker to place their property in the hands of the stronger and receive it back provisionally on condition of promising to defend the stronger against their enemies. Violence and a universal lack of rights are thereby transmuted through oaths of fealty into instances of private dependency and private obligation. Violence both precedes the system of feudalism and is simultaneously produced by it in turn.

The medieval Church eventually forfeited its own essence when it resorted to very similar means in its opposition to the arbitrary power and violence of the feudal lords and princes. This danger was all too obvious since the considerable worldly possessions of the Church turned it too into another 'terrifying worldly power'. Italy in the eleventh century provides the most brutal illustration of this fact. Why? Because this constituted the 'central focus of Christianity'. Depredation, bestial desire, treachery and deceit all flourished easily on such ground as this. The sale of offices, the arbitrary control over ecclesiastical property and eventually over the Papal seat itself were a matter of course.

This perspective clearly had nothing whatsoever in common with the idealization of the Christian Middle Ages as the great era of Catholic unity, such as Novalis had dreamt of in his work *Christianity or Europe*. On the contrary it was Hegel's emphatic counterstroke to all the romanticism he had encountered in Jena. Hegel also dealt with the feudalism which still enjoyed a strong economic base in the state of Württemberg as ruthlessly as he had with the institutions of medieval Catholicism, unfavourably contrasting the surviving system with the new monarchical principle. The celebrated nature of traditional German 'faithfulness and loyalty' was simply empty talk. In truth it represented 'the most utterly faithless thing of all' by virtue of its intrinsic one-sidedness: 'for the princes and vassals of the Emperor are loyal and faithful to nothing but their own interests, ambitions and passions, while they are quite faithless with regard to the Emperor and the Empire'.

Hegel sees evidence of historical progress in the transition from feudal forms of government to the monarchy. For the latter breaks the arbitrary power of the feudal lords and establishes the principles of law and right in its place. For Hegel the state essentially represents this new centralization of power in the hands of the monarch. The historical changes Hegel is talking about here had not of course transpired without considerable conflict, if we consider the situation in Italy and Germany on the one hand and in England and France on the other. In the former we witness a centrifugal movement of power away from the monarchy towards the vassal lords who for their part desire nothing so much as a weak Emperor; in the latter we see the Crown appropriating the rights of the vassal lords for itself and taking every possible measure to neutralize the opposing forces of dissension. This process already introduces the idea of the state as the proper realization of genuine freedom. The older powers and institutions gradually fall into oblivion as this development proceeds, along with the traditional Church which had formerly sought to control the wilder excesses of human behaviour with the threat of hell-fire that it constantly invoked before their eyes. For we were constantly reminded by the Church that man himself is evil by nature, and this belief provided its own justification for the necessity of such terrifying threats. Hegel regards this approach to enforcing social control as historically obsolete, having been superseded by the less conflictual influences of culture and education. In this general process the arts and the sciences have also played a crucial role in the dissolution of the medieval world view: the new humanism, the increasing knowledge of Platonic philosophy, the art of printing, the invention of gunpowder, the discovery of the Americas. Hegel celebrates the Reformation at the close of the medieval period as the great German achievement. Instead of pursuing the outer path of exploration by sea, Luther's path leads instead to the inner man and represents an essential accomplishment of the 'soul'. We should note Hegel's insistence that 'the Reformation arose from out of the corruption of the Church'. In the dialectical perspective of the Hegelian philosophy of history we can see how 'corruption' has played its necessary role in historical progress. The Reformation marks a mighty step in the historical advance towards the final goal of freedom. For henceforth there is no longer any particular estate, like the priesthood, which can claim exclusive possession of the truth for itself. Hegel's view here was clearly oriented towards his own image of the Prussian state around 1830, although the Hegelian philosophy had not removed every problem and ambiguity in this respect: it remained unclear whether this union of state, crown and the newly acquired freedom of the 'Protestant principle' had already attained this goal or merely represented an advanced station on the path towards it.

Hegel articulated this view with constant reference back to the old Empire which had been destroyed by Napoleon, and the passing of which, as we know, Hegel had certainly not lamented. The old system had left its mark on the German character: 'The Germans cannot deny that the French, the Italians, and the Spaniards possess more firmness and definiteness of character, and are more capable of pursuing a determined goal with total consciousness and the fullest of attention.' The reasons for this lay in the fact that as an 'elective state' Germany had never properly become a state in its own right. Germany's enemies, and even its own princes, had always known how to take advantage of this disunity for their own particular ends. When the Peace of Westphalia finally concluded the destruction of the Thirty Years War the principle of religious freedom was secured in Germany, and indeed by Richelieu. It should be noted that it was a Catholic cardinal who reluctantly achieved the very thing that his own countrymen had not desired and that his enemies gratefully recognized. The Protestant Church finally secured its established political status in Prussia through Frederick the Great. He was no cavilling theologian like some of the English monarchs had been, but rather a curious type of 'philosopher king' and an 'Enlightener' who took no interest whatsoever in theological disputes and thereby served to reduce their significance.

But it could not be denied that, generally speaking, France rather than Germany had taken the lead in advancing and realizing the cause of political freedom. Why was this the case? This is precisely what Hegel attempts to discover. The French were 'firebrands' whose revolutionary ardour was only encouraged by the obvious need for a transformation in political life. Before the Revolution the state found itself in a deplorable situation where 'shameless injustice' prevailed throughout the country. The entire state had become a single system of corruption. French theoretical insight into the greatness of the principle of freedom thus gave way to real historical praxis. In Germany, on the other hand, 'Protestantism had essentially moderated men's attitudes to the realities of law and ethics'. While the German Enlightenment generally sided with theology, the French Enlightenment explicitly took up arms against the Church. Thus it fell to the French people to play an essentially world-historical role through the realization of the revolutionary principle, to procure a historical breakthrough for the world spirit. That is why Hegel can describe the French Revolution as a 'splendid dawn'. We even find the Prussian state philosopher in the Age of Restoration adding in the lecture room of Berlin University that 'all thinking people greeted this epoch with celebration'. But although the Revolution itself must be regarded as an irreversible achievement of the world spirit for Hegel, there is much more to be said. For it is also necessary to look more closely at the ensuing course of events as the Revolution unfolded. And here Hegel points out the dramatic reversal whereby world-historical events can turn into their opposites. The 'course of the Revolution' followed a path which led from virtue exercised in the name of freedom, or from freedom exercised in the name of virtue, to a state of explicit tyranny. In the end it is not the people who come to rule as originally intended but rather 'the Terror' itself. At the beginning the vacillating Directory took over from the king, taking advantage of the military power which Napoleon had given it and would soon use himself to attain power. Hegel had followed the ascent of Napoleon with admiration. He had witnessed his military victories and been a victim of his wars in Jena. And in the end Hegel was also forced to recognize the 'impotence of victory'. This colossus had been brought down by national sentiments amongst the very peoples which had benefited from the liberal institutions originally disseminated by French power. None of this could now simply be reversed. Thus in Hegel's eyes the very fall of Napoleon had eventually furthered the cause of liberalism. For the latter consisted essentially in the establishment of rational laws, freedom of the individual and freedom to own property in the classical liberal bourgeois sense. What Hegel calls 'the abstraction of liberalism' began its career in France and subsequently expanded throughout western Europe. France can thus continue to play the leading world-historical role bestowed upon it through Napoleon and the Revolution in the new shape of the liberal bourgeoisie, the class which now represents political and economic progress over against the ancient feudal aristocracy which it had in principle overcome.

Hegel merely hints at possible future developments at the close of his *Philosophy of History*. He does not and cannot know the precise course of events to come. But Hegel also sees this ascendance of liberalism as something distinctly threatening on the threshold of the future. For liberalism naturally stands for an 'atomic principle', for the primacy of the individual will. In this sense it rests upon a continual process of dissociation. And nothing permanent can be erected, no firm institutional organization established, upon this basis. Hegel regards Prussia and the Protestant world in general as protected against the dangers of liberalism, in a way that the Latin cultures are certainly not. 'The Protestant world itself has already arrived through thought at the awareness of the absolute peak of self-consciousness.' Hence it requires a special force to enable it to oppose the persisting 'unfreedom' of the Roman Church. But the disintegrative atomistic tendencies of liberalism still exercise an unsettling and disturbing influence in the present: 'liberalism has prevailed within and indeed bankrupted all the Latin nations and the Roman Catholic world in general, in France, Italy and Spain'. And the process continues, fermenting new possibilities of conflict in the future.

Thus the philosopher who had closely followed the previous course of world history finally arrives at his own present. The way in which freedom had been articulated in liberalism must not be confused with the reality of freedom itself. But none the less the gains of the Enlightenment could not be relinquished either. The latter had placed its entire emphasis upon the efficacy of thought, and Hegel too recognized that the ultimate coincidence of thought and being in a Fichtean sense constituted the indispensable presupposition of his own philosophy. Hegel attempted harmoniously to combine this thought with the essential achievement of freedom in the Hegelian sense as the end purpose of history: 'man is not free if he does not think'.

Here Hegel stands firmly on the ground of that Enlightenment which he claimed had passed over from France to Germany. It was always the inner connection between the idea of freedom and the actual political constitution that formed the focal point of Hegel's interest and attention. He also pursued this theme in relation to the British parliamentary system. This friend of constitutional monarchy in Germany found no reason whatsoever to glorify parliamentarianism as some of his contemporaries did. In England, where monarchy, aristocracy and democracy were all of them influential forces in the working of the state, Hegel saw parliament essentially ruled by the same kind of 'republican corruption' which he had witnessed in Berne, in which particular individuals were able to buy their seats in parliament and sell their votes to others. This was part of what Hegel understood by the much-vaunted English 'freedom'. This parliamentary situation in England was justified by its capacity to produce an actual working government as a prime necessity. The country was characterized by its developed state of 'material existence': in marked contrast to Germany the wealth of the country was essentially based upon industry and world-wide trade, something which had turned the English into the missionaries of material civilization.

Hegel regarded the conditions in Germany on the other hand as agreeably stable. Precisely through the political oppression of the French, which the people had now shaken off, the inadequacies of its own earlier institutions had been clearly revealed and an optimistic Hegel radiated general confidence that these had now become intrinsically obsolete. The 'deception' perpetrated by the former Empire had disappeared along with its characteristic institutions: 'the obligations of feudal tenure have been abolished, the principles which guaranteed the freedom of property and person had been recognized as the fundamental ones. Every citizen now enjoys equal access in principle to holding political office.' Furthermore, the 'reconciliation of religion with the law had now been accomplished by the Protestant Church'.

As far as Germany and Prussia were concerned the outlook seemed hopeful. That the actual course of historical development had successfully brought us to this point represented the true grounds for a kind of 'theodicy' or justification of God's ways to man. In this sense Hegel therefore had no doubt that history could be regarded as the work of God! Hegel's philosophy of history had emerged from the whole European development of historicism which had been initiated by the Italian philosopher Giambattista Vico. Eduard Gans had already mentioned Vico in his Preface to the first edition of Hegel's *Philosophy of History*, although he also added that Vico had been unable, despite living in the midst of the Cartesian era itself, to see out beyond the confines of the pre-Cartesian age. Herder also represented an extremely significant philosopher of history, often more fertile in creative ideas in the field and better acquainted with many periods and cultures than Hegel himself. But what raised Hegel beyond Herder, and even in the era of post-Hegelian philosophy seemed to enable Hegel to reveal the true nature of historical advance, despite the questionable character of many of his particular judgements, was precisely the method. For with Hegel the method had become one with history and history had become one with method.

26

A Journey to the Low Countries

In the middle of September 1822 Hegel finally set out, and rather reluctantly at that, upon a journey to the Netherlands which had long since been planned for. His only purpose in travelling, apart from acquiring further general knowledge, was to visit Peter Gabriel van Ghert, a former student of his and now a cultural official employed by the government in Brussels. Hegel had scarcely arrived in Magdeburg, his first stop *en route*, when he began to regret leaving Berlin and seriously considered turning back again. The general conditions of travel and accommodation had been very poor, and would continue to prove so for the rest of the journey. At first Hegel felt unwilling to proceed any further because the post he was expecting from his wife had not yet arrived, the state of the coach he was offered for the next stage was wretched and he kept on dithering about different possible routes to his destination. While he was waiting to move on he wrote a substantial letter to Goethe on 15 September in which he supported the latter's experiments and results concerning the spectrum. A comparison of the cathedral in Magdeburg with the Gothic church in Nuremberg clearly fell out in favour of the North German building. Walking along the Elbe one day Hegel was delighted to behold thirteen vessels arriving from Hamburg in full sail, as he tells his wife in a letter. At the same time he was generally on the lookout for a suitable travelling companion, whom he finally believed he had found in a young Englishman he had met in Magdeburg.

At the very last moment Hegel decided to travel on via Cassel as his next stopping place, apparently because of the quality of the postal coach on offer. The route passed through Brunswick and then through Göttingen, which Hegel failed to visit even briefly in spite of its famous university. But he was particularly taken with Cassel. He found the town 'very much in the style of Berlin' as far as its facilities were concerned, well supplied with public parks and gardens like Potsdam with excellent verdant lawns. He was even able to drink coffee in the open air. On visiting the local art gallery he regretted the fact that the best paintings had been carried off to Paris and St Petersburg. He travelled out to visit the elevation of Wilhelmshöhe, with its chateau still occupied by the ruling prince, and felt himself richly rewarded by the resulting view of the town, the valley and the distant hills.

The next report of Hegel's travels which his wife Marie received came from Coblenz. The actual trip to the town seems to have been particularly trying. After leaving his English companion, who had got out at Cassel, Hegel was joined by 'nothing but German countrymen', now six of them in all, three to a seat and all huddled up together as a result. The speculative philosopher from Berlin, who was not generally one to give himself airs, was probably sensitive to a certain difference in rank with respect to an unnamed 'unofficial professor of theology' who was travelling with the group. He was also rather irritated that a student from Giessen had managed to hold on to the best seat throughout the entire uncomfortable trip. The journey took them through the beautiful countryside along the river Lahn. Marburg and its dilapidated dwellings made a rather depressing impression upon them all. In Giessen the small company divided. Some of them set off by coach to Frankfurt, while Hegel and the others, including 'my young colleague, the Israelite' as Hegel called him, travelled on towards the Rhine via Weilburg and Limburg. Conditions must have been very difficult in Limburg. The travellers arrived at two o'clock in the morning in pitch dark when it was raining, and they had to ask at several inns before they found suitable accommodation. Hegel arrived in Coblenz soaked to the skin and found it necessary to 'change his shirt for the third time' and catch up on lost sleep before continuing.

The next stage of the journey, along the Rhine by boat to Cologne with stops at Linz and Bonn, also proved a total disappointment for Hegel. The weather was windy, damp and very cold, and the passengers did not venture out of their quarters onto the open deck. There were students amongst them who had all embarked on their Rhine journey with large satchels from which their sharp-pointed boots projected on every side. Such a Rhine journey was supposed to be a major cultural event for Europeans! For his part Hegel was forced to confess that he 'could hardly take any conscious pride in undertaking this journey down the Rhine'. In fact he was sorry he had ever left Berlin. How much nicer it would all have been just to stay there with his studies, his wife and his children!

Hegel, however, was pleased by the open vista he found in Cologne. He described the cathedral with a kind of curiously detached admiration: it was like 'a mighty forest which just stands there independently on its own account and takes no heed of whether human beings crawl around and beneath it or not'. Hegel would have seen the massive building at that time in its still unfinished state, as 'a mighty enterprise of the city' which had decided to complete the edifice.

In Cologne Hegel found time to write to his friend van Ghert in Brussels about his own imminent arrival. He thought the journey would take another four days, travelling through Aachen and Liège with a small detour via Namur. Eventually Hegel did arrive on time as expected in Brussels, albeit without the planned excursion to Namur. In Aachen he had not missed the opportunity of visiting the cathedral, and nor had the philosopher of the absolute been able to refrain from sitting for a few moments upon the great imperial throne of Charlemagne himself. And Hegel explicitly admitted a sense of 'satisfaction' in having done so.

His first impressions of the Netherlands on crossing the border were very favourable. 'This is very rich countryside', he told his wife, noting the stark contrast with his Prussian homeland. 'It is a real pleasure to travel in the Netherlands.' He could enjoy the sights of towns like Liège and Louvain with their impressive public buildings along the road to Brussels, which passed through acres of rich cornfields. He was very surprised to find the main road from Liège to Brussels to be 'paved like the new Königstrasse in Berlin'. He was thus able to complete the journey – about 90 kilometres – within twelve hours, 'and that for 10 francs', as he added.

His wife learnt all about this and many other things in Hegel's letter home of 13 October, in which he informed her of his arrival at his final destination. Hegel's visit from Berlin was not only a very pleasant occasion for van Ghert, but probably did him good as well. He had only just recovered from an illness and had yet to assume his new post as a royal commissioner for religious education in the southern Catholic region of the country. As a result he was able to dedicate his entire time to his teacher and friend from the Jena days. They visited the castle of Laeken together, as well as the then famous botanical gardens. But what was most important of all, they hired a coach and travelled out to the battlefield of Waterloo where Hegel's great idol, 'the world-soul on horseback', had met his final military defeat only seven years before. It is intriguing enough to imagine the philosopher of the absolute standing on the very spot 'where Napoleon himself, the prince of battles, had set up his throne', as Hegel writes proudly back to his wife in Berlin. Van Ghert also accompanied Hegel further through Flanders to visit the city of Ghent. Hegel's correspondence shows just how taken he was with the untroubled serenity of the landscape. There were no beggars to be seen as there had been between Aachen and Liège, merely lots of well-dressed adults and children even in the villages along the way! And all this in an artist's landscape which was without equal. In the cathedral of St Bavo in Ghent Hegel stood in front of the paintings of van Eyck and also attended the rectorship ceremony at the city's university. And then after lunch the two friends set out together to visit Antwerp.

In Antwerp their paths parted: van Ghert himself had to return to Brussels, not least in order to arrange for Hegel's post from home to be sent on to him since he was now considering travelling on through Holland proper. It must have been an exhausting time for Hegel in Antwerp. Hegel felt himself perspiring all over after his numerous visits to the churches of the city. And given the extremely low cost of hiring a *diligence* to Paris – a mere 25 francs – Hegel was sorely tempted for a moment to pay the French capital a visit as well. Hegel had specifically undertaken to travel to Amsterdam via the town of Breda in order to see a piece of work supposedly by Michelangelo, which we now know is actually no such thing. From Breda he was forced to take a boat to Moerdyk and from Dordrecht onwards he was then able to enjoy the spectacle of the broad and verdant Dutch meadowland with its little canals, its cows that were milked out in the open and its towns of reddish brick.

Once Hegel found himself in The Hague he was particularly struck by the apparent wealth of the country. What did the city do with its poor? They were certainly nowhere to be seen on the streets. The latter, on the contrary, were marked by the most elegant shops stocked with gold and silver ware, with porcelain, tobacco and shoe-wares, everything beautifully arranged for view and illuminated by night. Hegel only mentions in passing his visit to the local 'gallery', presumably the Mauritshuis with its small but exceptional collection. A trip out to Scheveningen also proved indispensable in order to view the North Sea properly for once and to collect fresh mussels along the beach. Hegel spent the evening watching a French play at the local theatre.

If Hegel said very little about Amsterdam, which he describes as 'Queen of the Seas', this was partly because he had by this stage become rather weary of travelling and was already thinking constantly of the return-trip to Berlin, which he now wished to accomplish as quickly as possible. We do hear about some large paintings by Rembrandt, though no further details are supplied, about a certain Doctor Besseling with whom he lunched, and about an evening visit to a couple of synagogues in the city. He also reports generally about the 'innumerable canals' and 'ships', about the prevailing 'crowds' and 'tumult' of town life, and about the stock exchange – when the bell there rings at three o'clock people pour out of the place just like 'they do in Berlin coming out of the theatre'. But otherwise Hegel's general impressions now seem to have become altogether fainter in character. He had seen a great deal and constantly compared things with life back in Berlin. The prosperity and obvious wealth which he witnessed, and most especially in Holland, forced him to revise certain opinions he had earlier entertained, as the detailed reports in the letters clearly reveal. This is where the contrasts with a bleaker Prussia were at their strongest. Above all Hegel was quick to notice the over-population of this successful West European commercial and colonial state.

The return trip via Utrecht, Deventer, Bentheim, Osnabrück, Bremen and Hamburg was expressly planned to bring Hegel back to Berlin as directly as possible. Once Hegel had passed the Dutch border he clearly found the journey through the rather monotonous northern flat lands disappointing. In the Netherlands he had become accustomed to the spacious verdant meadows and now rather felt he had landed in the Steppes. He would later remember what he had learned from his journey and vividly relate the experiences of this Prussian from Württemberg: everyone ought to go and see such a highly civilized region as the Netherlands with their own eyes.

27

The Philosophy of Art

~~∞~~

Kant's aesthetics, developed in his *Critique of Judgement*, was essentially a theoretical analysis of aesthetic judgement as understood in the tradition of Wolf and Baumgarten, but in fact his intentions were quite different. Kant's work here represented a veritable crossing of the Rubicon in philosophical terms, even if he disguised its momentous character behind scholastic definitions like that of our feeling of beauty as a 'disinterested delight'. This was a definite achievement of Kant's with enormous implications for the past tradition of aesthetic reflection and its future development. Kant essentially claimed that wherever we encounter the beautiful, whether it is in nature or in art, we are dealing with an object of specifically aesthetic perception which has nothing whatsoever to do with questions of morality or religious belief, or, expressed in more modern terms, with political engagement.

Kant's perspicacious mind had fundamentally clarified the distinction between the aesthetic as such, the experience of which is based upon sense perception, and everything that could not be made available to such perception. In this respect Hegel did not preserve this highest insight of Kantian aesthetic thought. Although Hegel also recognizes the distinctions between the respective spheres of art, religion and philosophy, and delineates their limits much as Kant had done, he was also quite capable of integrating or fusing them if he felt it necessary. Hegel's notion of the Greek 'religion of art', for example, is thoroughly un-Kantian and seems to suggest a regression on Hegel's part to the perspective of pre-critical metaphysics. Nevertheless Hegel recuperates what he has relinquished in his own dialectical fashion and clarifies the obscurity with which traditional metaphysics had treated the aesthetic domain by appealing to his principle of 'both/and'. In this respect Hegel's thought on art marks a significant advance on that of Kant. But the original Kantian step had been taken and could not now be reversed, as Hegel's own attempt to rehabilitate the tradition itself reveals.

Thus if Hegel remained behind Kant in one respect, Hegel's actual treatment of art and works of art went quite beyond him in another. Kant's aesthetic philosophy, precisely as a critique of aesthetic judgement, related to the phenomenon of art, and the particular art-forms, in a purely formalistic fashion. It did not share or even seriously approach the characteristic insight of Hegel's aesthetics, for unlike the latter it was not essentially a 'philosophy of art' at all.

As a theorist of aesthetics Kant had not advanced beyond the tastes of the later Enlightenment. He even found Lessing unintelligible, as Hamann's report of his response to Lessing's play *Nathan the Wise* reveals. From his own perspective Kant quite naturally considered the contemporary cult of genius as expressed in works like Goethe's *Werther* to be a dangerous threat to reason itself. The classical movement in German literature, with Goethe and Schiller, and the incipient romanticism of the last decade of the eighteenth century seem to have made no impression at all on Kant in far-away Königsberg. Anyone who seeks to discover in Kant any trace of ardour or enthusiasm for the great works of poetry, painting or music will be utterly disappointed. We learn nothing whatsoever from his pages about the works of his younger contemporaries, like Goethe's *Egmont* or Mozart's *Magic Flute*. For Kant, who developed his critical philosophy on the basis of and in response to the thought of Locke and Hume, these things were non-existent. As Otto Pöggeler puts it: 'It was not the cathedral of Königsberg, but rather carpets, drawings, porcelain and the heads on walking-sticks which taught him the meaning of art.'

One distinction of Kant's, which Hegel takes up again in his own aesthetics, is that between 'nature' and 'art'. This is the great theme of Goethe's aesthetic reflections in his *Propyläen* where he distinguishes between 'natural beauty' and 'artistic beauty', although not at the expense of 'nature' as is usually the case with idealist thought. Goethe was disappointed to find that even Schiller followed this path in his interpretation of Kant's thought. This is where the real differences appear and the almost materialist side of Goethe's outlook reveals itself. In this respect Hegel finds himself closer to Schiller for he also ascribes a higher rank to art than he does to nature. The portrait-painter and the sculptor must go beyond the merely naturally given object; they must omit everything that offends the sense of beauty, if they are indeed to surpass the beautiful in nature. And that is precisely what they should be striving to do, like the classical sculptors before them who produced the *Discus Thrower* or the images of Venus. For the immaculate marble reproduction of a beautiful human body with all the right proportions is quite capable of surpassing mere nature itself with all its minor faults and blemishes.

The task is thus to lead us away from 'common actuality' and towards the ideal as the authentic actuality of art. Or as Schiller had expressed the idea in his poem *The Ideal and Life*:

> Yet in those regions of serenity
> Which pure forms alone inhabit
> There sounds no more the turbid storm of grief.

This relieves art of all oppressive gravity that would otherwise bind it to the earth, would destroy its character as art and obliterate its distinction from life. As Schiller also says: 'Life is earnest, art serene.'

According to Hegel, then, art must endeavour to raise itself above the prose of life. Thus the genre of epic poetry must transpire in a world of gods, kings and lords. This form of art must maintain its elevated status over against everything of baser character and quality. Why is this? Not out of any special homage to these typical aristocratic values as such, but because freedom and a form of individual independence are essentially at issue here. For in the epic the subject relies entirely upon himself rather than upon the external decisions of others. The freedom of the subject can be forfeited, and his fall depicted, but this is because one can only lose what one has formerly possessed.

This leads every art into what Hegel calls a determinate 'world-situation'. The way in which the latter is constituted depends upon many different factors which arise within it and shape it accordingly. Such a world-situation is not originally created by any established legal order of things, by any political constitutions or other social institutions, but through the actions of powerful men, through heroic figures who pre-exist all law and any state and live a life almost outside of or prior to history itself.

This heroic world-situation must therefore be regarded as the ideal or poetic world-situation as such. In the Christianized world these heroes appear as knights errant, like the Arthurian knights of the Round Table, or as military champions of Charlemagne, like El Cid as the paradigmatic image of the warrior who defends the Christian cause against the heathen. But the ideal condition which is essentially presupposed in all such action can be threatened, the world-situation can become internally corrupted and degenerate entirely, bringing down with it any semblance of right or justice. In his play *The Robbers* Schiller depicted a heroic individual in the shape of Karl Moor who took up arms against the existing world around him, but is eventually caught up himself in the perpetration of injustice and consequently destroyed. The transformation of the nature of the world-situation only reveals the unfolding work of history itself. In Schiller's tragic dramas – *Cabal and Love*, *Fiesco*, *Don Carlos* and *Wallenstein* – the heroic will of the individual is always attempting to renew the world around it. Goethe's play *Götz von Berlichingen*, on the other hand, presents rather the reverse of this: a medieval form of chivalric heroism opposing a newly emerging world that threatens its existence, only to find itself vanquished in the end.

For Hegel the art of poetry takes pre-eminence over all others, including music and the visual arts. Hegel tells us that architecture must be regarded as 'the most imperfect of the arts' because it is forced 'to work with material weight as its natural element and deal with it according to the laws of gravity'. Thus it is in the last analysis 'incapable of expressing the spiritual in an appropriate form'. Sculpture must be looked upon as a higher art in this respect since it makes 'the spiritual itself into its object', while music, in relinquishing all spatial characteristics, permits 'the total withdrawal into subjectivity itself'. Hegel here reveals himself as a friend of Italian opera, a man for whom Mozart hardly figured, apart from *The Magic Flute* which did appeal to him, and Beethoven his exact contemporary, born in the same year as Hegel in 1770, did not seem to exist at all. Hegel always seems to have been reluctant to go beyond a certain limit, afraid to venture into strange and unfamiliar waters beyond the operas of Rossini. The German musicologist Carl Dahlhaus was tempted to interpret Hegel's silence about Beethoven as an 'eloquent silence', one essentially grounded in Hegel's 'deep-seated mistrust of the direction in which Beethoven was taking music' and his belief that the very idea of 'absolute music' was a mistake. This silence on the part of the anti-romantic Hegel would also seem to fit in with his rejection of Carl Maria von Weber's opera *Der Freischütz*. This conspicuous distrust of the 'Dionysian' element is what most distinguishes him from his great philosophical opponent Schopenhauer. For the latter, music is essentially an objective art, an expression of the cosmic will itself, and therefore the very highest of the arts.

Up until the end of the eighteenth century the theory of art was constantly preoccupied with the idea of comparing painting with poetry. Do they really have anything in common with one another? How are the boundaries between them to be drawn? Lessing had explicitly asked this question. It should be noted here that the word for painting as the general art of depiction (*Mahlerei*) was also used to include the art of sculpture. For Winckelmann and for Lessing, for Herder and for Goethe, not to mention Kant, music seemed to occupy the lowest position in any potential hierarchy of the arts. Why was this? Too little was really known or understood of this art, which seemed to have its greatest periods behind it, and it was impossible for that generation to sense the important role it would soon come to occupy in future. In antiquity the art of music lagged behind literature and the visual and plastic arts. Hegel's aesthetics of music did make some attempt to integrate a philosophy of music into the overall philosophical system of the arts, but it cannot be said that he succeeded in entirely dispelling the very modest aesthetic reputation which the art of music still enjoyed. For Hegel music represents the art in which sensuous material itself is set in motion, thereby producing a specific sound or 'tone' as a result of 'quivering vibration'. But the proper definition of this art also requires further reference to the other arts.

A general comparative system of art, such as Hegel offers us, is really only meaningful for a philosophy of art, and not for art itself. Within his system of art Hegel holds fast to the idea of an overarching unity which comprehends the various individual arts in their relation to one another. In the individual art-forms of architecture, poetry and music art itself shows its many different faces, just as nature itself is to be discovered variously manifested in volcanoes, humans, animals, crystals, in water, air and fire. But there is an internal principle of order in Hegel's account. Architecture, for example, represents the 'beginning of the concept of art'. Architecture is indeed art in so far as it presents the 'first form of artistic embodiment', but it can also properly be regarded as a form of pre-art because spirit here has not yet taken shape explicitly as spirit.

Hegel's division of architecture into the three forms of 'symbolical', 'classical' and 'romantic' art is not strictly tied to historical chronology, even though Hegel does regard the buildings of ancient Greece as the very zenith of classical architecture. The essential beauty of classical architecture in Hegel's eyes consists in its purposive structure and character. The principle of utility governs the classical architecture embodied in the public baths, the theatres, the imperial palaces, the great aqueducts, and so forth. This art is in a sense 'freer' than the symbolical style which tries obscurely to express its meaning in obelisks and pictorial decoration. Friedrich Schlegel's expression about architecture as 'frozen music' clearly appealed to Hegel. Nothing more now remains to be discovered about the architectural beauty of the famous classical 'orders' – the Doric, Ionic and Corinthian columns of antiquity. Romantic forms of architecture, as Hegel sees the matter, cannot compare in this respect with the classical ones. The essential direction of romantic architecture is entirely different in character. Hegel uses 'romantic' here more or less as a synonym for 'Gothic'. Hegel felt it necessary to oppose the relative disdain for the Gothic style which had persisted so unjustly for many centuries. And here Hegel was siding with Goethe who had essentially rediscovered the significance of this form of art in his celebrated essay *On German Architecture*. Goethe had written it under the impression made upon him by Strasbourg cathedral. Hegel was thinking rather of the cathedral of Cologne which he had personally seen and in which, for all its incompleteness, he thought he could perceive the model Gothic building with a special function of its own apart from the classical style of architecture. For him the building represented not 'purposive function as such' but rather 'a purposiveness adapted to the subjective sentiments of the soul'.

According to Hegel it is the domestic house which forms the original 'anatomical structure' for classical architecture in general. For the house essentially fulfils the purpose of enclosure as such. The human form provides the fundamental basis for the art of sculpture. These basic distinctions determine the nature of the various arts: whereas the house is a human invention, the human form itself is 'an independent product of nature'. The art of sculpture thus finds its natural and appropriate subject in the human figure. The other forms of plant and animal have a much more secondary significance.

This judgement follows from Hegel's overall perspective and his classically Greek criteria here: sculpture more than any other art naturally corresponds to the ideal of the human figure, represents its objective character and free organic beauty, and is the focal point of all classical art.

The principles which Hegel thus reads into sculpture once again reveal the aesthetic superiority of art over the products of nature, for the latter could never bring forth such impeccable forms as these artistic representations of the human figure with their infallible sense of harmony and perfectly calculated proportions. But that also means that sculpture has to avoid all physiological extremes of bodily nature and preserve its own intrinsic ideality. If the eyes of classical sculpture are more deeply set than they actually are in nature, this appropriately corresponds according to Winckelmann with the sculptural ideal itself, which subtly corrects natural reality here. In its definite ideality the sculptured figure also typically lacks the depiction of the pupil in the eye, lacks as it were a momentary glance in the face precisely because it is elevated beyond any particular moment. The Greek artists of the classical age at its height took great care, on the other hand, to individualize features like the ears; the mouth, the most beautiful part of the face after the eyes, should possess lips which are neither too thin nor too full; the mouth itself may appear gently open as long as the teeth, which have no immediate connection with the 'expression of spirit', are not to be seen.

Romantic art, on the other hand, is essentially characterized by features which alleviate and soften the tendency to closed autonomous form. 'The story of the Passion, the sufferings on the cross, the Golgotha of the spirit, the poetry of death', all of this is infinitely distant from the subject matter of the 'classically plastic ideal'. The classical god lacked the penetrating glance of the eye, whereas the figure with the carefully painted eyes on the other hand is a seeing, self-knowing spirit. The supremacy of the human form is also characteristic of romantic art but is now marked by greater emphasis on the particular moment of experience. Where the material itself becomes increasingly 'contingent and external' the romantic form of art begins to dissolve. The 'abstract necessity' which marked the classical work of art now falls away. If a modern rather than a classical artist undertakes to produce the statue of a Greek god, or if a Protestant should paint an image of the Virgin, a distinct aura of pastness attaches to their products which themselves no longer seem fully to touch the artist concerned or to express the artist's own identity. There is inevitably a certain lack of earnestness involved, a certain distance from the object of representation, and an element of (romantic) contingency has entered into the work at hand. The 'reproduction of external objectivity' now no longer signifies objectivity as it was understood by classical art and already contains a certain 'disintegration of art'. Hegel believes that the 'objectivity' which constituted an unassailable characteristic of the classical in art has been progressively weakened over the course of time. The solitary greatness of such works cannot be further sustained indefinitely. Nor can it properly be imitated by artists of a later generation. The 'songs' of the more objective poets like Homer, Sophocles, Ariosto and Shakespeare have long since been sung. This kind of creative voice cannot possibly return in a different age, and if this were even to be attempted, it would inevitably be found incredible and unworthy of respect because such things are essentially unrepeatable. This 'disintegration of art' only brings the inherent limitations of art itself, and its possible 'end', more acutely to our conscious awareness.

In the world of ancient Greece the art of painting was relatively insignificant as compared with that of sculpture. It was therefore an easy matter for painting in the Christian era to surpass the classical achievements in this field. According to Hegel painting essentially reaches its culmination in the romantic rather than the classical age. But why is this? Hegel thought that painting could only now grasp its own authentic content, and only now learn to employ its own artistic means. In the art of painting the original spatial totality of three dimensions finds itself reduced to two alone. Where the surface as such becomes the very element of painterly representation this art finds itself even further removed from architecture than sculpture was before it. Its physical element is light and its natural opposite, the dark. But light and shade, luminosity and darkness cannot simply be separated abstractly from one another but inevitably involve various subtle transitions between each other. Colour is thus the proper material of painting. Hegel utterly repudiated the idea that light was essentially composed of the various colours and their different combinations, and that for quite concrete and particular reasons. For that had been Newton's theory of light, decisively rejected by Goethe in his own doctrine of light and colour. The visible differences between individuals, their separation from other objects in the environment, the sense of distance, the play of features in the human countenance, general expression, all of this is simply the work of colour and its appropriate application. Painting can thus relinquish the third dimension of 'spatial reality' precisely in order to replace it with the 'higher and richer principle of colour'.

Painting thus reproduces motivating human actions, while sculpture generally represents situations without the element of intrinsic conflict and can only really depict active processes and passions in the form of group reliefs of one kind or another. Giotto marks the point where painting decisively emancipated itself from its Greek models and allows images of real human individuality to appear against the flat golden ground of the picture. Painting would progress in the direction opened up by Giotto. But the further development of art would soon come to include other fields than that of the sacred in which the Italian artists were particularly at home.

The German and the Dutch artists, as Hegel explicitly notes, did not approach anything like the 'free and ideal forms of expression' characteristic of the Italian painters, either because they lacked the appropriate technical skill or because they were essentially interested in achieving something quite different. German painting tends rather to reveal an 'expression of a certain formal stubbornness on the part of wilful and unruly natures'. This defiance and resistance suggests an experience of intense struggle which has left deep wounds behind in these individuals. This is especially true for the tradition of North German painting. For Hegel, as for Goethe, the artistic deviation from ideal forms and proportions always implies distance from the ultimately perfect type of art. That is why he ranks Raphael higher than he does the van Eyck brothers. The classical criteria of Hegel's aesthetic thought found it difficult to do real justice to the achievements of authentic Dutch painting. Nor was it really possible to ascribe such art to the essentially romantic sensibility either.

Hegelian aesthetics did not really have the resources to appreciate this domestic Dutch world with its pleasure in depicting its accumulated riches, its glittering household objects, not to mention the dances and market fairs, its often crude humour, its busily populated landscapes, its genre scenes from military life, weddings and country feasts. This was art outside the pale of what was acceptable to a classical taste, and one which could only really appeal to a kind of immediate visual pleasure.

It would not be particularly difficult to show that Hegel's notion of progress within the history of art would obviously conflict with the facts if he had deigned to defend it within the domain of art in general. The fact that he did not feel the need to do so essentially results from the systematic placement of art in his thought which interpreted the ideal of classical antiquity as the intrinsic culmination of the fine arts proper, as a point beyond which there could be no aesthetic advance in principle. The feeling for the fine arts in this sense was indeed reawakened during the Italian Renaissance, and especially through Michelangelo, who is explicitly named by Hegel in this connection. But the 'plastic principle of the ancients' could only be united with the religious-romantic, i.e. the Gothic-Christian, element by the titanic audacity of a quite unique artist like Michelangelo. And why is this? Because two quite different worlds are involved here: 'the entire development of Christian sensibility is not essentially oriented to the classical form of the ideal at all'.

But this also means that the Christian outlook itself, which Hegel recognized in Michelangelo, was an intrinsically inappropriate one for furthering and developing the art of sculpture as attained by the Greeks. And this was because sculpture as such was essentially perfected in Greece. In the domain of painting, on the other hand, the situation is very different. For here Raphael represented a perfection of style, and the pictures of the ancient artist Apelles cannot be regarded as so many 'preliminary exercises' for the Italian painter, any more than the tragedies of Sophocles can so be regarded in relation to those of Shakespeare. And in fact neither modern artist knew the work of their ancient predecessors.

If the art of painting eliminated the third dimension, still represented in sculpture, and restricted its depiction of subject matter to the surface alone, then music expresses the elimination of all spatial exteriority. The sound or tone which arises from a vibrating body is entirely constituted by the element of temporality. The musical note is produced by the regular number of vibrations in an equal period of time. The physical body is not an immediate object of artistic treatment, but simply an instrument of the same.

'The authentic power of music is an elementary kind of force.' Here it is tone alone which artistically moves us, which grips the listening subject without the need of language, drawing the 'undivided self in the centre of its spiritual being' into the work of art and stimulating the activity of the subject at the same time. The ear can reach where the eye cannot, receiving and reproducing the signals of Bacchic enthusiasm and the tumult of human passion. So it was that Orpheus tamed the beasts and Amphion moved the stones. As an art which lives in the medium of pure temporality it is directly dependent more than any art upon the process of actual engagement and reproduction.

This signified a decided appreciation of the possibilities of music and a simultaneous limitation of its scope. Hegel regards music as 'romantic art' *par excellence*, albeit in a sense that diverges from the more usual understanding of the term. None the less, for Hegel music was one art amongst the others, it was certainly not the revelation of the world-ground as it was for Schopenhauer. Hegel finds some appreciative words for the art of J. S. Bach: 'A master whose marvellous, authentically Protestant, robust and yet learned brilliance has only recently come to be properly appreciated once again.' Hegel regards Palestrina, Lotti, Pergolesi, Gluck, Haydn and Mozart as exponents of a 'genuinely idealistic music'. His account of the art of music, generally speaking, does not advance far beyond the application of the 'method' to the idea of 'reconciliation' implied in 'harmony' and that of 'dichotomy' implied in the experience of 'dissonance'. The limits of this method are clearly enough revealed in Hegel's encounter with the modern and typically 'romantic' music of Weber. Hegel apparently sees his musical aesthetic threatened and potentially overwhelmed by such 'violent effects of musical contrast', by this 'laceration' of the emotions which does not permit 'the subject's enjoyment or return into itself'.

Hegel regards 'poetry' as the art of spoken language as the properly 'universal art'. For its content is supplied by the entire world of inner and outer experience. Poetry can give shape to every object of the imagination in every form, deriving as it does its essential material from the realm of inner perception. Taken in conjunction with the two earlier kinds of art poetry can be regarded as the third and highest type precisely because it is 'the totality which unites within itself the two extremes of the visual and plastic arts on the one side and that of music on the other at a new and higher level'. And language, as the essential medium of poetry, must be recognized as the most appropriate form of communication in the last analysis.

The proper content of lyrical poetry is the subjective dimension itself which is thereby expressed in all its 'individual intuitive character'. This is where the evocation of mood tends to predominate. Lyrical poetry takes human passion as its primary subject. Epic poetry, on the other hand, exposes the realm of the 'objective itself in its very objectivity'. The world-situation that finds expression in the language of epic poetry harbours truths of a particular kind. In the epic world-situation man is not yet presented as torn out of his immediate relation to nature. The people still willingly follow their kings, lords and rulers without question and their political authority is never challenged. At the same time there are no rigid institutionalized laws to which the people are expected to submit themselves. The whole world of machines and industrial labour and its characteristic products, the entire form of social organization in the state, all of this is utterly inappropriate to the world of the epic. The sphere of individual subjective desire and intention has not yet asserted itself in the context of the authentically epic view of the world.

The epic shares the general field in which the collision of human action takes place with the art of drama. Ever since the time of Aristotle the affinity between the epic and the drama has been recognized. The tragic drama in Greece originally developed out of the epic and its traditional subject matter. The epic poet Homer is also the father of Greek tragedy. In the epic the state of war must be regarded as the generally prevailing situation. It is here that the various peoples come into conflict with one another. And this is where Aristotle drew the boundary, in the fourth chapter of his *Poetics*, when he recommended that tragedy should locate its tragic conflict within the sphere of the family. *Orestes* and *Oedipus*, but also the historical tragedies of Shakespeare as Hegel points out, are tragedies of the family where dynastic struggles or fratricidal conflicts are played out. In the epic poem war must have a 'universal-historical justification', as in the case of the *Iliad* which depicts the conflict between the Greeks and Trojans, itself a crucial turning point in Greek history, or as in the case of Ariosto or Tasso when they present the wars of the Christians and Saracens. In the epic the universal element is always directly connected to the individual, like Odysseus or Achilles in Homer, for it is only individuals, whether they be gods or heroes, that can properly act in a decisive manner. In the *Divine Comedy* the author Dante is the individual who undertakes the great journey through Hell, Purgatory and Paradise. But the epic is not so much concerned with the action in itself as with the surrounding circumstances and events involved: it is interesting to see what transpires with the hero as he attempts to realize his desires and fulfil his purposes, as with the return of Odysseus to Ithaca, but the final realization itself is secondary. On the other hand, the fully-fledged individual activity of the hero, the actual realization of his ends and all the consequences of this form the appropriate subject of drama. In the drama the character produces his own fate, in the epic it is produced largely through the force of circumstances.

Hegel explicitly distinguished between an 'original' and an 'artificial' epic.

This is the distinction for him between Homer and Virgil. Epics of this second kind, which includes poems like Milton's *Paradise Lost* or Klopstock's *Messiah*, cannot attain the same heights as the ancient 'original epics'. For they depend upon 'a conflict between the content and the poet's own reflection upon this content'. Because Hegel discovers such serious defects at work in the German poem the *Nibelungenlied* he is unable to compare it positively with the Homeric epics. The novel represents the continuation of the ancient epic in bourgeois form. 'The novel in its modern sense', Hegel notes, 'presupposes a reality that becomes essentially prosaic', a world in which the 'originally poetic world-situation' of the ancient epic has finally vanished. The epic situation and its corresponding sensibility can no longer properly assert itself under the new conditions of the modern world, and finds itself reduced to the expression of nothing but grandiose sentiments. From its very beginnings in seventeenth-century England the bourgeois novel has essentially been based upon the schematic opposition of a 'poetry of the heart' and the 'prose of real life' which inevitably either destroys the former or forces it into compromise with the world.

Drama too has moved away from the epic world-situation and has lost the sense of the epic totality. The collisions involved in it are much simpler and the exposition of its themes cannot expand to anything like the same breadth and complexity as the epic. The form of tragic drama cannot afford to dwell upon a long and elaborate narrative of events, but rather demands a constant forward movement leading to the final catastrophe.

Dramatic poetry as it has developed from the works of antiquity through Shakespeare to the art of the modern age in Schiller and Goethe reveals the transformation which has transpired in the social world. The nature of the *dramatis personae* alone indicates this transformation. The kings and rulers in modern drama are not what they once were. The monarchs are no longer like the lords of the mythical age, and thus no longer represent the 'individual focal point of the social whole'. They have lost the capacity to make the most important political decisions on their own behalf, they no longer determine in person the nature of right and justice, and no longer decide 'the principal issue' of war and peace, as they once did. The difference between individuals and social classes cannot of course be eliminated. This is indeed what first makes the tragic action possible, constitutes the original eminence and status which precedes the eventual fall of the hero and which belongs essentially to the heroic individual in relation to the other figures, which marks him out and thus elects him, so to speak, for the coming catastrophe.

In Hegel's theory of dramatic art the tragic dimension does not necessarily possess the final word over against the comic dimension. 'In tragedy the individuals destroy one another through the one-sidedness of their substantial will and character . . . ; in comedy on the other hand the laughter of the individual who dissolves everything in himself and through himself reveals the victory of his own securely independent subjectivity.' But that is not the whole truth of the matter. For in comedy as the second arm of dramatic art the human being makes himself into 'the supreme master over everything that otherwise represents the essential content and significance of all knowing and acting'. The comedy of Aristophanes reveals a world in which the enlightened citizen plays the central role in the action. The aesthetic attitudes of the Berlin Hegel seem to express a decided dislike for this state of affairs: 'There is nothing that can be done to help a democratic people in this state, with selfish citizens who are contentious, superficial and self-important at the same time, lacking in all faith and knowledge, garrulous, boastful and vain. Such a people dissolves itself utterly in the exhibition of its own foolishness.' The emphasis of Hegel's theory of art in general thus clearly lies with the art of poetry. The most impressive sections of Hegel's lectures on aesthetics are those which deal directly with the epic and tragic works of world literature. What Hegel says about the lyrical dimension of poetry seems rather secondary by comparison. As far as his own aesthetic poetic tastes were concerned, Hegel did not advance beyond the work of Goethe, Schiller and Klopstock which he regarded as the *ne plus ultra* of contemporary lyric poetry. He seems to have been unaware of the uniquely expressive lyrical power of his former friend and room-mate Hölderlin. Or was it that he felt reluctant to speak about the poet and his fate?

The aesthetic values which find expression in Hegel's philosophy of art are thoroughly traditional ones. Hegel defends the basic position of aesthetic classicism with its orientation to what Goethe called the 'healthy' in art. Hegel attempts to justify this approach in detail by drawing upon Aristotle, undertaking to bring all the particular aspects of the individual arts together in a single systematic scheme. This led him to consider Winckelmann as authoritative for the visual and plastic arts, Herder and Lessing authoritative for the art of poetry.

It is true that the name of Lessing is rarely mentioned, and Herder disappears in the general tumult of the aesthetics of 'genius', but their influence decisively shaped the trajectory of Weimar classicism and the characteristic achievements of the so-called 'art period' of German culture, all of which finds its appropriate expression in Hegel's lectures on art. And here we see an otherwise surprising coincidence of views between Hegel and Schopenhauer, his unknown philosophical opponent. For Schopenhauer's doctrine of art is also classical and conventional, and is based, like Hegel's, upon Goethe. The work of Hegel and Schopenhauer in this respect reflected the same 'faith' that was cultivated in Weimar. But while Schopenhauer grasped art as born 'from the spirit of music', Hegel regarded it rather as born 'from the spirit of poetry'.

Yet according to Hegel there is also every reason to doubt whether art will enjoy a significant future at all. For precisely in his philosophy of art the idea of a continuous historical advance is decisively and abruptly called into question. Hegel thinks that we must seriously consider the possibility of an 'end of art'. It is perfectly conceivable that art will one day no longer exist. The idea of 'the eternity of art', which classical aesthetics took for granted, is now revealed as nothing but a highly questionable phrase. The appearance of art is like a momentary historical episode within a broader natural history of the world. Nietzsche, otherwise so far removed in outlook from Hegel, will later adopt this thought and develop it even further. Nietzsche's 'Overman' as a man of the future is also an overcoming of the artist. Who can say whether the future will not perhaps transpire without reference to art or to the artist? In Hegel's aesthetics this thought appears as a kind of rupture within the system or at least as an alien body in his philosophy. And this is certainly how the idea has often enough been interpreted.

In his biography of the philosopher, Rudolph Haym later made the historically and culturally revealing remark that 'although Hegel recognized and understood the specific nature of art, he misunderstood the religious dimension and demoted its significance'. Perhaps this authentically reflects the final impression which Hegel himself, surrounded with the aureole of Goethe's friendship, and his lectures on aesthetics actually left upon his listeners in Berlin. Hegel certainly believed that the 'aesthetic dimension' was essentially characterized by an intrinsic freedom towards the traditional subject matter and promises of religion. The aesthetic experience of 'the beautiful' in nature and art, the literally sensuous experience of objective reality in terms of body, material, form, shape, proportion, colour, word, sound and rhythm, is not an experience essentially tied to the past or the future, to the memory of an earlier age or the anticipation of future glory entertained in faith and hope. Rather such experience testifies to the infinite value of the present moment of time, something that essentially expresses itself in art rather than in religion.

This attitude was also profoundly confirmed by Goethe who, for all his genuine respect for religion and indeed especially for the Christian religion, still regarded himself as a 'pagan' and felt not the slightest need to be 'saved' through the promises of faith. And he openly expressed the reason for this outlook:

> He who possesses art and knowledge,
> Possesses religion also;
> He who possesses neither one nor the other,
> Let him have religion instead.

28

The Austrian Journey

We are well informed about the precise reasons which led our idealist philosopher to visit the Austrian dominions in 1824, the land of the imperial Habsburg dynasty which had ruled the former German Empire for many centuries. For once again Hegel himself provided very detailed reports of his travels in his letters to his wife. A Prussian from Württemberg in Austria! That must have involved direct contact with a world that was previously quite closed to Hegel, despite the Austrian historical connections of parts of Swabia, on account of his own background, general outlook and style of life. It is true that Austria had been an ally of Prussia, along with Russia, against their earlier common enemy, Hegel's 'world-soul on horseback', but the prevailing Prussian attitude to Austria was hardly positive or encouraging. Austria essentially represented not only the old vanished Empire itself, but all its characteristic faults and weaknesses, that backwardness which Hegel had always profoundly lamented and which in his view only met the fate it richly deserved with the eventual collapse of the Empire.

What, then, does Hegel say about Austria in his lectures on the philosophy of world history?

> Austria is not a kingdom but an imperial state, that is, an aggregate of several political organizations. The most important of these are not German in character and have been untouched by the influence of ideas. They have been elevated neither by general culture and education nor by religion; in some of them the subjects are still in a state of feudal dependence, and the more important of them have remained deprived and undeveloped, as is the case in Bohemia; and in some of them the crown has asserted its power under similar feudal conditions, as in Hungary.

Given Hegel's unqualified repudiation of feudalism as an unjust form of domination, his judgement could hardly be more negative than it was. It was with attitudes like this, also widely shared beyond Prussia, concerning the Habsburg Empire that Hegel set out on his journey in September 1824.

Dresden was his first stop, where he took the immediate opportunity to write to his wife in Berlin. He had always been particularly keen to visit this city. For Dresden, where he obviously felt so much at home, had been expressly chosen by Hegel as a natural meeting place where he could see his old friends from Heidelberg, especially Creuzer and Daub. In the event they were unable to meet him there after all. On this occasion therefore Hegel resigned himself to a short sightseeing visit and took up lodgings at the inn The Blue Star. He promenaded along the great terraces, attended a public lecture given by Karl August Böttinger, director of the museum of classical antiquities, and listened to the recitation of a play by Ludwig von Holberg at the home of Ludwig Tieck. Hegel actually visited the famous Dresden art gallery twice during his stay. When he announced the next stage of his trip to Prague, Hegel was particularly careful to tell his wife not to mention anything of a political nature in her correspondence with him since 'in Austria the letters are opened and read'. In the spa resort of Teplitz he went up the Schlossberg and enjoyed the resulting view of the valley. In the evening he watched part of Weber's *Preziosa*, which he remembered being rather better performed in Berlin. Then he went on to Prague. Hegel was reluctantly forced to extend his intended stay in Prague by a couple of weeks because all the available coaches to Vienna were already booked up. He also spent one evening at the playhouse. In the quarter known as 'Little Prague' he even got caught up in the midst of some military manoeuvres and was soon forced, as he put it to his wife, to beat a hasty 'retreat'. Hegel also made a trip out to Schloss Karlstein, four hours' travelling from Prague, apparently as a way of spending some of the long waiting time before he could depart for Vienna. He spent the journey in a coach which was divided by a window into two 'apartments' each seating four people. They covered a distance of 42 miles in about 36 hours.

We can see what it was about Vienna that had particularly attracted Hegel in the first place by his behaviour on arrival there. Even though he was still tired from the long journey, he immediately made his way, in his 'travelling clothes', to the Opera House where Meradente's *Doralice* was playing in the evening. And indeed it was Italian opera which occupied him throughout the next few days. Hegel found it incomprehensible how people could come and visit Vienna without thinking of going to hear Italian opera there. What he clearly enjoyed most of all on this occasion were not the works of Gluck or Mozart but those of Rossini, particularly as performed by native Italian singers. He was captivated by the 'sparkle' of this music, by the brilliant and sometimes superficial beauty of the vocal line itself with its glittering displays of coloratura. He explicitly mentions seeing a performance of Rossini's opera *Otello* and his *Figaro* (*The Barber of Seville*). He even went to hear the latter twice and had to confess that he had enjoyed it 'so much more than Mozart's *Figaro*'.

There were also some quite particular reasons why Italian music continued to occupy his thoughts during the rest of his stay and right up to his return to Berlin. For Hegel's friend Madame Milder, a singer whose salon the Hegels frequented in Berlin, had explicitly recommended him to visit Vienna specifically on account of the Italian opera, as well as the famous public gardens. Hegel duly followed her advice, immediately found her best recommendations fully confirmed by experience, and wrote directly to his wife asking her to pass on his appreciation to the famous singer.

Hegel visited the *Burgtheater* only once during his stay in Vienna, but there he met the actor Anschütz, whom he had not seen for twenty-five years. Hegel's letters reveal that he was particularly struck by his visit to the 'world-famous Kasperl' in Leopoldstadt. He provides an expert critical review of the disappointing playlet which preceded the pantomime, but he was delighted once Harlequin and Colombine made their appearance with full musical accompaniment, and he thoroughly enjoyed the restless antics and spirited acrobatics of the players. He was so pleased by the spectacle that he decided to go and see something similarly 'lowbrow' the next evening. He was equally delighted by a light play entitled *The Magic Pear* which he actually attended twice, also in Leopoldstadt, regretting only that his two sons had not been there to enjoy the evening with him.

It is small wonder that Hegel gradually began to detect signs of growing tiredness. He was generally on his feet from morning till night, and after ten days he was beginning to feel his bones aching. Although the thought of his own family back in Berlin had started more and more to occupy his mind, he still felt an enormous need to familiarize himself with things in the city which he had never been able to see before. 'As long as the money still suffices to pay for the Italian opera and the costs of my trip home, then I shall remain in Vienna.' This remark fairly represents the hopes and intentions of his Austrian stay as well as indicating its limits. Once the official grant which he had obtained from Privy Counsellor Schulz specifically for this journey was exhausted, Hegel was obliged to return to Berlin straight away. Some of the reservations he had initially entertained about Vienna as the capital of the much despised Habsburg Empire had clearly long since been dispelled by his experience of the 'rich world' he encountered there. The prospect of returning to his circumstances in Berlin suddenly seemed less inspiring after the splendid attractions of Vienna.

The Hegel who spent his time in Vienna rushing around between the play-house and the opera, the ballet and the light comedy – does he not initially seem a rather unlikely character? But it was quite true: the speculative philosopher had quite clearly allowed himself to relax from his profession for a good two weeks. The encyclopaedic philosopher of logic, nature, history, law and religion gave way to an extremely responsive adept of the arts. Perhaps this best reveals the aesthetic outlook of a man who learned much from his personal contact with Goethe.

Hegel returned from Vienna along the same route via Prague and Teplitz without stopping very long along the way. He was now clearly feeling the need to see his family again. He did make a stop in Dresden where he made a surprising appearance in the company of Tieck and Friedrich Schlegel, whom he had never met before. And Hegel there revealed himself, rather to the astonishment of his pupil Hotho, to be a fervent admirer of Italian opera. He also met with a certain rebuff on the part of Tieck. Hegel thought that, on account of some of his more formless dramatic pieces, Shakespeare had sometimes to be regarded as artistically confused. Tieck rejected this idea most emphatically. In his eyes Shakespeare was a man with a total clarity of vision. It is difficult not to agree here with Tieck, himself a brilliant translator of the English poet.

29

The History of Philosophy

Philosophy can never be separated from its own history. For Hegel the history of philosophy is itself philosophy. That is the central principle which governs the lectures on the subject that he gave in Berlin. The history of philosophy, in his view, reveals 'a gallery of the intellectual heroes of reason' and shows us how they 'penetrated to the very essence of things, of nature and of spirit'. We are essentially concerned here with acts of the spirit which, according to their content, have little to do with the personal or individual characteristics of men, with particularities, passions or expressions of singular genius; we are concerned rather with the essence of that free thought itself which belongs to the human being in general. The possession of 'reason in self-conscious form', Hegel reminds us, is not something that has simply 'grown up on the soil and ground of the present'. The 'deeds of reason' are initially a 'matter of the past' that lies beyond the immediate horizon of present reality. For 'what we are, that we also are historically'.

Thus philosophy, as a discipline mindful of its past, with the accomplished historical deeds of reason, preserves the legacy of the labour of all previous generations in the history of mankind and reveals its continuing significance for the present. Its content properly embraces the spiritual achievements of the world. But the spirit itself can never sink into indifference or inactivity: 'Its life is its deed.' The history of philosophy therefore relates the 'deeds of free thought', itself represents the 'history of the process in which thought discovers itself', in accordance with the Hegelian principle that spirit can only find itself in so far as it actively produces itself. What it produces are the various systems of thought. This labour of human reason has been performed within a time span of two and a half thousand years, a labour that is essentially directed towards the absolute itself. The history of philosophy is thus 'a part of the process in which the absolute grasps its own character', as Dieter Henrich puts it.

The history of philosophy as a philosophy of philosophy on the basis of history here rejoins Hegel's overall philosophy of history itself and covers some of the same ground. Like the philosophy of history, Hegel's history of philosophy is governed throughout by the thought of the advancing spirit and consciousness of freedom. In its history philosophy bears the epochs of its own consciousness within itself. For Hegel the Orient knew that only one was free, namely the despot, the Greek and Roman world knew only that few are free, namely the citizens, and finally the Germanic-Christian world properly knows that all are free. But since freedom essentially consists in the reciprocal recognition of equals, there was as yet neither a consciousness of freedom nor an expression of philosophy proper in the Oriental world. The latter could only arise where the idea of freedom had begun to dawn, as it had in Greece before passing on to influence the civilization of Rome.

But freedom is not the only condition for the activity of philosophy. There must also be a sufficient degree of general culture, certain conceptions must already have been acquired and developed, certain objects must have been present to reflect upon in the first place. A certain spiritual substance is required before philosophy can commence. Philosophy therefore does not simply arise in the very beginning but presupposes a cultural beginning has already been made. It inevitably has the morning freshness of youth behind it and beholds rather the world-historical evening in which the 'Owl of Minerva' takes its flight.

In addition to the incipient forms of culture and freedom, a third element, at least as a kind of premonition, is also required: a feeling for the possibility of approaching disaster. Freedom had scarcely begun to arise in Greece when it already found itself threatened by destruction as far as the Greek colonies of Asia Minor were concerned. And philosophy only reached its zenith precisely when the corruption of Athens had already begun to reveal itself, just as the dissemination of philosophical thought in Rome coincided with the real decline of the latter. When the Roman Empire began to disintegrate, philosophy experienced a final revival in the form of the Alexandrian School. This tradition was carried over into Neoplatonism, through Plotinus and Proclus, and became an intellectual element within Christianity, where it was adopted and baptized by scholastic philosophy. This process lasted over a thousand years and was not an entirely salutary one for philosophy in Hegel's eyes. The 'philosophy of the modern age' really only begins for him with the period of the Thirty Years War, with Francis Bacon, Jakob Böhme and René Descartes, and is thus essentially an achievement of recent date.

Hegel never loses sight of the fact that the Greek world, the only culture that is truly significant for the beginning of philosophy proper, also rests upon the legacy of the East and received much of importance as far as its art and religion were concerned from Syria and Egypt in particular. But it profoundly Hellenized this legacy and made it entirely its own. The Greeks possessed a gift, unparalleled by any other people, to turn what they inherited into a story of their own making. They transformed this material into tales about the origin of the world, of gods and men, of the earth, the sky and the winds, the mountains and the rivers. And they told these tales in such a beautiful and striking way that we can talk of original imaginative invention on their part. They made 'their world into a home for themselves' as Hegel says. They adapted the alien material before them and transformed it into something quite different. The feeling that the very name of Greece evokes is that of being essentially at home in the world. And that is also why philosophy itself always feels at home and at ease with the Greeks as it does nowhere else.

As far as the origins of Greek philosophy are concerned Hegel identifies two geographical locations as essential for the development of intellectual life: Ionia and the Greek mainland for the period which stretches from Thales of Miletus to Anaxagoras. The geographical distinction between East and West involves a broad distinction in patterns of thought. Amongst the Greeks of Asia Minor (Thales, Anaximander, Anaximenes, Heraclitus, Leucippus, Democritus, Anaxagoras and Diogenes of Crete) we find 'a predominantly sensuous and material emphasis' in philosophy, whereas with the western Greeks (Pythagoras of Samos, Xenophanes, Parmenides, Zeno and Empedocles) we find 'the priority of thought as such'. In the Greek philosophers of the Italian mainland the 'ideal conception of the absolute' is the most important characteristic. It is only with Socrates that the gravity of philosophy moves to Athens, where the two extremes are focused and mediated with one another.

Hegel subscribes to the traditional picture according to which Greek philosophy reached its culmination in the thought of Plato and Aristotle. The full significance of this interpretation would only be revealed after Hegel's death when it was first really contradicted. In his Jena dissertation on Democritus and Epicurus the young Marx placed a question mark over this evaluation, and much the same thing was done by Nietzsche too when he emphasized the enormous debt of his own thought to the so-called pre-Socratic philosophers and challenged the orthodox view. In the first case this indicates that Hegel underestimated the importance of the early materialist philosophers of nature, and in the second that the supposed advance of the world spirit in truth might involve a simple regression since the path traversed by philosophy from Thales and Democritus through to the dialectical dissolution of the later Greek city-states could thereby also be read under the sign of decadence.

Hegel, on the other hand, maintains the same sequential development here as in his philosophy of history and recognizes even in Thales, who explained everything in terms of water as his first principle, anticipations of what would be fully achieved by 'modern philosophy'. The development of nature out of some primordial stuff, like water, air, fire or earth, all transpires within an essentially unlimited time span. The atomists first attained philosophical insight into the existence of indivisible particles of matter which, according to Democritus, were extended, impenetrable, heavy and indestructible. These particles are all of exactly the same kind and are infinite in number. Thus being is here understood as split up into so many tiny ontological splinters which also presuppose the empty space within which they exist. Ontological speculation, which began with the earliest of the Greek philosophers and soon developed into an impressive body of thought, finds in Hegel the most penetrating interpreter imaginable. In Parmenides he discovers 'the most sublime form of dialectic there has ever been': all coming into being and passing away must reckon with non-being, characterized precisely by the fact that it is not, and shows that in the last analysis change is impossible and only unchangeable being truly is. Being and thought coincide as they do in the philosophy of identity that derived from Fichte. For non-being also *is*, carried along by being as its opposite without which it in turn cannot be, just as the principle of contradiction always operates within the nature of things and of human thought in general. Hegel sees Heraclitus as bringing this ontological speculation to its highest point. Heraclitus is for him the first thinker who grasped the essence of ideas as a unity of opposed moments and draws the appropriate conclusion: being and non-being are ultimately the same. This of course expresses a fundamental proposition of the Hegelian system, except that where the Greeks derived it from speculations on nature, Hegel derived it from his logic which necessarily precedes the philosophy of nature. Hegel emphasizes that there is not a single proposition of Heraclitus which he did not incorporate into the argument of his logic. Heraclitus also introduces the principle of living movement into philosophy, once again a major advance which Hegel is not slow to recognize: 'A great thought is involved in this passage from being to becoming.' This was an original insight of Heraclitus quite unknown to his predecessors, and Hegel regards such speculation in a certain sense as a mirror image of his own.

Hegel treated the atomists much more briefly, giving Leucippus more space than the much more important Democritus. But he finds them both more interesting than Empedocles. Natural science finds its outlook confirmed in these thinkers since they too regarded the world not as proceeding from some higher first cause but essentially as resting independently within itself. Hegel gives serious consideration to this materialistic version of the nature and origin of the world as one intellectual possibility, but certainly not as one which can compare with the Platonic or Aristotelian perspective on the question.

Philosophy amongst the pre-Socratics, according to Hegel, has not yet taken on the form of 'science' in his sense, i.e. a fully articulated body of systematic knowledge. Plato was the first thinker to accomplish this. And he could only do so because he already had the experience of Sophistic thought behind him. The Sophists, whose very frivolity reveals, as it were, the opposite side of Plato's own thought, were the fathers of the Greek 'Enlightenment'. They were the first to bring an explicit and self-conscious educational culture to the Greeks. For they encouraged the desire to acquire such culture in so far as they promoted the cause of rhetoric, the art with which the human affects and passions could be guided in the required direction. They did not regard 'truth' as a permanent object of thought. There are as many truths as there are individual minds, which is to say that there is no single truth at all. But what the Sophists offered their paying clients in return was by no means insignificant. As public teachers they undertook to make their students 'rational' in the only sense that really mattered, to supply them with the appropriate knowledge and skills with which they could accomplish their own subjective purposes and use the doctrine of truth to their own advantage. In the age of the Peloponnesian War, when Athens was being besieged by Sparta and the Greek mainland was declining as a political power, they exploited all the emerging doubts concerning absolute truth. Everything is in flux, caught up ineluctably in constant change and movement, and therefore ultimately relative. 'Man is the measure of all things', as the Sophist Protagoras expressed the idea. This proposition implied two things: man is essentially an individual and can therefore regard nothing as universally binding upon him, and yet as a human being he still possesses self-conscious reason. This is now the starting point for all genuine philosophy according to the Sophists.

Without the entire climate of thought first developed by the Sophists (grasping reflection as they did as a negative and essentially sceptical activity), without their notion that there is in fact no absolute truth, Socrates would have had nowhere to begin his attack upon such ideas, and no profound reason for doing so. In this sense the Sophists too were necessary for the progress of the world spirit.

But it is with Socratic thought that 'the principle of the modern age' is discovered. And the historical emergence of this principle amongst the Greeks coincided, as Hegel characteristically points out, with the decline and fall of Greece as a great political power. This weakness in the political domain itself helped to produce the epochal transformation of Greek thought in the philosophy of Plato and Aristotle, which had originally descended from Socratic thought and eventually became authoritative for subsequent speculation for the next two thousand years. In so far as Plato defended the view that 'the essence' dwells within human consciousness, that 'the absolute exists in the medium of thought and all reality is thought', in so far as he emphasized the fundamental 'right of self-conscious thought', to this extent Plato can plausibly be regarded as a direct follower of Socrates. For Plato the 'ideas' themselves are what is truly real. It is thought which produces them and first allows them to penetrate the inner being of consciousness. It is an illusion, by contrast, to consider the sensuous and external world as the pre-eminently real one. The intellectual production of the ideas constitutes a kind of recollection. In this process of recollection the soul and its thinking activity remembers what it has long since already experienced in a form of pre-existence. The Platonic doctrine of the idea in terms of pre-existence amounts to a doctrine of immortality, it recognizes the continuance of the soul after death and the associated processes of reincarnation and metempsychosis.

Hegel does not simply reject the idea of the immortality of the soul. The Platonic immortality of ideas, the immortality of the soul, is something that readily lends itself to the Hegelian concept of the 'world spirit' and the 'world soul'. In the Platonic version of the world soul the original architect of the world is pictured as arranging and co-ordinating matter in a rational fashion. Idea and material stuff are here conjoined, opposites in general here find themselves combined: order with chaos, reason with unreason, the living with the ideas.

But this also means that for Plato non-being belongs essentially to the realm of matter. The latter belongs in the dimension of negativity and plays an opposed role to that of spirit, thus revealing the fundamentally dualistic character of Platonic thought. Hegel perceives this dualism as its essential weakness. The opposed moments are not sublated, spirit appears as essentially separated from matter instead of including it within itself. In this respect Plato still lags behind the kind of idealism Hegel represents. His dualism with respect to the relation between the ideas and the material world, between form and substance, between philosophical speculation and immediate empirical experience – all of this prevents him from attaining a truly dynamic conception of being. Hence it is necessary to go beyond the philosophy of Plato, despite the profundity of his doctrine of the ideas, the beauty of his thought in general, and even the elevated conception of the divine which the Christian world itself would come to associate with his name. Hegel's view here was also directed against Schleiermacher, himself a great translator of Plato's works, who had already attempted to harmonize Platonic and Christian thought in his own fashion. For Hegel the progress of thought inevitably passes through Aristotle to attain a yet higher level of insight: 'He is one of the richest and most profound of intellectual geniuses who has ever existed, a man to whom no other age can find an equal.'

When Hegel deals with the philosophy of Aristotle, he is returning to his own intellectual origins. There is certainly no philosopher who reveals a greater propinquity to Hegel than Aristotle. Nicolai Hartmann has pointed out that Hegel felt himself to be an Aristotelian who had first properly discovered the original master after centuries of misunderstanding and essentially completed what he had begun. This is directly connected with a remarkable internal affinity in the structure of their thought and indeed with the fact that Hegel had devoted considerable close and careful study to Aristotle even during his early period in Tübingen. Hegel was more intimately acquainted with the thought of Aristotle than that of any other philosopher.

Hegel is quite explicit about the precise reasons why for him Aristotle was capable of continuing what the 'Platonic principle' had initiated: Aristotle is

truly 'comprehensive and speculative like no other thinker'. His was not the
sort of mind that was content merely to leave some 'systematizing whole'
behind him. For in his philosophy, on the contrary, the individual domains
(the disciplines of philosophy) are themselves empirically developed and co-
ordinated with one another. And 'yet they form a totality of essentially speculative philosophy'.

Hegel sees the relative superiority of Aristotle over Plato as grounded in
his greater speculative power. On the other hand, Hegel emphatically rejects
the usual opposition that is drawn between Plato's 'idealism' and Aristotle's
'realism', especially when the latter is understood in the trivial way it often
is. Hegel's affinity with Aristotle is based upon the latter's metaphysics and
its connected system of logic. In the eyes of Aristotle metaphysics is 'pure
philosophy' and distinguished precisely as such from all other sciences, which
naturally brings the subject into close proximity with Hegel's understanding
of the ultimate coincidence of logic and metaphysics. Aristotle could not fail
to impress him in this respect since his system of logic had also remained the
definitive one until Hegel's own science of logic comprehensively renewed it
in the same broadly Aristotelian spirit. As Hegel put it: 'Logic is thus the
science of reason; it is the speculative philosophy of the pure idea of the
absolute essence, not an opposition of subject and object, but an opposition
within thought itself.'

And here again we can also see the difference between Plato and Aristotle:
the 'idea' as Aristotle understands it is not the same as Plato's concept. Plato
recognizes the idea of the good, of the beautiful, of the ultimate end, etc. as
the universal. But the activity which essentially realizes the idea in question
is not explicitly 'posited' as such. The idea has not yet emerged from the
inertia of merely 'implicit being'. It has not yet been penetrated by 'the very
principle of life' itself. It is Aristotle who first permits the idea to fulfil itself
in subjective life, to emerge from the sheer objectivity of law and reason, to
enter into relationship with other ideas, to detach itself from the merely universal and thus to make itself effective in reality. The idea only reaches its
ultimate fulfilment in the concept of 'entelechy' in which the 'end' is authentically realized. Thus it is that matter is shaped and changed through activity, through form as intrinsic possibility and through dynamic power as
authentic capacity.

For Aristotle entelechy is the principal notion which contains all subsidiary
ones within itself. Here the process of thinking and the object of thought is
one and the same: 'Thinking is the thought of thought.' But they are also
separate because the energy of thinking as activity is higher than what thought
in each case actually thinks as its object. What, then, was the Aristotelian
philosophy *not* capable of properly comprehending in Hegel's eyes? This philosophy had no real 'principle for all particularities', no one 'absolutely unifying concept' for all the series of various subsidiary concepts. This is precisely
the task which Hegel ascribes to the subsequent history of philosophy.

The philosophers who immediately succeeded Aristotle were incapable of attaining the same intellectual heights as the great Stagyrite and rather prepared the way for the emerging Roman world. It is true that all these philosophies actually arose on Greek soil and their great teachers were all Greeks. But under the eventual world dominion of Roman power, which essentially suppressed the individuality of the different peoples, these systems of philosophy forfeited the original profundity of Greek speculation. Philosophy became an abstract affair and attempted merely to fulfil the dogmatic needs of the Roman spirit. In this process philosophy came increasingly to resemble a religious faith.

Hegel is thinking here of the various schools of Epicureanism, Stoicism and Scepticism. According to Hegel: 'The Stoic philosophy made abstract thought into its central principle, while Epicureanism made empirical sensation its principle; Scepticism was a negative procedure, the active negation of each and every principle.' In *one* respect, however, these philosophies are all alike: the inner freedom of the subject had to be maintained. A certain imperturbability, the indifference of the spirit towards pleasure and pain, was the common end they all strove to attain. This also included indifference towards the state, to which they no longer felt crucially attached as Plato had felt attached to the Athenian constitution in his time. In Rome political life was a cooler affair essentially remote from the Greek experience of joy and serenity. Rome possessed its excellent lawyers and the morality of a Tacitus instead. Philosophy was only invoked in the context of political life, at best, to ward off the influence of ancient superstition. Otherwise there is little positive to be said about it: 'in the misery of the Roman world everything beautiful, everything noble on the part of spiritual individuality was obliterated by the cold hand of harshness'.

At this stage Oriental philosophy also began to make its influence felt in the Alexandrian schools of philosophy, through the Kabbala, a hermetic Jewish doctrine of considerable obscurity, and through the new beliefs of the Gnostics. In Alexandria the Jewish thinker Philo attempted to explain the sacred Jewish scriptures by recourse to the philosophy of Plato. In the work of the Neoplatonist Plotinus the ideas of Plato finally became dominant once again, as he tried to understand the particular in the light of the universal. Plotinus recognized the mystic ecstasy which was required to understand the nature of 'true being', a feeling which can only be properly compared with the Brahman's total abandonment and 'absorption'. But it can equally well be identified with the 'blessed peace' which reason attains when it finally returns home to itself.

But there none the less remains a decisive problem with all these Alexandrian thinkers, as with Plato and Aristotle before them. For they also failed to reach the thought of 'absolute freedom', of the 'ego', of the 'infinite value of the human subject'. The 'world spirit' had not yet reached its destination in these philosophies. The human spirit required a sudden leap forward in order to wrest new insights and achievements from the activity of thought.

Philosophy essentially remained a matter of the Greek spirit right up till the time of Proclus, concluding a period that had begun with Thales of Miletus and had already lasted a thousand years. In the thought of Proclus 'the religiosity of late antiquity came to conceptual fulfilment and, in accordance with Hegel's epochal construction of philosophy, to its historical end', as Klaus Düsing puts it. The Christian philosophy which now began to emerge incorporated the Neoplatonic thought that God is essentially 'spirit' and finds his authentic realization in consciousness. The Arabs and the Jews played a merely external and subsidiary role in the perpetuation of philosophy upon a Platonic and Aristotelian basis. It was Christianity which now came to represent the 'universal consciousness of the world'. Here however one must take care in understanding Hegel's claim. For the idea of Christianity itself has been very differently interpreted at different times. Yet if one is to attach any serious meaning to the idea of divine providence in the world, then the emergence and establishment of Christianity must have something intrinsically rational about it and it cannot be entirely coincidental that this occurred at the time it did. Nothing that preceded this event was without purpose or significance either. But it cannot be said that Christianity was totally successful in incorporating and realizing the idea of philosophy even as it annexed the latter to itself. For amongst the early Christian Fathers and later amongst the scholastic thinkers philosophy never entirely lost its 'character of dependency' upon the Church. Even before going into any further details, Hegel takes great pains to emphasize this point against traditional 'Christian philosophy'. Medieval scholastic thought was not free: not 'the thinking idea in its freedom' but rather thinking under a fixed presupposition.

The presupposition in question is the 'Christian principle' as it is still understood at this stage. When scholastic thought draws its conclusions with regard to the separate spheres of reason and faith it is entirely governed by its understanding of this 'principle': 'In all this scholastic activity thought performs its allotted task in total independence of all concrete reality, all experience.' The general trajectory of Christianity and its effective establishment in the Middle Ages stands once again therefore under the law of dichotomy. The organization of the Church as a stable institution was intimately connected with the invasions and immigrations of the Germanic peoples who eventually overcame the Roman Empire and erected a new system of government on the ruins of the old. With the historic union of the Christian idea with the Germanic peoples a mighty advance was made with respect to the freedom that is the essential end of world history. But the crude and impulsive way in which the Church itself accomplished the transition from the spiritual to the worldly sphere of life also hindered the further development of this end. During the Middle Ages the power of the Church, as manifested by the actions of its popes, cardinals and legates, and the excommunications it was always ready to pronounce, was characterized as Hegel says by 'ambition, avarice, deceit, violence, robbery, murder, envy and hatred'. The Emperor and the princes were always defeated in this conflict with papal power. But the transgressions of the Church itself as a worldly power would also cost it dearly throughout the medieval period, as can be seen from the fate of the scholastic philosophy which served it. This philosophy in truth is nothing but a system of 'pedantic syllogistic reasoning' and the world spirit, intrinsically oriented to advance as it is, here finds itself checked and obstructed for nearly a thousand years. In the sixteenth century the spirit was still standing largely where it was in the sixth century.

This is where the spiritual breakthrough finally occurs and the spirit gathers its forces afresh: 'The spirit has collected itself and looked upon its reason as upon its own hands.' This is accomplished with the transition from the Middle Ages, with the gradual weakening, as Hegel emphasizes, of the formerly dominant feudal system whose principal claim to rationality, for all the suppression of freedom it entailed, consisted in the fact that the established order was better than no order at all. Hegel is thinking here in very large historical terms. For this revival of the spirit also signifies the reawakening of the arts and the sciences, the escape from the mausoleum of scholastic thought which had certainly developed the dialectical character of intelligence to a very high degree but still only in a purely formal manner.

The new humanism which expressed and encouraged this spiritual revival represented for Hegel a crucial intermediate stage on the way to an even greater revolution: the Lutheran Reformation in the German lands against the 'dichotomy', the 'hideous discipline', which had formerly been required by 'the stubborn German character'. The oppression of old harboured the inner necessity that man would eventually come to resist and overcome it by casting aside all false and extraneous authorities and thus 'returning into his own self': a mighty advance of the world spirit after a long stagnation and indeed a provisional end of the path on which it had long been moving.

As far as the history of philosophy is concerned the period of the Reformation as such has no great name to boast, apart perhaps from Giordano Bruno whom Hegel still regards as belonging to the Middle Ages although 'the subjective principle of his own thought' certainly already pointed towards the future. Bruno was intoxicated by the thought of individual self-consciousness, a man whom both Protestants and Catholics alike regarded as a heretic and atheist in one. But it was he who defended the cause of philosophy during this period of historical transition. He was an Aristotelian in the sense of the Alexandrian school, a Spinozist in advance with his thought of the ultimate identity of all things, and of a human reason which is capable of penetrating all reality. His principal idea was to 'grasp the unity of form and matter in everything'. Here is a spirit on a path which leads from Aristotle to Hegel. Bruno thought it was necessary to begin at the extremes of things, at the maximum and the minimum point of reality, if one was to disclose the ultimate secrets of nature herself. Hegel quotes what he calls a 'great saying' of Bruno's: 'The greatest thing is not simply to discover the point of union, but rather to develop its opposite principle from within itself; this is the real and most profound secret of the art.' Bruno paid for the boldness and freedom of his thought by being burnt alive at the stake at the express orders of the Church.

These were the first tentative skirmishes of a new kind of thinking which was destined to external failure in its own time when confronted with the entrenched power of scholastic philosophy. Even in decline the latter appeared to be strong enough to bring down the more audacious thinkers who were struggling ahead. But the new spirit of intellectual unrest was not be vanquished or repressed in the long run. It showed its vitality in many various ways, first of all in England with Francis Bacon's denunciation of the 'syllogistic forms' of abstract reasoning in favour of experience and observation. Hegel says it was an essential part of 'the new emerging spirit of the time and of the English way of thinking to proceed from the facts and frame our judgements accordingly'. Experience in this context means the observation of the nature of man and the world around him. This was a natural mentality in England given the realism peculiar to a nation of merchants and shopkeepers. In other countries the principle of empirical experience did not enjoy the same significance. 'Germany took as its point of departure the concrete Idea, the concrete emotional and spiritual life of the inner man.'

In this regard Jakob Böhme represented the opposite pole to the stress on external experience, with a doctrine which was rightly called the 'philosophia teutonica' although it had been obscured by the age of Enlightenment. Hegel regards Böhme as the first German philosopher really worthy of the name. And that means here that he represented the 'Protestant principle' in accordance with which 'the intellectual world is now located within one's own soul'. Hegel also recognizes that this first form of the Idea also includes a great deal of 'confusion' and explicitly says that 'the manner in which this is expressed here must be described as rather barbaric'.

When reading Hegel's account of Böhme we cannot avoid the impression that Hegel is now standing on his own ground, so to speak, directly describing a dimension of his own thought, planting his own heavy pedestal in the heart of traditional metaphysics. When he recognizes Böhme's 'principal idea' in the idea of the divine Trinity and interprets his entire philosophy and aspiration as the 'unveiling' of the same, we likewise recognize the importance of triplicity in Hegel's own logic as the expression of the identity of thought and being. 'The three-in-one is all' – this was a proposition already defended by Plato which naturally cohered with the Christian doctrine of the Trinity. Böhme grasped the three-in-one as a truth revealed in the nature of things in general. The 'revelation of God in all things' signified here that 'the son is born eternally from out of the essence of God, the quintessence of all forces and qualities' and that the 'spirit' is the 'unity of light with the substance of forces'. Arguments like these are to be found in Böhme, but they were also in a sense acceptable in Hegel's renewal of traditional metaphysics. Böhme's doctrine of light and colour as 'spiritual fire' naturally appealed to Hegel's own surviving Schellingian ideas about nature. 'All the stars betoken the power of the Father, and from them the Sun is derived' – high-sounding oracular remarks of this kind inevitably impressed Hegel the philosopher of nature with their speculative force.

The fact that the Church had also persecuted Böhme did not alter the fact that the true spirit of the Christian religion had penetrated his thought, but of course it did say a great deal about the intellectual deficiencies of the Church itself. But what Hegel calls 'the period of the thinking understanding' had still not arrived. In Böhme philosophical theology had not yet managed to emancipate itself from the dogmatic presuppositions of the Christian faith in the narrower sense. Philosophy was not yet autonomous and only really became so again, for the first time since the Neoplatonists, with René Descartes. This is where the thought of the modern age begins, the thought which builds upon itself alone, and explicitly rejects all 'authority' and 'dead externality'. Descartes begins everything from first principles. The Middle Ages had already known the 'Christian principle', but with Descartes 'thought' itself becomes the essential principle without any further qualification: 'What is to be regarded as true, is true only through thought.' All unproven presuppositions are to be suspended and a beginning is to be made with the simplest of propositions instead. Methodical doubt takes pride of place since we can always imagine ourselves subject to error in all our usual judgements. The senses can easily deceive us. But amongst all our supposedly certain or less than certain claims to knowledge the proposition 'I think therefore I am' is the most certain of all. Even if I reject belief in the existence of God, the heavens or bodies in general, I cannot reject the experience of thought itself: it is impossible that I who am now thinking should not exist as a thinking being. Being is present as thought, thought as being. The identity of the two is here secured beyond all question of doubt, is here demonstrated as a certainty which Hegel explicitly opposes to Kant who had declared the essential non-identity of thought and being.

Descartes bases everything upon this single certainty of the thinking self. Everything proceeds from thought and the essential freedom which it implies. No previously given judgement can be accepted at the start because nothing of this kind is absolutely certain or secure. The 'urge to freedom' does indeed strive after something secure and objective as its ultimate result: 'I wish to get to the nature of things through thought.' Thought is more certain than the body. One can doubt the reality of the body; one can, to repeat Descartes's example, believe one is feeling pain in a limb that has actually long since been amputated. Descartes posits thought as the primary reality in which the self becomes certain of itself.

However, Hegel explicitly criticizes Descartes because although he did indeed possess 'this most interesting idea of modern times', namely the idea of the ultimate identity of being and thought, he did not properly *demonstrate* it in its fullness. In Hegel's terms he did not take the step which leads from certainty to truth. Hegel is also thinking here in anticipation of Kant, who challenged the identity of thought and being, the very thing that still had to be concretely demonstrated. But Descartes did affirm bluntly that the ego possesses the idea of perfection within itself and necessarily compares itself with the idea of God as 'the most perfect being'. God is for him – and this will also become crucial for Spinoza – essentially substance. Substance is in turn defined as something which requires nothing else for its own existence, something which must be grasped as the original cause of matter. As the creator of matter God is the creator of the universe. But God as such is himself without extension.

What seems initially unintelligible here is only clarified by Spinoza. He was the best commentator on the Cartesian system, which he closely studied and developed even further. In fact he not only developed it but fundamentally transformed and completed it by rigorously drawing out its ultimate conclusions. Spinoza eliminated the dualism that still persisted in Descartes by recourse to the idea of the one and only single substance. Spinoza attempts to elucidate the identity of thought and being which Descartes had posited as self-evident. As with thought and being, so too the soul and the body also cease to be regarded as anything independent in their own right. They too are absorbed in the 'one' reality which the Jew Spinoza introduces into the European style of philosophy as the typically 'eastern thought' of the 'absolute identity'. Spinoza's substance = God acquires the attribute of extension as well as thought. Matter and form are represented together in the world, in nature, in the universe equally as extension and thought. No one had ever expressed this idea in such a way before Spinoza.

Hegel regards this thought as the culminating 'high-point of philosophy' and even asserts the proposition: 'either Spinozism or no philosophy'. All philosophy henceforth must take positive account of the Spinozist position. All genuine philosophical thought must begin from a comprehension of Spinoza's claim that 'all determination is negation'. If God represents the positive reality, or the ultimate single substance, then everything else compared with this can only be a particular 'modification' of the same, and cannot possibly attain the status of an independent reality which exists 'in and for itself'. As a finitely determinate something it is negativity over against the absolute determinacy of substance.

Hegel repudiates the frequently asserted identification of 'Spinozism' and 'atheism' as quite inadequate to this philosophy. This objection could only claim validity if Spinoza had interpreted nature as simply identical with God and God as simply identical with nature. But Spinoza opposed thought and extension rather than God and nature to one another. God, whose attributes thought and extension are, is rather the absolute substance into which the world and nature itself have completely dissolved and ultimately disappeared.

Instead of atheism, therefore, 'Spinoza's system' must rather be regarded as an 'absolute pantheism and monotheism articulated in thought': that is, all things and their particular determinations must be reduced to the one ultimate substance. One could also say that everything is 'cast into this abyss of destruction'.

Spinoza effectively completed the system of Cartesianism. Any future advance of philosophical thought could now only proceed in two directions. On the one hand, we can go forward to Malebranche, who can also be said to have brought the development which began with Descartes to a final conclusion and articulated 'Spinozism in another pious theological form' such as could never plausibly be accused of atheism. On the other hand, we can proceed to Locke, who represents the real alternative to the thought of both Descartes and Spinoza. Whereas Descartes had spoken of 'innate ideas', Locke explicitly denied the existence of such things. He regarded the soul as nothing but a *tabula rasa*, a blank tablet, which is filled up with the material of sense experience. Locke has no initially postulated definitions like those of Spinoza and he merely feels the need to show how such universal conceptions arise within in our minds in the first place. And that is solely through empirical experience. Every individual human being starts out with a number of simple experiences, psychological states, feelings and sensations from which he only subsequently builds up a set of determinations which possess permanent significance for him. The universal is developed out of the empirically concrete given. The question as to how far such apparently universal conceptions and determinations are indeed correct, as to how far they can properly claim emphatic truth for themselves, remains fundamentally an open one.

Locke thus continues the empirical approach first established by Bacon and contributes his share to the fact that such empiricism will henceforth remain characteristic of the English national character in philosophy. He thus defends a philosophy with very modest metaphysical ambitions, one which is easily intelligible, essentially popular in nature and intrinsically commonsensical. On account of its clarity such a philosophy was not particularly difficult to disseminate. It found considerable acceptance amongst the French and also served to prepare the way for the German philosophy of the Enlightenment. Locke's famous 'compound ideas' are highly plausible: space is experienced through the sense of sight; time through the uninterrupted sequence of empirical perception; substance through the connection which is made between 'blue' and the 'sky' to produce, for example, the notion of their identity in 'sky-blue'. If Locke proceeds not from first principles but from the empirical observation of things, not from prior theoretical commitments but from perception, towards this or that particular theory, then the question concerning the ultimate validity and justification of his conclusions is left open.

It was also with Hobbes in England that the preferential treatment of

social and political relations began, especially with regard to the fundamental opposition between the political state and the so-called original 'state
of nature'. Hegel thinks that the 'peculiar character of the English must have
led to such reflection upon these objects'. It was the English thinkers who
first properly raised the question concerning the 'state of nature' in modern
philosophy, soon to be followed in this by the French. The origin of civil
society is rooted in the fear each individual has of everyone else. Every individual is in a position, if he so wishes, to destroy the other, every individual
appears weak in relation to the rest. In the state of nature empirical power is
raised into the right to control those who cannot resist; everyone must mistrust everyone else and embark upon a 'war of all against all' in which it
would be most unwise to allow anyone now in one's power ever to become
strong in the future. Thus it is that man must leave this state of nature and
enter into a necessary relation with his fellows in which the laws of reason
are upheld and the general peace maintained.

It was Leibniz who entered the scene in basic opposition both to the empirical experience of the English as well as the single substance of Spinoza.
Hegel grasps the thought of Leibniz as a form of 'idealism' which upheld the
status of ideas and associated claims but was unable to demonstrate their
necessity and logical coherence. Thus he only ended up by producing the
equivalent of a 'philosophical novel'. Hegel was particularly critical of the
metaphysical optimism that Leibniz expressed in his famous *Theodicy*, his
misconceived attempt at a 'justification of God in the face of the evils of the
world' in accordance with the argument that the actual world must logically
represent 'the best of all possible worlds'. In the place of Spinoza's monism
Leibniz posits his 'monadology', the doctrine of innumerable individual and
independent bodies which are incapable of exerting a causal influence upon
one another. Each such body in turn contains an infinite number of atoms
and represents the 'totality in itself', or the 'entire world'. In the universe as
a whole everything is governed according to a system of 'pre-established
harmony' in which the slightest change or movement communicates itself to
the most remote extremities. One could therefore in principle grasp the whole
of the universe and its development from a single grain of sand if one only
possessed complete knowledge of the latter. God is the monad of all mon-
ads. For all his obvious admiration for Leibniz's 'intellectual brilliance' Hegel
mounts his own criticism of his thought: this ultimately 'burdens God with
everything that cannot otherwise be explained'. God appears here as a necessary 'expedient' in order to reconcile the unconnected claims concerning the
pre-established harmony on the one hand and the monad as an animated
microcosm on the other. Voltaire indeed had already recognized these intrinsic contradictions in the philosophy of Leibniz.

The content of Christian Wolff's philosophy is essentially a more thoroughly systematized version of Leibniz. Wolff finally brought the old scholastic Aristotelian tradition to an end, although his own highly pedantic division

of philosophy into various formally independent disciplines also introduced a different sort of aridity into the subject. Thought now entered upon a period of transition. The idealism of Berkeley attempted to include and transcend the thought of Locke by differentiating the empiricist account of experience. For Berkeley what appears large or small, fast or slow, cannot be determined from my individual experience alone since all such things are essentially relative. They can only be determined by reference to something else outside of me, itself possibly contingent, namely an intervening object. Hume adopted the standpoint of Bacon and Locke but developed it towards a form of radical scepticism which famously woke Kant from his dogmatic slumbers and provided the point of departure for his own philosophy. For Hume what is regarded as right or lawful, for example, is always different according to the different peoples at different times. Various individuals have interpreted the idea of God now in this way, and now in that, so that it is extraordinarily difficult to define the real universal characteristics of the deity to all men. There are certainly established and habitual ways of thinking about God, justice, truth, morality, and so on, but other people have developed quite different and for them equally habitual ways of doing so. Hume also extended his sceptical approach to the problems of freedom and necessity to the traditional proofs for the existence of God. The result of these critical reflections was a general distrust, or at least a certain suspension of judgement, concerning our knowledge of the universal nature of God, nature and immortality. Hume never flinched from dispassionately examining the state and limits of the human understanding.

The natural response to Hume's scepticism was first articulated in the Scottish philosophy of 'healthy common sense', which was also much concerned with issues of politics and the state. The Scottish thinkers in question (Reid, Oswald, Stewart) exerted a considerable influence in Germany, in particular with their distrust of all abstract philosophical speculation. The content of their own thought is eminently concrete and remote in principle from metaphysical reflection. Adam Smith is often regarded as the typical representative of this approach.

Hegel had a considerable respect for the authentic tradition of French philosophy. It stood out for the intellectual verve and brilliance with which it undertook to challenge the established ideas of the age. It was marked by a tremendous energy in contesting the prevailing structures of faith, power and authority. This philosophy recognized 'freedom' as the modern 'world-situation' and openly endorsed the 'concrete freedom of the spirit'. Everything that had formerly seemed stable was destroyed. In a sense there is nothing outside the realm of self-consciousness, nothing that is exempt from its criticism, whether it is the conceptions of good and evil, power, wealth or the prevailing notions of God and his relation to the world. It is self-consciousness which actively justifies these ideas, or otherwise, out of its own inner resources. The French philosophies of atheism and materialism were based upon a militant refusal to accept the presuppositions of religion, law or morality unless they have been made intelligible to reason first. Everything traditionally handed down from the past, everything based upon external authority is thus submitted to drastic critique in this negative approach to truth. And the priority of this negative orientation remained thoroughly characteristic of French thought. It therefore exerted a destructive effect upon the existing order, the legal system, political institutions, the Church, civil society, the morality of court life, the behaviour of governing officials, and so on. Philosophy had here succeeded in exposing injustice and hypocrisy to the derision and contempt of the world at large.

And that is what provided its intellectual justification. This philosophy only exerted such a destructive effect upon practices that were already destroyed from within, and in France it directly addressed a major conflict between state and Church that had no real equal elsewhere at the time. Hegel himself rejects a philosophy that would expressly desire revolution but he recognizes its historical significance. The Revolution in France was 'forced into being through the unyielding stubbornness of existing prejudices, principally through the prevailing arrogance, thoughtlessness and selfishness of the time'. And the philosophers as such were unable to give appropriate advice about how such problems were to be resolved.

The positive side of French philosophy is revealed in its appeal to real human needs, to the essential feeling of individual right, to the belief that religious faith cannot be compelled, in short to the importance of individual conviction. Reason had now been raised as 'the banner of all peoples', and rightly so since 'in the sign of the cross deceit and betrayal had been conquered' in principle. In future mankind must be present to himself in all he does. Helvétius did not regard it as strange to think that sacrifice for the sake of others is also intimately connected with one's own satisfaction. Rousseau, who saw the state and all political authority as based upon violence, force, conquest and the institution of private property, could thus appeal to the natural power of human feeling in opposition to the existing state of affairs.

Hegel accuses his fellow-Germans of a certain inertia here. They witnessed the events unfolding in France and merely accommodated themselves to the new situation like 'respectable slowcoaches who are easily satisfied with things'. They continued to hold on to the old Wolffian and Leibnizian definitions and demonstrations until they were 'gradually touched by the spirit from abroad'. Then at last they attempted to appropriate for themselves these new ideas from other countries, beginning with Locke's empiricism. The Enlightenment of the Germans was thus essentially an Enlightenment at second hand, in which the thoughts imported from France certainly became popular and widely appreciated, but were also reproduced in a weaker and less interesting form.

This all changed with Friedrich Heinrich Jacobi, who turned back to examine the thought of Spinoza, and above all with Immanuel Kant, who breathed new life into philosophy in Germany. He adopted a new stand-point which effectively confirmed Hegel's claim that thought is the root of all freedom. Reason had previously attempted to extend its domain and directly addressed the question of God 'as a transcendent reality beyond thought'. Now the question to be answered was the following: how can we properly retain a God who is still infinite and inconceivable in character, and how can such a God be restored now that reason has apparently driven him from the field of knowledge? Human reason and spiritual freedom, and the consciousness of self – these would seem to be subjective. How then can they really penetrate once again to objectivity itself, to the existence of God? This is the task that Kant, Fichte and Schelling had set for themselves, and the manner in which they treated these central questions in turn reflected and belonged to that historical transformation of the world produced through the French Revolution. In Germany these changes took on the intellectual form of thought, whereas in France they resulted in immediate political upheaval, but both responses were ultimately manifestations of a single historical process.

It is well known that Kant began by reflecting explicitly upon Hume, who had located the real basis of all knowledge in empirical perception and abandoned any strict claim to universality and necessity since the latter could never be empirically derived. But if universality and necessity could not be found in the processes of perception, Kant reasoned that they must spring from another and quite different source. For Kant this source is the subject itself. Universality and necessity thus belong to reason as self-consciousness, that is, to thought as such. Hegel regards this as the 'principal claim' of the Kantian philosophy. Thought thereby becomes the very object of thinking itself.

Kant, of course, was generally credited with having decisively overcome the 'old metaphysics' and was much praised for his critical achievement. This is not how Hegel saw the matter. He rejected the idea that reason must abdicate its traditional responsibility for thinking the infinite and the unconditioned, the sceptical thought that reason must withhold all final judgement on such matters. This seemed to him to ignore 'the living reality of nature and spirit'. Anyone who still believes that philosophy should be able to answer the question 'What is God?' will certainly find no intellectual succour in Kant. His view that 'we know only appearances' seems only to relieve reason of any further effort to examine such questions. In Hegel's eyes this merely represented an 'inconsolable epoch of truth'. Philosophy is robbed of metaphysics and thus becomes, as Hegel harshly puts it, 'a philosophy that is no philosophy'. In Hegel's perspective Kant had once more returned to that 'unknown God' to whom the ancients had once dedicated an altar in Athens. Hegel's final judgement on Kant's philosophy expressed the direction he would follow himself: 'The deficiency of the Kantian philosophy lies in the manner in which the moments of absolute form are still dissociated from one another.' And that meant that Kant's philosophy was still incomplete. This task of completion would fall to Fichte.

It must certainly be said that in interpreting Kant's critique of metaphysics as a lack of speculative power Hegel failed to recognize the true depths of this philosophy, as Ernst Bloch and others have claimed. Or is it rather that he shrank back in fear from these depths? Certainly Fichte could never be charged with any lack of speculative boldness.

Hegel distinguishes between Fichte's speculative philosophy, pre-eminently expressed in his earlier writings, and his later philosophy of the Berlin period, which came to overshadow the former in popular esteem. For the history of philosophy it is only the earlier phase of Fichte's thought which is really significant in Hegel's eyes. Here the subjective moment of Kantian thought is intensified to become an explicit philosophy of the ego. It is the ego which believes, thinks and doubts: 'the ego is the primordial fact', 'the ego is the first principle'. Everything can be doubted or challenged except the fact that the ego = ego. This is the first basic proposition of identity which requires no further determination. I am consciously identical with myself, even though I concede that other beings exist in addition to myself. The 'ego' is always related to the correlative 'non-ego', encounters limits where it ceases to be itself. But the non-ego is also limited when it encounters the ego. Since the ego is primary, the non-ego only presents itself as there for me. The ego only *becomes* what it is through the non-ego; if there were no non-ego, the ego could not exist either. The non-ego only possesses a meaning in so far as there is an ego. The one in each case depends reciprocally upon the other.

Hegel objects that Fichte's 'principle' of the ego, which allows it either to posit itself or not to posit itself, rests upon a contradictory presupposition. If there are indeed 'two principles' in question we cannot properly speak of one basic principle at all. The 'ego' would then be caught in an inevitable conflict with itself and could not exist. Furthermore, according to Hegel, Fichte's ego is abstractly separated from the 'spirit' of which it is a 'moment'. Thus Fichte does not attain to 'reason' proper as the 'real unity of the subject and object' or the unity of the 'ego and the non-ego'. Like Kant, he ultimately remains with the perennial 'ought' or with the standpoint of 'faith'. In other words: he failed to grasp the Hegelian identity of the identical and the non-identical.

In Schelling's path towards the systematic formulation of an explicit philosophy of nature Hegel could retrace the stages of his own earlier development. Schelling originally built upon Fichte's idea of the ego as 'pure activity' and 'pure act', but soon pursued a number of further steps which eventually led him to a system of his own. The philosophy of nature was now credited with the task of taking over from the empirical natural sciences and thereby 'rendering nature intelligible'. But Hegel had never completely shared Schelling's confidence in the philosophy of nature and soon expressed his doubts in the harshest of language. Above all, Schelling failed in Hegel's eyes properly to demonstrate the unity of objectivity and subjectivity, of the finite and the infinite, of the positive and the negative. Instead he merely asserted the 'idea of the absolute' without sufficient articulation of its necessity. He simply presupposed what had first to be convincingly shown.

The real achievement of the young Schelling was probably nowhere better expressed than in his philosophy of art, which decisively transcended the earlier standpoints of Kant and Fichte. Schelling's insight was to understand how the transition of subjectivity to objectivity transpired precisely in and as the work of art. Before Schelling no one had expressly dared to articulate the idea of the work of art as objective in this sense, as indeed 'the highest mode in which reason has objectified itself'. Nor did Hegel hesitate to recognize Schelling's significance as the authentic founder of the philosophy of art. For here, where the 'sensuous reality' of the work of art is directly grasped as the 'expression of spiritual life', Schelling did succeed in demonstrating the 'idea of the absolute' as the realized identity of the identical with the non-identical.

But Hegel also insisted upon the singular importance of the philosophy of nature in Schelling's thought, even as he distanced himself from the precise manner in which the latter had interpreted this domain. For the Schelling of the earlier and middle period one could plausibly claim that theology was essentially transformed into speculation on the essence of nature: in the sphere of matter the ultimate ground is the 'organism' as 'the highest expression of nature', while nature itself is described as the 'essence of God', the material existence of nature not merely as spirit but as concrete reality.

Hegel's presentation of Schelling's thought in his own Berlin lectures contains his final judgement concerning the philosophy of his former friend of the Tübingen days, with regard to its significance and its weaknesses. Hegel says that 'Schelling's great achievement in the philosophy of nature was to show the forms of spirit present within nature.' Schelling's merit consisted in demonstrating in a speculative manner that 'the true is the concrete'. His failure lies in his 'lack of dialectic'. He did not properly develop the conceptual dimension and the 'necessity of progressive development'. For Hegel that is the reason why Schelling constantly found himself forced to begin his philosophy afresh with a new approach. Schelling's philosophy is itself the history of its perpetual revision. It thus ultimately remained caught up in 'formalism' and failed to penetrate to the 'Idea according to its concept'.

Hegel viewed this result as the provisional completion of the ever-renewed and ever-advancing process of philosophical reflection through the ages. But it also contained the impulse to further advance in future. Although Hegel did not actually provide a summary outline of his own system at this point, the necessity of just such a necessary standpoint is clearly indicated without mentioning any names. Hegel claims that the task now is to 'recognize the Idea in its necessity', to 'expound the Idea in its totality' if the 'ultimate purpose' of philosophy is finally to be attained: namely 'to reconcile the concept with actuality'.

Hegel himself understands this purpose to be demanded by the new age the world spirit has begun to initiate. What has been accomplished before is not simply to be repeated. One cannot return to the thought of Plato. The sequence traced out by the course of the world spirit in history and philosophy alike has been a necessary one. The history of philosophy as the 'innermost heart of world history' is not determined by blind chance or contingent events. In a sense world history cannot err. Every particular standpoint is justified in its place. Even what is false bears truth within itself through the intrinsic necessity of its existence as false, through which the truth is stimulated and promoted in turn. The last genuine philosophy of an age grasps and comprehends all previous philosophies within itself and is also their product and result. Klaus Düsing has thus claimed that as far as Hegel is concerned 'the history of philosophy represents the genesis of his own speculative philosophy'. This means that an appropriate exposition of Hegel's own, the absolute, philosophy would have to involve *all* the great systems of the past in their place, clarified and purified in the system that stands at the end.

For his Berlin auditors Hegel chose a simpler and briefer method. He left them with a concentrated summary: the world spirit of the modern age in which his listeners share has, after a long period of protracted labour, reached the point where it can now 'relinquish everything of a fundamentally alien and purely objective character and finally grasp itself as absolute spirit'.

30

The Journey to France and the Stay in Weimar

Victor Cousin had been urgently imploring Hegel for months to come and visit him in Paris. Cousin made various concrete suggestions to his German friend in this connection, with an eye to the most suitable opportunity to meet and even the prospect of accompanying Hegel back to Germany on the return trip.

Thus when Hegel finally did set out for France in the middle of August 1827 he had a specific purpose in mind, just as he had with his earlier visit to van Ghert in the Netherlands. The journey itself was not as comfortable as it might have been. The coach was small, the four occupants had to squeeze up together, and Hegel was obviously relieved to reach Halle where he took the opportunity to visit his student Hermann Friedrich Hinrichs. Fortunately for Hegel the coach laid on for the next stretch of the trip was much more comfortable than the first. The only other passenger was a student and Hegel had a row of seats to himself which he used as a 'sofa' for resting and sleeping on (something he was well used to doing in Berlin). At the intermediate stops in Cassel and Marburg some other students joined the coach. In Marburg, which he described as a 'tumble-down place of a town', he visited the professor of theology David Theodor Suabedissen. He soon felt himself so out of place in his company that he 'scuttled off again as fast as possible', as he reports to his wife from Bad Ems on 23 August 1827. He continued the journey along the river Lahm to Coblenz and then on to Trier through the Mosel valley. Despite the beautiful scenery Hegel sometimes began to tire of his journey and to wish he were back home in Berlin. In Coblenz he was very impressed by the prospect over the Rhine (from the elevation of Ehrenstein) and a visit to a wine-growing area just outside the city. In Trier he was shown around the Roman ruins there by the innkeeper's brother. When he crossed the border in Luxembourg Hegel was still not yet securely on French territory, but rather in a part of the Netherlands which belonged at the time to the German Confederation. In Luxembourg itself he was particularly struck by the great fortifications, which he eagerly took the opportunity of visiting for himself. He was quite surprised to observe that although he was not really tired from the exertions of the travelling itself, he felt his energies rather sapped by temporary 'lack of intellectual labour' on his part. On 30 August, around three in the afternoon, he arrived in Metz. He took a look around the town, saw the cathedral from the outside and spent the evening in the company of some military officers from the local garrison. They went to the playhouse to see a slight and silly piece in French of which Hegel confessed he could hardly understand a word.

The rest of his trip through France itself went far more smoothly, as Hegel notes himself. In the small *coupé*, the front compartment of the coach, the three seats were arranged alongside one another and facing forward. Hegel was also pleased to note that the compartment was closed off on all sides with windows, unlike the *cabriolets* or express mail coaches generally used in Germany. Hegel was not much moved by the journey through the flat terrain of northern France and its countryside. On the other hand, the sight of the Ardennes soon aroused his interest, and especially the windmill at Valmy of which Goethe had written so strikingly. 'Memories of my youth, when I took great interest in these things' began to return, as Hegel later wrote to his wife on 3 September. He now found himself in the midst of the very landscape where the revolutionary wars of 1792 had been fought out.

Until they arrived in Paris the coach never left the banks of the Marne, with lovely villages and little towns to right and left, more attractive to Hegel than those he was familiar with in Germany. Hegel always undertook to appreciate the particular qualities and characteristics of the various places he visited on his travels. In Bad Ems he did not miss the opportunity of taking the waters there. In Coblenz he sought out the Rhine wine, and in Trier the local Mosel wine, which he drank as a toast to his wife in Berlin. In Châlons-sur-Marne he was able to sample champagne for the first time on French soil.

Thus the philosopher eventually arrived in the 'capital of the civilized world', as he enthusiastically described Paris to his wife. As seemed to befit his now eminent status in Berlin, Hegel actually alighted at the Hôtel des Princes. Hegel was immediately impressed by a city that provided such a marked contrast with the stiff formality and relative cultural insignificance of the Prussian capital. In fact he was quite overwhelmed by his first encounter with Paris. The Berlin of 1821 had almost nothing to compare with the great boulevards, the Palais Royal, the Gallery of the Louvre, the Tuileries and the ubiquitous palaces of the French capital. It was 'a city of ancient wealth' thanks to the past efforts of art-loving monarchs and, last but not least, of Napoleon himself. Hegel was struck by the spacious facilities everywhere, the fine menageries and zoological gardens which were all clearly 'open to the free use of the public'. He regaled his wife with tempting accounts of the elegant wares displayed in the boutiques in the quarter of the Palais Royal. Hegel felt surrounded by evidence of abundance on all sides. He was struck to observe how all the cafés offered a range of newspapers to their customers as a matter of course. Hegel also found little difficulty in making himself understood in the city.

The cost of staying at the eminent Hôtel des Princes, however, soon seemed rather in excess of Hegel's means. But he found no difficulty in finding a *chambre garnie*, a furnished room, in the vicinity of the Jardin de Luxembourg. He had already deposited his luggage with Cousin, who had placed his own study and library entirely at Hegel's disposal.

At this time Cousin himself was, for overtly political resons, without any official academic post under the restored Bourbon monarchy of Charles X and therefore lived in rather straitened economic circumstances. He regarded every 'cough' on the part of his highly esteemed guest as a matter for immediate and devoted solicitude. It was Cousin who was essentially responsible for that later and extremely significant chapter in intellectual history which could be entitled 'Hegel and France'. Cousin considered himself very much as a representative of Descartes and his particular form of rationalism, which he had promoted by editing the French philosopher's writings. But he also felt that this impulse had now largely been exhausted through changing historical circumstances, and he was therefore looking abroad for further intellectual inspiration through the 'new philosophy', and indeed specifically through Hegel as its leading figure. For Hegel the relationship with Cousin provided him with the best and most immediate opportunity for studying the contemporary 'French spirit' at first hand, for exploring the affinities between a modern form of Enlightenment thought nourished on the new logic and the older traditional form of French rationalism. This is essentially what grounded the rapport between the two men. Hegel's 'German philosophy' was thus directly acquainted with the typically West European mode of thinking that was quite naturally oriented to questions of fundamental political change. For a state like Prussia, which had strong leanings towards the east of Europe, this mode of thought equally naturally aroused suspicions that all appeals to reason, nature, an elaborately formulated constitutionalism and the cause of political freedom generally could only spell serious danger to the existing political order in the shorter or the longer term.

Thus in his own way Hegel found himself to be particularly at home in Paris, and was expressly conscious of the fact. This is the Paris that was only three years away from the bourgeois revolution of 1830 and hints of the latter could already be detected. The general spirit of 'progress' associated with the bourgeoisie could be traced back to its very roots here in Paris. Even if the decisive political events were yet to transpire, Hegel could clearly perceive the emerging developments, which would eventually have major consequences for Berlin as well. Hegel felt that people in France, and particularly in Paris, were intellectually and culturally in advance of those in Berlin. This much at least can be gathered from the letter Hegel wrote home from his more modest lodgings in the Rue Tournon, at the hotel 'Emperor Joseph II'.

Naturally enough Hegel did not miss the obligatory excursion to Versailles and also took time to visit Saint Cloud. He contemplated the site of the Bastille and went to see the actual place where Louis XVI had been executed. In Saint Denis he stood before the graves of the French kings; in Montmorency he visited the spot where Rousseau had once lived and which had now become a veritable site of pilgrimage for his youthful admirers of the present generation.

During his last few days in Paris Hegel once again spent his time in the cultural and academic institutions of the city. He found no difficulty whatsoever in gaining admittance to a session of the French Academy. Amongst the other guests at a shared lunch one day Hegel noted the presence of Mignet and Adolphe Thiers who had not yet begun their major political careers.

On 30 September Hegel wrote to his wife to inform her of his imminent departure from Paris. Cousin would be accompanying him, as originally planned, on the return trip to Germany. Hegel also intended to pay another visit to his friend van Ghert in Brussels, which lay on the return route. His stay on this occasion was only a short one. Hegel used the opportunity to visit Ghent, only about 50 kilometres away, and then travelled on to Bruges by horse-drawn barge. As Hegel's barge passed through the countryside of Flanders, he spent his time reading or playing whist with the other passengers. The main purpose of his trip to Ghent was to see the paintings of van Eyck, while he used the visit to Bruges to seek out a statue of the Madonna which was widely and fondly believed to be the work of Michelangelo. Hegel was familiar with the return route via Cologne from his earlier journey to the Netherlands. He was certainly not attracted to Cologne, this 'old and ugly city' as he called it, apart of course from its famous cathedral. Hegel spent his morning in Cologne in Cousin's company: they visited the cathedral and a local art collection, dined on oysters and tasted the Mosel wine. Hegel then decided he would like to go to Bonn and visit August Wilhelm Schlegel and his own friend Windischmann. In his letters home Hegel did not really conceal the general antipathy he had always felt towards the Schlegel brothers. In the meantime August Schlegel had become a professor in Bonn. The great literary critic and former lover of Madame de Staël kept a large and rather self-contained residence in the city and Hegel reports that he had to 'storm' its defences to gain admittance. But the two of them apparently enjoyed a conversation of 'cordiality and good cheer'. Hegel even noted with some surprise, he casually tells his wife, that there was no woman to be seen around the place as one would surely have expected.

As anticipated Hegel finally left Cousin in Cologne as he undertook the last stage of his journey, which he wanted to complete as quickly and directly as possible without any major stops. But there was one very important exception to this resolution: Hegel was particularly desirous of paying a visit to Goethe in Weimar since it was now a long time since he had seen the poet. As for his four-day trip to Weimar via Elberfeld, Hegel mentions Cassel, Eisenach and Gotha as stopping places. In Cassel he went to an evening performance of Goethe's *Egmont* but left the theatre after only half an hour. While he was travelling on through Westphalia, Hesse and Thuringia Hegel could not shake off the memorable impressions of his trip through the Netherlands. He missed the Dutch cuisine and complained to the coachmen about being taken to unsuitable accommodation along the route. When he finally arrived in Weimar he found Goethe's house all lit up: the Grand Duke himself was shortly expected for tea. Hegel notified Goethe of his arrival, who immediately received him 'in the friendliest and most cordial fashion', as Hegel reported to his wife in Berlin. The Grand Duke appeared half an hour later and Hegel was formally introduced to him by Goethe. The Grand Duke settled on the sofa and Hegel sat, at a respectable distance, immediately to his right. Hegel soon found himself being asked all about his visit to Paris.

It cannot really be said, however, that a very fluent conversation ensued between them. Goethe's friends Riemer and Zelter had already taken the precaution of withdrawing into a neighbouring room. For they were both well aware that the Grand Duke was extremely hard of hearing. Hegel followed Goethe's recommended social convention in this situation: he let the Grand Duke talk on about whatever he liked, and whenever he stopped the listener would wait patiently until something else occurred to the eminent guest. Thus Hegel found himself 'nailed' to the sofa for quite a while, as he put it, but he otherwise felt quite 'at ease' with the Duke none the less. Goethe, then in his seventy-eighth year, meanwhile looked on benignly and tactfully observed the appropriate protocol for the occasion.

The next morning Hegel followed the recommendation of the Grand Duke and went to visit the Botanical Gardens in the Belvedere, which had been considerably extended under the patronage of the Duke himself. Hegel walked with Zelter along the long since unfrequented paths of the beautiful park and along the banks of the river Ilm. He was also invited to lunch with Goethe for a couple of hours. Those present included Zelter, Councillor Vogel, Goethe's amanuensis Eckermann, the poet's son, two grandchildren and one Miss von Pogwitsch. Hegel took the seat of honour next to Goethe and the lady herself. It was mainly Goethe and Hegel who led the ensuing conversation. The other guests seemed to have been rather more reticent. Goethe was particularly keen to acquire a picture of the contemporary political and literary situation in France. The poet took a strong and lively interest in everything he was told. Hegel found Goethe to be 'extremely vigorous and healthy, the same old man as before, i.e. the ever-youthful one, a little more tranquil perhaps – altogether such a good, honourable and faithful character that one could quite forget the famous man of genius and inexhaustible energy that he is'. In his report of the occasion which Hegel specifically sent his wife from Weimar on 17 October, he left no doubt about his own powerful self-confidence and sense of satisfaction about conversing with his host as an equal: 'As old and faithful friends we are beyond the stage of cautiously observing what the other says or how he appears, and we found ourselves cordially reunited without the slightest vain honour of having seen or heard such and such from the man himself.'

The conversation dwelt in some detail on Hamann, a thinker with whom Hegel was certainly very familiar and whose works he had carefully reviewed in print. This obscure spirit, the 'Magus of the North', had once been a pupil of Kant before he was moved to break dramatically with the German Enlightenment and its sun of mere reason. Hegel felt a profound affinity with Hamann, who never ceased to stimulate a certain aspect of the philosopher's mind. Here it was Hegel again who did most of the talking. Goethe would often hesitate to express an opinion when such questions of philosophical speculation were broached. But on this occasion Goethe clearly desired to hear something about the 'dialectic' from such a privileged source as his philosopher-guest. Hegel thereby described it to Goethe as essentially 'the regulated, methodically developed spirit of contradiction which every human being innately possesses, and which reveals its great value in distinguishing the true from the false'. Goethe responded by saying: 'If only such spiritual arts and skills were not so frequently abused and employed instead to make the false appear true and the true false.' This was of course an argument that conflated the art of dialectic with over-sophisticated scholastic logic-chopping, and was surely thrown rather knowingly and playfully into the discussion by Goethe. Hegel showed himself armed to respond and said: 'This can certainly happen, . . . but only by people with sick minds.' Goethe was obviously not entirely satisfied with this answer and persevered in the attempt to clarify the problem:

> I take joy in the fact . . . that the study of nature does not permit such sickness to arise! For in nature we have to do with what is infinitely and eternally true, which immediately and unceremoniously rejects anyone who is incapable of observing and treating the subject matter with total clarity and honesty. And I am quite certain that many a dialectical affliction could find a benevolent cure in the study of nature.

In this conversation, which Eckermann recorded in his notebooks under 18 October 1827, both the poet and the philosopher had played their respective parts through to the end. If there was no immediate agreement between them, there was the common element of 'nature' which Goethe had brought into the discussion. Even if the dialectic and philosophy in general did not strike Goethe as all that significant, this clearly did nothing to diminish his personal liking for Hegel. And Goethe must have felt that if Hegel thought this way, then perhaps there was something to all this abstruse and apparently unintelligible speculation after all, something from which others at least could profitably learn.

Goethe was so delighted with Hegel's company that he invited him to pay him a third visit with Zelter the following day. As a result Hegel put off his departure for Berlin and spent the evening at the theatre. His wife thereupon received the news that her much-travelled 'Odysseus' would shortly be returning to 'the simple cares of everyday life'.

The trip by hired coach from Weimar to Berlin seems to have been a rather stormy ride. Zelter, who was accompanying Hegel in the expectation of enjoying some interesting conversation on the way, was somewhat surprised to see an irascible philosopher constantly scolding the driver and cursing the taverns. It was obvious that Hegel could hardly reach home quickly enough. He was impatient with the thought of stopping and giving the horses enough time to eat. He became anxious when he discovered he had lost his cap and the coachman had to get out and go back to look for it along the roadside. Zelter was only able to calm Hegel somewhat by offering his own hat as a temporary substitute. Zelter's recorded impression of Hegel on this occasion is particularly interesting, since it was clearly intended only for Goethe's eyes. The episode so amused Goethe that he responded immediately by numbering Hegel amongst those 'Lord Philosophers' who can certainly command God, the soul, and the world, but are hardly 'well-equipped against the trials and tribulations of everyday life' (as Goethe put it on 27 October 1827). In a third letter to Goethe Zelter returns to the subject of this irascible Hegel who regarded the coach-driver as a scoundrel because he insisted on charging the rate for 9 miles for 7½. He thought he had discovered in the meantime the real reason for Hegel's exasperation. 'Do you really imagine', he asks Goethe, 'that I failed to notice the direction in which that long neck, that busy backbone, that long nose was pointing? Fortunate the man in this situation!' (30 October 1827). Zelter now had unambiguous evidence that a 'gentle little doe' was anxiously awaiting Hegel's return home, one who had long been 'languishing' during the long absence of her husband and had been making daily enquiries at the Zelter household for news of his expected arrival. Perhaps this eventually convinced Goethe, who had always found it difficult to recognize the real human being behind the Hegelian 'concept'.

31

The Philosophy of Religion

With regard to Hegel's treatment of the various philosophical disciplines we can place the philosophy of religion right at the beginning of the others or we can equally regard it as their appropriate conclusion. Nor is it particularly difficult to see just why this should be so. On the one hand, Hegel's thought can be grasped from the perspective of the phenomenon of religion in general: in chronological-biographical terms religion stands at the very beginning of Hegel's intellectual career and Hegel always continued, in a sense, to think within a theocentric framework as such. On the other hand, his philosophy of religion also represents, in the sequence of the particular 'philosophical sciences' derived from the *Logic*, a natural culmination in so far as Hegel regards the subject matter of religion as the 'highest' and 'absolute' object of all thought. The object of religion is at the same time the absolute content of the philosophy of religion itself.

We can fairly easily come to a plausible understanding of what Hegel means by 'religion' if we approach the question from a number of different but related aspects. In the first place he describes religion as the phenomenon in which 'all the enigmas of the world, all the contradictions of thought, all the pains of feeling life are resolved'. Religion is the sphere of 'absolute truth': God himself. It is the beginning and the end of all activity, all thinking and willing. All human individuals and peoples have some consciousness of God. This is even true if we trace experience right back to a time in which there was still no explicit 'science' in a narrower philosophical sense: 'There was once a time when all knowledge was essentially a knowledge of God.' Religion is a phenomenon in which all experience is concentrated into a comprehensive 'single feeling'. That is why religiosity as such does not immediately require any 'knowledge' in the narrow sense, like that explicitly provided by the discipline of the philosophy of religion itself. Of course it is quite true that the philosophy of religion can lead the mind towards the dimension of religious experience, but that is not automatically the case and the latter does not directly depend on the former. The philosophy of religion, on the other hand, does presuppose that level of explicit 'reflection' which religion as such lacks since it functions quite naturally on its own without 'the additional effort of thought'. The philosophy of religion thus thinks both for religion and for itself: it is the demonstration of 'the infinite in the finite, of the finite in the infinite, and leads to the reconciliation of the *intelligence* and the *heart*'.

The phenomenon of religion, like every other domain of being according to the Hegelian method, is also subject to the principle of dichotomy. This is true of religion generally in its relation to the worldly sphere, 'mankind's general consciousness of the world'. Religion in itself turns away from the freedom of this worldly sphere because it has a different idea of freedom in view. This is also true of particular religions like Christianity, which actually presupposes that mankind is intrinsically 'evil'. It thus posits 'the dichotomy of the subject' where the original 'natural unity of the spirit' and the concomitant 'unity of man and nature' is torn asunder and 'natural freedom' is destroyed. Man must already have been born in a state of unfreedom if he is ever to attain freedom proper in the Christian religion. Christianity therefore must awaken certain needs, must produce a certain inner pain, must be convinced of the fundamental corruption of human nature. Otherwise it would be quite impossible to understand why such needs have to be satisfied, why such pain has to be relieved, why a more hopeful prospect has to be offered to the evil ways of the human heart. The discomforts of dichotomy and estrangement must precede the experience of reconciliation. The fact that the Christian religion insists so tenaciously on the 'principle of evil' in human nature explains its lack of joyful serenity. The 'joyfully serene reconciliation' characteristic of pagan religion, and Hegel is thinking of Greek religion in particular, is essentially foreign to Christianity.

As far as the separation of the religious from the secular dimension is concerned, Hegel distinguishes between 'two regions of consciousness'. Religion puts human beings in a position to transcend the realm of common temporality. The principled opponents of religion should always be reminded, whatever objections they bring against the phenomenon, that religion essentially carries the grounds of its justification within its actual existence. Religion draws its intrinsically rational character, in spite of all the particular irrationalities that may attach to it, from its very being, as Hegel's *Logic* would naturally suggest. For even those who would like to have nothing to do with the phenomenon can hardly deny that religion or, more precisely, the historical religions actually exist. As the fundamental discipline which enquires into all real being it therefore falls to philosophy to 'develop the intrinsic necessity of religion in and for itself'.

Hegel pursues this challenge to his own discipline by claiming that religion contains 'the moment of thinking in its total universality' and that here, moreover, 'thought thinks itself'. Religion only exists 'in and through the medium of thought'. And further: 'God is not the highest sensation, but the highest thought.' This immediately signifies a substantial switch of perspective. For Hegel here explicitly abandons the idea of religion as essentially a matter of 'simple feeling' and embarks on a very different approach. The very ambiguity and obscurity of religious language about God shows why this is necessary. Philosophy can certainly demonstrate that 'God is the absolutely true, the universal in and for itself, that which comprehends all things, sustains all things and preserves all things.' But that alone does not take us very far since while God here is certainly 'a very familiar idea, it is still one which lacks further systematic development and comprehension'. Those who claim to speak so confidently and authoritatively about the nature of God can never make their propositions genuinely plausible or perspicuous to others. All general talk about God and spirit leads nowhere specific, precisely because these terms themselves remain nothing but indeterminate words.

The existing tradition of Judaeo-Christian theocentrism already justified Hegel in developing his philosophy of religion with specific reference to the idea of God as the appropriate theoretical basis for understanding the phenomenon of religion in and for itself. This did not mean that Hegel simply rejected the significance of the older pagan 'divinities of nature', but they could now be understood as stages that have intrinsically been surpassed after the establishment of the Mosaic Law and the death and resurrection of Christ, all in accordance with the traditional Christian conception of the bounty of God. The theological-dogmatic scheme which Hegel incorporates into his entire philosophy of religion actually remains intact even in post-Hegelian philosophy, in the thought of Feuerbach, that great expert on Luther, for example. The scheme was only properly discarded and covertly replaced with another in the thought of Schopenhauer. The latter combined his contemptuous rejection of Hegel with a conspicuous sympathy for Buddhism and thereby deliberately reintroduced the idea of a religion without God.

It was Schopenhauer who did not properly fit in with the tradition in this respect and undermined the apparently stable consensus of the Christian bourgeois world. Hegel challenged the tradition in a different way by penetrating the theological veil which protected the structure of Judaeo-Christian belief – in his examination of Spinozist atheism which forms a crucial point of entry to an understanding of Hegel's thought. It is true that the former theological candidate who had studied under Flatt and Storr in Tübingen always starts by taking dogmatically impeccable Christian doctrine as his point of departure, as the *regula fidei*. According to the traditional view of God he is essentially God the creator of the world, who brings it into being out of nothing. Hegel takes the creation story in its orthodox accepted form as given, in order to draw his own philosophical conclusions from the narrative. God is the infinite who cannot do without the finite: he 'makes himself finite', Hegel says. God is movement and only through such movement is he the living God. His movement is this dynamic relation to the finite.

This idea naturally involves a number of contradictions. Every philosophy that deals with religion entangles itself in such contradictions because contradiction itself belongs to the essence of religion. This is a thought which Feuerbach would later develop in terms of a materialist philosophy of religion. Hegel himself presents the contradiction in question, which Feuerbach took over from him, in considerable detail but does not develop it in such a one-sided fashion. For example: God is the infinite and I am the finite. We could also say that God is the finite and I am the infinite. But that would mean that the opposition between the finite and the infinite was not functioning actively at all and we should simply be presented with the 'bugbear of opposition itself'. Hegel's own use of language in his analysis of this relation does justice to the slow and difficult insight that there is no simple opposition of terms here: 'In the ego as immanently self-sublating finitude God returns into himself, and is God only as such a return.'

To orthodox ears such a way of speaking sounds rather strange and indeed is strange. But it was not entirely new and is very close to the heretical speech of Eckhart's mysticism, and corresponded precisely with the structure of the latter's thought. Without the ego God himself cannot exist. There is no God who could simply be independently, exist entirely on his own account. The creation of the world first makes God into God: 'Without the world God is not God.' The subject becomes subject only in and as a relation to the object. And this relation is reversible.

This was also a return to the great and undeniable achievement of Fichte's philosophy of the ego. The ego – and not the existence of God – is the only certainty, the only absolutely sure knowledge that the ego can possess. Any potential certainty I may have of God's existence is derived from the ego. God's being has its source in the ego, and feeling is the place where God has entered into my being. Authentic certainty of God could be obtained in no other way. For God is no externally perceptible sensible object; he is rather the ideal object of our representation, one which not merely exists as representation but is identical with its object. If God cannot be perceived as a sensible object, we need some further ground for knowing something about the supposedly unknowable. According to Hegel we do know of God on this model, but we are also told that we should not reason further about his nature or try to comprehend that nature conceptually.

Hegel accepts the doctrine of feeling as the original source of our knowledge of God simply as the starting point of his own philosophy of religion. It is not enough, for Hegel, to remain fixated at this level, as most 'modern theology' of his time and in particular Schleiermacher has done, for whom 'feeling' is both the beginning and end of theological reflection. We know just how mercilessly Hegel could express himself concerning Schleiermacher's idea of religion as the feeling of 'utter dependency'. Hegel interpreted the idea in terms of a dog-like devotion that was quite inappropriate to the nature of genuine religious faith. Hence he thought that all talk of 'feeling' as the last word in theology was essentially superficial. For the advance to the stage of *reflection* and then of explicit *consciousness* is required if the ego is to attain its authentically specific and determinate character: 'For mankind is essentially spirit, consciousness.' Religion essentially exists *for* consciousness and possesses its reality *in* consciousness. This carries us far beyond mere feeling as the original site of our experience of God, even though it retains a subsidiary place in the structure of human consciousness.`

Kierkegaard later objected explicitly to the Hegelian philosophy as one which accords primacy to reflection. For Kierkegaard the individual consciousness involves an immediate self-relation that is not captured by this dialectical logic at all. He separates out the unity of thought and being into idea and actuality, and accuses Hegel of conflating thought about actuality with actuality itself. For Kierkegaard, life is a sphere *sui generis* over against thought as such, the sphere through which alone thought can become existential thought in any particular case.

With this approach, of course, the summit of metaphysical speculation and the 'concept' as its privileged means of acquiring ultimate knowledge has explicitly been abandoned. Thought falls back instead on the elaboration of a philosophical theology of another kind, namely that of 'faith' as a wager of existential resolve. But this thinking in turn is exposed to its own dialectic. Contradiction reappears within faith itself and philosophy transforms itself accordingly into a 'dialectical doctrine of faith', but one without the comprehensive support of Hegel's holistic speculation.

The theoretical attempt to penetrate the phenomenon of religion naturally tends to lead, given the very nature of the object itself, into a sphere not fully intelligible to reason alone. Thus the systematic study of religion brings philosophy, as the 'science' of reason itself, into a difficult predicament, involves it in contradictions which can only be dialectically resolved. In Hegel's doctrine of knowledge logic is the original philosophical discipline from which the others are derived. And the pre-eminent conceptual structure of the *Logic* is constantly present within the subsidiary disciplines, in history as a movement governed and directed towards its ultimate end by reason, and likewise in religion which is itself 'rational' to the degree that it represents God as the 'absolute truth'. The difficulties involved here, which result from the Hegelian identity of the identical with the non-identical, require preliminary theoretical explication. The philosophical study of religion thus appears as the end and culmination of the other partial disciplines: 'The science of religion is one science, indeed the last science, in philosophy, and thus presupposes the other philosophical disciplines, and is therefore essentially a result.'

But this science of religion which finally completes all the other partial disciplines was, chronologically speaking, the original starting point of Hegel's reflections. The religion he now describes as a 'result' was what once grounded his thought in the Berne and Frankfurt manuscripts, as in the early essay on *The Positivity of the Christian Religion* which led immediately to Hegel's first *Fragment of a System*. From its very earliest form the Hegelian system was organized in a hierarchical series of stages. Jewish monotheism rose above the primitive cults of nature religion, and was in turn superseded and built upon by the Christian religion of redemption with its trinitarian God. Nevertheless, the latter remained tainted by a kind of sacramental materialism which had still not totally renounced the necromantic character of ancient nature religion and its spells, and this indeed remained an element in the Catholic Church to his own day, in Hegel's view. The Protestant religion assumes a higher position through its much stronger emphasis upon the internal witness of 'spirit' rather than any external sacramental means. This signifies an essential 'freedom' from the exclusive importance of the sacraments and the priestly monopoly on their communication. Protestantism simultaneously emphasizes the realm of *Bildung*, of culture and education in the broadest sense, as a this-wordly human accomplishment. But while the religion of Protestantism is thus to be understood as the highest elevation of religion from the perspective of religion itself, it is not as such the highest sphere from the perspective of philosophy, which essentially deals with an absolute beyond all institutions, namely with 'absolute spirit'. In his philosophy of religion, which is directly oriented towards the ultimate 'totality', Hegel recognizes the expressly religious standpoint and remains rooted in the Christian religious principle of the reality of God, of salvation through the Son, the Crucified and Resurrected One, and the Holy Spirit. Hegel thus preserves in his own way the faith that he had originally absorbed and reflected upon as a young man. This principle remains valid for him because it is an essential reality in the present and therefore possesses its own immanent rationality. The theologian that Hegel essentially is remains firmly rooted in the old system of religion, especially the Protestant form of the same, but he none the less posits the philosophical principle as the higher, so to speak better, half of religion, as the authentic principle which must be grasped as such before anything else. As Hegel's commentator Vittorio Hösle puts it: 'Religion is a kind of philosophy for those who are incapable of pure thought: and that, precisely, is Hegel's basic view.' And into this same constellation of philosophy and religion Hegel also inserts, just as Schelling had done, the third dimension of art.

Hegel's conception of 'the religion of nature' and of what was traditionally called 'natural religion' is an extremely involved and complicated one precisely because the various religions in question, for all their particular differences, also form part of a continuum with one another. The religion of nature, which in its most rudimentary form is the religion of sorcery, is ultimately also connected with that 'natural religion' in which mankind attains to knowledge through the 'natural light of his own reason', one in which no special revelation is required. Natural religion in this sense, which Hegel also calls *metaphysical religion*, is well represented by the deism typical of the Enlightenment. In nature religion proper the unity of nature and spirit is still an undisturbed identity, one which has remained untouched by the dichotomy which necessarily transpires at the higher levels of religious experience. Religion of this kind still stands in a direct and immediate harmonious relation to art and knowledge in general or the rudimentary forms of the same. Hegel's thought here is essentially directed against those students of 'primitive' religion, who also have their representatives in the camp of Christianity and would like to preserve the notion of an original paradisal state of undisturbed harmony.

In the Lutheran theology which Hegel had studied in Tübingen there was little time for the idea of a 'natural religion' based on human reason, any more than there was for the related notion of 'natural law'. 'Faith' and 'revelation' were expected to deal with any objections that arose in this quarter, indeed to rule out such problems in advance. This traditional approach reasserted itself when the intellectual storms later broke over Hegelian philosophy and its supposed implications. As a dynamic developmental view of religion Hegel's system always implied an essentially comparative approach to the phenomenon. It has been claimed by Arthur Drews that, after Herder, Hegel was the first thinker to 'open the eyes of Christian theology to an objective appreciation of the other non-Christian religions'. That alone is already a stone of offence to Lutheranism in the narrower sense. Hegel displays a concern with natural religion as based on reason that is quite unwarranted from the traditional Lutheran perspective. Hegel connects the cults of the primitive religions with what he describes as the higher religions of measure, of imagination, of enigma – all of which are still a long way from Judaeo-Christian monotheism and display a marked sympathy for the beauty of natural phenomena and the human form itself. The realm of 'artistic beauty' can therefore also belong to the concept of God – once again an idea which directly contradicts Judaic monotheism and the iconoclastic impulses of strict Protestantism. In Hegel's view, on the contrary, the beautiful in art makes a justified and indeed 'necessary' appearance in the history of religion.

In this way Hegel preserves the realm of art from the harsher accusations of religion which have sometimes been tempted to reject it altogether as something essentially inimical to faith. This reveals Hegel's predilection for the Greek rather than the Judaic religious attitude to the world. In the Greek work of art everything is governed by a sense of clarity and measure. Jewish religion, by contrast, is for Hegel essentially a religion of 'sublimity'. This religion expresses the nature of the Judaic God as the One and Only Lord. Moreover, 'God is only the god of this single people, rather than human beings in general, and this people is the people of God'. All the other peoples are thereby excluded from participation in the One God in accordance with the traditional Oriental idea that religion is essentially bound to ethnic nationality. It was the Greeks and Romans who first undertook to incorporate foreign gods and associated forms of worship into their own religious practices. And amongst the Romans especially, religion was no longer considered as a purely national institution. If the Jewish people is expressly chosen by God, then its God must naturally be opposed to the universal in general. God here figures as the God of his created human servants, and is not yet the God of free human beings as such. In Jewish religion 'mankind enjoys no inner space of its own, no inner breadth, no soul that might enjoy a truly comprehensive satisfaction within itself, and the fulfilment and reality of the individual is that of temporal immediacy'. Judaism is concerned above all with the realm of temporal possessions, with the ownership of soil and cattle, with a long and prosperous life rather than with immortality. For the Jews there is no consolation for the fact of death. To seek to preserve life as long as possible is not the same as seeking eternal life. What does this signify for a religion whose doctrine of the original fall of man attempted to answer the question: how did evil first enter into the world? For a religion which punished the human attempt to attain equality with God, to know the difference between good and evil, with the loss of harmony with nature? But the very religion which imparted to mankind the idea of the One God is still marked, on the level of religious development which it has generated, by a fundamental shortcoming: Judaism has not yet attained to what Hegel calls 'the totality of religious consciousness'. That is only possible for the next stage of religion, namely Christianity itself. For it is an essential part of Christian teaching that God dies and is resurrected once again from the dead.

The thought of Greek religion for Hegel is always associated with the impression of friendly reconciliation. And many have loved to linger with that aesthetic beauty which seems wholly characteristic of the ancient classical world. According to Hesiod's account of early Greek thought it was 'chaos' or emptiness which stood at the origin of all things. We are not told who or what first created the chaos. It was always already there without any prehistory. As 'the dynamic unity of the immediate' this chaos generates 'particular powers' or forces which in turn give rise to further births: the earth begets the heavens, generates the lifeless mountains, the ocean, as well as the race of Cyclops who represent primitive natural forces as such. Earth and heaven together produce the inexhaustible reality of time which bears destruction within itself.

Amongst the Greeks these natural powers and forces assumed a personal shape. But like the Hegelian philosophy they also recognized the ultimate subjection of natural life by spirit. Zeus established the dominion of the spiritual gods through war and it is henceforth the spiritual powers which essentially govern the world. The purely natural powers were thereby relegated to the edges of the world, where however they continue to retain their rights and reveal their ultimately indestructible character. The great war of the gods, from which Zeus eventually emerged triumphant, expresses the entire previous history of gods, demigods and titans.

This essential propinquity of the human and the divine, of the divine and the human, and the ultimate coincidence of the one dimension with the other, was one of Goethe's own essential ideas, one he saw abundantly confirmed by the impression of Greek art in general. The gods manifest themselves here in human form, and indeed in an ideal and beautiful human form. In this regard Hegel takes up a position between Goethe and Feuerbach and already more than suggests what the materialist philosophy of religion will later claim: 'The gods have been produced, therefore, by the human imagination, and they come into being in a finite fashion, generated by the poet and the Muse.' They are essentially creations of the human spirit: 'Homer and Hesiod made the gods for the Greeks.' It was natural for the Greeks that the divine powers should be represented by the human form in its sensuous and natural appearance. The 'sensible character of the beautiful human form' is directly contrasted here with the Judaic conception that God only essentially exists in and for thought, i.e. without any concrete or external visible form. There was no true ideality before the Greeks. They revealed the nature of the ideal in their images and sculptures of the gods. The latter are presented in a perfect form but they are not to be understood in a merely symbolical sense. The Greek gods *are* what they represent. For the Greeks were capable of 'actually perceiving their God in the statue of Zeus by Phidias'. On the level attained by Greek religion the divine naturally manifests itself as a plurality of divinities with explicitly human characteristics and appearance. Greek art represents the perfect expression of this essential anthropomorphism. That also means that 'the reality of animal life' presents a very limited content for such art. Everything is directed rather to the human being and the human body itself. In this sense the Greeks could be seen as the most 'human' of peoples.

The Roman gods, on the other hand, are alien to the free beautiful individuality of the Greek deities and essentially lack their ideal humanity. It is true that Roman religion is often compared and brought into direct relation to the Greek precisely because the Romans took many of their own gods from the Greeks. But a quite different spirit lives in these borrowed gods. Hegel calls Roman religion a 'religion of purposiveness'. In the poetry of Virgil and Horace the Greek gods appear as cold imitations of their former self and there is something essentially rigid and lifeless about them. They are all supposed to satisfy certain needs and demands projected upon them. They represent fertility, war, trade, wealth or simply the power actually incarnated in the figure of the Emperor who is now himself regarded as a god. There is nothing here that recalls the original joy and serenity of the Greeks. When the Romans set foot on the Greek mainland they plundered the temples and shipped off the images of the gods back to Rome. In this way Rome itself became a veritable collecting house for all the religions of the time, the Greek, the Persian, the Egyptian, and became a pantheon where all the gods were represented. Rome was tolerant in this respect. But the presence of all these religions eventually produced a fundamental confusion as the various cults began to combine and merge with one another. The aesthetic form and the sensitivity to it that are essential to art proper, and so characteristic of the Greeks, were lost in the process.

Roman religion clearly reveals the purpose or end it existed to serve in the form of its cultus. The latter presupposes the truth of the divine as something universal and objective. But the interest expressed in the Roman cultus proceeds from the individual subject; it is the subject's indigence and sense of dependency that produces the feeling of sublimity, of reverence, of worship. The believer thereby expects his needs to be met or his predicament resolved. This expectation is the subjective root of devotion to the gods in Roman religion. The Romans thus also introduce a certain horrified awe into our relations with the inscrutable and mysterious gods. The Roman worshipper is preoccupied with pleasing or placating the gods and everything religious is constantly determined by this aim. The Romans venerate their gods because they need them – and especially in time of war. It is need which creates these gods and requires the introduction of new gods when the old ones no longer work.

This is a concept of God typical of the perspective of immediate instrumentality, or 'external purposiveness' as Hegel calls it. Every concept of God must first be explicitly 'posited' for Hegel. Although it may not be posited in a conscious theoretical fashion, the concept in question must eventually develop into its totality of determinations and this is what happened in the Roman world. The representation of the Emperor as a personal god is a good example. On the other hand it is also characteristic of Roman religion that the various national gods gathered together in the single pantheon should reciprocally *destroy* one another through this very process of unification. The divinities celebrated in the Roman cults are all indifferently reduced to one and the same reality and thus debased as such. The Roman spirit destroyed the joy that characterized the earlier religions. A terrible sense of universal grief arose as a result, something that would prove to be the birth pains of a new religion, the religion of truth. The ancient world entered into its final crisis at this point. The omnipotence of the Emperor eliminated all distinctions between free men and slaves. In its world-historical demise the Roman Empire thus prepared the ground for a 'truly spiritual religion'. For Gibbon, the rise of the Christian world is directly connected with the decline and fall of the Roman world.

In Christianity religion finally attains its highest level as the actual 'self-consciousness of God'. Religion realizes itself here in becoming the 'consummate religion', as Hegel calls it: 'The religion which is the very being of spirit for itself . . . , in which religion as such becomes objective to itself.' Thus the act of revelation enters into world history as the explicit manifestation of the fact that God has now become knowable in *objective* form. This corresponds with the Hegelian premise of the *Logic* that we can only properly speak of the being of the spirit when the latter has become 'object' to itself as such. The philosophy of religion is derived from the logical principle: 'A spirit which is not manifest is not spirit.' The manifest religion is also the one revealed by God.

According to Hegel this could only come to pass on the basis of the Roman Empire, where the 'grief of the world' met with its 'subjective preparation, the consciousness of free spirit, of the absolutely free and thus intrinsically infinite spirit'. This 'grief of the world', which the Jewish people continued to bear in so far as they did not share in the offered redemption, was the necessary condition for the emergence of Christianity. According to the Christian conception God himself became man. This alone finally signifies liberation and reconciliation: 'That only this idea is the absolute truth, the result of philosophy as a whole, is the logical principle itself in its pure form.'

Was this a transformation of theological into philosophical truth, or a transformation of philosophical into theological truth? Had the young theologian who officially graduated from the Tübingen Stift remained true to ecclesiastical doctrine all along, was the mature philosopher merely the 'secret theologian' speaking on behalf of the faith? Or had Hegel's theology always, from his earliest writings onwards, been nothing but philosophy? This question soon became a crucial one for post-Hegelian thought, and was answered in a variety of different ways. For Georg Lukács the early writings of Hegel never did contain any essential theological content in the first place, while for Hans Küng the mature theological thought of Hegel represents a useful starting point for a 'future christology' and is a sustained reflection on the 'incarnation of God'. It cannot be denied that in his philosophy of religion Hegel presents the fundamental truths of Christian doctrine in an impeccable dogmatic form which appeals directly to the trinitarian notion of God the Father, the Son and the Holy Spirit. Hegel also retains the basic theological idea of 'salvation history', which reappears as the accomplished 'freedom' of the worldly and political sphere and as the ultimate end of world history. Hegel regards 'freedom' as the essential attribute of Christianity, along with the 'redemption' and 'reconciliation' which it has brought into the world.

If the fundamental truths of Christianity have been maintained and preserved by philosophy, this was partly because these truths could be expressed in terms that went beyond what theology, and especially the typically 'modern' theology of Schleiermacher, understood by them. Philosophy therefore took Christianity under its wing as its own province and felt confirmed in doing so by the inherent 'logical truth' of this religion. In this way philosophy also seemed to assume a position beyond religion in general and thus occupy a higher stage itself. It did not reject religion but rather accepted its historical givenness. Its very being is the proof of its existence as 'positive religion', or religion which requires reference to the historically contingent, to that which enters into it 'externally' in such and such a determinate fashion.

In the lectures which Hegel gave on the traditional proofs for the existence of God in 1831 he paid particular attention to the 'ontological argument'. He thereby explicitly returned the question of God from the field of theology back to the immediate domain of philosophical enquiry as a question of ontology. God as posited refers back to being, being as posited refers back to God. Hegel uses the argument as an opportunity to compare and contrast his own notion of 'necessary being' with that of Kant. The difference between them consisted, as Dieter Henrich puts it, in the fact that 'Hegel contested Kant's claim that the concept of the necessary being is simply a name or word. Hegel's attempt to rehabilitate the ontological proof of the existence of God is an attempt to give an intelligible meaning to the concept of the necessary being.' Hegel appeals in this context to Anselm of Canterbury, for whom God was essentially the most perfect being of all, the conceptual summation of all reality. If God were merely identical with my subjective idea, then he would not be perfect. Only that can truly be regarded as perfect which is not merely subjectively represented but actually possesses existence in its own right.

The manner in which Hegel removes the question of God's existence from the exclusively authoritative realm of theology and appropriates it as the highest issue for philosophy itself represents one of the high points of his philosophy of religion. But it equally reveals the weakness of the latter, as Goethe immediately recognized. When the poet learned that Hegel had been lecturing on the proofs for the existence of God, he could not help feeling, for all his respect for Hegel, that this was merely reviving a dispute that had long since been settled. In comparing Anselm positively with Kant in this regard Hegel's dialectic seemed merely to have reverted to the scholastic subtleties of medieval theology, to have relapsed into that old tradition himself and thus fallen back far behind Kant's cautious examinations of all such proofs. This was surely the way back to the ancient dogmatic metaphysics which Kant had conclusively destroyed. In his descriptions of God as 'spirit', 'eternal Idea', 'the absolute', 'the Trinity', 'action', as 'beginning and end', and as 'love', Hegel was certainly a long way from Kant's modesty in filling out the concept of God itself. In his philosophical doctrine of God Hegel was developing the tradition of speculative mysticism in a logical form, was explicitly applying his *Logic* in accordance with his belief that every form of mysticism harbours a rational core which should not simply be abandoned to irrationalism itself. Mystical speculation attains to a knowledge of God which Kant either does not possess or repudiates as intrinsically uncertain.

With his doctrine of the trinitarian nature of God Hegel defended a Christian position on the character of God and translated it into philosophical terms. He had even defended it against the so-called 'modern' theology which no longer took the doctrine seriously at all. For Hegel the 'Father' represents the universal, the One, the depths of being, the abyss. But the One as the primary reality is not yet identical with everything. This initial being cannot yet be grasped as the true totality. The second moment is the realm of other-being, of difference and distinction. Hegel interprets this as the *Logos*, as the Word or divine activity. This is essentially represented in the form of 'the Son'. The distinction between Father and Son lies in the respective quality despite an identity of substance and person. Only with the addition of 'spirit' as a new quality can the totality in substance and person be properly grounded.

All of this is highly reminiscent of the mystical writings of Jakob Böhme. And Hegel does indeed mention Böhme, who was a source on which Hegel admittedly drew heavily. It is true that Hegel describes Böhme's notion of the Trinity as 'fantastical and wild' in character, but he clearly recognized that the mystic was struggling obscurely for a profound knowledge that would illuminate the presence of the threefold God in and as the ground of all things. If Hegel would like to tame the extravagances of Böhme's mystical intuition of God, he certainly regards these trinitarian speculations as a firm basis for his own philosophy. Hegel knew he was thereby returning to an archaic mode of speech about God. As he put it himself: 'The nature of God is not a mysterious secret in the usual sense, and least of all here in the Christian religion where God has revealed himself to knowledge, has manifested what he is, being essentially open and revealed to view.' If there are difficulties involved here they are not grounded in the object in question. The knowledge of God remains 'a mystery . . . for sense perception, for imaginative representation, for the sensuous perspective generally, and for the limited understanding', but certainly not for speculative reason itself.

Hegel places these various 'types of perspective' in a series, each of which is alien to the other: sensuousness, understanding, and the speculative idea of reason. This division belongs to the rupture which permeates nature and hopelessly separates out its original reality. But that is itself a necessary logical insight. Every individual concept is subject to internal self-contradiction and dissolves itself in this immanent contradiction: 'The logical principle itself shows how every determinate concept is essentially the process of sublating itself, consists in being its own contradiction.' The task of conceptual understanding would seem to be impossible. And for the understanding which thinks in unilateral logical terms, this remains impossible. But speculative thought demands its satisfaction. It welcomes the internal differentiation of the trinitarian God and takes that as its inspiring point of conceptual departure. Speculation loves, like Böhme, to decipher the images, the analogies, the legends, and the stories of religion and myth, because this is material which naturally invites philosophical interpretation. Thus in Adam himself God the Father creates man as a being who can be expected, or feared, to become 'like unto God'. God becomes man, Christ is the second Adam, a traditional interpretation of the story which Hegel is pleased to appropriate. But contradiction upon contradiction is already harboured in the narrative which leads from the original creation to the earthly paradise of Eden. For while this paradise presupposes eternal life, we are also told that it is only from the 'knowledge' forbidden to man that he will acquire true immortality. Is man as such good or evil by nature? Both views are possible and in a sense justified. It is impossible to give a unilateral straightforward judgement on the question. With its natural will the ego stands simultaneously in relation to the world from which it is nevertheless also separated. The consciousness of this separation creates an 'infinite pain'. Man is no longer satisfied in the world around him, and total reconciliation appears impossible. The kind of harmony of the ego with itself, the kind of reconciliation it attempts to find for itself in a philosophy like Stoicism, for example, remains simply abstract. Something else, something other, is still required as the condition of true reconciliation.

Hegel points out that authentic completion of desire can only be accomplished through another self: just as God himself requires his incarnation as the Christ if he is to become accessible to mankind, if he is to convince mankind that the weakness of human nature itself is not irreconcilable with God as the 'absolute Idea'. God demonstrates this very truth in the reality of the God-Man, in his birth and in his death.

This is the great turning point of Hegel's philosophy of religion. The expression 'God is dead', so popularly ascribed to Nietzsche, originally derives from Hegel. The logic of Hegel's thought implies that the living God must give way to the dying God, a monstrous presumption for those who have always been encouraged to believe in a God 'from eternity to eternity', and an occasion for 'the feeling of utterly helpless abandonment'. As the thought that 'all truth has ceased to exist' this thought is 'the most terrible one of all'. All faith in something higher seems to have been utterly destroyed.

But Hegel only lifts the veil on this derelict scene of a God-less world for a moment. For just as God sublates himself through death, so too death itself can be sublated in turn. The process of negation, a process 'itself included in God', does not stop with the death of God. There is also a death of death. God lets death die and arises himself to new life. He does not abandon the just in their graves. In this sense God provides a proof and witness of his own existence. God as 'spirit' is in fact 'only spirit precisely as this negation of the negation, which essentially contains the negative within itself'. In the death of Christ death is compelled to face its own death.

This is the circuitous path that leads Hegel from a sphere of total hopelessness back to the theocentric conviction, to the Tübingen doctrine of Christ that he never decisively broke with in his thinking. Hegel, expert on Greek natural philosophy as he was, could well have appealed to other sources here, like the atomic chaos of Democritus as an expression of the identity of being and nothing. But there is no mention of that in the lectures on the philosophy of religion. The great majority of Hegel's audience could not have noticed what intellectual contraband Hegel had smuggled into his philosophical baggage, apart from students like Ludwig Feuerbach, Arnold Ruge and Bruno Bauer. This insight only began to dawn later, when certain reactionary factions in Prussia, who had long sought support from Hegel's thought, were compelled to recognize the different potential harboured by this philosophical theology or theological philosophy. They made the fearful discovery that Hegel, in spite of his emphatic expressions of Christian conviction, had actually undermined the claims of Christianity and its monotheist foundations in the minds of many of his listeners. If pure being and pure nothing are indeed identical, then God and what is not God also coincide in the last analysis. The *Logic*, from which Hegel derived his philosophy of religion, could serve equally to support the doctrine of the threefold God or the demonstration of his non-existence. The same key fitted admirably for both positions. Hegel explicitly defended the one but apparently also left the other as a distinct possibility. 'The true is the whole,' Hegel had said. Schopenhauer later reproached Hegel for his apparent monotheism; Ferdinand Christian Baur composed his history of the Church largely according to the triadic Hegelian schema as he understood it; Schelling was called to Berlin in 1840 precisely to combat the virulent modern atheism which King Friedrich Wilhelm IV thought he perceived there. Paul Deussen, friend of Nietzsche, follower of Schopenhauer and respected Indologist, felt that Hegel had thoroughly misunderstood the domain of religion and regarded him as a deeply irreligious thinker.

This range of different responses resulted from the essential ambivalence of Hegel's philosophy of religion once it was read in close conjunction with his *Logic*. It appears as though what is often called Hegelian philosophy actually contained several different and mutually conflicting systems of thought. The first great rupture between the so-called Hegelian 'right' and 'left' interpretations of his philosophy manifested itself in the middle of the 1830s with reference specifically to the question of religion. While Ludwig Feuerbach and David Friedrich Strauss mobilized the resources of Hegel's thought to articulate their critical objections to the 'essence of religion' as it was understood in orthodox Christian terms, Philipp Marheineke explicitly defended Hegel's thought as the theological continuation of the Lutheran tradition, something he felt confirmed in doing by the oral and written support which Hegel himself had given him as colleague at the University of Berlin. An individual's own position in regard to these two competing schools of interpretation until about 1840 was essentially decided by this question of Lutheran orthodoxy. It was a matter of deciding either in favour of a dogmatically impeccable form of Lutheran belief with supranaturalist elements, which Hegel seemed on occasion to authorize, or in favour of a critically enlightened half-materialist or even explicitly materialist perspective. But the adherents of both schools still regarded themselves as authentic Hegelians. For Hegel himself had combined all these aspects: dogmatic Christianity, ancient metaphysics, mysticism, pagan Greek humanism, Spinoza and the spirit of the Enlightenment, all radically consummated in his conception of speculative reason. Taken together, these aspects constitute the 'totality' which

Hegel's philosophy attempted to articulate, which the philosopher sought to defend and protect in the context of the Berlin censor, Minister Altenstein, Ministerial Adviser Schulze, the Church authorities, hostile professors and recalcitrant students.

In the meantime there was always the 'Kingdom of the Spirit', this third moment through which the One God made flesh was represented in the actual world of the present: in a Prussia where throne and altar expressed the domains of worldly and spiritual power, a country which enjoyed religious freedom and could presumably look forward to further historical progress, animated by the conviction, shared alike by Hegel's philosophy and Goethe's *Faust*, that 'the human realm is the immediate and present God'. Heinrich Heine, who had heard Hegel lecture in Berlin and always retained his admiration even when the philosopher struck him as a rather grotesque figure, has left an unforgettable parody of this mentality in his *Memoires*: 'I was young and proud, and it flattered my presumption to learn from Hegel that the dear God did not really live in Heaven after all, as my grandmother supposed, but rather that I myself was the dear God down here on earth.' This stage had allegedly been attained by Christianity, namely the Christianity *of the spirit*, and not that of the Catholic Church, which merely represented the same in alien and 'external' form. Through the doctrine of personal immortality the human 'soul' had finally found fulfilment in the Christian religion: it was grasped as spirit in its 'infinite return to itself' and thus as 'actually present and immediate divinity'. Man at the final stage of spirit has become a 'citizen in the Kingdom of God'.

This was another culminating point of Hegel's philosophy of religion and recalls the programme he had originally shared with Schelling and Hölderlin in the old Tübingen days: the immanent preparation for the 'Kingdom of God'. The idea of the Kingdom of God had never actually disappeared from the minds of these three former friends. One could say that Hegel's philosophy of religion represented the first real steps in the eventual fulfilment of this early wish. In Christianity as the authentic 'religion of spirit' God had made himself a present reality in the here and now of human nature with its implications for state and society.

This might well sound like a glorious paean to Christianity and appear as a brilliant apology for the established religion of state, but that is not ultimately what it really was. This shows only one side of Hegel's ambivalent countenance. Hegel was a master of qualification who knew how to withdraw what had apparently been claimed, how to undermine dialectically what had apparently been asserted, and this could lead in the end to the total theoretical demolition of the thesis originally being sustained and defended. There is and can be nothing absolutely stable in the world of experience because every historical movement finally falls victim to the principle of 'dichotomy' and disintegrates as a result.

Hegel presented his series of lectures *On the Proofs of the Existence of*

God as a supplement to his philosophy of religion, and one expressly designed to convince his 'listeners' that the entire philosophical treatment of religion had to be understood in the light of his *Logic*. The traditional proofs, however antiquated they might initially appear, did spring as Hegel notes from the real need to satisfy the demands of a logically thinking reason, even though the object in question, namely God, was not treated in accordance with speculative reason proper and was subsumed instead under the methods of the 'old metaphysics'. In this handwritten manuscript Hegel clearly reveals what he had otherwise rather shrouded in a mist of obscurity in the lectures on the philosophy of religion themselves. Hegel here largely ignores the physico-teleological and the cosmological proofs of the existence of God and emphasizes the ontological proof as central. Being itself implies and involves the existence of God. But we know from the lectures on the philosophy of religion that the existence of God depends on the thinking subject. Just as God as posited being is posited being through me, so non-posited being is non-posited being through me. Behind this lies the old notorious formula of Hegelian logic according to which A = non-A, the negation of A which must always be thought along with A. This looks like something that might have been magically conjured up by Hegel's kinsman Dr Faustus from Knittlingen, but it perfectly encapsulates the abstruse character of the *Science of Logic*, which Hegel himself admitted. This abstruseness was at once an element of logical reason and of the actuality of nature, law, the state, religion, art and history, and is directly involved in the progressive movement of that actuality. There is a cold and sober insight here for all the apparent extravagance of its expression. Logic in Hegel's eyes is entirely removed from the sphere of human caprice. It is concerned solely with a thinking that is identical with being, with thought in and for itself.

One must consider the later effects of these ideas in order to appreciate the enormous realism of Hegel's *Logic*. Although Hegel formally claimed to speak for the principle of the 'Church', there was not much left of it in practice. The 'Church' exists for Hegel only as the 'community' of believers 'in the spirit'. He had no more sympathy for the 'externality' of the Catholic religion than he had for feudalism as a form of political and social life. Luther certainly provides the most 'insightful' account of the relationship between God and the subjective will of the individual, but even he failed to develop the idea effectively. The communion meal is rightly recognized as the centre of Christian doctrine because it offers the enjoyment of partaking in God's presence. But the truly sacramental aspect of the practice is threatened by a materiality which is alien to spirit. In the Host 'God is presented as an external thing for religious devotion', as Hegel puts it in paragraph 552 of the *Encyclopaedia*, where he expresses his distrust of an immaterial divine power which has to prove its efficacy by embodying itself in something material after all. Hegel here attempts what neither Augustine, nor Aquinas, nor Luther, nor Kant had ever attempted, namely an interpretation of Christianity as a form of religious freedom which must precede and prepare the actual 'liberation' of mankind in the world: a thought which would prove enormously important in the future when Christianity was finally grasped as a political force for liberation. But Hegel would not be Hegel if he did not apparently abandon such a provocative view as well. A 'Christian philosophy', he tells us in his lectures on the history of philosophy, can never be a 'free' philosophy because the attributes 'free' and 'Christian' refer to a different content after all.

It was hardly surprising, therefore, that people in Church circles moved over increasingly to join the ranks of Hegel's accusers and detractors, once the general drift and purport of Hegelian teaching had emancipated itself from its veil of linguistic obscurity. Such people had not failed to notice, as Ernst Bloch put it, that Hegel had 'allowed Christianity to arise more from the soil of Greece and Rome than from that of Galilee and Jerusalem'. How should that form part of an officially recognized and politically sanctioned philosophy of the Prussian state? They were not wrong in their suspicions and had not entirely misrepresented Hegel's position here either. Schleiermacher had warned against Hegel's influence long before. The time when Hegel could count on the enthusiastic support of theologians had already reached its zenith, and he was now on the point of becoming a bugbear of the profession instead. The 'Church' as an institution had been harshly handled by Hegel on account of the particular way it had traditionally sought 'reconciliation with the worldly sphere' at the cost of inner spiritual 'laceration'. Theology and its theologians were forced by Hegel to hear what they did not like to recognize: 'Everything in the spiritless actuality of worldly life reappears within the Church itself because of the domination exercised by the latter.' The Church has thus been overtaken by 'dichotomy' and experienced its self-alienation as the loss of its own principle. This only lends the state, which Hegel appeared to represent, further justification for the mistrust it already shows towards an institution inwardly threatened by such 'corruption'.

All of this could be read in Hegel and belonged to the massive influence his doctrines would have, with all their numerous cracks and fissures, throughout the rest of the nineteenth century. Hegel had also placed the various religions in a hierarchically articulated order of value. It was not only Feuerbach or Marx, when he reviewed Bruno Bauer's *Essay on the Jewish Question*, who clung to this same schema. Even when the churches turned explicitly against the Hegelian philosophy they could not escape the powerful influence of his own system of religion in this respect and ended up by appealing to it all the same.

32

Absolute Monarch in the Empire of Philosophy

On one occasion the official sitting of the Society for Scientific Criticism, the association essentially responsible for publication of Hegel's journal, had proved a rather tempestuous affair. It was appropriately called a 'Society' because a shared evening meal generally took place immediately after the regular sittings. Everything about the arrangements strongly suggests that Hegel himself also regarded this institution as something of a compensation for the fact that Schleiermacher had succeeded in preventing his membership of the prestigious Berlin Academy of Sciences. Acceptance in Hegel's 'Society' had no real formalities attached to it. Hegel himself had expressly gone about recruiting interested members and he had never raised any objections concerning any of the proposed candidates. But there was one exception: namely the proposal that Schleiermacher should also be invited to become a member! When Varnhagen explicitly raised the idea in one of the Society's official meetings, Hegel suddenly sprang up from his chair in considerable annoyance and started wandering around the room muttering that this would mean his leaving the Society himself. The situation was eventually resolved: it was decided not to invite Schleiermacher after all, since in the event he was unlikely to accept and that would only make the Society look foolish.

The establishment of the Society and its associated journal not only encouraged a greater solidarity amongst Hegel's explicit opponents, but had a similar effect as independent observers, like the otherwise quite sympathetic Wilhelm von Humboldt, chose to maintain a certain distance from the Hegelian faction. Humboldt, who as Altenstein's predecessor had himself been Secretary at the Prussian Ministry of the Interior with responsibility for cultural affairs, warned the Society against accepting a government subsidy of 400 imperial thalers: 'since Herr von Altenstein would hereby be expected to procure money for the Society, he would also most certainly have certain intentions with regard to the former, and it would have to take care to maintain its freedom from unwelcome interference'. This is what Varnhagen recorded in his private diary. Humboldt was well aware of Altenstein's ambition to maintain the profile of his supporters, with Hegel at the helm, and to keep them on board in future. Ludwig Börne recommended general caution in view of the anti-liberal Berlin tendencies which could be expected to emanate from Hegel's journal and therefore advised the German academics not to contribute to it.

It was only natural, of course, that the public expression and establishment of Hegel's philosophy in such a visible form as the journal would only serve to multiply the number of his explicit opponents as well. The Germanist Karl Lachmann knew he could count on the support of Jacob Grimm in speaking of the 'Hegelian clique' as he did in a letter of 11 April 1827. Hegel himself could have rejected this claim, and with some justice, since the journal's opening issue also presented contributions by scholars like the classical philologist Philip August Boeckh and the archaeologist Alois Hirt, who were certainly not part of Hegel's circle and indeed were rather remote from it. And Goethe and the two Humboldt brothers, all of whom Hegel strove to interest in the journal, were tangentially involved in the project.

Hegel also had close connections with the advanced bourgeois Jewry of the Berlin salons. He liked to visit the home of Rahel Varnhagen where he felt free to talk about political issues with her husband, while his wife took the opportunity of conversing with the hostess. According to an undated letter to Hegel's student and future biographer Karl Rosenkranz, Varnhagen himself believed that the sympathetic intelligence of his wife Rahel had certainly recognized Hegel's 'full spiritual stature', but doubted whether Hegel for his part had been able to appreciate 'the authentic nature of her true spirit'. This may well have been the case, but it is certainly true that at the zenith of his influence Hegel found what he desired in this private social sphere: an intellectual milieu where science and learning, philosophy, politics, literature and music all seemed for a moment to come together – and where the presence of Italian singers like Angelica Catelani was also to be expected.

In Hegel's private life the official philosopher is not always very far from the surface either. And towards the end the philosopher also tended to become 'increasingly difficult and increasingly despotic' in his behaviour, as Varnhagen reports in the same letter to Rosenkranz: 'In official meetings he would sometimes behave so oddly that the whole Society felt that things could not go on like this much longer.' The somewhat absolutist spirit, to which Hegel felt increasingly drawn in the political sphere, also began to reveal itself as a peculiar stubbornness of character in his private dealings as well. But again these occasions were often only momentary ones that were soon relieved by generous expressions of honest goodwill on Hegel's part, with an attitude which clearly recalled the pleasantly easygoing and generally phlegmatic nature of the earlier student Hegel under the motto of the

German saying 'All good things need their time'. On one occasion, when Eduard Gans returned from a trip undertaken to recruit suitable contributors for the *Yearbooks,* he found Hegel in a green dressing gown, wearing his characteristic black cap rather resembling a beret, taking a pinch of snuff with one hand and groping through a disorderly pile of papers with the other. A veritable sentimental picture of comfortable academic life around 1827! Even the slightly sleepy atmosphere of the scene is captured here.

The needs and demands of Hegel's immediate academic pupils were also beginning to make themselves felt at this period. They wanted to be promoted, recommended and employed in secure official positions of one kind or another. A certain rivalry between some of them revealed itself, like that between Hinrichs, whom Hegel's praises had helped to employment in Halle, and Gabler, who sought Hegel's assistance in moving over from Bavarian to Prussian government service. There were difficulties with Hegel's student Leo for both personal and professional reasons. Altenstein had left him in the position of a non-titular professor in Berlin, a financial situation which made it impossible for him to contemplate marriage. But now, so he tells Hegel in a letter, he is actually grateful to the minister after all since on more mature reflection he felt he could no longer marry the woman in question anyway and had accordingly broken off the relationship. In the meantime he had fled to Jena and now hardly dared to show his face in Berlin. Obviously Hegel's sympathy for friends was difficult to lose once it had been acquired. As long as he lived Hegel amply fulfilled his reputation for securing professorships for his academic followers, whether through patient diplomacy or more clandestine intrigue. This was itself one source for continued conflict between the university faculty and the government ministry: whereas the majority of the faculty would oppose Hegel, Altenstein would support him unreservedly. When the ecclesiastical Lutheranism represented by the theologian Hengstenberg boasted of its powerful opposition to Hegel and his school, there was an attempt to appoint Hengstenberg as non-titular professor in distant Königsberg. This soon provoked complaints about Hegel's 'deification' in Berlin, and even Wilhelm von Humboldt, who had participated in Hegel's journal although he found some of the contributions too obscure and hesitated himself to take a conclusive stand on Hegel's philosophy as a whole, was ready in private circles to accuse Hegel of a certain 'despotism'. The philosopher of freedom was beginning to appear as a man who was actually endangering freedom.

Humboldt was no insignificant figure and his judgement may well have been justified. In this situation Hegel was seen as the state philosopher, as the intellectual advocate of Altenstein, who was himself playing an increasing role in the affairs of the university with the ever-growing power of the Restoration. Humboldt could no longer recognize this approach as representing the spirit of the Reform age he had once known. On the other hand, voices were also being raised against Hegel from a quite different quarter, accusing him of secretly harbouring English-style constitutional ideas and thereby deceiving the stricter adherents of monarchy. What was to be believed here? In the sense of Hegelian logic and the actual situation in Berlin both at once! At this time Hegel found himself at the height of his influence thanks to the *Yearbooks* and the success with which the power of his method seemed wedded with the enormous significance of his philosophy in general. Hegel seemed to preside as judge over all the most important issues of earlier and modern philosophy alike. One only needs to consider Hegel's letter to Cousin of 25 March 1828 where he refuses to place the thought of Kant below that of Plato in philosophical importance. In Hegel's opinion, that would only be appropriate in certain respects, whereas from another perspective the modern philosophers occupy a different and higher plane with regard to the earlier thinkers on account of the inner depth and range of their principles. And Hegel naturally stands for these modern philosophers too.

The rise of Hegel's philosophy and its dissemination as an intellectual approach had now completely overshadowed the thought of the man who had assisted at its first emergence and considered himself as its authentic founder. After years of silence Schelling had resumed his lecturing activity in Munich and that now inevitably involved an explicit engagement with the man who had apparently borrowed his 'method' for himself and successfully applied it under a different name with different trimmings to fields originally of less immediate interest to Schelling himself. Hegel, who had still widely been regarded as a 'Schellingian' up till the end of his period in Heidelberg, had by now become a European celebrity, while the formerly famous Schelling was forced to endure a series of misfortunes in the Bavarian South: a cultural climate that hardly favoured Schelling's intellectual gifts, the death of his first wife Caroline, and finally, though he would be the last to admit this, the fateful contact with the mysticism of Baader and Görres. He was of course inwardly predisposed to influences and interests of this kind, which first showed themselves in his enthusiasm for the mysteries of the 'divining rod' – something which Hegel had tactfully avoided mentioning in his correspondence with Schelling. During his time at Munich Schelling developed this characteristic fascination with the 'dark side' of nature even further and became increasingly interested in 'the magical dimension of the will'. He believed that will-power could impart motion to the pendulum. 'Thus in effect our own muscles are nothing but so many divining rods which move inwards or outwards according to the action of our will', as Schelling observed in a letter to Windischmann of 16 September 1804. It was part of Schelling's programme to rediscover the 'key' to the art of 'ancient magic'. The Schelling of these later years has already become 'mystical-religious' in outlook, something which can certainly never be said of Hegel the religious phenomenologist even when he seems to speak on behalf of religion itself. Moreover, Schelling was increasingly drawn to the (by now) Catholic Friedrich Schlegel, which must have suggested evidence of final intellectual and spiritual exhaustion in Hegel's eyes, given his own extremely critical attacks on Schlegel's views. This was certainly the current attitude to Schelling in Prussia. But not only there: in Germany as a whole Schelling's reputation had long since begun to appear suspect amongst the leading literary circles, far beyond the borders of the politically progressive and liberal movement. Perhaps one can ignore the malicious tone with which Heinrich Heine would later speak of Schelling in his book *Religion and Philosophy in Germany*, but one cannot simply reject the claim that even the Restoration itself could no longer endure Schelling, that he actually ended up rehabilitating things that 'merited comparison with the French Restoration in the worst sense'. Why had Schelling sunk so low in public esteem? According to Heine, 'public reason itself no longer found him bearable' now that he was 'rummaging around in the hidden recesses of Jesuitical obscurity, busily forging more spiritual fetters, and all the while presuming to tell us he is just the same old enlightened man of reason that he once was . . .'

But Schelling could not forget the early beginnings when a somewhat perplexed Hegel had first sought his assistance, when the older man Hegel had actually felt himself a pupil of the rather younger Schelling. Schelling always continued to insist on his priority with regard to the philosophical method of idealism. Victor Cousin, who had originally travelled to Germany to study with Schelling and had accidentally encountered Hegel in Heidelberg and thus familiarized himself with contemporary 'German philosophy' through the latter, received a letter written in French by Schelling from Munich on 27 November 1827.

> You have begun to acquaint yourself with the system that originally derives from me only in the shape which certain ill-informed or intellectually weak individuals have given it, and in a form which it has temporarily assumed in the limited mind of a man who believed he could simply appropriate my ideas, just as a crawling insect believes it may take over the leaf of a plant once it has embroiled it within its spidery web.

If this is how Schelling saw the matter it could only be because he necessarily felt himself deprived, in the public consciousness, of the original credit for initiating the new philosophy. On the other hand, Schelling could no longer properly recognize himself in what Hegel had done with the 'system' anyway. The original 'system', so he told Cousin, possessed a 'living principle' which Hegel had never been able to grasp and had merely distorted like a sensitive flower whose precious life had now been killed as a result.

Here in Munich we see the emergence of the first really important critique of Hegel, one which essentially already contains the seeds of all the arguments later directed against Hegelian thought. On this view the artificial character of Hegel's philosophy had simply severed the living thread of organic life. This reproach was not far from what Goethe hesitated to say in so many words, but which surely revealed its unspoken presence in his various remarks concerning the philosophy of his otherwise dear friend. But if there is some justice in this reproach, Schelling was not justified in emphasizing his own absolute priority in every respect and simply rejecting Hegel's further elaboration of the 'method'. He overlooked the fact that Hegel intended to elevate the dialectic into a total method and develop it through his logic into an instrument that could be applied to all areas of scientific knowledge, that could subject nature and spirit, past, present and future, to its sway: in short, that Hegel had effectively made dialectic into what it would soon prove so influentially to be in the outside world. Thought 'in itself' and 'for itself' is dialectical thought; being 'in itself' and 'for itself' is being with its own internal dialectical dynamism. Above all, Schelling overlooked Hegel the Enlightenment thinker at a time when the Enlightenment as an intellectual movement had already long since appeared dead and gone, enjoying a kind of afterlife only in eccentrics like Paulus in Heidelberg. Hegel was not Paulus, but the most fateful thing about Schelling's harsh judgement here is that he seems in a sense to have forgotten himself, seems not to have realized how much the light of Enlightenment, which had once burned so brightly in him, had become such a feeble glimmer now.

The direction in which Hegel's thought had generally been moving, and the degree to which it now diverged from Schelling's, can be appreciated from the letter which an unknown correspondent sent to Hegel from the Bavarian town of Ansbach. The author, a young man who had just become a doctor of philosophy, sent Hegel his dissertation on 22 September 1828 and in the accompanying and rather laborious lines attempted to epitomize his current views concerning religion. Although the correspondent describes himself as an 'immediate pupil' of Hegel's who claimed to have attended his lectures in Berlin for two years and merely wanted to express his 'personal respect and extreme admiration' to his teacher, the absolute philosopher could not remember ever having heard his name or ever having exchanged a single word with him. But on reading the enclosed text and accompanying letter, if he ever did so, Hegel would have had to conclude that the unknown correspondent had indeed understood his teaching, and understood him even in the moment of intellectual separation from his influence. For the writer of the letter, Ludwig Feuerbach, here confronted the Berlin master, with the maxims, clumsily expressed as they were, and the essential task of the 'new philosophy', namely:

> to penetrate to the very ground of truth, really and truly to destroy all of the previous world-historical conceptions of time, death, the beyond, of this world, of the ego, the individual, the personality, of the person intuited in the absolute as independent of all finitude, namely the absolute person of God himself, all those conceptions which provide the ground of all previous history and the

original source of the system of Christian ideas, whether orthodox or more rationalist in character.

That was something which Hegel had never publicly proclaimed from his lectern, but it was a perspective that could be plausibly developed if the constituent parts of the official system were dismantled and rearticulated in a correspondingly new form. In his letter Feuerbach even dared to contradict the letter of Hegel's teaching when he concludes by adding: 'Christianity cannot therefore be regarded as the perfect and absolute religion.' For that is precisely what Christianity was according to Hegel. And yet in another sense that was not what Christianity was in so far as Hegel also claimed that its truth was merely subsidiary in respect to the full truth vouchsafed only by philosophy: 'For if philosophy as you understand it, and as the knowledge of history and philosophy itself teaches us, is no longer to be considered merely as a matter of the school, but rather as a matter of humanity itself, . . . then the task now is to establish a kingdom as it were, the kingdom of the Idea.' And he goes on:

> Philosophy has worked over the centuries at the realization and perfection of itself, and has gradually advanced step by step to grasp the totality, the All (however one wishes to describe it) according to one particular form and in accordance with one particular concept . . . , but its task now is finally to dispel the thought that something other than itself, something still subsidiary, should continue to claim, whether only in appearance or with justice, a second subsidiary truth of its own, like the truth of religion, and so forth.

And in the eyes of this correspondent at least that implied nothing less than 'the uncontested sovereignty of reason'. To establish such a realm it would first be necessary to 'dethrone that conception of the ego, of the self in general, that has hitherto ruled the world, and especially since the beginning of the Christian era'.

Here Hegel could see a simplified version of his own teaching that he would never himself have expressed in these terms, although it is a view that could be read in his ever so carefully and subtly qualified *System of Philosophy*. For here, in the solitude of a tiny south German town, in the name of Hegel's method, a barely 24-year-old man could lift the protective camouflage which the master himself had draped over the structure of his own thought and thereby reveal the prospect of an activist application of these ideas in the service of radical change. Feuerbach, who was here laying the foundations of his own philosophical approach, found himself advancing to a doubly one-sided interpretation: a reading of Hegel entirely from the perspective of material reality, and an explicit identification of Hegel's whole philosophy with his philosophy of religion. Hegel's philosophy had always harboured the possibility of its own inversion, had always been capable of inferring the non-existence of God from his very existence, just as Feuerbach himself did when he expressly spoke in his letter of 'destroying . . . God', of relegating him to all those other hallowed and withered ideas and beliefs now approaching their final demise. In the place of such conceptions the true realm of the Idea would now be able to establish its own truth, which is no longer a truth of a religion or of a church. Things had already come as far as this by the end of 1828.

Even in the philosopher's own lifetime, therefore, the first chapter of the story 'Hegel and his Influence' was already being written. It was a peculiar characteristic of Hegel that the whole of Feuerbach – including the materialist who broke with Hegel and explicitly turned against him – is contained within the orbit of his thought. Feuerbach did not really go beyond what Hegel's logical reflections on the being, or the possible non-being, of God had already suggested, apart from bringing new empirical materials to the study of the historical religions. Feuerbach's atheism is already implicit in Hegel, especially in the form of the Spinozist doctrine of the *one* substance, which Hegel understands on the one hand as pantheism, as the all-permeating 'world soul' or 'world spirit', something with which no personal relationship is really possible. On the other hand, Hegel can also describe this view as a kind of atheism, while admitting all the dangers which are inevitably connected with the use and the understanding of such a word.

All of this implies once again that the Hegelian philosophy in fact consists of at least two mutually opposed philosophies which are only held together by means of the 'method' and thereby synthesized into a third system. The philosophy resembles Hegel himself as a man who harboured the most profound differences and discontinuities within himself: in his family; in his professional capacities; in his relationship to colleagues; in his insights into nature, the state, politics, history, law and religion. Dialectic always functions as the means by which to resolve the contradictions between the essence of being and appearance in the self-presence of spirit.

Particularly under the influence of the *Yearbooks* in the late 1820s, this led to a situation in which the unfolding ideas of the 'school' also became directly involved with those of Hegel's critics and could not always easily be disentangled from the latter. When Immanuel Hermann Fichte, the son of Hegel's famous predecessor as Rector at Berlin, sent his work *Contributions towards the Characterization of the more Recent Philosophy* to Hegel for an appropriate judgement on its merits, something which he considered as a positive step for his intended academic career, the author was taking quite a risk. For the piece already contains all the basic elements of a fundamental critique which the younger Fichte would eventually mount against Hegel. The reasons why Ch. H. Weisse regarded himself as a 'pupil' of Hegel's, as expressed in his letter to the philosopher of 11 June 1829, were of a very different nature. Weisse was the first person to make two significant discoveries with regard to Hegel's philosophy, both of which threatened to expose it to a potential misunderstanding which has not perhaps been avoided to this day. And he explicitly mentioned them in his letter to Hegel. The first concerned the peculiar identification of logic and metaphysics and the second touched upon the idea of the constant progress of the world spirit which seemed to contradict Hegel's assumption that his own philosophy represented the 'highest of all conceivable forms of spiritual activity' and had thus already attained the 'final goal of all development, not only of the human spirit but of the divine spirit as well'. In our own century thinkers like Karl Barth and Ernst Bloch have once again only endorsed the full significance of Weisse's questioning of Hegel in this regard. If Hegel's philosophy truly claims to be the vehicle in which the 'spirit' authentically realizes itself, then any further historical advance in the future can only mean one of two things: 'the spirit has the choice either of falling back again from its present position or of now simply repeating itself in an eternally monotonous cycle'. Weisse himself thought that Hegel would have to reject the latter possibility. The correspondent from Leipzig does not appear to have received an answer to his questions.

There were two factors which essentially determined the status of Hegel's philosophy in the intellectual world at the height of his public influence: its intrinsic obscurity and its transformation into a kind of 'secret doctrine' through its further development and elaboration in Hegel's lectures. As far as written and therefore generally accessible works were concerned, Hegel's ideas were only to be found in the *Phenomenology*, the *Logic*, the *Philosophy of Right* and the two editions of the *Encyclopaedia*, together with a few contributions in the Berlin *Yearbooks*. What Hegel ultimately thought in detail about the realms of nature, history, aesthetics and religion could only properly be discovered from his lectures, which were circulated in student transcripts which Hegel himself found extremely unsatisfactory whenever he had occasion to examine one. The question as to what Hegel had actually said about the various disciplines in accordance with his specific logical approach was by no means easy to answer. On 5 April 1829 one Herr Ravenstein, first lieutenant with the second cavalry regiment in Pasewalk, formally contacted Hegel and expressed his desire to obtain a transcript of his lectures on the philosophy of religion. He already possessed transcripts of the other lectures which he guarded with his life – they were apparently being regularly exchanged amongst disciples of the philosopher in this tiny garrison town. In his reply to the lieutenant, Hegel had to confess that he was unable to offer any further concrete help to this enquiring friend of his philosophy.

After travelling many paths, upon which he was hardly richly rewarded in material terms, Hegel had now finally attained in Berlin his ultimate station in life. But in spite of all his direct experience of wealthy and important towns like Frankfurt and Nuremberg, Hegel had always remained in many respects a man from the provinces. The later protagonist for 'Young Germany', Carl Gutzkow, who had listened to Hegel's last series of lectures on the philosophy of history in the winter semester of 1830/1, described Hegel in his literary portraits of the Berlin world as very much the typical 'Swabian master of philosophy as far as his external appearance was concerned'. That says quite a lot about Hegel. The gradual and rather deliberate nature of his character and thought can easily obscure the many problems and anxieties to which he had been exposed in life. His decision to pursue philosophy in the first place was a decided risk, and remained something that often weighed upon him like a 'curse', as he explicitly admitted. New sources of anxiety were constantly arising to gnaw at his essential being and he frequently left a rather wretched external impression on his visitors. The winter following his trip to Paris brought him considerable illness, which he himself described as a 'chest complaint'. As a result he had to cancel his lectures for quite a while. The physician recommended him to go and take the waters somewhere to restore his health. Hegel's letter to Minister Altenstein of 16 May 1829 revealed the somewhat straitened nature of his finances at the time. The costs that would be incurred by such a journey exceeded his means, all the more so now since Hegel had only held a closed seminar during the winter semester and had suffered a considerable drop in income as a result. There were no longer any financial reserves: 'During my residence in Berlin we have had to use all of the independent capital which my wife formerly possessed, because my official income was insufficient to meet the various costs incurred in living here, even though I have never exceeded the limits of our real needs and sense of propriety.' The original prospect of an increase in salary once he entered into Prussian academic service never materialized during the ensuing eleven years in Berlin. Hegel received a letter from Altenstein eleven days after his submission to the minister in which he was duly promised 'a special grant of 300 thalers'.

All of this clearly revealed one thing at least: for all his devotion to the cause of the state, the enthusiastic fulfilment of his official duties and the public influence of his thought, Hegel had gained very little in financial terms. In order to dedicate himself entirely to philosophy he had had to draw on his wife's own insubstantial dowry. Hegel was no better off in Berlin than he had been as a debt-ridden Rector in Nuremberg, and certainly worse off than he had been as a newspaper editor in Bamberg when he had no family to support. The only thing left now was the pension scheme for himself and possibly his wife in case of his early death. This did not amount to very much. And the new Prussia still actually enjoyed the reputation of providing more generous pensions than most of the other German states.

Hegel's ingrained love of stability had found its ultimate expression by the autumn of 1828. He was in no mood for any further changes of circumstance. When his domestic rent came up for renewal he left his wife in charge of all the details in his absence. But he clearly wanted to continue living in Kupfergraben and eventually to die there. He would far rather undertake the necessary alterations to the place, and undergo a few months' inconvenience, than contemplate moving house altogether.

Persisting in the accustomed ways had always been an old and characteristic Württemberg feature of Hegel's personality. By July 1829 Hegel was able to move back into his newly renovated home. His wife organized the library by subject areas. In her eyes he had become the most agreeable of socialites. Thus she could write to Hegel's sister Christiane on 24 July 1829: 'the more seriously engaged he is during the day, the more enthusiastic he is about taking a stroll or going to play whist, and enjoying company or listening to music in the evenings; if there is anything fine to be seen or heard, he is sure to be there.' At the end of August Hegel travelled to Karlsbad via Prague. He alighted at The Golden Lion, took the obligatory walk around the area, enjoyed the famous view of the town from a local hill and betook himself to the recommended spa. After two or three days he was already beginning to feel much better. He did not actually take the waters, in marked contrast to another guest who just happened to be there at the same time. When Hegel learned of this fact he set out to find him. 'Just imagine,' so Schelling wrote to his wife at the beginning of September 1829 from Karlsbad, 'I was sitting in the baths when I suddenly heard a rather unpleasant half-familiar voice asking after me. Then the unknown person announced himself: it was Hegel from Berlin.'

It is extremely instructive to compare the respective reports which the two men sent to their wives about this unexpected meeting. From the beginning Hegel attempted to revive the old familiarity he had once enjoyed with Schelling. But the latter was very wary indeed. 'In the afternoon he turned up again', so Schelling continues, 'very importunate and uncommonly cordial, as if there were nothing between us at all; since we have not discussed philosophical matters as yet, something I would like to avoid, but since he is a bright enough person, we did spend a couple of hours conversing together in the evening.' In Hegel's letter to his wife of 3 September the reunion is very differently described: 'We were both pleased to see each other and felt like good friends together.' Indeed Hegel also gave Varnhagen the distinct impression that the former amity between the two founders of systematic idealism had now been re-established. In fact Schelling was not prepared for such a reconciliation. Hegel had actually encountered a very embittered man. They did not exchange a single word about philosophy and its 'method' during their conversations in Karlsbad.

In October 1829 Hegel was elected Rector of the University of Berlin. Hegel's one-year tenure of the office marked the first time that the position was combined with that of Deputy Government Representative. This arrangement hardly corresponded to the spirit of Humboldt's original university reforms. The government clearly saw Hegel as the appropriate man to discharge this new double function and they were certainly right in this. As the philosopher of freedom and the philosopher of a state where freedom and law essentially came together at least in his eyes, Hegel was pleased to celebrate the academic freedom of teaching and learning at the University of Berlin in his Latin rectorial address delivered on 18 October.

Hegel's time as Rector coincided with a rather turbulent period. The revolution of 1830 was already brewing, and there were symptoms of coming change even in certain German university towns, although the existing system was never seriously threatened when the trouble came. It was a very different situation in France and Belgium, where Hegel could see the storms blowing freely. As far as the discontent in Belgium was concerned, Hegel sided with the old Netherland party, to which his friend and former student van Ghert belonged, and encouraged this group to act decisively without delay. As far as France was concerned the situation for Hegel appeared rather more complex. Here his other friend Cousin had attempted to win the philosopher over to the cause of political freedom as he himself understood it, and it was under this banner that the liberal bourgeoisie effectively took power under the monarchy of Louis Philippe. Naturally the principle of political legitimacy, which was now also at stake in France, inwardly impeded him from immediately supporting the advancing liberalism, which he had always basically distrusted anyway. In Berlin he was able to keep all political problems and disturbances at bay as far as the university was concerned, and during his period as Rector no student was expelled. The fourteen students who were detained during this time were all punished for the usual kinds of institutional transgression. The government appreciated Hegel's efforts and in January 1831 rewarded him, long after he had discharged his period as Rector, with the Order of the Red Eagle, Third Class.

Hegel had inevitably performed his rectoral duties as a figure-head for the Karlsbad Decrees, originally promulgated in 1819, which had dissolved the student fraternities and increased press and university censorship generally. But he discharged his role in the mildest way possible. On the 300th anniversary of the Augsburg Confession on 25 June 1830, Hegel's position gave him the opportunity to express in public, once again in Latin, his principled conception of the authentic union of throne and altar, of Prussia and Protestantism. Luther is praised as the true saviour of religious freedom from the Catholic Church and the irreconcilable gulf which it posits between man and God. Two months later, on his sixtieth birthday, Hegel's students presented him with a commemorative medallion they had specially commissioned for the occasion. The front of the medal shows Hegel in profile, while the reverse side displays an allegorical scene: a radiant spiritual youth is flanked on the right by a female figure bearing a cross and on the left by a scholar poring over a book beneath a watchful owl of Minerva. Naturally everyone was so delighted with the idea of such a medal, which obviously enough represented the union of faith and wisdom, that any other aesthetic reservations were forgotten. Goethe immediately felt rather differently when he received his own complimentary copy of the medallion: what on earth does the cross have to do with the owl of Minerva, and the owl of Minerva with the cross? Hegel himself could not be held directly responsible of course. Perhaps the allegorical representation evoked a certain painful dichotomy that Hegel had long since overcome in his own thought, but Goethe himself was not at all impressed by it. On I June 1830 he wrote to Zelter about

> how much the reverse side of Hegel's medallion displeases me. One cannot properly see what it is supposed to mean. I have demonstrated in my own poetry that I have always known how to honour and to beautify the cross both as a poet and a man; but I can hardly take comfort from the fact that a philosopher has led his students along the darkest pathways and byways of being and non-being to such an arid conclusion as this.

Goethe's profound, and even physically obvious, discomfort at the conjunction of philosophy and Christianity naturally found an immediate object in Hegel. On the other hand, this response was not justified after all since Hegel's 'method' could easily also lead, as the next couple of generations would show, emphatically to kinds of anti-theological systems of thought never really seen before, namely the philosophies of Ludwig Feuerbach and Karl Marx.

In Hegel's period as Rector of Berlin University the original 'school' of his followers that was formed during his own lifetime reached the zenith of its power. But signs of imminent decline were also quick to reveal themselves. On account of various editorial ineptitudes the *Yearbooks* had not quite enjoyed the success or made the favourable impression originally expected of them. They actually exerted a somewhat disintegrating effect instead, being too loosely and arbitrarily put together, combining at once Hegelian and non-Hegelian perspectives without much sense of a unifying connection. And some of the more remarkable and eccentric contributions only exposed the journal to explicit and most unwelcome attacks from its opponents. Even the projected financial support from the government failed to materialize as expected, and Altenstein's monies were not forthcoming in the end.

Hegel's pragmatic rectorship, so welcomed by the government, had somewhat weakened Schleiermacher's resistance to Hegel's admission to the Prussian Academy of Sciences. Wilhelm von Humboldt had always regarded it as rather 'inappropriate' that Hegel had never been granted membership of the institution, but he did not want to give the impression of trying to interfere personally in the issue. But now, when Schleiermacher was prepared to agree to the idea, it was the natural scientists who registered the opposition. It seems as though the ancient quarrel in matters of theology had finally been buried. This is certainly suggested by the fact that shortly before his final illness Hegel had actually engaged in a stimulating conversation with Schleiermacher on the street in Kreuzberg and both of them had apparently come to a positive understanding with one another.

33

The End

~

Hegel's rectorship had scarcely come to an end when he fell seriously ill. In September 1830 Hegel and his wife were both confined to bed because of fever. An apparent improvement in their situation soon turned out to be deceptive. On 1 November Zelter wrote to his friend Goethe about the matter: 'Hegel and his wife have both contracted fever again and I am very concerned about both of them.' Twelve days later Zelter wrote again to Goethe informing him of a certain Frau von Wahl who had fled her Russian homeland to escape a cholera outbreak there and had gone to spend the winter in Berlin. She had entrusted her son to the care of the Hegel family with the philosopher as a kind of 'foster father' and was herself a frequent visitor of the household. Once again Hegel began to feel he was firmly on the road to recovery and, despite a continuing fever, insisted on delivering his lectures on world history. It was at this time that Hegel received news of the death of Goethe's son. Varnhagen von Ense, a mutual friend, communicated Hegel's condolences to the poet on 16 November: a man like 'Goethe shows resolve before all things . . . he is prepared to face everything, steady above all with himself, that was his greatest task and his greatest power'.

During the ensuing winter Hegel fulfilled his professional lecturing responsibilities despite his continuing poor state of health. His lectures meant a great deal to him. In a sense he dedicated more effort to them than he did to his current publications and writing projects, which now included a new edition of the *Science of Logic* and the essay on the English Reform Bill. Zelter himself had witnessed the intensity of Hegel's activity in Lecture Room 6 of the university and would later tell Goethe that Hegel had almost 'read himself to death'.

As the cholera infection which the Berliners had already dreaded now began to spread, Zelter's remark takes on an added significance. But it is of course also possible that Hegel's work-load is quite irrelevant in this connection. The Hegel family had in fact taken all the practical precautions they could. When the epidemic was already claiming its first victims in Berlin, the Hegels were living on the first floor of a Garden House in the Kreuzberg region, then a remote and protected country suburb of the city. At the beginning of the academic vacation his wife had implored Hegel to spend his time out of doors away from the city. He had thus spent the summer in the country where the danger of infection appeared much reduced. His friends came out to visit him there and always found him in exceptionally good spirits and happily surrounded by his family. Kreuzberg is also where Hegel celebrated his last birthday amid champagne and general rejoicing.

But the autumn already showed a much changed Hegel. 'Pale and sunken, he would stagger up the steps to the lectern', so reported Hegel's student Johann Jacoby with regard to Hegel's afternoon lecture on the history of philosophy delivered on 1 November 1831. To judge from the remarks of this student and those of Schulze to Altenstein, Hegel's final Friday lecture would seem none the less to have made a great impression on his listeners. After the lecture was concluded Hegel went directly, in spite of very bad weather, to the publishing house Duncker in order to sign an agreement for a projected new edition of the *Phenomenology of Spirit*.

Marie Hegel wrote to her mother in Nuremberg to inform her of Hegel's death, telling how her husband 'after one and a half days of sickness had finally passed away, easily and without pain, gently and peacefully without enduring a final death struggle, without suspecting his death and in clear consciousness until his last sleep'. And she also added the interesting observation: 'He showed none of the usual symptoms which might have alerted us to the mortal threat, no pain in the calves, no chilling in the arms and legs or the chest.' The two doctors in attendance applied mustard plaster to Hegel's entire body, which made no difference to his condition, and warm compresses of camomile. These measures, deemed appropriate for 'cholera in its acutest form' – the officially registered cause of Hegel's death – must obviously have been approved by Hegel's wife. But she also recorded 'abdominal pains' as one of Hegel's immediate symptoms. These stomach pains may actually have had a much earlier source. His repeated attacks of nausea were now producing emissions of bile. At his bedside his wife expressly noted 'icy coldness and cold sweat on his forehead'. In fact these could well have been symptoms of an earlier medical problem of Hegel's. His sister Christiane was able to remember similar difficulties in Hegel's Württemberg period when he had suffered an almost 'fatal illness' which she simply described as a 'cold fever'. 'I encountered this with Wilhelm even in his student years', as she wrote to her sister-in-law on 6 February 1831. When Christiane finally received news of her brother's death she was already in a state of great mental confusion and it took some hours for the news to sink in properly.

If the death certificate mentioned the epidemic as the cause of death, an explanation accepted by Hegel's wife although she had some reason to be sceptical about it, this can be seen as a readily understandable cautionary measure in the interests of public health. None the less, Hegel's friends and family were still able, obviously through the good offices of Schulze or Altenstein, to prevent Hegel's body from being taken away at night in a cart with other cholera victims to rest in a specially designated graveyard. In fact, Hegel was buried at about three o'clock in the afternoon next to Fichte and very close to Solger. Hegel's student Marheineke was chosen to deliver the funeral oration in the great lecture hall of the university. When he did so Marheineke indulged in a rather exaggerated comparison, albeit one that clearly corresponded to the general mood of the Hegelian school that almost felt it had reached the appointed end of history:

> Like our Saviour himself, whose name he had perpetually glorified in his every thought and action, in whose divine teaching he had recognized the deepest essence of the human spirit; who as the Son of God had given himself over to pain and death, in order to return to his community for ever as spirit; so too he has now returned to his true homeland and attained to glory precisely through his death and resurrection.

If Marheineke's ambitious rhetoric was prepared to place Hegel alongside Christ himself, Friedrich Förster's oration at Hegel's graveside compared the philosopher with the disciples: 'Although no Peter will ever arise who could presume to be his representative, his kingdom, the kingdom of thought itself, will continue to spread, not indeed without contestation, but with ultimately unhindered power.' In addition to the Saviour and his representative on earth Förster also mentioned Alexander the Great and Frederick the Great in this connection. This is how Prussia celebrated its most outstanding sons through the mouths of two prominent Hegelians of the time. Even the Prussia of the Restoration period had not entirely forgotten that it was its famous king who had 'placed philosophy upon the throne'. Without Frederick the Great, no Kant. Without Prussia, no Leibniz and also no Fichte, whom the country had once adopted and preserved from persecution. And without Prussia, certainly no Hegel, who only really found 'his true homeland' here, as the orator clearly implied. The oration finally concluded: 'Fichte and Hegel! These are the Pillars of Hercules.' Prussia, which had formerly shown itself a veritable Sparta in the wars of liberation against Napoleon, had now become, through the efforts of its philosophers, a true Athens.

For all its high-flown rhetorical exaggeration the peculiar thing about such a pronouncement was that it could none the less claim a certain truth. The proof of this lies in the influential future of Hegelian philosophy itself, including its imminent disintegration into mutually conflicting schools as well as the attacks and persecution to which it would be exposed, and which were indeed already beginning to manifest themselves the moment Hegel's eyes had closed in death.

It might well seem as though another widely discussed matter had contributed to Hegel's death on 14 November 1831, apart from the very real stomach pains and the not very likely cholera infection. This was Hegel's argument with Eduard Gans. Hegel had announced two lecture courses for the winter semester: one on the philosophy of right, the other on the history of philosophy. At the beginning of the semester Hegel discovered that Gans had announced his own forthcoming lectures on the philosophy of universal right. That would mean that the teacher and the pupil would be lecturing at the same time on the same subject according to much the same method. There were certainly some rather significant differences between the respective approaches of Hegel and Gans. Gans was the more progressive spirit, a republican with a liberal outlook, a man gifted with the capacity of making the material of his teaching much more immediately intelligible. Hegel, by contrast, inevitably appeared rather as a man of the Restoration, a convinced monarchist and opponent of liberalism, with a style of delivery and presentation which made it very difficult for his listeners to penetrate quickly to the heart of the issues. Students were saying that one would do better to study the Hegelian philosophy with Gans than with Hegel himself. As compared with the original, the reproduction seemed to have become the more accessible coinage.

It was the ministry that suggested that Hegel should resume lecturing on the philosophy of right, which he had formerly delegated to Gans, since the government wanted to prevent Gans from turning 'all the students into republicans'. Hegel had never worried about Gans's lectures before and had never attempted to interfere with them, although he was well aware of Gans's political position, which he did not share himself. To Hegel's surprise Gans interpreted the idea of parallel treatment of the same material according to the same Hegelian method in a rather flexible way. What was Hegel to do in this situation?

Gans had actually made things rather difficult for his teacher. For it soon emerged that the students Gans was attracting to his lectures did not really want to attend Hegel's, but preferred to wait until the rather more contemporary Professor Gans treated the same subject matter instead. When Hegel entered the university he now found Gans openly recommending his students to attend Hegel's lectures. It was as if the student had now suddenly become Hegel's protector and was clearly anxious lest his own teacher start losing students. The very last thing Hegel wrote was actually a letter to Gans on 12 November in which the philosopher expressed his dissatisfaction about the current situation in an extremely formal and stylistically convoluted fashion. He claimed that Gans 'through his express recommendation had permitted the impression to arise that there was some competition for students'. Hegel subsequently delivered only two more lectures on natural law before he fell seriously ill and was unable to attend the university again.

There is indeed much to suggest that the extreme irritation Hegel experienced at this time suddenly encouraged his old abdominal problems and finally brought him to his deathbed. Arnold Ruge, who described these incidents from first hand experience in his memoirs *From an Earlier Age*, also suspected a connection between Hegel's anxious irritation and the onset of illness. We already know from Varnhagen von Ense that Hegel could be subject to terrible rages. Perhaps on this occasion Hegel found himself forced to recognize an unpalatable fact. In taking over the lectures again, Hegel 'was expected to exert his own authority on behalf of the Court', Ruge observed in the same passage, 'but it soon transpired that he no longer had any'. As far as the university and its students at least were concerned, the times themselves had long since begun to overtake Hegel. And the somewhat subversive student Gans, in contrast to his teacher Hegel, had certainly realized as much.

Bibliography

Primary Texts

Hegel, G. W. F. *Werke* (*Freundesvereinausgabe*) 18 vols (in 21), Berlin: Duncker and Humblot, 1832–45. *Ergänzungsband* 19, various editors, 12: *Briefe*, ed. K. Hegel, Leipzig, 1887.
—— *Hegels theologische Jugendschriften*, ed. H. Nohl, Tübingen, 1907.
—— *Briefe von und an Hegel,* 4 vols, ed. Johannes Hoffmeister and Rolf Flechsig: F. Meiner, 1961.
—— *Sämtliche Werke* (*Jubiläumsausgabe*), 26 vols, ed. H. Glockner, Stuttgart: Fromanns Verlag, 1965.
—— *Gesammelte Werke,* ed. Rheinisch-Westfälischen Akademie der Wissenschaften, Hamburg: F. Meiner, 1968—.
—— *Werke in zwanzig Bänden*, ed. E. Moldenhauer and K. M. Michel, Frankfurt am Main: Suhrkamp Verlag, 1970–1.
—— *Vorlesungen über Rechtsphilosophie 1818–1831*, 6 vols, ed. and introduced by K. H. Ilting, Stuttgart-Bad Cannstadt, 1973—.
—— *Vorlesungen*, 10 vols, various editors, Hamburg: Meiner, 1983—.
—— *Dissertatio philosophica der orbitis planetarum*, German translation, introduction and commentary by W. Neuser, Weinheim, 1986.
—— *Frühe Studien und Entwürfe*, ed. J. Gellert, Berlin: Augbau-Verlag, 1991.
Hoffmeister, Johannes (ed.), *Dokumente zu Hegels Entwicklung*, Stuttgart: Fromann Verlag, 1974.
Nicolin, G. (ed.), *Hegel in Berichten seiner Zeitgenossen*, Hamburg: F. Meiner, 1970.

English Translations of Hegel

Hegel: *Aesthetics*, 2 vols, trans. T. M. Knox, Oxford: Clarendon Press, 1975.
—— *Difference between the Systems of Fichte and Schelling*, trans. H. S. Harris and Walter Cerf, Albany: State University of New York Press, 1977.

—— *Early Theological Writings*, trans. T. M. Knox, with an introduction and fragments translated by Richard Kroner, Chicago: University of Chicago Press, 1948; reprinted Philadelphia: University of Pennsylvania Press, 1971.

—— *Elements of the Philosophy of Right*, ed. Allen W. Wood, trans. H. B. Nisbet, Cambridge: Cambridge University Press, 1991.

—— *The Encyclopedia of Logic*, trans. T. F. Geraets, W. A. Suchting and H. S. Harris, Indianapolis: Hackett, 1991.

—— *Encyclopedia of the Philosophical Sciences in Outline* [Heidelberg, 1817] (containing first edition of the *Encyclopaedia* and Hegel's review of Solger's works), ed. E. Behler, trans. S. H. Taubeneck, New York: Continuum, 1990.

—— *Faith and Knowledge*, ed. and trans. W. Cerf and H. S. Harris, Albany: State University of New York Press, 1977.

—— *Hegel and the Human Spirit* [Second Philosophy of Spirit, 1805–1806], trans. L. Rauch, Detroit, Michigan: Wayne State University Press, 1983.

—— *Introduction to the Philosophy of History*, trans. L. Rauch, Indianapolis: Hackett, 1988.

—— *The Jena System, 1804–1805, Logic and Metaphysics*, trans. and ed. J. W. Burbidge and G. Di Giovanni, Kingston and Montreal: McGill-Queen's University Press, 1986.

—— *Lectures on the History of Philosophy*, trans. E. S. Haldane and F. H. Simpson, 3 vols, London: Routledge and Kegan Paul, 1892; reprinted 1955.

—— *Lectures on the History of Philosophy* [The Lectures of 1825-1826], vol. 3, trans. R. F. Brown and J. M. Stewart, Berkeley: University of California Press, 1990.

—— *Lectures on the Philosophy of World History: Introduction*, trans. H. B. Nisbet with an introduction by D. Forbes, Cambridge: Cambridge University Press, 1975.

—— *Lectures on the Philosophy of Religion*, 3 vols, trans. P. Hodgson et al., Berkeley: University of California Press, 1984–7.

—— *Lectures on the Philosophy of Religion*, 3 vols, trans. E. B. Speirs and J. B. Sanderson, London: Kegan Paul, 1895.

—— *The Letters*, trans. Clark Butler and Christiane Seiler, commentary by C. Butler, Bloomington: Indiana University Press, 1984.

—— *Natural Law*, trans. T. M. Knox, with an introduction by H. B. Acton. Philadelphia: University of Pennsylvania Press, 1975.

—— *Phenomenology of Spirit*, trans. A. V. Miller, with introduction and analysis by J. N. Findlay, Oxford: Clarendon Press, 1977.

—— *The Philosophy of History*, trans. J. Sibree [1857], New York: Dover, 1956.

—— *Philosophy of Mind*, trans. from *Encyclopaedia of the Philosophical Sciences* by W. Wallace and A. V. Miller, Oxford: Clarendon Press, 1971.

—— *Philosophy of Nature*, trans. from *Encyclopaedia of the Philosophical Sciences* (1830) by A. V. Miller, Oxford: Clarendon Press, 1970.

—— *Political Writings*, trans. T. M. Knox, with an introductory essay by Z. A. Pelczynski, Oxford: Clarendon Press, 1964.

—— 'Relation of Scepticism to Philosophy' (trans. H. S. Harris), in G. Di Giovanni and H. S. Harris, *Between Kant and Hegel, Texts in the Development of Post-Kantian Idealism*, Albany: State University of New York Press, 1985, pp. 313–54.

—— *Science of Logic*, trans. A. V. Miller, London: Allen and Unwin, 1970.

—— *System of Ethical Life and First Philosophy of Spirit*, ed. and trans. H. S. Harris

and T. M. Knox, Albany: State University of New York Press, 1979.
—— *Three Essays 1793–1795* ('Tübingen Fragments' and the 'Life of Jesus'), trans. Peter Fuss and John Dobbins, Notre Dame, Ind.: Notre Dame University Press, 1984.

Periodicals and Bibliographies

Bulletin of the Hegel Society of Great Britain, the University of Warwick.
Hegel-Jahrbuch, ed. W. R. Beyer, Munich/Meisenheim am Glan, 1961— and Cologne, 1974—.
Hegel-Studien, ed. Friedhelm Nicolin and Otto Pöggeler, Bonn: Bouvier verlag, 1961—.
Hegel Bibliographie, compiled by Kurt Steinhauer, Munich, New York, London, Paris, 1980.
Hegel-Bibliographie der Dissertationen aus sieben westeuropäischen Ländern 1885–1975, ed. G. U. Gabel, Hamburg, 1980.
The Owl of Minerva. Biannual Journal of the Hegel Society of America, Villanova University.

Secondary Literature on Hegel

Adorno, Theodor W., *Negative Dialectics*, trans. E. B. Ashton, New York: Seabury Press, 1973.
——, *Three Studies on Hegel*, trans. S. W. Nicholson, Cambridge Mass.: IT Press, 1993.
Avineri, Shlomo, *Hegel's Theory of the Modern State*, Cambridge: Cambridge University Press, 1972.
Beiser, Frederick C. (ed.), *The Cambridge Companion to Hegel*, Cambridge: Cambridge University Press, 1993.
Bloch, Ernst, *Subjekt-Objekt. Erläuterungen zu Hegel*, Frankfurt a. M.: Suhrkamp, 1962.
Caird, Edward, *Hegel*, Edinburgh: Basil Blackwood, 1883.
D. E. Christensen (ed.), *Hegel and the Philosophy of Religion*, The Wofford Symposium, The Hague: Nijhoff, 1970.
R. S. Cohen and M. W. Wartofsky (eds), *Hegel and the Sciences*, Dordrecht: Reidel Verlag 1984.
Coplestone, Frederick, *A History of Philosophy*, vol. VII: *Fichte to Hegel*, New York: Doubleday, 1963.
Croce, Benedetto, *What Is Living and What Is Dead in the Philosophy of Hegel*, trans. D. Ainslie, London: Macmillan, 1915; reprinted New York: Garland, 1984.
Cullen, Bernard, *Hegel's Social and Political Thought*, Dublin: Gill and Macmillan, 1979.
Dickey, Lawrence, *Hegel: Religion, Economics and the Politics of Spirit (1770–1807)*, Cambridge: Cambridge University Press, 1987.
Düsing, Klaus, *Hegel und die Geschichte der Philosophie*, Darmstadt: Wissenschaft-

liche Buchgesellschaft, 1983.

—— *Das Problem der Subjektivität in Hegels Logik*, 2nd edn, Bonn: Bouvier Verlag, 1984.

Easton, Lloyd D., *Hegel's First American Followers*, Athens, OH: Ohio University Press, 1966.

Fackenheim, Emil L., *The Religious Dimension in Hegel's Thought,* Bloomington: Indiana University Press, 1967.

Findlay, John N., *Hegel: A Reexamination,* London: Allen and Unwin, 1958.

Flay, Joseph C., *Hegel's Quest for Certainty*, Albany: State University of New York Press, 1984.

Gray, J. Glenne, *Hegel's Hellenic Ideal*, New York: King's Crown Press, 1941. (Reissued as *Hegel and Greek Thought*, New York: Harper and Row, 1968.)

Hardimon, Michael O., *Hegel's Social Philosophy*, Cambridge: Cambridge University Press, 1994.

Harris, Errol E., *An Interpretation of the Logic of Hegel,* Lanham: University Press of America, 1983.

Harris, H. S. : *Hegel's Development I: Towards the Sunlight (1770–1801)*, Oxford: Clarendon Press, 1972.

—— *Hegel's Development II: Night Thoughts (Jena 1801–1806)*, Oxford: Clarendon Press, 1983.

—— *Hegel. Phenomenology and System*, Indianapolis and Cambridge: Hackett Publishing Company, 1995.

—— *Hegel's Ladder*, 2 vols, Indianapolis: Hackett, 1997.

Hartmann, Nicolai, *Die Philosophie des deutschen Idealismus*, 2 vols, Berlin: de Gruyter, 1929.

Haym, Rudolf, *Hegel und seine Zeit*, Berlin: 1857 (reprinted Darmstadt: Wissenschaftliche Buchgesellschaft 1962).

Heidegger, Martin, *Hegel's Concept of Experience*, New York: Harper and Rowe, 1970.

—— *Hegel's Phenomenology of Spirit*, trans. P. Emad and K. May, Bloomington: Indian University Press, 1988.

Heiss, Robert, *Hegel, Kierkegaard, Marx*, New York: Dell Books, 1975.

Hinchmann, Lewis P., *Hegel's Critique of the Enlightenment*, Gainesville: University Press of Florida.

D'Hondt, Jacques, *Hegel in his Time*, trans. J. Burbidge et al., Peterborough, Ontario: Broadview Press, 1988.

Hösle, Vittorio, *Hegels System. Der Idealismus der Subjektivität und das Problem der Intersubjektivität*, Hamburg: Felix Meiner, 1988.

Houlgate, Stephen, *Reason, Truth and History*, London: Routledge, 1991.

Hyppolite, Jean, *Genesis and Structure of the Phenomenology of Hegel,* trans. S. Cherniak and John Heckman, Evanston, Ill.: Northwestern University Press, 1974.

—— *Logic and Existence*, trans. L. Lawlor and A. Sen, Albany: State University of New York Press, 1997.

Inwood, Michael, *A Hegel Dictionary*, Oxford: Blackwell, 1992.

Jaeschke, Walter, *Reason in Religion*, trans. J. M. Stewart and P. C. Hodgson, Berkeley: University of California Press, 1990.

Janicaud, Dominique, *Hegel et le destin de la Grèce*, Paris: Presses Universitaires de France, 1975.

Kainz, Howard P., *Hegel's Phenomenology*, 2 vols, Athens, OH: Ohio University Press, 1983, 1988.

Kaufmann, Walter, *Hegel. Reinterpretation, Texts and Commentary*, New York: Doubleday, 1965.

—— *Hegel's Political Philosophy*, New York, 1970.

Kelly, George Armstrong, *Hegel's Retreat from Eleusis*, Princeton: Princeton University Press, 1978.

Kojève, Alexandre, *Introduction à la phénoménologie*, Paris: Gallimard, 1979. (Abridged English translation as Kojève, *Introduction to the Reading of Hegel*, trans. J. H. Nichols, New York: Basic Books, 1960.)

Kroner, Richard, *Von Kant bis Hegel*, 2 vols, Tübingen: Mohr, 1921.

Küng, Hans, *The Incarnation of God*, trans. J. R. Stephenson, Edinburgh: T. and T. Clark, 1987.

Lauer, Quentin, *A Reading of Hegel's Phenomenology of Spirit*, New York: Fordham University Press, 1976; 2nd edn, 1994.

—— *Essays on Hegelian Dialectic*, New York: Fordham University Press, 1983.

Lukács, Georg, *The Young Hegel*, trans. Rodney Livingstone, London: Merlin; Cambridge, Mass.: M.I.T. Press, 1976.

Macintyre, A. (ed.), *Hegel. A Collection of Essays*, New York: Doubleday, 1972.

Marcuse, Herbert, *Reason and Revolution. Hegel and the Rise of Social Theory*, 2nd edn, London: Routledge and Kegan Paul, 1968.

McTaggart, James, *A Commentary on Hegel's Logic*, Cambridge: Cambridge University Press, 1910.

Merklinger, Philip M., *Philosophy, Theology, and Hegel's Berlin Philosophy of Religion, 1821–1827*, Albany: State University of New York Press, 1993.

Mitias, M. H., *The Moral Foundation of the State in Hegel's Philosophy of Right*, Amsterdam: Rodopi, 1984.

Mueller, Gustav Emil, *Hegel: The Man, his Vision and Work*, New York: Pageant Press, 1968.

Mure, G. R. G., *A Study of Hegel's Logic*, Oxford: Oxford University Press, 1950.

—— *The Philosophy of Hegel*, Oxford: Clarendon Press, 1965.

—— *An Introduction to Hegel*, Oxford: Oxford University Press, 1970.

O'Brien, George D., *Hegel on Reason and History*, Chicago: University of Chicago Press, 1975.

O'Malley, J. J. (ed.), *Hegel and the History of Philosophy*, The Hague: Nijhoff, 1974.

O'Regan, Cyril, *The Heterodox Hegel*, Albany: State University of New York Press, 1994.

Pelczynski, A. (ed.), *The State and Civil Society. Studies in Hegel's Political Philosophy*, Cambridge: Cambridge University Press, 1984.

Petry, Michael John, *Hegel and the Newtonianism*, Dordrecht, Boston and London: Reidel Publishing Company, 1993.

Pinkard, Terry, *Hegel's Phenomenology: The Sociality of Reason*, Cambridge: Cambridge University Press, 1994.

Pippin, Robert B., *Hegel's Idealism*, Cambridge: Cambridge University Press, 1989.

Plant, Raymond, *Hegel. An Introduction*, 2nd edn, Oxford: Blackwell, 1983.

Pöggeler, Otto, *Hegels Idee einer Phänomenologie des Geistes*, Freiburg and Munich: Alber, 1973.

Ritter, Joachim, *Hegel and the French Revolution*, Cambridge, Mass.: MIT Press, 1982.

Rockmore, Tom, *Hegel*, Berkeley: University of California Press, 1994.

Rosen, Stanley, *G. W. F. Hegel. An Introduction to the Science of Wisdom*, New Haven: Yale University Press, 1974.

Rosenkranz, Karl, *Georg Wilhelm Friedrich Hegel's Leben*, Berlin: Duncker und Humblot, 1844 (Reprinted Darmstadt: Wissenschaftliche Buchgesellschaft, 1963).

Rotenstreich, Nathan, *From Substance to Subject. Studies in Hegel*, The Hague: Nijhoff, 1974.

Singer, Peter, *Hegel*, Past Master, Oxford: Oxford University Press, 1983. (Also available in *German Philosophers: Kant, Hegel, Schopenhauer, Nietzsche*, Past Masters, Oxford: Oxford University Press, 1997, pp. 105–14.)

Solomon, Robert C., *In the Spirit of Hegel: A Study of Hegel, 'Phenomenology of Spirit'*, New York and Oxford: Oxford University Press, 1983.

Stace, Walter, *The Philosophy of Hegel. A Systematic Exposition*, New York: Dover Publications, 1955.

Sterling, James H., *The Secret of Hegel*, 2 vols, 1st edn, London: Longman, Roberts & Green, 1865; 2nd edn, Edinburgh: Oliver & Boyd, 1898. (Reprinted: Bristol, Thoemmes, 1990.)

Stern, R. (ed.), *Hegel: Critical Assessments*, 4 vols, London: Routledge, 1993.

Taylor, Charles, *Hegel*, Cambridge: Cambridge University Press, 1975.

—— *Hegel and Modern Society*, Cambridge: Cambridge University Press, 1979.

Toews, John E., *Hegelianism. The Path towards Dialectical Humanism 1805–1841*, Cambridge: Cambridge University Press, 1980.

Travis, D. C. (ed.), *A Hegel Symposium*, Austin (Texas): University of Texas Press, 1962.

Wahl, Jean, *Le Malheur de la conscience dans la philosophie de Hegel*, Paris: Presses Universitaires de France, 1951.

Westphal, Merold, *History and Truth in Hegel's Phenomenology*, Atlantic Highlands, NJ: Humanities Press, 1979; 2nd edn, 1990.

Wilkins, B. T., *Hegel's Philosophy of History*, New York: Cornell University Press, 1974.

Williamson, Raymond K., *Introduction to Hegel's Philosophy of Religion*, Albany: State University of New York Press, 1984.

Willman, A. (ed.), *Hegel on the Ethical Life, Religion and Philosophy*, The Hague: Nijhoff, 1989.

Wood, Allen W., *Hegel's Ethical Thought*, Cambridge: Cambridge University Press, 1990.

Yerkes, James, *The Christology of Hegel*, Missoula, Mont.: Scholars Press, 1982; 2nd edn, Albany: State University of New York Press, 1984.

Index